The Artful Mind

The Artful Mind

*Cognitive Science and the Riddle
of Human Creativity*

EDITED BY MARK TURNER

OXFORD
UNIVERSITY PRESS

2006

OXFORD
UNIVERSITY PRESS

Oxford University Press, Inc., publishes works that further
Oxford University's objective of excellence
in research, scholarship, and education.

Oxford   New York
Auckland   Cape Town   Dar es Salaam   Hong Kong   Karachi
Kuala Lumpur   Madrid   Melbourne   Mexico City   Nairobi
New Delhi   Shanghai   Taipei   Toronto

With offices in
Argentina   Austria   Brazil   Chile   Czech Republic   France   Greece
Guatemala   Hungary   Italy   Japan   Poland   Portugal   Singapore
South Korea   Switzerland   Thailand   Turkey   Ukraine   Vietnam

Published by Oxford University Press, Inc.
198 Madison Avenue, New York, New York 10016

www.oup.com

Library of Congress Cataloging-in-Publication Data
The artful mind : cognitive science and the riddle of human creativity / edited
by Mark Turner.
p. cm.
Includes bibliographical references and index.
ISBN-13 978-0-19-530636-1
ISBN 0-19-530636-8
1. Art—Psychology.   2. Cognition.   3. Creative ability.   I. Turner, Mark, 1954–
N71.A762 2006
701'.15—dc22   2005031824

9 8 7 6 5 4 3 2 1

Printed in the United States of America
on acid-free paper

Acknowledgments

We are grateful to the Center for Advanced Study in the Behavioral Sciences, our host during the 2001–2002 academic year. As a token of our gratitude, we have assigned the copyright and the royalties for this book to the Center. The Center hosts the permanent supporting website for this book at http://theartfulmind.stanford.edu.

Generous support for our research was provided by the J. Paul Getty Grant Program. The Institute of Neuroesthetics and the Minerva Foundation arranged a conference at the University of California, Berkeley, that involved many of our members in January 2002. We are exceptionally indebted to Cynthia Read and Arthur Evenchik for their editorial work.

Mark Turner is grateful to Wildlife Education, Limited, for permission to reprint in his chapter the image from *Dinosaurs*, an issue of Zoobooks.

"The Neurology of Ambiguity," by Semir Zeki, was first published in *Consciousness and Cognition*, Vol. 13, Issue 1 (2004), pages 173–196. It is reprinted with permission from Elsevier. The author is grateful for permission to reprint it here with minor changes.

Full color images that accompany this book are presented on the web at http://theartfulmind.stanford.edu. The site additionally presents supplementary documents, a history of the research activity surrounding this volume, and notes on further activities and research on the artful mind.

Contents

Contributors, ix

Prologue, xv

PART I Art and Evolution

 1. Art and Cognitive Evolution, 3
    Merlin Donald

 2. The Aesthetic Faculty, 21
    Terrence Deacon

PART II Art and Emotion

 3. A Cognitive Account of Aesthetics, 57
    Francis Steen

 4. Composition and Emotion, 73
    David Freedberg

PART III Art and the Way We Think

 5. The Art of Compression, 93
    Mark Turner

6. The Cognitive Tango, 115
   Lawrence M. Zbikowski

7. Dynamics of Completion, 133
   Shirley Brice Heath

PART IV Art, Meaning, and Form

8. The Neuroscience of Form in Art, 153
   George Lakoff

9. Form and Meaning in Art, 171
   Per Aage Brandt

10. Slippages of Meaning and Form, 189
    Stephen Murray

PART V Art and Sacred Belief

11. Making Relics Work, 211
    Robert A. Scott

12. Architectural Space as Metaphor in the Greek Sanctuary, 225
    Gloria Ferrari

PART VI Art and Ambiguity

13. The Neurology of Ambiguity, 243
    Semir Zeki

14. Mastering Ambiguity, 271
    Marc De Mey

Epilogue, 305

Index, 307

Contributors

PER AAGE BRANDT is Department Chair and Emile B. de Sauzé Professor of Modern Languages and Literatures at Case Western Reserve University. Formerly Professor of Semiotics and Director of the Center for Semiotics at the University of Aarhus, he is author of a dozen books and some 150 published papers on cognitive and semiotic theory, the semantics of literature (especially poetry) and language (clause structure), the cognitive aesthetics of works of art, and music (tonal dynamics). In 2002, he received the Grand Prix de Philosophie from l'Académie française and was made Officier de l'Ordre des Arts et des Lettres by the French Ministry of Culture. He was also a fellow at the Center for Advanced Study in the Behavioral Sciences in 2001–2002.

TERRENCE DEACON is Professor of Anthropology at the Helen Wills Neuroscience Institute at the University of California, Berkeley. He is author of *The Symbolic Species: The Co-Evolution of Language and the Brain*. His neurobiological research focuses on the nature of the human divergence from typical primate brain anatomy, and on the correlations between anatomical differences and special human cognitive abilities, particularly language. His longstanding interest in developing a scientific semiotics that could contribute to both linguistic theory and cognitive neuroscience will be reflected in his next book, *Homunculus*, which explores the relationship between evolutionary and semiotic processes.

MARC DE MEY is Professor Emeritus of Cognitive Science at the University of Ghent. He is the author of *The Cognitive Paradigm: An Integrated Understanding of Scientific Development* and a member of the Royal Academy (KVAB) in Brussels. At the Flemish Center for Advanced Studies (VLAC), which is a unit of the Royal Academy, he has pursued a research project on Jan van Eyck with Carol J. Purtle, Benjamin Rawlins Professor of Art History, University of Memphis (*Looking at Jan van Eyck*, forthcoming). A scholar of the dynamics of conceptual systems as well as an analyst of specific discoveries, he is currently exploring the perspective paradigm and the study of visual perception. His three-dimensional computer reconstructions of paintings (Masaccio, van Eyck) and scientific discoveries (Kepler) illustrate the intertwined nature of science and art.

MERLIN DONALD is Department Chair and Professor of Cognitive Science at Case Western Reserve University. He is author of many scientific papers and two influential books: *Origins of the Modern Mind: Three Stages in the Evolution of Culture and Cognition* and *A Mind So Rare: The Evolution of Human Consciousness*. He is a fellow of both the Canadian Psychological Association and the Royal Society of Canada, and a former Killam Research Fellow. His research interests center on hominid cultural evolution, and the effects of cultural and technological change on human cognition.

GLORIA FERRARI is Research Professor (Emerita) of Classics at Harvard University. Before joining the Harvard faculty in 1999, she taught in the Departments of Art History and Classical Languages and Literatures at the University of Chicago. Her publications deal with both Roman and Greek art and include *Il commercio dei sarcofagi asiatici* and *Materiali del Museo Archeologico di Tarquinia XI: I vasi attici a figure rosse del periodo arcaico*. Her most recent book, *Figures of Speech: Men and Maidens in Ancient Greece*, explores issues of method in the interpretation of pictures, focusing on the representation of gender. The book was awarded the 2004 James R. Wiseman Book Award by the Archaeological Institute of America. Her current research interests are in the area of archaic and classical Greek art and poetry, particularly vase paintings and iconography, with special attention to the relationship of images to texts.

DAVID FREEDBERG is Professor of Art History at Columbia University and Director of the Italian Academy for Advanced Studies in America. He is the author of several well-known books on psychological responses to art, including *Iconoclasts and their Motives* and *The Power of Images: Studies in the History and Theory of Response*. His earlier books include *Dutch Landscape Prints of the Seventeenth Century* and *Rubens: The Life of Christ after the Passion*

(OUP 1984). His many works on the intersection of art and science in the age of Galileo culminated in *The Eye of the Lynx: Galileo, His Friends, and the Beginnings of Modern Natural History* (2002). He is currently preparing a book on art and the brain, following his neuroscientific researches, which have substantially refined and superseded the approach only broadly adumbrated in the essay in this volume.

SHIRLEY BRICE HEATH is Professor at Large at the Watson Institute for International Studies at Brown University and Margery Bailey Professor of English and Dramatic Literature and Professor of Linguistics (Emerita) at Stanford University. She works primarily in the fields of language and human development, community development, and social entrepreneurship. Her books include *Ways with Words: Language, Life, and Work in Communities and Classrooms*, *The Braid of Literature* (with Shelby Wolf), and *ArtShow: Youth and Community Development* (with Laura Smyth). She also directed the award-winning documentary film *ArtShow*. She has been a fellow of the Spencer Foundation, the National Endowment for the Humanities, the John D. and Catherine T. MacArthur Foundation, the Center for Advanced Study in the Behavioral Sciences, and the John Simon Guggenheim Foundation.

GEORGE LAKOFF is Richard and Rhoda Goldman Distinguished Professor of Linguistics and Cognitive Science at the University of California, Berkeley. He is also the Founding Senior Fellow at the Rockridge Institute. He is author of *Women, Fire, and Dangerous Things* and *Moral Politics*, and *Don't Think of an Elephant!*); co-author (with Mark Johnson) of *Metaphors We Live By* and *Philosophy in the Flesh*; co-author (with Mark Turner) of *More Than Cool Reason*; and co-author (with Rafael Nunez) of *Where Mathematics Comes From*. In 1971–1972, he was a fellow at the Center for Advanced Study in the Behavioral Sciences at Stanford. His current research concerns include conceptual analysis within cognitive linguistics, implications of cognitive science for philosophy, the cognitive structure of math, and the neural foundations of conceptual systems and language. He is also engaged in the development of cognitive social science, which involves practical applications of cognitive linguistics to help social advocates frame social and political issues.

STEPHEN MURRAY is Professor of Art History at New York University and Director of the Media Center for Art History, Archaeology, and Historic Preservation. He is author of *Building Troyes Cathedral: The Late Gothic Campaigns*; *Beauvais Cathedral: Architecture of Transcendence*; *Notre-Dame, Cathedral of Amiens: The Power of Change in Gothic*; and *A Gothic Sermon:*

Making a Contract with the Mother of God, Saint Mary of Amiens. His current work is on medieval sermons, storytelling in Gothic, and the Romanesque architecture of the Bourbonnais. He is also engaged in projecting his cathedral studies through electronic media, using a combination of three-dimensional simulation, digital imaging, and video.

ROBERT A. SCOTT is Associate Director Emeritus of the Center for Advanced Study in the Behavioral Sciences and former Professor of Sociology at Princeton University. His most recent book is *The Gothic Enterprise: A Guide to Understanding the Medieval Cathedral.* He is also co-author (with Arnold Shore) of *Why Sociology Does Not Apply;* author of *The Making of Blind Men;* editor of several collections of essays about stigma, deviancy, and social control; and author of numerous articles, book chapters, and essays on related topics.

FRANCIS STEEN is Assistant Professor of Communication Studies at the University of California, Los Angeles. He has published in such journals as *Auto/biography Studies, Philosophy and Literature, Style, Journal of Cognition and Culture,* and *Poetics Today,* for which he edited a special issue on "Literature and the Cognitive Revolution." He is currently involved in several research projects that investigate various dimensions of art, literature, and play—activities that appear to have no functional purpose and are in some central sense undertaken for their own sake. These projects include a multi-site study of pretend play among preschool children, an investigation of children's perceptions of monsters, and experiments concerning people's perceptions of art. He is also writing a book articulating a cognitive and evolutionary framework for art, literature, and entertainment.

MARK TURNER is Institute Professor at Case Western Reserve University. His books include *Cognitive Dimensions of Social Science: The Way We Think about Politics, Economics, Law, and Society* (OUP, 2001), *The Literary Mind: The Origins of Thought and Language* (OUP, 1996), *Reading Minds: The Study of English in the Age of Cognitive Science,* and *Death Is the Mother of Beauty.* He has been a fellow of the Institute for Advanced Study, the John Simon Guggenheim Memorial Foundation, the Center for Advanced Study in the Behavioral Sciences, the National Humanities Center, and the National Endowment for the Humanities. He is external research professor at the Krasnow Institute for Advanced Study in Cognitive Neuroscience and distinguished fellow at the New England Institute for Cognitive Science and Evolutionary Psychology. In 1996, the Académie française awarded him the Prix du Rayonnement de la langue et de la littérature françaises.

LAWRENCE M. ZBIKOWSKI is Associate Professor of Music in the Department of the Humanities in the college at the University of Chicago. He is author of *Conceptualizing Music: Cognitive Structure, Theory, and Analysis* (OUP, 2002), which received the 2004 Wallace Berry Award from the Society for Music Theory. His research focuses on the application of recent work in cognitive science (especially that done by cognitive linguists and cognitive psychologists) to various problems confronted by music scholars. These problems include the nature of musical syntax, text-music relations, the organization of improvisational traditions, and the structure of theories of music. During 2003–2004 he was a fellow at the National Humanities Center, where his project concerned the development of a cognitive grammar of music. This work is the basis of his next book, *By Crystal Fountains: Music, Language, and Grammar*. He is presently director of a special project for the University of Chicago Division of the Humanities on creativity and cognition.

SEMIR ZEKI is Professor of Neurobiology at University College London. A Fellow of the Royal Society and a foreign member of the American Philosophical Society, he is author of *Inner Vision: An Exploration of Art and the Brain* (OUP, 2000) and *A Vision of the Brain*, and co-author (with Balthus) of *La Quête de l'essentiel*. Among his awards are the Rank Prize, the LVMH Science for Art Prize, the Yngve Zotterman Prize of the Swedish Physiological Society, and the King Faisal International Prize in Biology. He has established the Institute of Neuroesthetics, based in Berkeley and London.

Prologue

The great riddle—of archaeology, cognitive science, neuroscience, anthropology, sociology, political science, linguistics, religious studies, and the humanities from literature and music to dance and art—is how we became human, how we acquired modern minds.

Human beings with mental architecture like ours came into existence only yesterday, evolutionarily speaking—perhaps fifty thousand years ago. At least, the archaeological record as we have it shows no robust evidence of cognitively modern behavior before that epoch. The staggering behavioral singularities that come with cognitively modern minds—advanced tool use, decorative dress, language, culture, religion, science, mathematics, art—present us with the greatest scientific embarrassment, for they appear to indicate a mysterious and unexplained discontinuity between us and the entire rest of Life.

To have a cognitively modern human mind is to be robustly artful, and conversely. This equivalence provides the inevitable starting point for a research program aimed at answering obvious yet hard questions: What is the evolutionary path from our remoter ancestors, who somehow lacked artful minds, to the existence of cognitively modern human beings, who cannot fail to be artful? How did the artful mind emerge? In a leap, or through slow development? What are the basic mental operations that make art possible for us now, and how do they operate? What neurobiology subtends these abilities? What is the interplay, in the phenomena of artfulness, between biological dispositions, individual experience, and cultural history?

The individual human being, in form and movement, in thought and action, is a seamless intersection of powerful histories—phylogenetic history, individual development, and social and cultural history—all profoundly influential. A human being is a unified agency of biology, psychology, and social, environmental, and cultural patterns. And yet, the academic study of human beings is fragmented into scattered disciplines. How can science overcome this academic incoherence to launch a tradition of research in which neuroscientists, cognitive and developmental psychologists, archaeologists, vision scientists, evolutionary theorists, artists, art historians, semioticians, sociologists, and cultural historians join to explain the artful mind and its expression in cultures? How, in short, can inquisitive twenty-six-year-olds inspired to explain the artful mind discover a unified intellectual framework and institutional setting in which to begin thinking about it? Can their path be prepared to any degree by their elders, who lack their enviable plasticity and their exciting prospects, but who presumably command some of the knowledge, methods, and intuitions they might find useful?

This book has been designed with these goals and questions in mind. Its contributors collaborated over the course of a year, 2001–2002, at the Center for Advanced Study in the Behavioral Sciences. This year of collaborative residential research was made possible by a generous grant from the J. Paul Getty Grant Program. Some of the members of the group were in residence for the entire year, others for a month or two, a few for only short intervals here and there. We read each other's work; offered ideas, hints, and data; convened for more than thirty seminars; participated in three conferences; and conducted innumerable open-ended conversations over lunch and dinner or before and after screenings and shows.

This book is addressed to the next generation of scientists and scholars who seek to explain the wonders and mysteries of the artful mind. We hope it provides directions for a new field of research that, embryonic at present, can play an informative and eloquent role in answering the great riddle.

PART I

Art and Evolution

I

Art and Cognitive Evolution

Merlin Donald

This chapter offers an overview of the cognitive principles of art, the origins of art, and the cognitive function of art. Art is an activity that arises in the context of human cultural and cognitive evolution. Its sources include not only the most abstract integrative regions of the brain but also the communities of mind within which artists and audiences live. The interaction of these sources creates complex cultural-cognitive domains, which are reflected in art. Art and artists are active players in the co-evolution of culture and cognition.

In this chapter, I use the word *art* to refer to a wide class of expressive forms and media, including music, dance, theater, various multimedia categories (such as opera and cinema), painting, sculpture, aspects of the built environment, and architecture. The word can reasonably be extended to include most forms of written literature. I do not include any of the broader applications of the word *art*—as in, for instance, the art of mathematics, engineering, baseball, or carpentry. It may be said that there is an art to performing virtually any activity elegantly or well (including art: there is an art to good art, one might say), but that is another matter. Here I am concerned with the origins and functions of artistic forms and media themselves, rather than with issues of artistic creation, merit, beauty, or transcendence.

What cognitive principles govern art? And where should we begin a cognitive exploration of its origins? There is no consensus on this, but a few guidelines might help establish the territory to be explored.

(1) Art should be regarded as a specific kind of *cognitive engineering*. As a first principle, art is an activity *intended to influence the minds of an audience*. It involves the deliberate construction of representations that affect how people (including the artist) view the world. This reflects a very deep human tendency for the reciprocal control of attention, which carries with it a propensity to deliberately *engineer* the experiences of others (especially of our own progeny and peers). Joint and reciprocal control of attention is the foundation of human social communication; just as parents guide their children's attention to certain aspects of the world, most artists attempt to control their audience's attention, leading it by the hand, so to speak, into a carefully engineered experience. To achieve this, the artist must be an effective pedagogue, anticipating the audience's reactions (this principle applies even if the artist wants to elicit an apparently unpredictable result, in which case, of course, uncertainty itself is engineered into the outcome).

(2) Art is always created in the context of *distributed* cognition. Human cultures can be regarded as massive distributed cognitive networks, involving the linking of many minds, often with large institutional structures that guide the flow of ideas, memories, and knowledge. Artists are highly placed within these cultural-cognitive networks, often serving as the creative engine that drives much of the enterprise. They influence the cognitive activity of their particular tribe or generation (for artists, like everyone else, are situated in space and time), both by preserving and by modifying its symbols, images, and other expressive forms. In a sense, they are one with the network: they derive their most basic ideas and techniques, as well as their inspiration, from it, and must operate within the limitations it imposes.

(3) Art is *constructivist* in nature, aimed at the deliberate refinement and elaboration of mental models and worldviews. These are the natural products of cognition itself, the outcome of the brain's tendency to strive for the integration of perceptual and conceptual material over time. The term *large-scale neural integration* refers to the nervous system's cross-modal unification of many sources of experience into a single abstract model or percept. The canonical example of this kind of integration is event-perception, which can unify a blur of millions of individual sensations of sight, sound, touch, taste, smell, and emotions into unitary event-percepts. This ability is very limited in simple organisms, where the "stimulus" of behavior is often an uncomplicated one-dimensional property, such as a pheromone or a color, but it is common, and very highly developed, in most social mammals and especially in human beings, where it has evolved into a very abstract capacity to integrate not only the raw materials of experience but also the constituents of memory itself.

Thus, a dog is able to understand complex social events, such as "begging" behavior or "submission," which involve socially relativistic percepts that unfold over time. Humans, of course, navigate much more abstract versions of social behavior, which culminate in worldviews that frame their interpretation of events. The Stoic, scientific, Puritan, and Romantic worldviews share a basis in the need to achieve abstract integration of smaller events. Such worldviews are collective, or cultural, products of the inherent drive toward integration.

Large-scale integration might be regarded as the major adaptive advantage conveyed by the complex of special brain capacities often labeled *conscious processing* (Donald 2001). As the nervous system's capacity for conscious processing evolved, selected species achieved increasingly more abstract kinds of cognitive integration, which gave an accordingly wider temporal and spatial range to their behavior. Hence these species' ability to perceive distant, complex, and very abstract events that occur in the social environment, such as changing alliances, whose complexity exceeds the perceptual capacities of simpler creatures. In humans, this constructive integrative capacity evolved into a communally shared capacity: human culture is essentially a distributed cognitive system within which worldviews and mental models are constructed and shared by the members of a society. Artists are traditionally at the forefront of that process, and have a large influence on our worldviews and mental models.

(4) Most art is *metacognitive* in nature. *Metacognition* is, by definition, self-reflection. Art is self-reflective. The artistic object compels reflection on the very process that created it—that is, on the mind of the artist, and thus of the society from which the artist emerged. Ultimately, art derives from the innate human capacity for self-observation. That is why art has been so instrumental in defining cultural periods and in providing tribes, of whatever size and complexity, with their self-identifying symbols and allegories. Art is thus inherently metacognitive in its cognitive function on both the individual and social levels. Though the term *metacognition* customarily refers to individual self-reflection, I use it especially to denote art's crucial role as a collective vehicle for self-reflection and as a shared source of cultural identity.

At various points in human cultural history, artists and writers have built comprehensive metacognitive systems that served to reflect on society and human nature; typical examples are the complex pictorial representations of knowledge so common in medieval European alchemy, and the multitude of very large Italian paintings that tried to sum up the conventions of Renaissance social order. These artistic objects reflected the predominant mental models and worldviews of those societies back to their members, and placed artists in a position of considerable metacognitive influence, even though they derived their material from the society itself. The power of the artists arose because they often subtly (and sometimes not so subtly) altered the prevailing images and worldviews of their societies in a highly selective manner. The worldviews of communities have often been permanently changed through the efforts of a single artist (e.g., Verdi's revolutionary impact on nineteenth-century Italian politics). On such occasions, art sits high in the hierarchy of cultural-cognitive governance. Traditional religions have long recognized (and, consequently, relied on) the cognitive influence of art. Much the same can be said of modern secular states, such as Maoist China, and of modern corporations. The social-reflective role of art has always been controversial. But the ferocity of the arguments revolving around this topic testifies to the fundamental nature of art's contribution to the collective processes of thought, memory, and perception in society. This contribution is evident in the art of Christianity, Buddhism, and Islam, which conveys highly formal, integrated worldviews. It is also evident in the chaotic and fluid imagery of modern secular society, which conveys many different worldviews.

(5) Art is a *technology-driven* aspect of cognition. Although it may have begun as a natural expression of our collective need to represent reality, the media of artistic expression affect what can be represented, and these media differ tremendously between societies. The effect of technology on art is far-reaching. Technology affects the kinds of cognitive networks artists can construct, in part by setting limits on the kinds of ideas and images that can be represented and created. Major works of art constitute a crucial part of society's attempt to engineer, manipulate, and reflect on its own experience and occasionally to fabricate *de novo* its defining ideas and images. In historical context, technique and technology are central in defining what artists do and what choices they can make. Moreover, technology can actually alter the properties of the distributed cognitive systems of society and change the nature of the cognitive work that is done.

(6) The role of the artist, viewed as a component in a distributed cognitive system, is *not necessarily fixed*. As the system goes, so goes the role of art—and, indeed, the very definition of art. Elsewhere (Donald 1991, 2001), I have argued that symbolic technology (including the many technologies involved in making art) can deeply affect the architecture of cognition, both inside the head and outside, in the social network. In particular, such innovations as writing systems, new graphic media, and external memory systems can change the kind of art, and the range of worldviews, that are possible *because they influence memory itself, through both the media of storage and the pathways of retrieval.* Symbolic technologies ultimately enabled Brunelleschi to

build the dome of Santa Maria del Fiore in Florence. Similarly, they enabled Rodin to conceive of, and cast, his bronzes, while setting limits on what he could represent. Technology often determines the parameters of thought and creation (mathematical thought is a particularly clear example of this— mathematics is all about finding the right set of symbols to capture an idea).

This point has been largely missed in cognitive theories of art. When one is dealing with a distributed network of many individuals linked together, rather than an isolated individual, as a major source of creativity, the properties of the network, particularly those of network memory, become highly relevant. These are typically affected much more by technology than by the properties of biologically defined memory in the individual, which are largely fixed in the genome.

(7) Art is always aimed at a *cognitive outcome*. The conventional engineering of, say, a bridge or a drug compound is aimed at a specific physical outcome. In contrast, art is aimed at a specific cognitive outcome. It is designed to engineer a state of mind in an audience (even in cases of extreme narcissism where the only intended audience is the artist). The work is judged by its success in achieving this aim. Thus, in its ends, art is essentially different from other kinds of engineering, because its purpose is primarily cognitive. Cathedrals, and films, are specific kinds of cognitive machines. Their major social functions are cognitive: they influence memory, shape public behavior, set social norms, and modify the experience of life in their audiences. In these terms, the various techniques and media of art are a small but important part of the larger evolutionary trajectory of the human mind.

Art Viewed in an Evolutionary Context

Art is universal to all societies and unique to humans. Inevitably, when a phenomenon is both universal and species-unique, the question of its evolutionary origins arises. Within the reach of evolutionary theory, human evolution is special, and unusually complex, because it entails the co-evolution of biological and cultural forces. Art is central to that process, and one of the most interesting phenomena of human culture.

The cognitive domains of human cultural and cognitive evolution have emerged in three cascading stages, which I have labeled, successively, as Mimetic (~2 million years ago), Mythic (~150 thousand years ago), and Theoretic (last 2 thousand years, approximately) (Donald 1991, 1993, 1998a, 2001). These dates are only rough approximations; it is the sequence, rather than the specific dates, that is important. The progression is cumulative and conservative, with each preceding stage remaining in place, and continuing to serve its specialized cognitive function in human society, as each new stage emerges. Even though art is a relatively recent development in the long history of the human species, it has an investment in all these cognitive domains, and its many forms reflect the very rich cognitive accumulations of human culture. Indeed, in many instances art has been a major factor in evolving these domains, and constitutes our primary evidence in determining the nature of prehistoric culture.

Because evolution is conservative, the modern mind retains all previous stages within its complex structure. The Mimetic domain (of which I shall have more to say later) comprises gesturing, pantomime, dance, visual analogy, and ritual, which evolved early and formed an archaic layer of culture based mostly on action-metaphor. Mimesis allowed for the spread of tool-making technology and fire-tending, through imitation and ritual. It also set the stage for the much later evolution of spoken language.

Mythic culture is based on spoken language, and especially on the natural social product of language, storytelling. Most societies have a specific subset of stories that acquire the status of myths, and these play a governing role in defining how to behave in a given culture. Myths also preserve notions of authority, gender, and morality. Mythic culture retains a subsidiary mimetic dimension, manifested in ritual, costume, and gesture, which are epitomized in various forms of art. We might even say that the mimetic dimension tends to fall under the governance of myth; thus the art and ritual of Christian civilization have been greatly concerned with the mythic content of that civilization. The same applies to Islamic, Jewish, Buddhist, and Hindu art. Traditional religion has often been the core institution for the regulation of what might be called "high" Mythic culture, and art has fallen under that kind of regulation in many societies.

Theoretic culture is a more recent historical development. It started very slowly, with the emergence of sophisticated writing technologies and scientific instruments, and then, after a long gestation period, became (somewhat) dominant in Western society after the Enlightenment. Over the past few hundred years, however, it has evolved very rapidly. Theoretic culture is symbol-based, logical, bureaucratic, and heavily dependent on external memory devices, such as writing, codices, mathematical notations, scientific instruments, books, records, and computers. It is the culture of government, science, and technology, and of many forms of art. In a global context, relative to the influence of the Mimetic and Mythic domains, Theoretic culture is still a minority culture. However, it is disproportionately influential because of its place in the distributed cognitive systems that determine such things as our collective representation of the past and our tribal and class identities. Of necessity, even Theoretic institutions retain a Mimetic and Mythic element; human society cannot function without these more basic forms of representation, which carry out specific kinds of cognitive work. Whereas Theoretic modes of thought are dominant in planning, science, technology, and government, Mythic and Mimetic forms continue to dominate the vast majority of human transactions, including those that take place in the political and interpersonal domains.

Even though art is a relatively recent development in the long cognitive history of the human species, its forms reflect all these cognitive and cultural domains. The diversity of art, and its modern proliferation of forms, reflect the rich historical background of modern cognition and culture. Table 1.1 illustrates this point, by mapping various current artistic forms onto the proposed major domains of human cultural-cognitive emergence.

Note that this process is cumulative and scaffolded. By implication, the breakthrough adaptation, and the one from which all else that is distinctive about the human mind follows, is mimesis. The strong form of my hypothesis about art might be phrased as follows: the new is always and inevitably scaffolded on the old, and as a result, art is ultimately a reflection of the

TABLE I.I

External Form	Cognitive Domain
Pantomime	Whole-Body Mimetic
Prosody, Chant	Vocal Mimetic
Most Rituals	Whole-Body and Vocal Mimetic
Acting, Body Language	Facial, Vocal, Whole-Body Mimetic
Costume, Dress, Makeup	Technologically Amplified Mimetic
Most Styles of Painting	Visual Mimetic
Sculpture, Crafted Objects	Visual, Tactile, Kinematic Mimetic
Popular Music	Auditory Mimetic
Oral Storytelling	Linguistic/Mythic
Epic Oral Poetry	Linguistic/Mythic
Lyric Poetry	Linguistic/Mythic
Novels, Other Extended Narratives	Linguistic/Mythic
Traditional Architecture	Mimetic/Mythic
Comic Books, Cartoons	Mixed Mimetic/Mythic
Formal Public Ritual and Spectacle	Mixed Mimetic/Mythic
Cinema, Opera, Theater	Mixed Mimetic/Mythic
Modern Architecture	Mixed Mimetic/Mythic/Theoretic
Modern Painting	Mixed Mimetic/Mythic/Theoretic
Modern Poetry and Music	Mixed Mimetic/Mythic/Theoretic

deepest and most ancient form of human expression, mimesis. This hypothesis is discussed further in a later section.

Art, Neuroscience, and Distributed Networks

Before embarking on this section, I should offer a caveat about the uses of neuroscience in this kind of very broad cognitive theorizing. All things cognitive—and art is no exception—are ultimately products of brain activity. It may seem to follow that, to understand art, we need only track its origins to some specific brain structure or function, such as the neural systems underlying human vision or human mimetic capacity. While there is undoubtedly some truth in this, the situation is not so simple.

When we speak of the mind, we usually invoke a theoretical entity called the *cognitive process*, which can be broken down into various component functions, such as perception, working memory, spatial attention, lexical search, episodic recall, and so on. Any complex mental task, including the production and viewing of art, is made up of chains of these cognitive components, arranged in functional architectures, or operational hierarchies that resemble the algorithms of computation. A major objective driving what might be termed the cognitive deconstruction of artistic experience is to analyze the functional architecture of its underlying component operations.

The act of looking at a painting, for example, might be deconstructed into a series of very brief components, each of which produces a "glimpse" of the object. These components include such things as moving the eyes, fixating and focusing them, processing the fixated image, storing that image in some form of temporary, or buffer, memory, and synthesizing the whole series of remembered images into a unified perception of the painting. This percept might then be subjected to further scrutiny in working memory. The sequence might be repeated and reflected upon many times before the viewer acquires any "expertise" or familiarity with the painting. This process provides the higher interpretative centers of the brain with multiple frames, spread out over time, much like a cinematic sequence. This is true even if the object is a static thing, such as a sculpture, because such objects are always viewed in several glimpses taken over time, from various distinct fixations, from different angles and distances.

It is evident that this type of cognitive sequence, which is typical of everyday cognition as well as of the experiencing of art, entails a complex and somewhat idiosyncratic series of brain operations. Some of the neural activity that drives these operations (to date, only the most elementary ones) can be observed by electrical recording and brain imaging (see, for example, Zeki, this volume). Predictably, most works of art activate many brain regions and engage a variety of neural resources, depending on the modality of the artistic medium and the type of representation offered. Every creative or interpretative act, regardless of its input modality or conceptual demands, can be broken down, or deconstructed, in this way, into its neuro-cognitive "atoms."

In every case, these will translate into a series of elementary brain operations that unfold in a complex sequence. The sequences will be quite different for various kinds of cognition, and for dissimilar artistic media, but the component operations will be basically alike. These complex sequences can become habitual and automatic. Thus, my reaction to one of my favorite paintings, Gustav Klimt's *Hope 1* (located in the National Gallery of Canada, Ottawa), always follows a familiar course: my gaze starts in one of a few possible places, and moves around the painting in a fairly predictable order, with emphasis on certain key features. These features lead me to a certain state of mind, and elicit memories which govern how I see the painting. This is a well-studied aspect of visual perception, and involves little or nothing by way of operations that are unique to the artistic experience.

The uniqueness of the artistic experience produced in my brain by that painting can undoubtedly be traced back, if not to the elementary components in the sequence, then to the high-level neural consequences of the sequence of meanings and associations uniquely triggered by the painting. Such sequences, which I have referred to elsewhere as *Condillac sequences* (Donald 2001), lead to, and sustain, the cognitive endpoint of the artistic experience: a unified state of awareness that such a work of art ideally sets up in my (or any viewer's) mind. Unfortunately, neither brain imaging technology nor neurobiology has solved the problem of how to measure, let alone model, these abstract chains of meanings or the specific states of awareness they induce. The technology to do this may come in the future, but it is not yet available.

However, the real limitation of this approach is not our lack of knowledge about the physical basis of Condillac sequences, or states of consciousness; presumably it will eventually be within our powers to advance our knowledge in these areas. A more serious long-term limitation of any strictly neuroscientific solution lies in the fact that the common component processes of experience in the nervous system are not the only drivers behind the experience of art. It may be argued that the most important drivers are largely cultural, or cognitive-cultural, and depend not only on what is experienced, but also on interpretative algorithms that may be peculiar to individuals or societies and have no fixed neural instantiation. These algorithms are embedded in the "distributed" cognitive processes of social networks.

Distributed networks constitute a higher level of cognitive control that exists on a social level, and exerts a tremendous pull on the minds of the individuals in the network. It combines the memory storage capacities of many brains with whatever memory technology a given social network has at its disposal, and weaves these into a cognitive system that extends far beyond the individual brain. Within such a system, the location of memory itself is problematic. Memory can reside anywhere in the network. Perceptions can emerge and undergo major transformation anywhere in the network. Representations become a shared resource, and the sources of creative change can be found in many different locations at once. By definition, the neural component of distributed cognition is almost impossible to track down. Moreover, it is not clear that tracking down the neural responses of participating brains would extend our understanding of network-level cognition itself, except perhaps by clarifying the nature of the interface between brain and network.

Large distributed cognitive networks, such as those commonly found in corporations, can achieve cognitive objectives that exceed the capacity of individual brains. This is especially true of memory retrieval and storage, but it also extends to thought and representation. Distributed cognition can exploit the specialized talents of individuals by combining them into a collective cognitive organ; in theory, such an organism has at its disposal all of the relevant capabilities of an entire population, plus whatever additional cognitive power technology can contribute to the system. In other words, the system prevails, and even the most brilliant individual's intellectual contribution will be judged by the standards of the system itself.

But even the distributed system is not the ultimate arbiter of artistic experience. There is an unpredictable, sometimes rather quirky individual contribution to the interpretation of any work of art, and despite careful crafting by the artist, a work of art itself can never be entirely in control of the neural end-state it produces in a given recipient. Individual memory is so complex as to become unpredictable in practice, and it is the way Condillac sequences are juxtaposed in the memory of the individual viewer that will ultimately lead the viewer to a specific end-state. It is unrealistic to expect that a common pattern of neural processing will ever suffice to "explain" our individual reactions to art.

Artists might insist that the main driver of artistic experience is the engineer of that experience—namely, the artist—and this holds partly true. Certainly, the way the artist manipulates events so as to set up an end-state in the minds of the audience starts the process running, and some techniques (such as those of film) can be extremely compelling in controlling the audience's experience. But the brain might deconstruct the world presented by the artist in many different ways, and through many different paths, while the goals and methods of the artist are largely set by larger social-cognitive networks that are distributed. The artist controls only a fraction of this process.

The major underlying challenge for cognitive science is not to discover all the possible cognitive processing paths by which artistic experience comes to be; that would be impossible, and pointless. Such an endeavor would not be unlike a particle physicist's trying to track every electron in, say, a roomful of people at a cocktail party. Why would one want to do this? It would explain nothing about cocktail parties or people. Nor would such an analysis explain a work of art. It is the very source of art-based cognition we should be chasing here, and that source will not be found in either the brain or social networks, taken by themselves.

Therefore the relevant research question is: What question should we be asking of art with empirical brain research? One answer might be: We should ask how art has historically enriched or modified the cognitive processes of human beings, both individually and collectively. To a cognitive scientist, art represents a singular, rather peculiar way of knowing the world. Art attacks the mind, not usually through its logical or analytic channels, but more commonly through its senses, passions, and anxieties. Under the distant guidance of the artist, the brains of the viewers gather the disparate pieces of evidence placed before them, while they draw on their own experiences to reconstruct the artist's intent. The challenge for the scientist is to interpret the cognitive source of the audience's perception of the worldview intended in the work. This can rarely be reduced to the solving of a simple static stimulus, or to any moment frozen in time. It almost always entails the integration of many complex perceptions over many viewings. Such interpretations are inherently dynamic in nature, and mostly, they engage large-scale neural integration over time.

This is done by an unknown integrative process, in what we euphemistically call the "higher regions" of the mind, where the work is ultimately interpreted. In terms of the laws of higher neural processing, we have no idea how this final step is achieved. We know much about the neural principles underlying such processing, and we know roughly which geographic regions are involved, but we still have no adequate theory of how large-scale parallel neural networks can create such an abstract and detailed conceptualization of the world.

We do know, however, that many species have roughly the same elements of sensory and perceptual intelligence as we do, despite having produced nothing like what human beings call art. The basic processes of the nervous system are very similar in monkeys, apes, and humans, and the overall design of the brain is virtually identical. The human brain is much larger than those of apes and monkeys in certain areas, but as far as we have been able to determine, it has no qualitatively new regions or features. This might tempt us to think that the primate brain is a good starting point for a cognitive theory of art, and there is probably some gold to be mined by such studies. However, this is a self-limiting strategy and cannot explain much about the interpretation of art, since it avoids the central question: What makes humans so different?

The answer seems to lie elsewhere—and not entirely in the brain by itself. In the case of human beings, there is an additional factor that must be taken into account in explaining art: the distributed cognitive processes of culture. Human culture is uniquely cognitive in its function. Human culture is a marketplace of ideas and images, feelings and impressions. Indeed, it is a vast cognitive network in its own right. The cultural network introduces an entirely new element to human life: immersion in a cognitive collectivity, or community of mind. This is perhaps the primary source of the enormous cognitive differences between human beings and our closest genetic relatives. Monkeys and apes solve the world alone; we do not. Human culture is based on the sharing of mental representations, and we are tethered to that network. It allows us to achieve things that are far beyond the capabilities of an ape or, for that matter, a socially isolated human brain.

Artists may sometimes have the illusion of separateness, of isolation from society. But in reality they have always been society's early warning devices. The best of them are connected, and more deeply enculturated than most. It follows that the sources of their creativity, although partly personal, are also public, outside the nervous system, in the distributed system itself—that is, in culture, which encompasses, but supersedes, the individual nervous system.

The Evolutionary Origins of Art

The various expressive domains of art correspond roughly to major stages in the cognitive and cultural evolution of the human species. In previous publications (Donald 1991, 1993, 1998a, 2001) I have argued that art is an inevitable by-product of mimesis—a primordial, and truly human, cognitive adaptation that occurred very early in hominid prehistory and became the signature feature of the human mind. Mimesis had enormous cognitive consequences on the group level, resulting in a characteristically human form of communicative culture that later increased its influence with the emergence of language.

Mimesis is an analogue or holistic style of thought that is more basic to our uniquely human way of thinking than language or logic. Indeed, on present evidence language and logic evolved much later, from a mimetic platform. Mimesis is a foundation skill that arrived early in evolution, and defined the human style. The components of mimetic cognition are present to some degree in primates, but are vastly more developed in humans. This makes mimetic culture a logical, but radical, extension of the primate mind. It remains an important force in human affairs, and produces such typically human cognitive patterns as ritual, skill, gesture, tribal identification, personal style, and public spectacle. It explains our irresistible tendency to imitate one another and conform to patterns of group behavior, especially group emotional expression. It sets the tone of human social life, and it is the ultimate driving force behind art, which might be viewed as the ultimate refinement of the mimetic mode.

Mimesis is an innate capacity, and its universality allows human society to function smoothly. Then again, the mimetic tendency to copy others and conform is also a potentially fatal flaw that might someday destroy the human race; but that is quite another question. If humanity had somehow managed to evolve language and symbolic thought without first establishing an evolutionary platform for it in mimetic cognition, we would have very different minds. And very different cultures.

What is mimesis? The easiest answer to this question is simply to list some of the behaviors it encompasses. The term *mimesis* describes a cluster of capacities that were made possible by a single neuro-cognitive adaptation. They go together historically because they share certain key neural components. The four central mimetic abilities are mime, imitation, gesture, and the rehearsal of skill. Human beings are uniquely good at these. Apes have some small degree of competence in these areas, and this strengthens the case that these capacities might have been subjected to selection pressure early in hominid evolution, primarily to improve our ancestors' ability to obtain a high-quality diet in a changing environment.

Mimesis seems to have evolved as a cognitive elaboration of embodiment in patterns of action. Its origins lie in a redistribution of frontal-cortical influence during the early stages of the evolution of species *Homo*, when the prefrontal and parts of the premotor cortex expanded enormously in relative size and connectivity. The cognitive significance of this lies in the fact that, in virtually all social mammals, the frontal regions are concerned with the control of action and behavior, as opposed to the posterior areas, which are broadly concerned with the elaboration of perception. The disproportionate expansion of frontal influence gave hominids greatly improved motor control. More important, the expansion of the prefrontal cortex was crucial in improving conscious self-regulation and metacognition. This created a new metacognitive field, a greatly expanded and differentiated working memory, in which hominids could observe themselves as actors, and rehearse and refine whatever they were doing. This also gave them some ability to reflect on the cognitive process itself, and the option of deliberately reflecting on, and shaping, their own actions.

The latter point is worth some elaboration. Only human beings reflect on their own actions, and modify them accordingly. Human children pass large amounts of time in skill-related play—that is, in rehearsing and altering their own actions. For instance, they might spend an entire afternoon improving their ability to bounce a ball, skip stones, make faces, assume odd postures, or create novel sounds. No other creature does anything like this. Many species engage in play, of course, and innate skills need to be exercised frequently in developing organisms. But most species play in a stereotyped manner, and do not generate truly novel patterns or engage in role-playing or imaginary games. It is as if their attention were fixed on the external world, and unable to redirect itself toward the internal world of action. That is a great limitation, because it precludes what humans know as culture. If attention is exclusively outward-directed, then motor activity, generated internally, remains fixed and stereotyped. And this rings true when examining what virtually all other mammals can do. They appear much less self-conscious than humans. Their awareness is other-directed, not self-directed.

Mimesis is therefore the direct result of consciously examining our own embodiment, of the brain using its body as a reduplicative device. The cognitive engine of this expressive skill is a much more powerful working-memory space, an inner theater where imaginary actors play with actions and expressions, and where the embodied self performs various possible roles in the social world. It is also a place where self-initiated actions can be judged, altered, and exposed to internal critical scrutiny. The outcome of this remarkable process is a characteristically human capacity for reenacting events in a nonverbal, gestural, fuzzy, quasi-symbolic manner. A child's simple pantomime of a tea party or bedtime is a good example. It is an imaginary *playback* that tries to reduplicate an aspect of perceived reality, but alters reality in the process. *Reality* does not in fact look anything like its putative reenactment, and every successive mimetic act in such a sequence will become another variation on the initial reenactment. The metacognitive part of the mimetic mind can reflect on this scenario, which can be altered until the child judges it to be *right*. Unlike the stereotyped play of animals, the details of such a performance are never fixed. Mimetic expressions, even the simplest of them, are inherently creative and somewhat arbitrary. Mimesis can produce a virtual infinity of specific forms, even in the simplest reenactment, charade, or pantomime.

Moreover, mimetic expressions can potentially engage any part of the body. Unlike the songs of birds, they are not limited to one sense modality. Rather, mimesis is truly amodal, and can map virtually any kind of event-percept onto virtually any set of muscles, using many different specific read-outs. This leads to flexible analogue motor expressions, or action-metaphors. I might normally indicate anger with my face and low-level voice modulations, but at a distance I can substitute larger body gestures and very different sounds to achieve the same communicative effect. In a boardroom I might limit my expression of the same emotion to polite finger-tapping or searing glances. The point is that a mimetic production is never limited to one set of muscles or one fixed set of expressive forms. Mimetic creativity is *domain-general* or supra-modal, and fully accessible to consciousness. It meets all the criteria for what Fodor called a *nonmodular adaptation* (Fodor 1983) because it can range across all the perceptual and motor domains given to the actor's awareness. It creates a very abstract mimetic *mapping* of an act model onto a perceptual model, and this capacity allows the actor to use any part of the body to formulate and transmit intentions, ideas, and skills.

At the same time, mimesis is the supporting adaptation of many other human endeavors. It enables athletes, skilled craftsmen, and other performers to refine their skills by generating variations on their actions and selecting the most successful ones. Mimesis is always an attempt to reduplicate some aspect of reality in action, and in the case of skilled rehearsal, the rehearsal itself is a mimetic act: the performer is imitating his or her own previous actions, and creating variations of those actions. The result is a personal repertoire that can be altered toward achieving some ideal of action. This is the cognitive path to a multitude of human skills. People acquire an incredible number of skills in a lifetime—they play sports and music, drive, and talk, to mention a few—and all these skills have been learned and improved through mimetic action.

Mimesis is the original source of human culture—that is, communities of mind linked together in a public expressive domain. Taken together, the mimetic actions of a small group of primate actors will inevitably generate a social theater of some complexity, and a rudimentary version of human culture, limited in its range of expression. On a larger scale, the same abilities will establish the implicit customs and folkways of a truly human culture. Even in the absence of language, this process carries out its work, as happens in communities of nonsigning deaf people. Mimetic role-playing and fantasy constitute a basis for a limited worldview, but one that is at least partially public, and subject to some degree of cultural change. When this capacity was amplified through an interaction with spoken language, the expressive potential of mimesis was fully realized, resulting in an expressive culture of great power.

Where did mimesis come from? Our closest relatives are the chimpanzees, with whom we shared a common ancestor five or six million years ago and whose genes are very close to ours. But while chimps and humans have virtually similar cognitive capacities, chimps are very different from humans. We have traveled an inordinate distance, and this needs an explanation. It is true that our brains have tripled in volume, doubling their number of neurons, and that certain brain areas have expanded disproportionately. But there do not seem to be any new neural modules or neurochemical transmitters in the human brain. The most radically novel factor in our evolution is culture itself, as a collective storehouse of knowledge, and our brains have evolved specifically for living in culture. We are the species that made cultures into distributed cognitive systems, and those systems have reshaped our brains. In fact, the human brain cannot realize one of its key design potentials, symbolic cognition, without extensive cultural programming.

If we concede that human infants get language and all the tools of symbolic thought from culture, then we should ask: Where did cultures come from? What generated them *de novo* in the wild? The answer is: mimetic action. Apes are notoriously poor at mimetic action. A species cannot generate a culture until it can escape the autochthonous solipsism of the central nervous system and generate a common cultural space that can accumulate knowledge. Apes never managed to do this, primarily because they are so poor at gesture and imitation, and virtually incapable of deliberately self-supervising the rehearsal of their own actions to refine them. However, they have some of the key elements of mimetic ability, and this provided natural selection with the opportunity, once conditions gave fitness value to improved mimetic skill, to nudge and shape archaic hominids in the direction they eventually took.

The importance of mimesis can be seen in the limitations of even the most brilliant encultured apes, who can manage symbol use much more easily than the gestural or skill-related dimensions of human culture. It may seem odd that Kanzi (the star performer of encultured chimpanzees, who can segment the speech stream, understand some of the rudiments of grammar, and employ a vocabulary of several hundred symbols) cannot manage even a simple iconic gesture or engage in the kind of role-playing common in two-year-old children. Nor can he play basketball, as his trainer observed. But this is not odd at all; it is entirely consistent with what I have said about the crucial importance of mimesis in human cognition.

The central role of mimesis is relevant to determining the cognitive role of art in human history and prehistory because all art is essentially mimetic in style. Even literature, which appears to depend more on language than on mimesis for its superficial forms, is ultimately shaped by mimetic tendencies emanating from the deepest part of the writer's mind. This idea was articulated very clearly by the eminent critic Erich Auerbach a generation ago (1953/2003). In a similar vein the French philosopher René Girard recognized the role of mimesis in forming the fundamental dramatic tensions driving human social life (Girard, 1979).

In short, art is the expressive culmination of the most ancient domain of the human mind, as manifested in the rituals, public actions, and gestures that characterize any human society. It is woven into the deepest layer of meaning that can be called uniquely human. The power of mimetic expression can be furthered by technology, but the roots of that very special expressive style go deep into the earliest evolutionary layer of human emergence.

Summary and Conclusion

Art is a distinctively human form of cognitive activity that is characterized by the following features.

1. Art is aimed at influencing the minds of an audience, and may therefore be called a form of cognitive engineering.
2. It always occurs in the context of distributed cognition.
3. It is constructivist in nature, aimed at the deliberate refinement and elaboration of worldviews.
4. Most art is metacognitive in its role—that is, it engages in self-reflection, both individually and socially.
5. The forms and media of art are technology-driven.
6. The role of the artist and the local social definition of art are not necessarily fixed and are products of the current social-cognitive network.
7. Nevertheless, art, unlike most conventional engineering, is always aimed at a cognitive outcome.

Viewed in an evolutionary context, art originated in the earliest stages of hominid evolution, the so-called Mimetic phase. Newer forms have been scaffolded onto the older ones, and as human beings have evolved complex languages and technologies, artists have developed new forms that contain within them all the elements of our evolutionary history. Every newly evolved artistic domain has a unique combination of these elementary components. Surveyed as a whole, the domains of art ultimately reflect the entire evolved structure of the human cognitive-cultural system. The challenge to cognitive scientists and neuroscientists is to develop a methodology that will allow them to fathom the abstract amodal processes of large-scale neural integration that transform the complex representations imposed by artists on their audiences into meaningful experiences. The ultimate engine of art, and the common force that makes art so distinct in its cognitive style from science, is mimesis. Therefore the genesis of art will not be understood, even in principle, until the neural and cognitive principles and mechanisms of mimesis are better understood.

REFERENCES

Auerbach, E. 1953/2003. *Mimesis: The representation of reality in western literature* (fiftieth anniversary edition). Princeton, N.J.: Princeton University Press.

Donald, M. 1991. *Origins of the modern mind: Three stages in the evolution of culture and cognition.* Cambridge, Mass.: Harvard University Press.

———. 1993. Précis of *Origins of the Modern Mind* with multiple reviews and author's response. *Behavioral and Brain Sciences,* 16:737–91.

———. 1998a. Hominid enculturation and cognitive evolution. In *Cognition and material culture: The archaeology of symbolic storage,* ed. C. Renfrew and C. Scarre, 7–17. Cambridge, England: McDonald Institute of Archaeological Research.

———. 1998b. Mimesis and the executive suite: Missing links in language evolution. In *Approaches to the evolution of language: Social and cognitive bases,* ed. J. R. Hurford, M. Studdert-Kennedy, and C. Knight, 44–67. Cambridge, England: Cambridge University Press.

———. 2001. *A mind so rare: The evolution of human consciousness.* New York: W. W. Norton.

Fodor, J. 1983. *Modularity of mind: An essay on faculty psychology.* Cambridge, Mass.: MIT Press.

Girard, R. 1979. *Violence and the sacred.* Baltimore, Md.: Johns Hopkins University Press.

2

The Aesthetic Faculty

Terrence Deacon

This chapter asks the question: Why is it that only human beings spend time and effort to produce and acquire aesthetic experience? It focuses on the role of juxtapositions, bisociations, and blends in human cognition, and proposes that symbolic abilities are a critical basis for these kinds of mental operations. Symbolic juxtapositions force further juxtapositions of correlated emotional responses, which are presumably independent of the logic of symbolic juxtaposition. These symbolic juxtapositions can thereby induce emergent and highly novel emotional experiences.

To discuss art as a biological phenomenon divorced from a particular culture at a particular historical moment seems almost ludicrously artificial. And even within such constraints, it is still difficult to use-fully define and categorize what constitutes art. As is often remarked, one man's junk is another man's art. Indeed, it seems to have been a postmodern preoccupation of artists to produce works that insistently undermine any effort to define it. Within our current (and largely culture-dependent) understanding, "art" often refers less to a defin-able class of objects and performances than to an economic and commodity-status category. But this somewhat disembodied concep-tion is mostly confined to large, stratified societies. Indigenous peo-ples from Third World societies often find Western buyers' art-commoditization of their cultural objects to be strange, even as they eagerly oblige by specializing in the mass production and sale of these same objects. If, however, we step back from "art" both as commodity and as intellectual valorization, and consider the general phenomenon that is the object of this fetishization, quite a few useful generalizations are possible.

First, there are few if any societies in the world that do not engage in the production of some artifacts whose form conveys more than literal or simple use information, and essentially no society is devoid of all forms of music, dance, or storytelling. This clearly indicates the existence of a species-wide predisposition to create and use means *to express or evoke experiences* in ways that cannot be approached through what might be called *literal modes* of communication— for example, unmarked forms of language, physical instruction, or species-typical calls, displays, and facial expressions. In "art," then, we recognize two key elements: (1) an extraction from direct instrumental communication; and (2) a duplicitous logic of representation: there is what it is or presents, and there is what it conveys only in some figurative form.

For the sake of this biological reflection on the nature and basis of this human phenomenon, I will use the term *art* in this most generic and culture-independent sense to refer to any conventionalized semiotic activity that has these characteristics, with the caveat that this is at once too broad and too restrictive a definition, and may need to become progressively more sophisticated as we move on. My general (but also limited) purpose is to analyze the special cognitive features of this communicative-cognitive-emotional phenomenon in such a way that it helps us to understand the idiosyncratic evolution of art in just one lineage.

There is another important caveat as well. The neurological modifications of human brains that underlie this faculty are almost certainly neither necessary nor sufficient to explain artistic activities or even the mental phenomena associated with them. This follows from the fact that art is not a product of some autonomous neurological development process, as is the ability to walk or to articulate speech sounds. Like language acquisition, the development of even modest artistic expressive abilities takes effort and extensive cultural experience. Language, however, though also dependent on social input, is far more canalized in its development, doesn't appear at all counterintuitive to young children, and is highly constrained in its possible variation. Also, unlike linguistic abilities, the ability even to appreciate what a given culture considers artistic (in this broadest sense) depends on cultural experiences with these or related forms and with others' interpretations of them. To make matters worse for this comparison, most modes of artistic expression and communication involve modifications of extrinsic media, and even those that utilize modified vocalization and social behavior—that is, singing and acting—involve rather special conventional re-framings of "mundane" speech and social life.

So, not only is it unlikely that there has been direct selection for these capacities, but they also share with reading and writing the status of being supported by cognitive capacities that probably evolved for other reasons. Consistent with their being capacities that require considerable training and cultural support to develop, there is wide individual and cultural variability in artistic phenomena. Yet despite this cultural boundedness and a fundamental break with biology, there is surprising species universality as well. Even though artistic expression does not "come naturally," as does language and much social behavior, it is essentially culturally universal in some form or other. That is to say, there are extensive cross-cultural, historical, and developmental commonalities that are widely recognized in artistic activities and creations. Even the very earliest paintings of animals on cave walls, made tens of thousands of years ago, are as easily recognizable as if they had been painted today. They evoke an unmistakable sense of psychological identification with the painters.

Development of these abilities shows evidence of both art's alien character and its tie to species-general predispositions. Children in both Western and Eastern societies, for example, are actively encouraged and trained to express themselves in the various media that these cultures associate with the arts—drawing, sculpting, dance, music, acting, and so on. Children from these diverse cultural backgrounds seem to acquire an understanding of what pictorial depiction is all about in roughly similar recognizable stages. At early ages, when children are first confronted with the opportunity to "draw something," they tend to appear "unclear on the concept" and require both example and encouragement to get it. But once they do, their subsequent development of concepts of spatial relationships, and their development of the ability to depict these relationships, seem to follow surprisingly parallel tracks.

In these respects, art seems to have a sort of cognitive complementarity to language. A correlated neurological complementarity is also highlighted by the curious dissociation between linguistic and artistic capacities that is common in so-called savant syndromes, often associated with autism. Here the disruption or delay of linguistic and social capacities apparently facilitates the development of paradoxically augmented nonlinguistic expressive skills, such as artistic depiction or musical imitation.

So, the cultural variety, historical transformation, and significant individual variance in artistic expression and appreciation suggest that it is a cognitive capacity that is far from genetically prefigured, and yet the near universal presence of art, the curious links it shows with neurological disturbances, and its uniquely human status all make it a hallmark of a "cognitive style" that is unprecedented in the animal kingdom.

Uniqueness

The species uniqueness of this capacity is humorously exemplified by one of my favorite coffee-table books: *Why Cats Paint: A Theory of Feline Aesthetics* (Busch and Silver 1994). This tongue-in-cheek review of the "works" of selected cat artists probes their styles and motivations and considers the meanings hidden in cat paintings and sculptures (my favorites are claw-work sculptures rendered in the medium of sofas and overstuffed chair arms). Of course the real question that this suggests is: Why *don't* cats paint? (assuming that you agree with me that the book is a spoof!). Indeed, why don't any other species engage in quite this form of behavior or even seem to appreciate its products? And why is it so nearly universal in some form in humans if it is so culture-dependent and culture-bound? And, of course, why do these activities produce the special kinds of experiences that they do, which can be both powerful and seriously sought after?

Stating the claim to species uniqueness in such black-and-white terms is to some extent an exaggeration. I do not mean to suggest that no other species makes and appreciates elaborate constructions whose primary purpose is communication. There are many examples to indicate that the sensory attractiveness of certain objects matters to many species.

Insights into both animal analogues to art and the processes relevant to its evolution are found in male bower bird behavior. Males construct nestlike structures and decorate them with brightly colored objects to attract females. The bower building is clearly evolved from ancestral nest building, but it no longer serves that purpose. This has almost certainly contributed to freeing the behavior from functional constraints and has allowed the associated behaviors to begin to incorporate merely communicative flourishes. This pattern of "deletion" of prior functional constraint from some object or behavior, allowing it to assimilate purely signal-altering features, will show up as a recurrent theme in the story of the evolution of both play and art. It is also often the origin of new subjects and substrates appropriated for artistic purposes. This freedom from one set of selection constraints in bower birds has apparently released (or unmasked) the possibility of selection for communicative elaboration, and it has apparently instilled something like "appreciation" for what makes a good trinket for incorporation into the bower. A covetousness about objects with attention-grabbing properties is exemplified by the fact that these birds constantly raid one another's bowers for bright colorful objects. It is doubtful that they consider anything like the "significance" of what they are doing, or what it may convey to another bird, other than being an attractant. As an analogy, we might consider human body decoration for the purpose of potential mate attraction—a species-wide preoccupation that also borders on and crosses over into art.

There are also numerous accounts of apes, birds, elephants, and various pets (like the cats mentioned above) being coaxed into expressing themselves by painting. Exhibits of animal "art" have periodically drawn crowds to art galleries, and animal paintings have been sold to support animal research. This is not new. On the back cover of *Why Cats Paint* there is a picture of a poster, apparently more than a century old, advertising a showing of the paintings of an "amazing" cat named Clarissa; reports of similarly amazing trained animals have been around since the Renaissance. Where the process of inducing animals to express themselves in this way is described, it often suggests only very partial recognition by the animal "artists" of what the human trainers intend or interpret. Much like very young children on their first exposure to making art, the animals seem to find the process and the associated social feedback reinforcing, though it is not clear that they advance to an understanding of the "something more" that we humans come to take for granted.

But what is this "something more" that I have alluded to? Art objects and artistic performances are created to communicate something that they are not. They are *signs*. In contrast to most other species, we humans find reason to seek the "significance" of some crafted form, seeing it as a vehicle for expressing or representing something beyond its specific physical form or uses. I think that this is true not just with respect to art, however, since we also have difficulty suppressing the urge to find "meaning" in natural events, coincidences, and natural forms. Perhaps we can't say for certain that a particularly crimson sunset isn't capable of evoking melancholy for lost love in a robin or that a rock cliff profile doesn't suggest the silhouette of a conspecific face to an ape, but there is little evidence that it is so, and an overabundance of evidence that this sort of tendency is almost a defining feature of humanness. We almost can't help ourselves. So then, to the definition of what I am considering to be the *human aesthetic faculty*, I would have to add this easily activated compulsion to treat objects or actions as signs (icons, indices, or symbols) for something beyond themselves.

This curious difference between humans and other species demands an evolutionary and neurological explanation no less than does the uniqueness of language. But this uniqueness raises two evolutionary questions prior to any neurological questions that might be asked:

1. Is this capacity-predisposition a primary adaptation or a side effect of some other selected cognitive traits (e.g., language adaptations)?
2. To what extent is it an acquired feature dependent on the development of linguistic symbolic abilities, or an expression of predispositions that are in some way developmentally antecedent to any cultural symbolic overlay?

If we postpone considering these questions, and do not proffer at least provisional answers to them, we run the risk of confounding aesthetic cognition with its superficial correlates in perception and emotional arousal.

There is one more critical component that must be incorporated into this provisional consideration of the features that make aesthetic cognition unique: a difference in the motivational orientation that characterizes the production and experience of art. (This description, in turn, raises the question of whether differences exist between the motivational structure of human cognition and that of other species.) More precisely, the aesthetic experience, and especially the predisposition to assume a representational stance (see below) with respect to a very wide range of stimuli, reflects a phylogenetically atypical linkage between certain kinds of perceptual experiences, cognitive assessments of those experiences, and the emotions that derive from these assessments. The human predilection for artistic endeavors thus also hints at the possibility that human emotional architecture may have been tweaked, along with other cognitive capacities, during our evolution. Whereas most discussions of human mental evolution invoke ideas of modified intelligence, linguistic computation, or domain-special computational modules, a consideration of human artistic predispositions suggests that these hypotheses may have entirely missed something at least as fundamental: the likely possibility that human cognitive and neural evolution includes a significant modification of typical mammalian motivational systems. So an exploration of the neural-evolutionary underpinnings of this characteristically human attribute may alert us to important aspects of human evolution and brain function that have otherwise gone completely unnoticed.

The arts and humanities are often treated by evolutionary biology and the neurosciences as peripheral epiphenomena with respect to more instrumental cognitive domains. This seems to me to be a serious intellectual blindspot. The human fascination with the perceptual experiences and activities that we broadly classify as aesthetic seems to be one of the clearest indices of the existence of a broader cognitive penumbra—extending beyond increased intelligence or language ability—cast by our neural evolution. These phenomena provide what I would regard as the equivalents of signature neurological signs (in the clinical sense of that term), pointing to an important species-specific modification of the typical primate brain plan. Thus, an investigation of the cognitive foundations of artistic expression and appreciation in all its forms promises to offer a special window onto our uniquely human neurology.

To be able to mine the data, we must first develop a clearer functional account of what the human difference actually amounts to, and of its antecedents in nonhuman cognitive functions. The comparative cognitive side of this question does not, however, immediately suggest clear experimental methodologies, precisely because of the evolutionary non sequitur nature of these behaviors. It is not at all clear how these human abilities can be functionally parsed so as to foreground exactly those component cognitive operations that map onto nonhuman cognitive homologues.

Compositional Homology of the Art and Language Faculties

In this era of brain imaging, the empirical study of the neural basis of human aesthetic and artistic cognition would appear to be a straightforward project. Analyze the cognitive tasks involved, collect *in vivo* images of the brains of artists "creating" and observers of the arts "appreciating," and compare these data to that from other cognitive processes that do not involve aesthetic cognition (as controls). What would this tell us? Something like brain region X is activated by the perceptual analysis of some patterned stimulus and that brain areas Y or Z are variably active as well, depending on whether the perceptual object is being considered as a potential tool, say, or as an artistic expression. What would such a result mean? Is the differential activity of areas Y or Z telling us that these areas house an aesthetic evaluation module?

As materialists, we can trivially agree that when it comes to brains and cognition there is "no free lunch"—that is to say, for every distinguishable cognitive state, perceptual operation, mnemonic-attentional orientation, and so on, there will be a distinct pattern of neurological activation and inactivation. So to go on a fishing expedition to isolate some *in vivo* metabolic activity pattern in response to a presumed aesthetic judgment (or whatever) will not *ipso facto* contribute useful information about the neurology of aesthetic experience. A too greedy reduction of artistic cognition to regional brain activities will rightfully be dismissed by serious scholars of the arts as contributing little more than verification that *something* is happening in the brain. We must be precise about the distinctive features of the phenomenon before we can go about investigating its physical correlates, and this must begin with a careful assessment of what it is about this activity that is not just mammalian cognition as usual.

One great aid in this investigation is the likelihood that brain structures involved in aesthetic experience have homologues in nonhuman species' brains. I am willing to bet that there will be perceptual judgments made by monkeys that light up their brains according to a similar combination and yet will have little to do with art or the interpretation of art. Activation of these areas may be necessary for this experience, but this does not mean that it is sufficient to explain what is going on and why. I have no doubt that brain function in aesthetic cognition is in some way distinctive and unique (and below I will offer some hints as to how), but there may be no simple mapping that is evident, given our current technologies and paltry understanding of the more subtle neural processes that are likely involved. More important, there may well be a significant aspect of aesthetic cognition, such as its social-cultural framing, that is extraneuronal—for example, dependent on something outside the brain.

Human cognition is both deeply continuous with nonhuman cognitive capacities and yet also significantly modified. Its modification is most enigmatically exemplified by our linguistic adaptations, which in many ways can serve as a model for thinking about the evolution of aesthetic cognition as well. As far as can be discerned—as assessed in terms of histological regional distinctions, neuronal response characteristics, effects of structural damage, and general connectivity patterns—language processing depends on modifications of otherwise rather typical primate neural architecture.

For example, classic language areas in the cerebral cortex appear to have primate homologues with respect to topology, cell architecture, connectivity, and functional responsiveness (Deacon 1997; Romanski et al. 1999). No unambiguously "new" (i.e., nonhomologous) cortical or subcortical structures have been identified, even though there appear to have been significant quantitative shifts of components and possible connectional changes related to language processing (Deacon 1997). It is as yet highly controversial how radical those modifications related to language might be, to what extent they are language-domain specific, and exactly how the cognitive constraints and biases that result interact with complex developmental and cultural processes to produce languages within the known limits of their variation. There can be little debate, however, about the existence of *some* level of neural reorganization responsible for our language-processing capacity. It is the specificity of this reorganization with respect to linguistic functions, and the extent to which it determines or constrains language structure and language processing, that provokes the controversy.

My own view is that the critical neuroanatomical changes are unlikely to consist of anything like a direct mapping to linguistic functions. Rather, I believe that we must approach language processing as an emergent complex system effect. In other words, what I prefer to call *language adaptations* likely constitute a diverse set of subtle modifications to many neural and vocal system structures, none of which could properly be called language-specific. Each modification of an otherwise conserved pattern of neural signal processing also changes higher-order system relationships, and it is these complementary effects which constitute the predispositions that support language acquisition and use.[1] I will discuss some details of these neuroanatomical predispositions, and their relevance to the evolution of aesthetic cognition, below; but first let me return to the issue of social factors.

An emergent view of the language faculty also suggests that brain evolution will tend to fall short of localizing all major supports for this capacity inside brains. In this regard, important clues are provided by recent simulation studies, which suggest that many characteristic attributes of language structure, such as compositionality and structural regularization, can be generated as a result of the constraints of language learning and transmission alone (e.g., see Hurford 2000). To the extent that some consistent structural organizing processes can be reliably generated by these self-organizing (and transgenerational) social-communicative dynamics, selection that might otherwise instantiate these biasing influences in the form of neuronal structure will be weakened. Thus, what has been described as the language faculty may be constituted only in part within brains. I think we tend to consistently underestimate the constructive power of extra-neuronal, supra-cognitive factors, and correspondingly overestimate what must be contributed by special features of human brains.

In summary, we humans do not appear to use wholly unprecedented (in a phylogenetic sense) neural resources to support our unprecedented language abilities, although we probably use these neural systems in novel combinations in order to respond to the atypical demands of language processing. Also, it seems that this novel functional synergy was achieved via the contributions of many supporting systems, including, critically, a dependence on social processes and, quite likely, modified motivational systems to maintain these external supports.

Play and Representational Stance

As I noted above, one of the key elements of the "something more" that distinguishes art from mere adornment is the enigmatic tendency to communicate significance or meaning, to function as a sign of something it is not. Borrowing a trope from Dan Dennett (1991), I will call this predisposition a *representational stance*. Dennett uses the phrase *intentional stance* to describe a predisposition to treat other people, most animals, and certain animate objects (such as personal computers) or surrogates for animate creatures (such as puppets and stuffed animals) as having intentional states—that is, as having minds with beliefs, desires, and so on. Although we do not treat everything in the world as standing for something else or as conveying some cryptic content (as Freud is reputed to have retorted at one point, "Sometimes a cigar is just a cigar"), we humans are nevertheless notorious for these kinds of projections. In almost all societies, people routinely interpret natural disasters, diseases, the appearances of comets, bad luck, and even simple mechanical failures as "signs" of something. I have elsewhere (Deacon 1997) wryly described this as a sort of *symbolic savant syndrome*, by which I mean to emphasize the almost compulsive tendency to apply this one mode of sensory-cognitive evaluation to a far wider scope of objects and events than is instrumentally warranted.

To describe the "representational stance" as uniquely human would be to overstate the case (though below I will defend a narrower interpretation of this claim with respect to symbolic representation specifically). Probably the most widespread expression of this stance in nature is found in play behavior. In an influential account of what constitutes the representational character of play in animals, Gregory Bateson (1972) describes how a play nip conveys the "significance" of a bite without the correlated physical consequence, and thus becomes behavior *about* fighting without *being* fighting. The resemblance of the actions of play fighting to actual fighting clearly evokes memories or activates behavior patterns associated with fighting, but the failure to produce the pain typically correlated with and expected of the act of biting indicates that this activity is only a surrogate, and not what it appears. The participants thus maintain a representational stance toward these behaviors (at least until one accidentally does cause significant pain).

Play is of course a widespread mammalian behavior, especially common in younger animals. It clearly indicates that, at least in such special circumstances, many other species are capable of conceiving of things as representations, and recognizing that certain consequences and responses do not follow that would follow were this not play. We see this phenomenon even in cross-species play behaviors between humans and their pets. In semiotic terms, the play fighting behaviors are *iconic* of fighting, but the critical deletion of certain key consequences *indicates* that it is a mere representation. To an outside observer, even sometimes one of the same species, this semiotic transformation may not be obvious (though usually there are many redundant indices of it). Human play also includes these elements and can extend (as may also be common in other species) to peek-a-boo (which might be described as a sort of abandonment-reuniting play), maternal play (with the infant replaced by some surrogate), sexual play (with copulation deleted), hunting play (with the prey replaced), and so forth. But there is an additional overlay in much human play: conventionalization and the introduction of symbolic relationships.

By early middle childhood the establishment and regulation of a "play frame" becomes increasingly dependent on rules and roles, many of which are part of the cultural heritage. These include both transmitted conventions explicitly for play (as in games) and culture-specific roles that are transformed into play roles by appropriate deletions and substitutions. Although the term *symbolic play* has been used somewhat differently—for example, by Jean Piaget (1951) to refer more generally to all forms that involve representational transformation—I would distinguish these conventionally established frames as *symbolically mediated*, whereas play fighting and at least some maternal and sexual play, for example, could be mediated merely by the indexical role of critical deletions and substitutions. I think that the use of symbolic information (mostly expressed in linguistic form) to establish the play frame, as in "let's make believe..." play, identifies a critical difference between humans and other species. Even when we use symbols to initiate play between pets and their owners (e.g., a dog responding to "You wanna play fetch?"), it is likely to be the habitual predictability of the following interaction and not the symbolic content of the utterance that matters. (The utterance itself, in such cases, serves as an index.)

It is this distinction I want to draw upon to characterize art and aesthetic cognition as compared to their near neighbors in human and nonhuman cognition. My hypothesis is that our capacity to assume the representational stance—to function in what I have called "a sort of duplicitous state of mind"—has been radically transformed by the use of symbols and also by human adaptations that have come to serve as ancillary supports for making symbolic communication easier over the course of our evolution. A corollary of this is that the human symbolic tweak of the more general nonhuman capacity amplifies it to nearly unrecognizable extremes. But it amplifies and embellishes something already there and phylogenetically prior. Like the bower bird and its nest building or the play-fighting with respect to agonistic behavior, these phylogenetically prior capacities are the cognitive-emotional substrates recruited in the aesthetic experience. And these have old neural substrates as well. But as they are recruited—out of context, so to speak—they can be expressed, embellished, and recombined in radically unprecedented ways. How, though, might these cognitive-emotional patterns have been freed from more ancient, functionally grounded constraints?

What Is a Symbol?

I believe that the key to this release from strict functionality of cognitive-emotional states occurred through the aid of our recently and idiosyncratically evolved capacity to comprehend and use symbols. So to understand the evolutionary anomaly of aesthetic capacity, we must first understand another equally anomalous phenomenon. We need to ask what is so different about symbolic reference and why it does not appear to be in use by any other species.

Asking this apparently simple definitional question opens a pandora's box of philosophical, linguistic, and semiotic debates. The tendency, especially in animal behavior studies, but also in the cognitive and neurosciences and even linguistics, is to finesse the problem by making do with simple operational definitions, and move on to other topics such as syntax or behavioral functional correlations. Unfortunately, with respect to the study of human cognition, especially from a comparative perspective, to avoid the problem is to black-box the primary mystery.

The capacity to easily acquire symbolic competence, productively use symbols in novel combinations to refer to novel referents, and effortlessly decode these novel combinations on the fly is unique to humans. Although other species have been successfully trained to communicate in limited contexts with small systems of symbols, this generally appears to be a rather difficult task and is sufficiently counterintuitive for them as to limit most generative use or spontaneous new symbol acquisition. Even this claim is controversial, but there is considerably more disagreement about what our symbolic capacity entails and how it came about. There is almost unanimous agreement about one claim concerning symbols, however: the ability to communicate and think with the aid of the symbolic tools of language accounts for much that sets humans apart from other species.

As I argued above, however, this novel capacity does not appear to be based on some phylogenetically novel human brain structures. There is no human neural "essence" that explains this capacity; no new symbol module (or language module) that can be anatomically identified as being without an antecedent primate neuroanatomical homologue. I have argued elsewhere (e.g., Deacon 1997) that our capacities to employ symbolic representations, and language more specifically, were achieved by a largely quantitative reorganization of regional proportions within the brain, coextensive with the enlargement of the hominid brain as a whole. From this perspective, I argued that these symbolic capacities were *emergent capacities*, in the sense that their synergistic functional attributes were never expressed nor subject to selection in any nonhominid lineage, and yet the component cognitive functions that contribute to this composite function were all present and subject to selection previously. What I believe distinguished human evolution and made human cognition and communication so singularly distinctive was that an initial modest incorporation of symbolic communication in our distant ancestors (as far back as 2.4 million years) shifted selection on human cognitive capacity to this emergent synergistic composite function. This selection was both independent of and in some cases even contrary to the selective forces previously responsible for honing the component functions on which this higher-order capacity was based. The combinatorial consequence— symbolic communication—became the tail that wagged the dog, so to speak, and has now produced a brain significantly biased to make symbol learning and manipulation almost effortless.

What were the tweaks in cognitive processing that made an unnatural form of communication seem natural? What brain differences in humans reflect these aids to symbolic cognition? Or perhaps we might ask this inversely: What are the cognitive limitations that make symbolic representation nearly inaccessible for nonhuman species?

The answer to these questions largely depends on how one conceives of symbolic reference. There are both semantic and theoretical difficulties contributing to the widespread differences of opinion regarding what constitutes a symbol. For many, it is sufficient to define symbols in terms of the arbitrariness of the reference relationship or the use of a conventional token as a sign. Understood this way, there is little to suggest that other species lack symbolic capacities. After all, even pigeons can be conditioned to peck at arbitrarily chosen patterns to request food or drink, or even to alert other pigeons to their presence. And species from Vervet monkeys (Cheney and Sayfarth 1990) to chickens (Hauser 1996) produce distinctive alarm calls to alert conspecifics of the presence of one of a few of their most commonly encountered predators. This understanding of symbolic reference, however, misses an important distinction between features prominent in both the sign vehicle and its object, on the one hand, and features that actually serve as the basis for a given interpretation. Although lack of obvious formal similarities with the object suggests non-iconism, and lack of directly observable physical involvement in the object suggests non-indexicality, these superficial assessments ignore the basis on which an interpretation is made. In each of the animal communication studies mentioned above, there is a constant con-junction of sign and object that supports the referential inference (in the pigeon case, via trainer machination across training trials; in the alarm call case, via statistical conjunction as well as increased survival over evolutionary time). In both cases, mere correlation is the driver.

In contrast, pointing at a bird and exclaiming "Hawk!" invokes a node in a network of other words and combinatorial possibilities, where innumerable cross-cutting semantic categories carry information about the bird's material form, animacy, type of mobility, typicality, linguistic gender, mythical sig-nificance, and so forth. These are implicitly encoded as an interpretive system with respect to which, in addition to the perceptual-emotional gestalt of the hawk experience, the word is generated and understood. It is this systemically mediated form of representation that I think we generally intend when we describe language as being symbolic in nature. Acquiring this system in the first place may involve learning reinforced by repeated physical co-occurrence, but once the system is in place, co-occurrence of word and object is no longer critical, since the reference is held together and maintained indirectly via the vast, repeatedly explored web of symbol-symbol associations.

In contradistinction to the negative definition of symbol that is typically invoked, we implicitly recognize that symbolic reference does not depend on an absence of form or an absence of habitual correlation. A failure to recog-nize this nonexclusivity of symbolic and other forms of reference long im-peded recognition that manual languages of the deaf, such as American Sign Language (ASL), were full-fledged languages despite their widespread use of iconicity as a mnemonic aid. Making the figure-background shift from using physical comparisons to using interpretive operations to distinguish between sign modalities allows symbols to be defined positively rather than negatively (i.e., not iconic, not indexical, but arbitrary).

Symbolic reference is indirect, mediated by reference to an intervening system of relationships established between the symbol tokens (see the de-piction of this logic in figure 2.1). If (as the negative definition holds) it is not determined by any intrinsic properties of the sign vehicles, neither is it un-dermined by the presence of formal (iconic) or correlational (indexical) properties also linking sign vehicle and object. This positive definition applies equally well to linguistic, mathematical, and even ritual and mythical symbols.

Ignoring the interpretive operations necessary to discover the reference of a symbol, and just thinking of it as an arbitrary mapping, gives the very misleading impression that the symbolic interpretive process is simple compared to that involving other forms of signs. In many respects, the very opposite is true. The reason icons are so useful internationally (as restroom

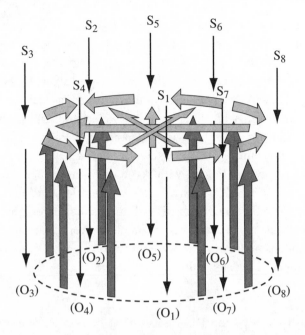

FIGURE 2.1. A schematic depiction of the logic of symbolic relationships in terms of their component indexical infrastructure. Arrows depict indexical relationships and letters depict symbol tokens (Ss) and objects of reference (Os). Downward directed arrows represent the interrupted transitive indexical relationship between symbol tokens and their typically correlated objects of reference. The upper arrows point to loci in the semantic space that has been virtually constructed by token–token relationships (depicted by the horizontal system of arrows). If the symbolic reference is simple (not combinatorial), indexical reference continues from there down to a given instance of a typical object. Otherwise this referential arrow should originate at an intermediate position in the semantic space (determined by a sort of vector summation of the relationship of the combined symbols) and proceed to some other position in the object space. Upward arrows depict an extrapolated correspondence between physical relationships and semantic relationships on which this extrapolative and indirect mode of reference depends for its pragmatic fit to the world (text and figure reprinted from Deacon, 2003b).

and road sign markers, for example) is that they, in effect, carry their interpretation on their sleeves. Words are not so helpful. One needs to have internalized a large system—a significant part of a language—to accurately interpret them in a given context. And although one can get by while traveling by simply memorizing a few words and phrases in a foreign language, these are useful only as mapped onto first-language equivalents with all their complex detail. The competence to interpret an icon is generally simple to acquire, whereas the competence to interpret a symbol can require extensive learning and experience.

Symbols are to this extent analogous to encrypted signs. Without access to the mediating system, we will perceive them, at best, as isolated indices and interpret them (often with quite minimal understanding) via their regular conjunction with events or objects. But precisely because of its mediating system of relationships, symbolic reference gains a degree of disconnection from formal or physical linkage with its ground of reference. Consequently, the dimensions of potential combination, composition, and juxtaposition of symbols make symbolic reference nearly limitless in its referential capacity. It is this implicit mapping into a vast semantic network, supplemented by explicit conventions about allowable combinations and compositions, that allows the generative open-endedness of language.

A Guess at the Processing Differences That Make a Difference

What makes the interpretation of symbols difficult, then, is not the arbitrariness of the symbol tokens or the need to remember many uncued mappings between sign vehicles and objects. Rather, the difficulty lies in initially generating the interpretive competence required to take advantage of this indirect form of reference. It is intrinsically difficult because this competence requires acquisition of and mnemonic facility with a complex relational scheme. And this scheme must be initially acquired by comparison and trial and error. Since systemic relationships are combinatorial relationships, the domain of possible combinations can be huge. Sorting through them to find the appropriate systematic, intrasystemic correspondences could be an enormous task, for which memory of the details is unlikely to be sufficiently large and robust.

This mnemonic sorting problem thus creates a significant threshold that makes even simple symbol systems difficult. So how have human nervous systems been aided in this process? The short answer is, by an improvement in working memory. The more complete answer is that short-term memory has become more resistant to interference effects, and prepotent salience effects of stimuli have been minimized by increases both in the relative strength of independently generated attentional arousal and in the relative salience of any associated alternative associations of the same stimuli. Many of these functions are associated with the relationship of the prefrontal lobes with other systems, especially the sensory cortices and mnemonic and arousal systems. And one of the most prominent (though still debated)[2] features of human brains is the disproportionate expansion of eulaminate cortex (often misleadingly labeled "association cortex" because it does not serve either exclusively sensory or motor functions) and especially prefrontal cortex.

Unique Human Emotions?

Emotion is not distinct from cognition. Emotion cannot be dissociated from cognition. It is the attached index of attention relevance in every percept, memory, or stored motor subroutine. Emotional tone is the *prioritizing marker* attached to every cognitive object that enables an independent sorting of it with respect to other competing cognitive objects, irrespective of pattern-matching processes. One acquires not only patterns of perception, categorization, and norms of action but also information about the set of attached prioritizing markers. This information can often be far more important, because of the precognitive role it can play in organizing interpretations and activities according to a largely hidden and sometimes orthogonal matrix of emotional associations.

The question of what aspects of aesthetic cognition have phylogenetic antecedents and what aspects are uniquely human can also be framed in terms of emotion. The preceding discussion of the problems posed by symbolic reference suggests that means to reduce the emotional salience of specific prepotent stimuli and associations between stimuli would aid the capacity to explore alternative conditional relationships more effectively and so to more easily discover optimal systemic patterns. A relative enlargement of the prefrontal system could well have led to a greater resistance of its operations to perturbation by emotional, perceptual, or mnemonic associations generated elsewhere, owing to a shift in connections increasing the relative proportions of intrinsic to extrinsic links. This can be understood as both a cognitive and a motivational modification of human cognition. But there is also a way in which an initial symbolic system, once it begins to be available, can directly aid in its own development and expansion. Symbolic representation itself provides a reduction in the relative differences in associative salience by virtue of the partial dissociability of a symbolic reference from more direct associations with other correlates and features of its object. Thus, prepotent sensory and arousal influences are reduced, which in turn almost certainly reduces bias on further symbolic associations and combinations. This increasing cognitive flexibility and ability to explore ever more indirect and subtle representational relationships is clearly the most important contribution of symbolizing to mental modeling of the world.

This capacity to resist cognitive interference from the arousal correlates of represented stimuli may also, in turn, similarly deconstrain the correlations and intrinsic interdependencies between emotional states—relations that are otherwise highly preprogrammed and phylogenetically conservative. This could make possible a kind of associative experimentation, so to speak, with a wider and more facile range of represented emotional experiences. But also, it may open the possibility for human-unique emotions.

In general, what I am suggesting is that human aesthetic experience is both a function of an intrinsic shift in motivational structure favoring combinatorial associative exploration—a reflection of adaptation to ease the mnemonic difficulties of symbolization—and a function of the increased combinatorial freedom for manipulating mental representations and their emotional correlates with respect to one another. And this same freedom can also apply to the emotional correlates of these representations. Thus, aesthetic cognition may involve representational manipulation of emotional experiences that causes them to differ in significant ways from the emotions common to other primates (and mammals in general).

In what follows I will outline some reasons for thinking that art is used to generate and experience emotional states that are deviant in unprecedented ways from more phylotypic patterns, and I will also begin to sketch a theory of symbolically mediated cognitive states that suggests that human aesthetic experience is one form among a larger set of symbolically transformed cognitive-emotional domains. I do not pretend to offer a new categorical scheme to make sense of the whole enigmatic domain of emotionality. But I do think it is possible and useful to distinguish the somewhat special class of symbolically transformed emotions that are of relevance to the problem of aesthetic cognition.

I have a number of candidate emotions in mind that I would argue exhibit a peculiarly human character. These include awe, nostalgia, righteous indignation, agape, aesthetic appreciation, and the experiences of humor, irony, and eureka. The list could probably be expanded extensively and might even be open-ended. I do not want to make a strong claim that any of these emotions are impossible to find in the experience of nonhuman species, though I will give a number of reasons for suspecting such instances to be rare at best. What these emotional states all share is a complex compositional structure and a rather paradoxical mix of typically alternative or opposed component emotions. They can be considered to be *emergent* emotional states because what distinguishes them from other primary or secondary emotions is their basis in the interaction effects of other component emotional states. They are not merely co-produced and juxtaposed states but are transformed by their interactive relationship. I think they are also partially or wholly reliant on symbolic representation processes to create their eliciting conditions.

The semiotic freedom provided by symbolic representation is achieved by virtue of the interpolation of a system of relationships between the symbol and what it represents. This implicit system-dependency ultimately grows out of icons and indices associated more directly with the reference and depends on these for its grounding, so although there is a degree of semiotic "distance" (to the extent that consideration of these links can be postponed or deleted temporarily), these correlates—especially the emotional ones—are nevertheless loosely correlated with symbols. In literary contexts, many of these correlates "leak out" in the form of connotations. But the independent symbolic links of the intervening semantic network of associations also import, via these associations, some of the near-neighbor emotional correlates as well. And since the semiotic distance can be selectively biased using symbols and their web of connections—for example, by deleting an additional functional constraint—symbolic associations can play inordinately more powerful roles in the construction of complex compositional forms of reference, and, along with this, in selected amplifications and deletions of emotion.

All the emotions I cite as specially amplified in humans and rare to nonexistent in other species are the results of complex, symbolically mediated juxtapositions and compositions of otherwise exclusive emotional states. The fear and appreciation of beauty or grandeur that come synthesized in feelings of awe may juxtapose both the joy of appreciation and the terrifying recognition of fragility. The recollection of happiness and the sense of present and potential loss that come entangled in nostalgia similarly require the mental representation of mutually exclusive experiences and possible experiences. In short, I think these emotions can best be described as emergent synergies of blended cognitions and emotional experiences, which the mind transfigures by symbolically re-representing them.

I suspect, too, that these sorts of emotional experiences are the rule, not the exception, for modern humans. Transfigured emotions clearly constitute a major organizer of human social behavior. They likely occupy extensive processing space and time because they are in some sense supernormal internal stimuli, even compared to primary emotions. As mutually competitive juxtaposed states, they demand the special attention that must be accorded to unresolved perception-action linkages. And because they are often virtual— that is, about possible futures and possible pasts—they are not constrained from amplification (though this also means that they can be suppressed in other circumstances). In general, I am suggesting that we humans live in a very much more complex realm of emotions than any other species on earth.

And we have an urge—with respect to internal as well as external control of emotional experience—to master the ability to manipulate this generative possibility. Art, I believe, is an expression of this urge.

Bisociations, Blends, and the Juxtaposition of the Mutually Exclusive

The use of symbols to re-represent experiences reduces the salience differences between representations of alternative experiences and possible experiences. This enables more effective cognitive "search for"/"sampling of" their possible correspondences and higher-order iconisms. Symbols are thus the cognitive tools of choice for mental simulation. They allow the activation of mutually competitive action schemes (with action deleted), the activation of recollections of predicted consequences (with emotional consequences largely deleted), and the juxtaposition of many such alternatives within one's working memory capacity. This amounts to a kind of mental play, bringing together both the reinforcing experiences characteristic of play and the correlated symbolically transfigured emotions. Art to some extent externalizes this process, but as a result, it may offer a means for observing features of the architecture of this process in a more accessible way.

The importance of the human ability to cognitively juxtapose complex representations has been recently brought to the attention of humanities and cognitive science scholars by the work of Gilles Fauconnier and Mark Turner (whose ideas are well represented in other chapters in this volume).[3] The aim of the concluding sections of this chapter is to show some links between the core ideas of this theoretical scheme and the sketch of symbolically mediated emotionality I have presented above. I will not review the theory of cognitive blends here, but will instead assume many of these concepts and try to show how each of our approaches may augment the other.

According to Fauconnier and Turner (2002), the capacity for what they call double-scope blends may be unique to humans. So the question is posed whether symbols derive from blending or blending from symbolic abilities. Blends can involve polyvalent iconic representations, or otherwise ambiguous multiple interpretations. But the ability to fuse them cognitively—that is, systematically deconstruct and reconstruct them into novel syntheses in which there is selective projection of compositional semiotic elements from each of the two systems—already presupposes a systemic representational "space" underlying each. This is the defining feature of symbolic representation (indirect representation mediated by a system of representations).

This raises two questions: How have these systems (spaces or schemas in blend theory) come to be constructed? And what allows them to be brought into juxtaposition so easily without their mutually exclusive attributes conflicting and interfering by grabbing attention away from the otherwise unnoticed consonances?

The essence of the blend is the spontaneous discovery of a third interpretive schema (space/system/mediating coordinate space) that is a subset of both antecedently represented schemas with respect to some set of common dimensions. It is my suspicion, given the constraints on iconic and indexical representation, that this emergent synergistic space can only be made available by symbol tokens that bring them into virtual representation antecedently and allow consonant iconic and indexical mappings to emerge after the fact and spontaneously, so to speak, as they percolate into the new symbolic option that has been posited. These virtually present systems of representations may also include additional orthogonal dimensions, able to be selectively evoked precisely because the symbolic displacement allows selectively shallow interpretive use of the underlying mediating systems of relationships.

If not for the ability to hold an independent symbolic token representation of two potentially competing semiotic interpretive systems in working memory, it would be nearly impossible to create cognitive conditions from which an intersection system could emerge. So it seems to me that double-scope blends (which are considered uniquely human) could not appear in any stable form were the component spaces not able to be represented as symbols.

As argued above (and elsewhere, Deacon 1997), selection pressures coordinate with the evolution of symbolic-linguistic abilities in humans have produced a suite of neurological biases supporting the attentional, arousal, and mnemonic demands of symbolic processing. Not surprisingly, these same cognitive biases have also enhanced many of the cognitive capacities that make humans predisposed to interpret ambiguous or juxtaposed symbolic references as blending. Blending, in a sense, is the basic iconic interpretive process that allows symbols to be projected to novel referential roles.

But there are two other ways in which I would augment blend theory to be in better consonance with this approach to aesthetic cognition-emotion. The first is to link it to a theory of emergent emotional states—that is, to recognize the inescapable interweaving and interdependency of the dimensions of mind we divide into cognition and emotion. The second is to recast it in dynamic terms, in order to be able to trace the structure of the symbolic transformations and their relationship to emotional emergence.

It should not be surprising that similar theories invoking a synthesis of ideas and emotions have a long history, with the most important and influential examples traceable to the thinking of Kant, Goethe, and Hegel. In the modern era, however, I find the closest affinities with Arthur Koestler's theory of bisociation (Koestler 1964). Koestler's Germanic influences also trace to Gestalt psychology, and so it is not surprising that he, like Fauconnier and Turner, employs a spatial metaphor. What he describes as "matrices" of thought are bisociated—that is, brought together conceptually—by the discovery of a point of conceptual coincidence that shows them to intersect. Koestler's way of depicting this is shown in figure 2.2. It is clear from his description of this bisociation event, however, that he is imagining it as a mapping, in which the "moves" through the matrix in one plane correspond to "moves" through the other, and that discovering this creates the bisociation: a new synthesis in which they are unified. Koestler's bisociative logic captures many key aspects of blend theory (missing many others, of course) but also introduces time, structure, and emotion in ways that are only hinted at in blend theory. Trisociating blend theory, bisociative theory, and an understanding of how symbolic reference can underlie these may provide a new way to reintegrate the aesthetic into a cognitive theory of art.

There is a central correlation in bisociation theory between involvement with and production of classes of emotion that may offer insights into a

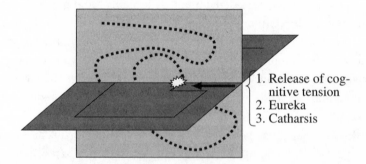

1. Release of cognitive tension
2. Eureka
3. Catharsis

FIGURE 2.2. Arthur Koestler's way of depicting the bisociation of "planes" or "matrices" of ideas (roughly equivalent to schemas or cognitive spaces) in which two conceptual systems are either: 1. reversed so that one is undermined (jokes, humor, irony), 2. fused into a new larger synthesis (scientific discovery), or 3. juxtaposed to illuminate oppositions, tensions, symmetries, paradoxes, etc. (ritual, arts). The lines traced on each plane reflect parallel inferential or narrative "moves" on which the bisociation will be based. A sudden discovery of the existence of a bisociative possibility (e.g., in a eureka experience) is depicted by the tiny explosion cartoon indicated by the arrow, though the suddenness or single-point mapping is not intrinsic to the general model.

feature of aesthetic experience I have not touched on: different semiotic constructions themselves have a logic that determines major features of the emergent emotional experience. One central aim of Koestler's bisociation theory was to explain how the structure of a semiotic process (e.g., joke, discovery) could influence the "structure" of an emotional experience (e.g., humor, eureka).

How the mapping occurs and how valences in each matrix/space inter-relate in the bisociation/blend matters for the emotion generated. For ex-ample, the bisociation in a joke blends two mutually incompatible matrices and yet is carefully constructed so as to disguise the fact that the semiotic moves in the one matrix exactly track an allowed set of moves in the cryptic matrix; this mapping is suddenly exposed by the punch line. The bisociation in a scientific discovery involves a similar semiotic parallelism, except that the primary and secondary matrices are ultimately concordant and the bisociation involves recognition of this. In the case of humor, the emotional eruption (associated with incompatible arousal states) results from suddenly pointing out the implicit absurd mapping. The rug is pulled out from under one emotional frame, and all moves are reframed in the absurd alternative, often undermining some threatening connotation of the primary matrix—hence the importance of the matrices' emotional load. In the case of a discovery, the fusion may be as sudden as in the joke (hence "eureka!"), but the result is actually a fitting of one matrix within another, with a corresponding expan-sion of scope and explanatory power. Figure 2.3 schematically depicts the generic logic of conceptual blend theory augmented with the implied emo-tional juxtaposition of Koestler's bisociation theory.

In the terms of blending theory, these might be described as single-scope blends because of the primary-secondary, overt/cryptic structure of the rela-tionship (though this is not a necessary correlate of either more complex humor or discoveries). Koestler's conception of bisociations in art, however, has a different kind of resolution. Here, often two or more matrices are juxta-posed, but neither is cryptic or necessarily more primary, and their roles can shift over the course of appreciating the bisociation. In art, according to Koestler, the matrices are shown to be only partially compatible, and often it is the incompatibilities that are the focus of the fusion and which drive the dynamic of the bisociative process. For Koestler, it is the sustained juxtaposi-tion and incomplete fusion that is key; for this tension, resolved in various ways, is the source of what he describes as *catharsis*, or a sort of eventual grounding of emotion. In the vernacular of blend theory, this is a double-scope blend, where there is no dominant or subsumed space, but an equal juxtapo-sition status, where each space contributes equally to the blended space.

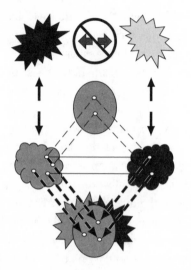

Mutually exclusive
primary emotions

Generic conceptual space
(associated arousal states)

Blended symbolic
conceptions

Synergistic symbolic conception
with the *emergent* experience
of juxtaposed but competing
emotional states

FIGURE 2.3. This figure follows the depiction logic of cognitive blend theory
(lower half: cloud = contributing spaces, and lower oval = blended space)
but introduces the additional depiction of the correlated emotional "spaces"
of each contributing space (jagged shapes). The network/matrix structures
of the emotional spaces need not be in any way correlated with one another,
as the conceptual spaces are. Emotional spaces are thus depicted as juxtaposed but not integrated in the background of the fused blended
conceptual space.

Notice that what we gain with bisociation theory is a clear prediction of
how the course of the semiotic process plays a determining role in the
emotional experience. This is a final piece in the puzzle. The different ways
that emergent emotional spaces can be created adds a dynamic that is often
skipped over if we imagine emotions to be static states. All are hints about
how to develop a higher-order cognitive theory of semiotic juxtapositions that
contains all three approaches as subsets.

The Realm in Which Aesthetic Cognition Dwells

Different categories of emergent emotional experience thus depend on the
particular logic producing the bisociation, as well as on the fit between
the fused emotional associative networks. Figures 2.4 and 2.5 attempt to
use the above augmentation of the blend diagram to depict the contrast between the bisociative structures of jokes and of aesthetic experiences, re-
spectively (following Koestler). The critical difference is that whereas jokes

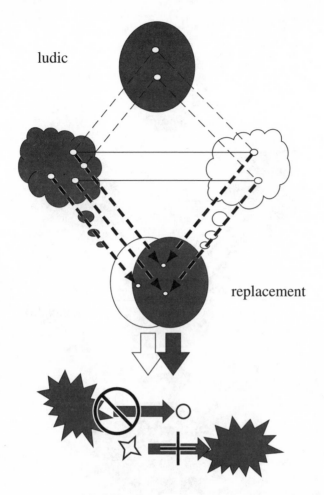

ludic

replacement

rapid shift of arousal commitment

FIGURE 2.4. The blendlike structure of jokes. Following the diagrammatic conventions of figure 2.3, conceptual spaces are cloudlike or oval, and emotional spaces are jagged. Humor begins on one presumed conceptual frame (depicted as a dark cloud) and then executes a shift to a different and conventionally unlikely parallel frame of interpretation (depicted as a light cloud). The blend is achieved by some trivial mapping of phonology (as in a pun) or semantics (circles) but inverts the weakly activated conceptual frame in background attention (depicted as the light cloud; probably a predominantly right hemisphere activity). In the bait-and-switch blend of the joke, this conceptual and attentional relationship is reversed and an unlikely background frame is indicated. Correlatively, there is also a shift in arousal commitment from one correlated emotional frame to another (usually from a more socially loaded to a less loaded one; here indicated by the deflation of one and inflation of another emotional state), which triggers the rapid transfer of attention and arousal.

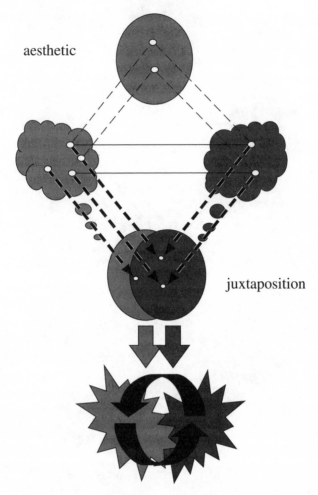

aesthetic

juxtaposition

alternating emotions

FIGURE 2.5. The blend structure of aesthetic experiences. Using the
same conventions of depiction as figures 2.3 and 2.4, this figure depicts
the difference between humor and art as an incompletely resolvable
juxtaposition where the cognitive blend relationship creating the conceptual
juxtaposition and a correlated juxtaposition of correlated emotional spaces
remains in flux. This is depicted as dynamically alternating emotional schemas, often in conflict with one another.

result in a replacement or substitution of one cognitive-emotional space pair
with another previously cryptic one, the artistic experience juxtaposes them
without immediate resolution, perhaps even creating a sort of necker-cube
oscillation effect of alternating or transforming emotions. The dimensions
that define emotional spaces and their relations and those that define semiotic

relations are mostly based on nonconcordant logics. So a semiotic relationship that brings a correlated emotional juxtaposition into being will often do so in an emotionally atypical way.

Jokes and other sources of humor and irony depend on something like cryptic or incipient blends. Humor typically establishes one conceptual frame presented as though it is to be interpreted literally. The analysis of its semantic and syntactic consistency is probably mostly maintained by left hemisphere function. Humor occurs with the shift to another frame of interpretation that is conceptually absurd or conventionally antithetical to the first in some sense, with some strand of linking logic (phonological, semantic) smoothly linking the first interpretive analysis to the second. This is the ground of the blend or bisociation. The cryptic alternative is one among many possible weakly consistent but conventionally unlikely parallel frames of interpretation. The tracking of the non sequitur nature of this shift of interpretive frame is probably a predominantly right hemisphere activity. But whereas the phonological or semantic processing continues unbroken in the unfolding of the joke or humorous story, the interpretive frames are mutually exclusive. The result is that mental resources committed to developing one context of analysis become irrelevant and must be released.

Laughter appears to be correlated with dorsal medial frontal activation (probably involving either or both the anterior cingulate and supplementary motor cortex). This region plays a critical role in attentional monitoring and is the only cortical area involved in production of primate vocal calls, especially with respect to the intentional suppression of calls. In this sense, we may be able to conceive of laughter as a sort of release call.

In scientific discovery, there is also a juxtaposition of conceptual schemas, but although they may originally appear incompatible on the surface, it is the discovery of a mapping by a similarly unnoticed isomorphism of components from the one to the other that creates the blend. In this kind of blend, moreover, it is the tension of mystery itself, rather than correlated emotional states, that is central—the cognitive incompleteness of some explanatory schema that lurks in the emotional background. The cognitively imposed tension released by "seeing the connection," so to speak, between schemata is a bit like the release of the joke, but the bait-and-switch results not in the abandoning of one schema for another but rather in a probable synthesis which supersedes both initial schemata. The conceptual blend serves not merely as a juxtaposition but also as a synthesis and consequent expansion of the now unified schemata—the creation of a new cognitive space. It is of course only a "probable synthesis," because the perception of an apparently deep constitutive isomorphism can often be mistaken. Often, too, the conceptual task of tracing a complete mapping from schema to schema will take from hours to months more before it is confirmed. Nevertheless, the same experience and cognitive architecture is constituted by false discoveries as by true ones; the discovery that an apparent unity or explanation is after all based on a false synthesis or only a partial isomorphism (e.g., a superficial analogy) effectively turns the eureka architecture into the architecture of a joke. Of course, the emotional juxtaposition created by this new replacement of the sublime with the trivial is seldom the cause of humor. It is more like being the butt of a practical joke, the flip side of humor.

Finally, let me return to the topic of this chapter and book as seen from this broader perspective. In art, unlike either humor or discovery, the principal emotional architecture of the multilevel blend is neither one of bait-and-switch nor of resolution, but one of tension. A conceptual juxtaposition creates a blended space that often brings together uncharacteristically associated emotional schemas, or else merely explores the various possible juxtapositions, tensions, transitions, and transformations that can be evoked by manipulating this juxaposition. The simplest aspect of this kind of sustained juxtaposition is the "make believe" state of subjective projection we refer to as willful suspension of disbelief. An audience at a play involves itself in the projected emotional experiences of the characters but does not entirely lose track of the fact that this is a represented and juxtaposed state. The emotional distance afforded by the incompleteness of the mapping in this juxtaposition is critical to creating the virtual experience. The tensions between juxtaposed emotional schemata are themselves emotional states, but of a higher order than the components. In this relationship, the semiotic development of the conceptual juxtaposition contributes its structure to the dynamic of the emotional space juxtapositions, and thus may create complex changing oppositions, tensions, and resolutions of emotional experience. The sign vehicles incorporated in this sort of blending may be semiotically far more diverse and multiply superimposed (e.g., images plus words plus music plus dance) than in either jokes or discovery processes, because there is no intention to fully resolve or completely map between either conceptual or emotional schemata. So it is in this realm that it is possible to create the most highly atypical and complex dynamic emotional juxtapositions, with little constraint on the semiotic vehicle or mode of representation.

Art need not involve symbolically mediated juxtaposition, any more than simple play requires it, and may evoke its effects irrespective of symbols. Consider music, with its weaving of harmonies and dissonances, rhythms and timbres. Its ability to engender the participatory exploration of emotional transitions is not itself mediated symbolically (except in the special case of singing or explicitly programmatic music) but involves the construction and modulation of sound iconisms and contrasts that simultaneously play on many mappings—for example, to recognized musical context and tradition; to dynamics of strangeness, surprise, analytic difficulty, and familiarity; to simple auditory perceptual processing differences of consonant and dissonant sound juxtapositions; and so forth—which by listener participation evoke what might be called emotional parallelism with this architecture. Yet to focus on the structure of the aural experience *in order* to also appreciate the spontaneously correlated, simultaneous emotional states and transitions that it brings about requires a state of mind much like that required to access symbolic reference itself, a predisposition to follow the form of the communication in search of systematicity behind it. Thus, the tendency to approach complex patterns of all sorts with the expectation that they are merely the superficial expression of some deeper cryptic systematicity is both a prerequisite to being a facile discoverer of symbolic systematicity and a bias toward experiencing the world as representation.

In summary, extrapolating from Koestler, I have tried to integrate emotional architectures more fully into blend theory. I have also attempted to show how symbolic capabilities open up cognitive blending to a realm of "play" that is vastly larger and more emotionally complex than it otherwise would be. Also following Koestler, I have attempted to identify a much broader system of human-unique emotional-cognitive states that have emerged from the capacity to symbolically juxtapose representations of otherwise exclusive experiential states and force the blending (bisociation) of the correlated emotions. But the examples of emergent emotional experiences I have only superficially explored suggest that this realm of symbolically mediated emergent emotionality is much more extensive than I initially suggested. There are different architectures of cognitive-emotional juxtaposition which have not been considered and which are likewise and for similar reasons likely to be largely confined to human experience because of their reliance on symbolic means. Among these would be members of the list of human-unique emotions I listed earlier. The combinatorial logic I have described could also be used to organize these emergent emotions into a taxonomy. To give only a flavor of the sort of approach I think this might yield, I offer a simple multidimensional taxonomy that attempts to show the relationships between the three experiences that Koestler describes—ludic, eurekic, and aesthetic—and additionally interdigitates other intermediates. Each of these also involves a juxtaposition-blend-bisociation of emotional schemas that would be mutually inhibiting and unlikely to be brought into juxtaposition (much less sustained in such a relationship) in the absence of the capacity for symbolic re-representation. These experiences appear to form a graded closed circular spectrum of cognitive-emotional states (see figure 2.6). Although this depiction collapses many dimensions of arousal and semiotic dynamics into two and inevitably is only a tiny sampling of the range of possible forms, it makes apparent, I hope, the symmetry of relationships that arises among these emergent states as a result of the underlying architecture of the blending of symbolized schemas.

In many ways, the arts appear to continually expand the space of emergent emotional states we can experience. This ever-expanding exploration of

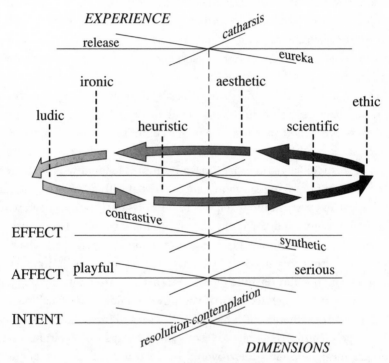

FIGURE 2.6. A very tentative map of the interrelationships of some emergent emotional forms. This figure represents an elaboration of a chart from Koestler (1964) in which he links humor, science, and art in a continuum. Here I have interdigitated his with other domains of emergent cognition-emotion. This diagram collapses a multidimensional space of possible relationships to depict these relationships with respect to how they map onto four dimensions of semiotic and psychological functions. These are inferential effect, affective value, communicative intent (dimensions depicted below), and the dynamic development of the bisociative-blending process (depicted above).

newly emergent experiences is clearly one of art's great attractions. It is literally an exercise in expanding the space of consciousness.

The logic of this link between classes of emotions and the specific dynamics of conceptual integration is a mostly unexplored domain. The simplest way to conceive of how cognitive semiotic-pattern relationships can become the basis for unprecedented emotional experience is by assuming that the symbolic fusion forces a bisociation of any emotional attachments associated with the contributed planes/spaces. But as the examples of jokes, discoveries, and artistic experiences indicate, this is much too simple. These emergent emotional states are also distinguished by a kind of intrinsic dynamism and transience, unlike what is intrinsic to the more basic emotions from which they emerge. This fleeting and fragile nature is also characteristic of the whole realm of what might be called "transfigured experience" because of the way it has become both recoded and re-experienced in coded form. Hearing a sad song only weakly and transiently makes one sad (except where it invokes an actual sorrowful experience), and in a complex piece of music or well-crafted poem, our emotional experience may be quickly whisked from one state to another in ways that are also uncharacteristic of the inertia and momentum of endogenously generated emotions. Aesthetic emotions are thus not quite emotions as we usually understand the term, precisely because they are essentially emotional relationships between emotions. They are not false emotions and yet are virtual in some sense. Their facile nature is what makes it possible for semiotic tricks to drag them on roller-coaster-like trajectories over the course of hours or seconds. And like carnival rides, even quite negative emotions experienced in this partially deleted, fleeting manner are also enjoyable.

But they are not just enjoyable, not merely cognitive ice cream that titillates sensibilities that evolved for something more instrumental. The evolution of symbolic abilities and correlated interpretive predispositions, along with the cultural elaboration of supportive symbolic interpretive systems, has made possible the creation and exploration of unprecedented cognitive and experiential domains. The exploration and expansion of this domain has been of immeasurable importance for our species. The same predisposition also drives scientific and ethical analyses; all emergent capacities such as these are to some extent "educated" and exercised by the least constraining realm—that of aesthetic juxtapositions. Precisely because the only ultimate constraint is the "attractiveness" of the resulting experience (in all the ways that this term can be rendered), it often demands the most flexible and facile use of these capacities.

We see, then, that the unprecedented domains of emergent emotions, synthesized by virtue of the power of symbolic material to present us with novel juxtapositions of cognitions-emotions, includes within it much more than aesthetic experiences in the classic sense. Most important, as suggested above, we can place ethical experience and moral cognition among these emergent domains. These too are inextricably bound to the capacity to juxtapose emotional frames of reference, to create the virtual world of intersubjective experiences. Like other blend-dependent experiences, this capacity is a product of more basic emotional and cognitive states, and yet it transforms these in the self-other blend.[4] Like art, ethics is emergent in the sense that its function is more a reflection of the form of the relationships that have been brought into being than of the component emotions that are necessarily constitutive of the experience. Understanding the functional and evolutionary logic of artistic expression and experience can help to illuminate our understanding of the superset from which it grows, and on which the capacities that make us unique among animals depend.

NOTES

1. See Deacon (1997) for a more detailed account of the specific anatomical correlates and developmental mechanisms discussed here with respect to language adaptations of the brain. An analysis of the special selection dynamics required to account for such a coordinated complementary evolution can be found in Deacon 2003a.

2. Many back-and-forth results have left this issue unresolved. Some of the reasons for apparently differing results from these studies are discussed in Deacon 1997.

3. Fauconnier and Turner (2002) contains a recent elaboration of these ideas. See also Turner, this volume.

4. An expanded argument for the emergent emotional-cognitive structure of ethical experience and moral cognition, mediated by symbolic capacities, is presented in Goodenough and Deacon 2003.

REFERENCES

Bateson, G. 1972. *Steps to an ecology of mind.* New York: Ballantine Books.

Busch, H., and B. Silver. 1994. *Why cats paint: A theory of feline aesthetics.* Berkeley, Calif.: Ten Speed Press.

Cheney, D., and R. Sayfarth. 1990. *How monkeys see the world.* Chicago: University of Chicago Press.

Deacon, T. 1997. *The symbolic species: The coevolution of language and the brain.* New York: W. W. Norton.

———. 2003a. Multilevel selection in a complex adaptive system: The problem of language origins. In *Evolution and learning: The Baldwin effect reconsidered,* ed. B. Weber and D. Depew, 81–106. Cambridge, Mass.: MIT Press.

———. 2003b. The hierarchic logic of emergence: Untangling the interdependence of evolution and self-organization. In *Evolution and learning: The Baldwin effect reconsidered*, ed. B. Weber and D. Depew, 273–308. Cambridge, Mass.: MIT Press.

———. 2003c. Universal grammar and semiotic constraints. In *Language evolution*, ed. M. Christiansen and S. Kirby, 111–139. Oxford, England: Oxford University Press.

Dennett, D. 1991. *Consciousness explained*. New York: Little, Brown.

Fauconnier, G., and M. Turner. 2002. *The way we think: Conceptual blending and the mind's hidden complexities*. New York: Basic Books.

Goodenough, U., and T. Deacon. 2003. From biology to consciousness to morality. *Zygon*, 38, no. 4: 801–19.

Hauser, M. 1996. *The evolution of communication*. Cambridge, Mass.: MIT Press.

Hurford, J. 2000. Social transmission favors linguistic generalization. In *The evolutionary emergence of language: Social functions and the origins of linguistic form*, ed. C. Knight, M. Studdert-Kennedy, and J. Hurford, 324–52. Cambridge, England: Cambridge University Press.

Kirby, S. 1999. *Function, selection, and innateness: The emergence of language universals*. Oxford, England: Oxford University Press.

Koestler, A. 1964. *The act of creation*. New York: Macmillan.

Piaget, J. 1951. *Play, dreams and imitation in childhood*. London: Heinemann.

Romanski, L., B. Tian, J. Fritz, M. Mishkin, P. Goldman-Rakic, and J. Rauschecker. 1999. Dual streams of auditory afferents target multiple domains in the primate prefrontal cortex. *Nature Neuroscience*, 12:1131–36.

PART II

Art and Emotion

3

A Cognitive Account
of Aesthetics

Francis Steen

The study of aesthetics within an evolutionary framework has focused on the appetite for beauty as an engine for driving adaptive behavior in habitat and mate choice. In this chapter, I propose instead that aesthetic experience is its own goal, in the sense that the experience implicitly provides adaptively useful information utilized for purposes of self-construction.

At the cognitive roots of art is a subjective phenomenology of aesthetic enjoyment. Private and intimate, or ostentatiously public, such feelings constitute, on the one hand, a centrally gratifying dimension of being alive, and, on the other, a mystery, a gift without a card. To the project of reimagining and reconstructing the full depth of human history, of situating our current cognitive proclivities and capabilities within a renewed narrative of human origins, the phenomenon of aesthetics presents a crucial and delicate challenge. Current work in evolutionary theory is animated by the seductive promise of a functional explanation for every key human trait. Yet the variety and complexity of the aesthetic impulse, along with its myriad expressions, may make us conclude, very sensibly, that reality simply overflows our theories.

Nevertheless, I submit wholeheartedly to this seduction, with the caveat that a functional analysis of aesthetic enjoyment must be shifted into a new dimension. The field of evolutionary aesthetics (for an overview, see Voland and Grammar 2003) has principally focused on landscape preferences as a function of adaptations for habitat choice and the experience of human beauty as part of mate selection. While these perspectives are not unsupported by credible evidence, they leave out vast tracts of aesthetic experience—from neolithic symbolic art to what Robert Hughes (1991) called "the shock of the new," from the frivolous to the sublime. What evolutionary aesthetics has so far failed to provide is a credible framework for understanding the surprising range of aesthetics. Just as significantly, the implicit underlying assumption that aesthetic pleasure is comparable to the pleasures of sex and food in driving adaptive behavior (Orians and Heerwagen 1992, 555) is clearly false: the subjective phenomenology of aesthetic enjoyment differs qualitatively from desire. In contrast to hunger and lust, the experience of beauty is prototypically its own reward; unlike these, it does not find its release, fulfillment, and satiation in possession. To the extent that this is so, we must look for an explanation that honors beauty itself as a resource, without seeing it as a proxy for something else.

In the following, I argue that the aesthetic impulse and experience is an appetite for certain types of information—in a word, that beauty is a kind of truth. I take my cue from John Keats's "Ode on a Grecian Urn," which famously and rather fatuously proclaims that beauty is the only kind of truth we have or need. My claim is both more modest and in some ways more far-reaching: while beauty is certainly not the only kind of truth we need, we appear to use it for a most intimate and crucial task, that of constructing ourselves. Not to skimp on the complex subjective phenomenology involved in this process, let us turn for a moment to the poet's animated description before I elaborate.

In the first stanza of "Ode on a Grecian Urn," the speaker addresses the artifact as a "sylvan historian," praising its skillful telling of a "flowery tale." Although urns, as everyone knows, don't talk—Keats obliquely acknowledges this by calling it "foster-child of silence"—the object can be used to convey a story through images. The scenes depicted on its exterior are understood as snapshots of a fictive or historical narrative, the details of which the onlooker may attempt to infer: "What mad pursuit? What struggle to escape?" In this narrative, the characters portrayed have both a past and a future. To understand the scenes as adding up to a story, the onlooker must see them as iconic representations of entities whose existence is independent of the urn itself, illustrations of events to be filled in by memory and imagination. In Korzybski's explanation (1933), they are no more to be confused with the events themselves than a map with the territory.

In the second stanza, however, this is no longer true. Here, the poet immerses himself imaginatively in the depicted scenes, pretending that the

bas-relief marble figures are in fact real human beings in a state of permanently suspended animation, yet with a fully intact consciousness, including
perceptions, emotions, and intentions. In a surprising attempt to console
them, he informs them about the peculiar nature of their situation, of which
he assumes they are unaware:

> Bold Lover, never, never canst thou kiss,
>   Though winning near the goal—yet, do not grieve;
>   She cannot fade, though thou hast not thy bliss,
>   For ever wilt thou love, and she be fair! (Keats 1820)

In this perspective, the world imaginatively reconstructed on the basis of the
artwork on the urn exists only on the urn itself. No longer depictions of independently existing events, each of the scenes is now perceived as a mini-world of
its own, subjectively as real for its inhabitants as ours is for us. Keats highlights
what he sees as the salient feature that distinguishes this reconstructed world
from our world: it is uniquely characterized by the absence of time. So implausible is this conceit that no attempt is made to explain how a whole community and its natural environment ended up in a waking and blissful but
otherwise cryogenic state in the permanent exhibition of the British Museum.
Somehow, and we are not invited to contemplate how, the people in the story
have become trapped by their representation—life has transformed into art.

In the third stanza, the poet argues that this artistic and imagined world
is preferable to our own. In the real world, "breathing human passion" leaves
people in pain, either through deprivation or surfeit; in contrast, in the world
on the urn, there is "More happy love! more happy, happy love!" By removing
time, art achieves an uninterrupted and unvarying delight. It may be coun-
tered that art objects are just as subject to change over time as are other
objects, people, and events, and that it is only in the imagination that the
depicted worlds are frozen in time. In his description of the urn, the poet is
blurring the vital distinction between what is constructed as it were out of
whole cloth on the basis of memories, supplemented by some curiously
shaped marble, and what originates in a genuine perception of reality.

If the poet is committing a category mistake, however, he does so know-
ingly and on purpose. In order to construct and contemplate the rich possibilities of an artistic, fictive world, it appears to be necessary to dedicate our
working-memory capacities to this task, unburdened by the challenges of
reality. Retracing his steps, Keats unwinds the fancy, performs a controlled
retreat from the depicted world, and resumes his address to the urn itself in
the last stanza. He praises it for its capacity to "tease us out of thought"—the
implication being that beauty is strongly experienced as its own reward and

that the mind is inherently attracted to it, to the point that it will temporarily set aside its own engagement with reality in favor of the aesthetic and imaginatively enhanced worlds of art. Finally, handing the microphone to the urn, the poet imagines that the urn itself formulates its enduring meaning and significance to future generations:

> "Beauty is truth, truth beauty,"—that is all
> Ye know on earth, and all ye need to know. (Keats 1820)

The claim is clearly exorbitant, even if we make allowances for the speaker's being an urn. Coming on the heels of a sequence of imaginative projections and self-evident counterfactuals, the artistic object's claim to referential truth is weak. If beauty is truth, what kind of truth is it? In the following, I provide a strong if partial defense, situating the poet's intuition of the importance of aesthetics within a cognitive and evolutionary framework.

Natural Aesthetics: An Appetite for Beauty

In order to accomplish the complex task of constructing a functioning brain, the information contained in the genes does not suffice. While important target values appear to be genetically specified, the paths taken to reach them are not (Turner 1996, 25). For this, the organism depends on information that is reliably present in the environment. We can think of the genes as a series of switches activated by an orderly progression of environmental conditions, starting with the sheltering and nurturing enclosure of the womb. The power of the genome to determine the development of the organism is wholly subject to the structure of the environment in which it finds itself. Natural selection operates on functional outcomes; these are joint products of the complex order of the environment and some additional genetic information. If the environment reliably contains the information required to construct the brain, natural selection can be expected to favor mechanisms that effectively access this information.

In many cases, the information required is ubiquitous. A famous series of experiments showed that cats raised in an environment without vertical lines failed to develop the capacity to perceive them (Stryker et al. 1978; Tieman and Hirsch 1982). In the long course of mammalian evolutionary history, there was never an environment that lacked vertical lines. During critical periods of development, infant cats from snow leopards to jungle jaguars have been able to tacitly count on the recurring presence of vertical lines around them. Over tens of millions of years, the inability of feline genes to provide the information necessary to build a brain that perceives vertical lines in the temporary absence of such lines has had no functional consequences, and has therefore not been subject to deselection. Since the necessary information was an inherent and ubiquitous part of the structure of their environment, a relatively passive mechanism for accessing it would have sufficed.

In other cases, the information may be unevenly distributed and vary in quality. Here natural selection can be predicted to favor mechanisms that detect relevant quality differences and exhibit an active preference for features of the environment that present high-quality information. The information will in effect constitute a scarce resource to be monitored and sought out. When found, it can be absorbed and utilized by the brain to pattern a targeted function. The active case is what concerns us here, as this is where I propose to ground aesthetics.

Consider the recurring necessity of calibrating the embodied brain's perceptual systems. These are highly complex and sophisticated mechanisms, implemented in organic systems undergoing constant change and upheaval. Some of the work of the senses is dull and monotonous. Under these conditions, the system may rely on certain features of the environment for recalibrating itself. It may be important, for instance, to obtain reliable information about baseline values as well as a rich sense of the full range of sensory phenomena the system is designed to handle. As long as all this information is reliably present in the natural environment, even if it is scattered in time and space, natural selection can be predicted not to favor potentially expensive mutations that engineer it into the genome. In this sense, it is more like food than gravity or vertical lines: reliably present, but requiring an active search, discriminating capacities, and a set of preferences expressed as appetite.

It is in this territory, then, that I propose to locate the phenomenon of aesthetics. In general terms, the suggestion is that our attraction to beautiful objects and events, and our experience of aesthetic enjoyment, may coherently be understood as the results of a biological need to locate certain types of information in our environments, as a supplement to genetic information, for the purpose of constructing and maintaining our own order. More narrowly, the prototypical function of aesthetics is to bring our senses back to life, or to an optimal state. In this sense, it constitutes an ancient evolutionary solution to the problem of calibrating various components of our multidimensional sensory systems. Natural selection, according to this model, has produced a set of adaptations designed to search the environment for certain types of information, and to engage in activities that will make this information salient. We can be predicted to show an active preference for a class of features of the environment—namely, those that in evolutionary history our ancestors were able to rely on to supply information complementing that supplied by the genome. The aesthetic impulse would be an appetite for information that in our distant past was recruited and relied on for optimal self-construction, regulated by a developmental chronology.

I'm not suggesting we know we're doing this. If aesthetics is an evolved mechanism for constructing and maintaining complex patterns of order in the brain, it does not advertise itself as such. We do not seek out aesthetic experiences as the result of a conscious and deliberate intention to reach a specific goal; in fact, the distal cause of aesthetics is cognitively impenetrable. In order to gather the necessary structuring information, the conscious mind does not need a conceptual model of the distal purpose and function of aesthetics, nor does it need access to the complex internal logic of the operation of this function, any more than it needs access to the intricate nano-technology of digestion in order for digestion to occur. The biological function of aesthetics is complex in principle and execution, and from the standpoint of selection, there is nothing to be gained and much to be lost by clogging up the limited bandwidth and processing capacities of the conscious mind. What is made available to consciousness is a phenomenology of aesthetics that is experienced as an end in itself and inherently motivating, an experience that is rich and delightful, confirming the exquisite order of the world and indeed our place within it. Inversely, under conditions when our senses for long periods are deprived of an aesthetic order, we experience a palpable dissatis-faction with the quality of our sensory environment, a nagging and aversive sense of boredom, and a longing for change.

Is this a credible theory of aesthetics? I should note here that my aim is not to construct an all-encompassing theory; as Prigogine and Stengers (1984, 1) note, reality always overflows our descriptions of it. Aesthetics is a delicate and subtle cognitive event, and these qualities, I suggest, reflect back on the complex and fluid organic order that forms and sustains a human being. The social and cultural uses of aesthetics presuppose rather than negate a bio-logically grounded explanation. If it had not existed, surely the phenomenon would have been unimaginable: all culture can do is tap into the capacity, in endless variations. While aesthetic preferences themselves vary, for reasons I explore below, the presence of art in all documented cultures, past and present, indicates that the phenomenon itself is universal (cf. Brown 1991). The purpose of an adaptationist account of aesthetics, then, is not to reduce a complex phenomenon to a simple one, but to gain genuine insight into its complexity.

This is a trivializing view of aesthetics only if we view the order of the universe as trivial. Primary aesthetic events and objects include the vast silence of the stars at night, the brilliant play of colors in the clouds at sunset, tumbling and crashing waters, the complex fluid dynamics of a rushing river, birds' songs, the delicate shape and coloring of flowers and leaves, a bare tree, the shape and movement of a healthy animal. Our evolved aesthetics has to be a natural aesthetics, responding to an order that is reliably present rather than to one that is manufactured. Prototypically beautiful natural events are characterized by a dynamic and ordered complexity, or by evidence of what we might term a generative order (Bohm and Peat 1984). By this I mean that we experience the complexity of beauty as a complexity that emerges in an orderly manner through the operation of an underlying generative process; for instance, a waterfall is continuously generated by gravity acting on water in motion, the slowly changing pink hue of the clouds at sunset is generated by the gradually changing refraction of the light from the setting sun, and the delicate leaf is produced by a patterned order of growth. The aesthetic response appears to pick out these dynamic processes, and the intrinsic delight of aesthetics appears to stem from an appreciation of the inferred but invisible underlying order that generates the manifest phenomenon. The present proposal is that we unconsciously make use of such complex natural orders in wiring the brain and calibrating our perceptual systems, that our self-construction relies on them, and that natural selection has constructed a motivational system that leads us to seek them out.

As long as it is embedded in nature, a society might not feel the need to celebrate the beauty of its environment explicitly. In the West, it was the large-scale industrialization and urbanization of the eighteenth and nineteenth centuries that spurred an interest in the importance of natural aesthetics. The poet William Wordsworth became a primary spokesman in England for this growing cultural movement. In "Lines Written a Few Miles above Tintern Abbey, on Revisiting the Banks of the Wye during a Tour. July 13, 1798," looking back on his childhood, he contemplates the impact the sheer sensory experience of nature had on his formation as an individual. He emphasizes that he experienced a wide range of natural forms as enjoyable and meaningful in themselves, a passion and an appetite that did not rely on any conscious purpose or perceived utility. "For nature then," he writes,

> To me was all in all.—I cannot paint
> What then I was. The sounding cataract
> Haunted me like a passion: the tall rock,
> The mountain, and the deep and gloomy wood,

>Their colours and their forms, were then to me
>An appetite; a feeling and a love,
>That had no need of a remoter charm,
>By thought supplied, or any interest
>Unborrowed from the eye. (Wordsworth 1798, 76–84)

In "Tintern Abbey," Wordsworth provides a particularly rich account of the phenomenology of the experience of natural aesthetics. He describes the mental state involved as distinct and characteristic, as deepening and intensifying through a sequence of stages orchestrated by emotions, and culminating in a suspension of the body similar to sleep, in which the mind perceives a profound truth:

>—that serene and blessed mood,
>In which the affections gently lead us on,
>Until, the breath of this corporeal frame,
>And even the motion of our human blood
>Almost suspended, we are laid asleep
>In body, and become a living soul:
>While with an eye made quiet by the power
>Of harmony, and the deep power of joy,
>We see into the life of things. (Wordsworth 1798, 41–49)

Truth, in this case, is "the life of things": a hidden and generative order that is the target of the aesthetic faculty and that delivers a climactic and perfect satisfaction to the appetite for beauty.

Imagination and the Virtual Agent

By focusing on the dynamics of natural aesthetics, I have attempted to sketch a model of how our appetite for beauty may have a basis in biology, as an aspect of an adaptation that dates back millions of years. This model, however, does little to account for the truth claims made for art, understood as the objects and events that we design and manufacture for their aesthetic effects. Natural forms and events actually take place, and an insight into their underlying generative order, if accurate, carries a credible claim to an interesting kind of truth. Yet the cognitive processes that animate Keats's "Ode on a Grecian Urn" appear to be qualitatively different from those at work in Wordsworth's sensory rhapsody, dealing as they do with imaginary situations that we have no reason to believe are in any exact sense historical, and centrally involving the wholly implausible claim of a transformation of in-animate depictions into conscious agents. Who needs a notion of falsehood if this is truth?

To get a handle on what is going on here, let us consider some simpler examples of the same phenomenon. The elementary guiding principle of artistic creation is to trigger a controlled series of sensations that awaken an aesthetic response. This definition is less vacuous and circular than it might seem: the detailed characteristics of our aesthetic response system are un-known to us, but in the making of art, it can be systematically probed. At the same time, the proposed adaptive design of the aesthetic response engine is to detect and acquire information in the environment that is not present in the genes or in its own structure, for the purpose of wiring the brain. This means that through art, an individual can not only acquire a certain type of self-knowledge about his own aesthetic preferences, but also use the art itself to propose new orders. These new orders can then be selectively incorporated into his own perceptual system, in effect teaching him to perceive and sense the world in new ways.

As long as these orders tap into the adaptive design of our aesthetic response system, they need not replicate natural aesthetics. Adaptive design is by necessity a product of particular if usually prolonged historical circum-stances, and gets constructed within the context of a certain environment because it solves a present problem. Any adaptation will have a built-in slack—areas where it may function in interesting and potentially useful ways even though it was not designed to do so (for a discussion, see, e.g., Sperber 1996). By proposing new perceptual orders, artists tap into both the core and the unused fringe capacities of the aesthetic response system to explore complex sensory orders that have no precedent in nature.

Experiments have shown that, when provided with the means, nonhu-man animals are capable of formulating and carrying out the intention of creating aesthetic objects. The lowland gorilla Koko, whose work was featured prominently in a primate art show at the Terrain Gallery in San Francisco in December and January 1997–1998, uses broad strokes of primary colors to achieve a remarkably lively and complex aesthetic effect. (See http://theartful mind.stanford.edu for an example of this work.)

I leave open the possibility that much of the distinctive effect is due to the human scaffolding: the laying out of the canvas and the paint, the focused encouragement, the choice of the moment of completion, and of course the selection of canvases to exhibit. Moreover, I find it intriguing to contemplate the difference it makes for my appreciation of the painting to consider the mind of the creator. Are these lines clumsy strokes that arbitrarily criss-cross and fortuitously suggest a complex order, or are they the intended results of a delicately sensitive mind, sharply aware of the subtle play of form and color? In the former case, it would be misleading to call this art—or, to put it differently, the artistic act should be attributed to their human friends and handlers rather than to the gorillas themselves. A distinctive feature of art as communication is that at some link in the chain must be the act of declaring something to be an aesthetic artifact. Treating Koko's paintings as art carries with it the necessary implication that gorillas have a sense of aesthetics.

In fact, the anecdotal evidence strongly suggests that our closest simian relatives have an independent and self-motivated urge to create art, and that this enjoyment drives and orders their activities toward end results that humans have no difficulty relating to as art, even high-quality art. Desmond Morris (1962) reported in the early 1960s that chimpanzees would get so absorbed by their painting that they forwent food, evidently finding the activity inherently enjoyable. When they were systematically given a reward for each painting, however, their work would degenerate to a minimal smear as their motivation shifted to obtaining the reward. This suggests that the animals have aesthetic response systems very similar to ours, that they experience aesthetic pleasure, and that, just like us, they are capable of targeting this aesthetic pleasure through their own exploratory and original creations in ways that are unprecedented in their natural history.

Koko's work is not obviously figurative, but the paintings are given titles that suggest a subject (for example, one is titled "Bird"), based on signs exchanged with humans at the time of painting. Representational art relies on a complex suite of cognitive adaptations, some of which are clearly present in apes. The gradual development of the capacities required to make sense of images can also be observed in infants.

I sometimes read picture books with a friend; younger than two years, she likes to point at various items she is familiar with and name them. The items, of course, are depictions and not the objects themselves; they are two-dimensional, stylized, small, and feature-poor versions of the actual things she names. In order to utilize the affordances of the depictions of hats and balls and to interpret them as iconic, rather than as colored blots on a piece of paper, she must activate her personal memories of these objects, memories that are laced with emotions and motor activity. "Ball!" she exclaims with passion, likely the same passion she feels for the real object. In her mind, there is a simulation of a ball—or more conservatively, a simulated response to a ball—and it is this simulation that constitutes the act of understanding the image. This act of making sense of an iconic depiction is very similar to the act of pretense: it involves the reinterpretation of perceptual input based on a counterfactual scenario, one in which there is a hat (for a more detailed treatment, see Steen 2005).

It may appear excessive to invoke the notion of simulation to explain something as elementary as understanding a picture. After all, pictures of hats and balls look like hats and balls; why should it be any harder to understand one than the other? The point here is that since images are not what they represent, it is not adequate to respond to them as if they were. Understanding a picture is not a matter of making a mistake, of momentarily confusing pictures of hats with hats, and then realizing that you missed the mark. At the same time, understanding a picture of a hat involves precisely something very like this type of confusion: it requires activating the response system that handles real hats. Only by activating the appropriate target response system will the picture of a hat make sense to you as a hat. In less paradoxical terms, understanding the picture of a hat requires that your brain respond to it as if it were a hat, but that it simultaneously track the fact that it is just a picture. In this sense, the picture prompts a simulated response—a response that duplicates key features of the real experience, but lacks its real consequences.

In this view, the act of responding to an image is an act of pretense. It requires that you set up a distinct mental space in consciousness to handle the perceptual input of the image as well as the output of the target response system. While the cognitive machinery of pretense can be utilized for executive purposes such as symbolic communication and planning, it seems likely that the capacity to pretend first evolved to enable behavioral simulations such as chase play and play fighting—that is to say, to solve problems related to self-construction (Steen and Owens 2001). As such, pretense represents one of the central cognitive innovations of the organizational mode. It is designed to solve a particularly complex adaptive problem—that of improving performance on a task in the absence of the normal eliciting conditions. Pretense allows the young mammal or child to make use of affordances in its environment to devise learning situations that are safe, readily available, and developmentally appropriate. This amounts to saying that natural selection acts on the organizational mode to elaborate what might be termed an evolved pedagogy. We can thus make sense of the developmentally and contextually calibrated boredom and thrill of play as motivational and regulatory mechanisms designed to optimize the kind of learning that benefited our ancestors in the environment of evolutionary adaptedness.

In representational art, aesthetics and play join forces. When we engage with an artistic representation, such as Keats's Grecian urn, the mental spaces created are neither precisely counterfactual (they are not primarily contrasted with a real state of affairs) nor hypothetical (they are not primarily formulations of a possible state of things). Rather, they are defined in a deliberately playful manner to optimize the conditions for self-construction. A striking feature of this optimization is the creation of virtual agents, which permit an intense and likely extremely effective first-person learning.

Consider the situation when you encounter real human beings. You know they see you and that what you do will make a difference. In order to act coherently, you need to track who you are and what your goals are as well as your available resources and possible obstacles. These elements constitute what we may term your agent memories. When you encounter a human being in a piece of representational art, you realize that there is no need to respond to him or her—the person isn't there; it's just a picture. She cannot see you, and you are not called upon to act. In this case, what do you do?

First, you may lower your defenses and enter an aesthetic frame of mind; this may play a role in the effective implicit information gathering. Because you do not need to respond, you may set your own agent memories aside—an act that frees you from worrying about the real problems in your life. In this way, the aesthetic attraction and imaginative possibilities of the object tease you out of thought, to use Keats's expression. Second, you may use your imagination to fill in the blanks, to attempt to reconstruct a past and a future that fit the cues provided. In doing this, you are in effect constructing a model of the fictive agents in the representation, attributing to them a social and biological identity, a goal, and a set of resources and obstacles relating to reaching this goal. This act of reconstruction creates a complete set of agent memories—wholly fictive, of course, and attributed to the individuals depicted. In the third stage, you may swing your wand and undergo yourself a temporary transformation into the person represented, handled either as a personal identification or as an imaginative projection. You do this by, as it were, writing your own agent memories to disk and reading in the fictive ones you constructed in stage two, thus becoming a virtual agent. By creating a virtual agent, you are able to enter the fictive scenario and contemplate from a first-person perspective the full experience presented in the representation.

This virtual agent allows the pretending individual to use fiction to access and to explore the vast space of possible human action. Human beings are not born with operating manuals, and the competitive nature of social and natural reality means that there will always be a premium on new and original strategies of action. Discovering the small subset of useful strategies among the vast number of possible actions is a nontrivial problem, especially in domains where the cost of an attempt is high and the tolerance for failure low. In pretense, we can explore this abstract and unmanifest but nevertheless real phase space of human thought, feeling, and action in a manner that is safe and sheltered from real consequences, and we can do so at a negligible cost. Great representational art, in this perspective, provides a set of affordances that allow us to open up this phase space in new and original ways, suited to our local individual and cultural conditions.

Conclusion

If we agree to use the term *beauty* for whatever qualities it is that attract us to aesthetic objects and events, we can now return to the question raised by Keats's ode: what kind of truth is beauty? In the first approximation, this model of natural aesthetics suggests that beauty can meaningfully be thought of as an important type of truth. Referential truth makes a claim about a systematic relation between an external manifest and an internal symbolic order; in natural aesthetics, there is no symbolic order. Instead, aesthetic truth makes an even more basic claim: that there is a significant and systematic relation between certain orders that are externally manifest and the internal manifest order of certain aspects of our being. The truth of beauty, in this view, is that particular subset of truths that we are designed to feel inclined to seek out and enjoy as an end in themselves, and that are relied on by the organism and by natural selection for the purpose of constructing and maintaining our own order.

In the second approximation, the truth of beauty encompasses the use of imaginative immersion and the creation of virtual agents in representational art. In this case, beauty's claim to truth is more diffuse. It is centered in the proposition that the set of actions, thoughts, and feelings—modes of relating to the world—that are possible but not yet manifest or realized constitutes a genuine and important truth. It has supreme practical value, for it is in this state space that new strategies can be found. Art provides us with the occasion and some of the tools to explore this possibility space in ways that are cheap, safe, and effective.

Both of these types of truth—the aesthetic and the imaginative—are precarious. It is not the case, pace Keats, that aesthetics and the imagination are the only kinds of truth we have or the only kind we need. This matters, as they are not infallible paths to truth. First, the processes of natural selection that have endowed us with these admittedly very powerful modes of acquiring truth are effective only with regard to truths that have persisted and mattered for survival for very long periods, and even then only to some pragmatic degree of approximation. Second, cultural innovations in the arts rely in part on deliberately exploiting the slack in our adaptive machinery; in these cases, the truths we discover, if any, can be chalked up to our own account. Third, the fact that the real work of beauty takes place in large part below the horizon of conscious awareness, but according to principles that can be at least in part discovered, creates a situation where the instinctive conviction that beauty is truth lends itself to manipulation for political and other purposes. Finally, according to the present argument, the very design of aesthetics and imaginative play is to explore a vast phase space of human action, much of which has not been realized and thus cannot have been acted on by natural selection. In brief, we are on our own. Beauty is a profound guide to a kind of truth we might term "existential": if it has a referent, it is the order that unites us with the cosmos.

REFERENCES

Bohm, D., and F. D. Peat. 1984. *Science, order, and creativity.* New York: Routledge.

Brown, D. E. 1991. *Human universals.* New York: McGraw-Hill.

Hughes, R. 1991. *The shock of the new* (rev. ed.). New York: Knopf.

Keats, J. 1820. "Ode on a Grecian Urn." In *Lamia, Isabella, The Eve of St. Agnes, and other poems.* London, England: Taylor and Hessey. Also available in J. Keats. 1982. *Complete poems,* ed. Jack Stillinger. Cambridge, Mass.: Belknap Press, Harvard University Press.

Korzybski, A. 1933. *Science and sanity: An introduction to non-Aristotelian systems and general semantics.* New York: International Non-Aristotelian Library.

Morris, D. 1962. *The biology of art: A study of the picture-making behaviour of the great apes and its relationship to human art.* New York: Knopf.

Orians, G. H., and J. H. Heerwagen. 1992. Evolved responses to landscapes. In *The adapted mind: evolutionary psychology and the generation of culture,* ed. J. H. Barkow, L. Cosmides, and J. Tooby, 555–79. New York: Oxford University Press.

Prigogine, I., and I. Stengers. 1984. *Order out of chaos: Man's new dialogue with nature.* Boulder, Colo.: New Science Library.

Sperber, D. 1996. *Explaining culture: A naturalistic approach.* Cambridge, Mass.: Blackwell.

Steen, F. 2005. "The paradox of narrative thinking." *Journal of Cultural and Evolutionary Psychology,* 3(1): 87–105.

Steen, F. F., and S. A. Owens. 2001. Evolution's pedagogy: An adaptationist model of pretense and entertainment. *Journal of Cognition and Culture,* 1, no. 4: 289–321.

Stryker, M. P., H. Sherk, A. G. Leventhal, and H. V. Hirsch. 1978. Physiological consequences for the cat's visual cortex of effectively restricting early visual experience with oriented contours. *Journal of Neurophysiology,* 41, no. 4: 896–909.

Tieman, S. B., and H. V. Hirsch. 1982. Exposure to lines of only one orientation modifies dendritic morphology of cells in the visual cortex of the cat. *Journal of Comparative Neurology,* 211, no. 4: 353–62.

Turner, M. 1996. *The literary mind: The origins of thought and language*. New York: Oxford University Press.

Voland, E., and K. Grammer, eds. 2003. *Evolutionary aesthetics*. Berlin: Springer.

Wordsworth, W. 1798. Lines written a few miles above Tintern Abbey, on revisiting the banks of the Wye during a tour, July 13, 1798. In *Lyrical ballads*, W. Wordsworth and S. T. Coleridge. 1798. Bristol, England: T. N. Longman. [Also available in *Lyrical ballads*, W. Wordsworth and S. T. Coleridge, ed. W.J.B. Owen (2nd ed., 1969). London, England: Oxford University Press.]

4

Composition and Emotion

David Freedberg

In The Power of Images *(1989), I described some of the recurrent symptoms of emotional responses to paintings and sculptures throughout history. Here I take the problem one step further and suggest that one of the tasks of future interdisciplinary work between the neurosciences and the history of art might be to examine the relationship between how pictures look and the emotional responses they evoke. This chapter rejects the notion that such a relationship may be too ragged to plot. In it, I give some examples—from the history of painting and the history of music—where efforts have been made to connect particular compositions with particular emotional states. Poussin's proposal (1647) suggests future possibilities for research in this area.*

What are the protocols for conducting an experiment on the relations between pictorial composition and emotional response? Underlying this question is the problem of establishing and defining correlations between particular kinds of compositions and particular emotional responses. In a preliminary group of experiments conducted by Pietro Perona and myself in May 1999, we attempted to establish the possibility of arriving at conclusions about the relationship between the immediate perception of an image and emotional responses to it. Context, of course, conditions and contaminates response, but we were concerned with such responses as might arise from vision unmitigated by prior circumstantial knowledge and as uncontaminated as possible by contextual factors, whether individual, social, or historical. We acknowledged two initial sets of difficulties. The first had to do with the isolation of compositional features from everything else in a picture (color and subject matter, for example) that plays a role in the evocation of emotion; the second concerned the definition of types of response. We have continued to assess the problems of evaluative criteria; of modes and modality; of parallel processing; and the more general problem of moving from aspects of vision (say, saccadic eye patterns and the issue of saliency) to emotion. The latter move is the crux.

We took two broad kinds of compositions: relatively simple geometric ones, and more complex ones such as paintings. Some paintings from the past contain compositional elements so plainly salient that they may usefully be compared, in terms of the responses they evoke, with plainer geometric compositions devoid of color or iconography. They thus offer the possibility of testing the correlations between composition and emotion more satisfactorily than pictures where the elements of composition are less obvious or less overtly striven for by the artist. The work of the seventeenth-century French painter Nicolas Poussin offers a large number of possible examples. Many of his paintings have compositional structures so clear (and so self-consciously devised, as we know from his writings, his drawings, and his own experiments in composition[1]) that the elements of their geometricity appear much stronger, and leave a more lasting impression in the mind, than those in most other figurative paintings in the history of art. Thus, Poussin offers a superior test case for the emotional effects of overall compositional structure, apart from the interferences of color, subject matter, and more apparently decorative structural elements. All this might seem to be a matter of mere impressions, but it hardly needs to be said that mere impressions are to be taken seriously when it comes to the relationship between pictures and the potentially correlative mental effects they generate. Moreover, Poussin offered an interesting set of reflections on just the problem of the relationship between composition and the arousal of emotions in the "soul of the beholders" (as he himself put it). These reflections will form the central text of the first part of this paper. They revolve round an old notion of the musical modes.

I remain unmoved by the argument that the kinds of emotions pictures (and music) arouse are too refined to fall within the scope of the neurosciences. The argument that the most we can now say about the emotions is on a relatively gross level ought not to block research into the correlations between visual composition and emotion, however refined such emotion may be declared to be (or however contaminated by contextual factors). In the meantime, I offer a case study in the history of the modes that seems to me to constitute an interesting prolegomenon to the problem, not only because of the following:

- The paintings of Poussin present a kind of compositional clarity not often found in other pictures (in them, I believe, composition is indeed so clear that it is less likely, at least in the context of immediate or "early" vision, to be contaminated by issues of color, iconography, expression, etc.).

But also because:

- The historical problem of the modes offers an entirely different way of thinking about modality from current conceptions of that notion;
- The historical parallel with the musical modes—see the skeletal post-lude here—points once more to the single issue that has for so long stymied serious study of the relations between aesthetic objects and emotion—namely, that the emotions are too ragged and irregular to be amenable to any kind of rule or law.

The commitment here is to a belief that neuroscientific work (by Damasio, Le Doux, and many others) may introduce order into the general raggedness of talk about emotion and counter our loose inclination to regard emotion—especially when not gross or strong—as a psychoanalytic issue rather than a neural one.

The Modes

The idea of the modes in art (and in painting in particular) was not a common one, at least not until the middle of the seventeenth century. But from then on, it enjoyed a fairly long vogue. Its introduction into the mainstream of the history of art is due to the influence of one man alone.

On November 24, 1647, the French painter Nicolas Poussin wrote a long letter from Rome to his friend and patron Paul Fréart de Chantelou in Paris. "Those fine old Greeks," he said at one point, "inventors of everything that is beautiful, found several modes by means of which they produced marvelous effects" (Poussin 1911, 372–73).[2] What did Poussin mean by the "modes," and what meaning could they have for us?[3]

In 1647, Poussin painted a *Finding of Moses* for Jean Pointel (see http://theartfulmind.stanford.edu), one of several he did of this comparatively un-usual subject, and a scene of *Ordination* (part of a cycle of the Seven Sacra-ments) for Paul Fréart de Chantelou (see http://theartfulmind.stanford.edu).

Pointel and Chantelou were Poussin's most important French patrons, though certainly not as important for his art as Cassiano dal Pozzo in Rome, for whom he painted the first series of Sacraments just before his brief return to Paris in 1641–1642. Pointel was a banker and a bachelor, and he eventually owned twenty-one of Poussin's loveliest paintings. He was also the most private of men—unlike Chantelou, who along with his brother Roland Fréart de Chambray was instrumental in what might be called the classicization of French art under Richelieu, Mazarin, and Colbert. It isn't surprising that Chantelou should have commissioned a series of the Seven Sacraments (an extremely unusual subject) in direct emulation of the earlier set, painted for Cassiano, in which Poussin displayed his famous knowledge of the archaeology both of early Christianity and of classical antiquity.

But Chantelou was evidently not satisfied with his painting of *Ordination*. He was constantly looking over his shoulder, and as we learn from a famous letter by Poussin to him in November 1647, he seems to have felt that Pointel's *Finding of Moses* was the better picture. Art historians may think that this is a bit like comparing apples and oranges, and Poussin obviously thought so, too. Quite exasperated by Chantelou's nagging, he wanted to settle the problem once and for all.

"[I]t is easy to dispel your suspicion that I honor you less and that I am less devoted to you than to others," he wrote in a petulant letter to Chantelou.

> If this were so, why should I have preferred you, over a period of five years, to so many persons of merit and quality who ardently desired that I should do something for them and who offered me their purses? Why was I satisfied with such a modest price that I would not even accept what you yourself offered me? And why, after sending you the first of your pictures composed of only sixteen or eighteen figures—so that I could have made the others with the same number or fewer in order to bring such a long labor to an end—why did I enrich them further with no thought except to obtain your good will?
>
> If you find the painting of the finding of Moses in the waters of the Nile which belongs to M. Pointel so attractive, is this a reason for thinking that I did it with greater love than I put into your paintings? (Poussin 1911, 371–72)

Then he had an idea. He would try to explain something very basic about pictures to Chantelou. Not having quite the right arguments to hand for painting, however, he turned to an example from the theory of music to explain what may seem obvious to us: that different subjects require different treatments. But he went still further than this, suggesting that different treatments might have different effects on the beholder.

Can't you see that it is the nature of the subject, and your state of mind [*disposition*], which has caused this effect, and that the subjects I am depicting for you require a different treatment? The whole art of painting lies in this. Forgive my liberty if I say that you have been too hasty in your judgment of my works. To judge well is very difficult unless one has great knowledge of both the theory and the practice of this art. Our senses alone ought not to be the judge, but reason too.

This is why I want to tell you something of great importance which will make you see what has to be observed in representing the subjects of paintings.

Those fine old Greeks, inventors of everything that is beautiful, found several modes by means of which they produced marvelous effects.

This word "mode" means, properly, the *ratio* or the measure and the form we use to do something, which constrains us not to move beyond it, making us work in all things with a certain middle course or moderation. And so this mediocrity or moderation is simply a certain manner or determined and fixed order in the process by which a thing preserves its being.

The modes of the ancients were composed of several things put together; and from their variety there arose certain differences between the modes; and from these one could understand that each mode retained in itself a certain distinctiveness, *particularly when all the things which entered into the composition were put together in such proportions that there arose the capacity and power to arouse the soul of the beholders to diverse emotions* [emphasis added]. Observing these effects, the wise ancients attributed to each [mode] particular effects arising from each one of them. For this reason they called Dorian the mode that was stable, grave, and severe, and they applied it to matters that were grave, severe, and full of wisdom.

And passing on from this to pleasant and joyous things they used the Phrygian mode because its modulations were more refined [*plus menues*] than those of any other mode and its aspect sharper. These two manners and no others were praised and approved by Plato and Aristotle, who deemed the others useless; they held in high esteem this vehement, furious, and highly severe mode that strikes the spectators with awe.

I hope within a year to paint something in this Phrygian mode; frightful wars provide subjects suited to this manner.

Furthermore, they considered that the Lydian mode was the most proper for mournful subjects because it has neither the simplicity of the Dorian nor the severity of the Phrygian.

The Hypolydian mode contains within itself a certain suavity and sweetness which fills the soul of the beholders with joy. It lends itself to divine matters, glory, and Paradise.

The ancients invented the Ionian which they employed to represent dances, bacchanals, and feasts because of its cheerful character.

Good poets have used great diligence and marvelous artifice in adapting their choice of words to their verse and disposing the feet according to the propriety [*convenanse*] of speech. . . . So, when [Virgil] is speaking of love, he has cleverly chosen certain words that are sweet, pleasing, and very gracious to the ear. Where he sings of a feat of arms or describes a naval battle or accident at sea, he has chosen words that are hard, sharp, and unpleasing, so that on hearing them or pronouncing them they arouse fright. If, therefore, I had painted you a picture in which this manner was followed, you would imagine that I did not love you.

Were it not that it would amount to composing a book rather than writing a letter, I would like to bring to your attention several important things that should be considered in painting, so that you could fully realize how much I exert myself to serve you well. For though you are very knowledgeable in all matters, I fear that the company of so many insensitive and ignorant people of the kind that surround you may corrupt your judgment by contagion.

> I remain, as always, your very
> humble and most faithful servant,
> Poussin.

(Poussin 1911: 373–74)

Obviously there is much here that requires comment (the relation between reason and the senses, for example, and the predictable parallels between painting and poetry); but I want to concentrate on what may seem the most arcane part of the letter—namely, the part in which Poussin talks about the modes and his strange references to the grave Dorian, the sharp and warlike Phrygian, the suave Hypolidian, the cheerful Ionian, and so on.

Where does all this come from? It comes, as Anthony Blunt discovered in 1933,[4] from ancient music theory. In fact, what Poussin wrote about the modes is little more than a direct plagiarism from Gioseffe Zarlino's *Harmonic Institutions*,[5] first published in 1553 and reprinted many times for the rest of the century. But this is no reason not to take his ideas seriously. After all, while most of us can recognize the possibility that different kinds of music might stir us differently, the idea that different kinds of pictures move us in different ways would seem rather more resistant to formulation in any clear-cut or systematic way. Indeed, scholars of Poussin have mostly avoided the topic altogether. The usual approach to this letter has been either to dismiss it as simple plagiarism or to see it in terms of the twin doctrines of decorum and of the *affetti*.[6] That is, Poussin has been understood to be making the rather conventional claim that the expression of the emotions *within* the paintings should somehow be appropriate to the kind of subject to be depicted. Poussin himself wrote in 1637 of another painting which he did for Chantelou, the now almost unreadable picture in the Louvre of *The Israelites Gathering the Manna*, that there were "certain natural attitudes within it" that enabled one

> to see in the Israelites not only the misery and hunger to which they
> were reduced, but also the joy and happiness in which they found
> themselves, the amazement by which they were touched, the respect
> and the reverence they had for their leader; with a mixture of women,
> children, and old men, and of different temperaments.[7]

It was this kind of reading of a picture that was taken up in the famous *Conférences* or lectures in the French Academy of Painting from around 1667 on;[8] and this is exactly how almost all scholars have tried to deal with the problem. Much of the literature on Poussin and very many of the early commentators on his work, from the late seventeenth century onwards, have expended great effort analyzing the ways in which one or another of Poussin's modes was expressed within one or another of his paintings.[9] Large quantities of ink have been spilt in order to establish what the particular "modes" of individual paintings could be, and whether a particular subject was expressed in a mode suitable or adequate to that subject. But this is not what Poussin intended, however much his descriptions of the modes may suggest this.

Of course, it may be that we perceive a picture or a piece of music to be severe, say, but that it does not make us feel severe. Expression of emotion, however, is not the real subject of Poussin's letter; the excitation of the emotions is. Expression is evidently bound up with more than composition alone entails (such as, for example, color and subject matter). The stimulation of a feeling[10] may be dependent on expression in a picture, too, but the aim of the project outlined here (as well as the central focus of Poussin's letter) is to move toward the establishment of correlations that precede the contextual information on which, to a large extent, expression depends. This, however, is not the place to offer distinctions between expression and the excitation of emotion.

To return to Poussin: he was not simply pointing to the difficulty of finding the right modes by which to express the relevant emotions of the actors in pictures. Nor was he making a case for the expression of the moral and emotional character (the *ethos*, as it was then called) of a picture or its actors. The basic issue for him, as the letter makes clear, is the arousal of emotion, not the putative expression of emotions within a picture. Nor was he especially concerned with the issue of how correctly to read the emotions expressed in a painting or by its protagonists.

To view Poussin's letter in any of these ways seems to me to gloss over its most crucial and interesting passage. After all, he himself clearly and articulately observed that "each mode retained in itself a certain distinctiveness, particularly when all the things which entered into the composition were put together in such proportions that there arose the capacity and power to arouse the soul of the beholders to diverse emotions." This is the central claim of the letter. It goes far beyond the injunctions in his letters of ten years earlier about the *Gathering of the Manna* to "read the story and the painting [*lisez l'histoire et le tableau*] in order to know whether each thing is appropriate to the subject [*afin de connaître si chaque chose est appropriée au sujet*]" (Poussin 1911, 21). This notion, certainly, was based on the old parallelism between texts and paintings and on the notion of decorum and appropriateness. But the point now was much more radical. It had little to do with *reading* a picture. It implied—or rather, it stated outright—that a composition may be put together in such a way as to arouse the soul of the beholders to particular emotions.

With music this seems self-evident, commonsensical, intuitive, and consistent with our experience—but with painting? Or sculpture? Or architecture? And could such modes be specifiable for pictures? Could, furthermore, the correlative emotions for the way particular pictures are put together be established? I think that anyone who reflects on these questions will realize instantly that a positive answer would entail a view of the relations between pictures and spectators that is not solely dependent on context. Such a view is predicated instead on the possibility of being able to establish certain rules, and assumes that particular kinds of responses are in fact innate. One has, therefore, to ask whether the kinds of correlations Poussin was suggesting might be both universal (which is what the letter implies) and universally applicable. After all, Poussin said that the modes were specifiable and that the effects of pictures on their beholders could be directly correlated with how they were composed and how they looked.

No one, as far as I know, has taken any of this sufficiently seriously to analyze the possibility that Poussin might indeed have been claiming not only something important about responses to images, but also something basic. I think he was. Furthermore, I believe that what he had to say has powerful implications for the philosophy of mind and for how we think about the architectonics, as Kant would have put it, of mental operations. None other than Bernini, that most sensual of sculptors, seems to have caught something of this when, pointing to his forehead, he remarked (upon seeing the painting of the pictures in Paris in 1665) that "*Signor Poussin è un pittore che lavora di là*"—"Signor Poussin is a painter who works from here" (Thuillier 1960, 127, and also in Thuillier 1994, 177). When I wrote *The Power of Images* (Freedberg 1989), I deliberately refrained from suggesting anything either about human nature or about the possibility of innate levels of response— although some critics caught some hint of that. But I now believe that I was not radical enough. My own sense is that Poussin was right, and that one ought to be able to establish a syntax of correlations between pictures and responses— and that this syntax is in principle discoverable through the idea of the modes.

In his letter, Poussin does not, of course, offer anything remotely approaching a full-blown theory. It is not simply (or at all) the traditional problem of justly expressing the emotions of the figures painted in accordance with the subject of the painting. Nor is it just a matter of decorum. Rather, it entails the production of effects in the mind of the spectators, "*une puissanse de induire l'âme des regardans à diverses passions*," as Poussin so clearly put it (Poussin 1911, 373). It is true that Poussin has simply substituted *l'âme des regardans* for Zarlino's *gli animi de gli ascoltanti*. However clear the borrowing, the changes are crucial. And there are two significant ones. First, the change from "hearers" to "beholders"; second, from "souls" to "the soul." Implicit in this latter change is the notion, however unconscious in Poussin, that one may indeed speak of the generic soul rather than of particular souls. The mind is singular, not plural, and as such is analytic.

But what is it in pictures that actually causes the soul to be moved to different emotions? Let us turn to the body of the letter. Most of it, as Blunt noticed, comes from Zarlino. There seem to be three factors at stake: first, variety—that is, the varied ways in which the elements of the composition are put together; second, difference—that is, the difference that produces variety; third, proportion—that is, the proportional relationships between the elements of a composition upon which the diversity of emotional effects actually depends. If we remained solely concerned with the problem of the *difference* of effects, then all this has some logic to it; but if we think of how the effects themselves are actually produced, then it all seems rather abstract and vague.

And the idea of the regulatory possibilities of proportion seems much easier to grasp in the case of music than in that of pictures, since in music they are so obviously confirmed by repetition. How, for example, could one speak of the beat of pictures or of the beat of pictorial effect? The pulse of music may be slow, languid, frenetic, or insistent, and stir one's body to approximately concomitant feelings; but how could one begin to speak of the pulse of pictures? Poussin's letter leaves the problem wholly unresolved.

At the heart of the letter lies the definition of the modes. "Mode," says Poussin, *"signifie proprement la raison,"* and reason is *"la mesure et forme de laquelle nous nous servons à faire quelque chose. laquelle nous abstraint à ne passer pas oultre."* Reason is measure, and as shape or form entails boundedness, constraint, and limit. Constraint and limit (*"ne passer pas oultre"*) are constitutive of the reason that is mode. At this point the letter seems to take a disappointing turn, for Poussin goes on to speak of the *"médiocrité et modération"* which reason makes us apply to all things.

But we should be careful not to take *"médiocrité"* in its modern sense of a quality that betokens something somewhat ordinary. Nor is this *mediocritas* simply to be understood in terms of the *via media* so beloved of seventeenth-century neo-stoic philosophy. This, of course, at least partly anticipates its modern meaning, referring to something that avoids the excitement of one extreme or another—something tame, safe, ordinary, *not* extreme. But when Poussin (like Zarlino) speaks of *"médiocrité et modération,"* he deliberately makes explicit his awareness that measure entails limits and that its extremities are formally bounded. Indeed, the claim he makes in the final section of this paragraph is what ties it together and gives it its profound consistency: "this mediocrity and moderation is nothing else but a certain determinate order, and has a closure to it by which the thing conserves its being."[12]

This is the fundamental and complex core of the paragraph, and it forms the basis of the ideas of variety, difference, and proportion set out in the next part of the letter. Poussin himself may not have been fully aware of the dense philosophical implications of his extract from Zarlino, but they are fundamental to any understanding of the efficiency of the modes. Being entails conservation; it has to be conserved in order to be; it can never be purely open. Pure openness is the enemy of being. If being were purely open, it would lose its life, terminating in nonbeing; and nonbeing can have no effect. The being of being consists of its own immanent closure and determinacy, or rather, as Poussin puts it, its determinate order. But how is this affective order preserved?

Poussin omits (or rather, he probably forgets to transcribe) Zarlino's crucial addition to his definition of the mediocrity that constitutes being—namely, the fact that the closed and determinate order that conserves something in its being does so "by virtue of the proportion to be found in it": "*Imperochè tal mediocrità, o moderatione non è altro, che una certa maniera, over ordine terminato e fermo nel procedere per il quale la cosa si conserva nel suo essere*, per virtù della proportione, ch'in essa si ritrova" [emphasis added], says Zarlino.

Order and closure in music, just as in pictures, are only possible by virtue of proportionality. It is proportion that drives the conservation of order and determinacy. Proportion determines closure and thus constitutes order itself. Order changes with changes in proportion, and the distinctiveness of each form depends on proportional variety, the *"je ne sais quoi de varié"* of the next paragraph. Both Zarlino and Poussin insist that it is the proportion used in a composition that generates the power to induce the soul of viewers (or listeners, as the case may be) to different emotions. Each proportion has its peculiar, distinctive, and describable effects. None of this may seem to be sufficient to explain the actual *production* of effect, only the difference between effects. But to conclude in this way would be a mistake. Since proportion always entails rule—each proportion must have its own rule—there must also be a rule-bound correlation with effect. Consider how traumatic it would be, in this kind of reading, if one could stipulate nothing more specific about the relation between proportion and effect! This is one task that must be undertaken.[13]

All this is likely to arouse deep skepticism. I am not now primarily speaking of the relations between perceptual rules and how a picture looks. These, too, are relations whose rules may presumably be discovered, and much cognitive work has been done in this domain; but in proposing a *tertium quid* I am indeed taking a further leap. Even if we assume that we may establish a syntax for the relations between how pictures look and how we cognize them, I believe that there is a further syntactical level: between the look of a picture and the emotions it arouses. And the rules for that syntax, I believe, are innate and specifiable. The general view, of course, is exactly the opposite. This more popular view holds that the emotions are not subject to reason or to any specifiable set of rules; and that very little if anything can be said about the relations between pictures and feeling that is not purely contextual or idiosyncratic. That, of course, is not a view I share.

Key Characteristics

If the idea of the modes and the specific emotional qualities associated with them was uncommon in painting (though perhaps more common than usually assumed), this was not at all the case with the idea of the modes in music. As we have already seen, it was at least as old as the Greeks, and it has played an important role in all musical theory and much musical practice (from chant through Beethoven) ever since. But one of the problems in music was whether the modes were somehow equivalent to the keys; and with respect to the keys and the emotions associated with them—what have appropriately been called key characteristics—the evidence is abundant, much more so than has generally been acknowledged. "The search for pertinent material was full of surprises; I never knew where I would stumble upon another list of key characteristics," wrote Rita Steblin in her book on the subject. "It is clear," she went on, "that the topic cannot be ignored" (Steblin 1983, xi and 1). Here is one such list from the seventeenth century:

PROPERTIES OF THE MODES

C Major	Gay and warlike
C Minor	Obscure and sad
D Minor	Grave and pious
D Major	Joyous and very warlike
E Minor	Effeminate, amorous, and plaintive
E Major	Quarrelsome and peevish
E-flat Major	Cruel and severe
F Major	Furious and quick-tempered
F Minor	Gloomy and plaintive
G Major	Quietly joyful
G Minor	Serious and magnificent
A Minor	Tender and plaintive
A Major	Joyous and pastoral
B-flat Major	Magnificent and joyous
B-flat Minor	Gloomy and terrifying
B Minor	Lonely and melancholy
B Major	Severe and plaintive[14]

Much plaintiveness, as if to cover the possibility of some more precise emotion.[15]

It was in the air, this association of particular emotions with particular aspects of musical composition, this need to introduce rule into the correlation between the composition of a work and the emotions it aroused. Our list comes from Marc-Antoine Charpentier's *Rules of Composition*, written around 1692 for the young Philippe d'Orléans; it was by no means the only such list in the seventeenth century, but perhaps the most detailed. About thirty years later, Jean-Philippe Rameau's chart *De la propriété des modes & des Tons,* from his *Traité de l'harmonie,* would make a similar set of connections;[16] but by then such ideas, however much they may have been theoretically renewed, adapted, and refined, were stale. In all of them, as Rameau's heading makes clear, and as Poussin insists in *his* letter on the modes, the classical idea of decorum remains in the foreground. The emotions a piece of music expressed, or aroused, had to be fitting to its subject, just as with painting. Let us turn the clock back to times when these ideas were more urgent, less overtly mechanistic, and then remind ourselves of the central period—Poussin's—when they were articulated in such a way that they might still be of relevance to the neurophilosophical problems we are pursuing.

Charpentier's list is headed "properties of the modes," but it seems to provide nothing more than a list of keys with their emotional correlates. This was the commonest way in which the modes were understood in the seventeenth century and after. For the ancient Greeks, too, the modes (the Greeks had only eight) corresponded, very roughly, with our notion of key signatures; and they, too, thought of the modes both as representing particular emotions and as capable of provoking them with similar particularity. But can it be only a matter of key, however understood? Of course not. As everyone knows, there is much more to music than key that can affect its hearers—modulation from one key to another, rhythm, harmony, and melody, for example. Not surprisingly, the modes were often taken to be something else besides these, or a composite of various aspects of a musical composition. Then there was the perpetual issue of the relationship between music and its texts. In fact, this remained the central issue, if not always explicitly so, in every discussion of the relationship between the modes and the emotions, from the earliest times at least until the eighteenth century. And so it is not at all surprising that in his letter about the modes, Poussin should have begun by insisting that Chantelou attend more carefully to the determining role of the subjects of the pictures that had provoked their *contretemps* in the first place.

Charpentier offered two justifications for his list. First, and straightforwardly enough, there was the need to accommodate different vocal ranges. But second—and much more importantly—there was the list's potential utility as a guide to "the expression of the different passions, for which the different key properties [*energies,* significantly enough] are appropriate." (Always the need for the appropriateness and propriety of properties, as if propriety were the chief constitutive element of property.) But if it all were simply a matter of key, the task would be relatively simple, at least in principle. It would not be much different from, say, attempting to establish the *moods* of particular colors in pictures (in which case "mood" would not implausibly serve as a rough substitute for "mode," and color as a rough equivalent for key). But just as there is more to music than just key, so too there is more to painting than color. Certainly to speak only of color would not satisfy the full implications of Poussin's letter at all.

In 1640, in the wake of a cruel musical competition set up for him by Marin Mersenne, Johan Albert Ban, a slightly crazy and certainly obsessive priest and music theorist of Haarlem, wrote a letter to the famous Dutch bluestocking Anna Maria van Schuurman, in which he assigned emotional qualities to the consonances, thus:

minor third:	soft, bland, and languid
major third:	energetic
fourth:	harsh, because it cannot be divided into two harmonic intervals
fifth:	heroic and martial
minor sixth:	more flattering and languishing than the minor third, because it is a wider interval
octave:	merely pleasing, because it has no power of moving[17]

Ban went on to observe that the dissonances could also affect the emotions in specific ways, but these he did not outline, as they were in his Latin treatises on music, which are now lost. The issue of musical modulation intervenes here, too;[18] but all this raises another and conceivably more crucial possibility for the ways in which cognition and emotion may be understood to interact in works of music and the visual arts—namely, the matter of intervals between notes or what in painting could be called proportion. This is an issue that will be developed in future work on our project. But first the project must identify the ways in which emotions issue from the engagement of the body by the picture (or by clusters of pictures).[19]

To appeal to the mimetic powers of music to explain its effects on its listeners is even more vague than to appeal to mimesis in the case of pictures, unless we also attend to the *means* of mimesis (or "expression," for that matter). It could perhaps be argued (although I think it should not be) that for Poussin and other seventeenth-century writers about art, the idea of the modes did not entail the formal means of a picture; but still one would be left with the problem of the relations between how a picture looks and the emotions it arouses. One approach to the problem may be via theories of music often said to be irrelevant to Poussin and his contemporary commentators. Obviously, I believe that those theories *were* relevant—that the seventeenth-century view of the modes as adumbrated by Poussin contains a key to understanding the relations between seeing pictures and reacting to them with the body and mind, and with the emotions that spring from the incorporation of the body into cognition.

NOTES

1. See, for example (and especially), Blunt 1967, 241–47.

2. My translations from Poussin are adapted from Blunt's generally excellent ones (Blunt 1967), which I have modified where they seemed wrong or in need of clarification.

3. For the ways in which the general problem of the modes was viewed with regard to the visual arts, see the fundamental article by Bialostocki (1961). Bialostocki, however, overlooks the interpretation of the modes outlined in the present article.

4. In his unpublished Trinity College, Cambridge, Fellowship thesis "Poussin's Contribution to the Theory of Painting" of 1932, as noted (and partly published) by Alfassa 1933, 125–43.

5. Zarlino's text on the modes is to be found as Chapter I of Part III of the *Istitutioni harmoniche*; the passages adopted and adapted by Poussin are also reproduced by Alfassa 1933, 138–43.

6. For incisive remarks about the *affetti* (the expression of emotions in the characters of a painting—or even of a story—in such a way, sometimes, as to elicit comparable emotions in the beholder), see Cropper and Dempsey 1996, 13, as well as Dempsey 1989.

7. Poussin 1911, 4–5; Poussin to Stella, ca. 1637, as reported by Félibien 1725, 26.

8. As published in Jouin 1883 and Félibien 1725. See, for example, Jouin 1883, 48–65 and 93–94, as well as Félibien 1725, 412–13.

9. For instances of both modern and earlier attempts, see Freedberg, 1999, 311–38.

10. For a critical distinction between emotion and feeling, see Damasio 1999, 279–95.

11. Now in the Walker Art Gallery in Liverpool.

12. In the interests of clarity I have eliminated some of the vagueness of the original: "*telle médiocrité et modération n'est autre que une certaine manière ou ordre déterminé, et ferme dedens le procéder par lequel la chose se conserve en son estre*" (Poussin 1911, 373). "*Mediocrità o moderatione*" are exactly the words Zarlino uses in his chapter on the modes; cf. Zarlino 1589, I, 378.

13. A strong argument, however, has been made against doing anything of the kind. In his 1985 essay on Roger de Piles, Thomas Puttfarken argued vigorously against the view that the modes entailed the formal and abstract means of expression in a work. He denied that an understanding of Poussin's use of the modes could be attained by anything approaching what in modern terms would be called "formal analysis," or "by describing a composition using abstract terms like horizontal or vertical" (Puttfarken 1985, 30–34). For a further outline of Puttfarken's position and a refutation of it, see Freedberg 1999.

14. My translation from the transcription in Ruff 1967, 250–51.

15. For an important discussion of the distinction between emotions, feelings, and background feelings, see Damasio 1999, especially 275–95. Damasio's distinctions are plainly applicable to lists such as these, in which emotions and various forms of more or less conscious feelings are lumped together—in a way that does not, in my view, harm the project outlined in this paper. When a version of this paper was published for the Web conference Art and Cognition, 2002, several respondents objected to my claims on the grounds that these particular keys may evoke responses other than the ones cited here (see http://www.interdisciplines.org/artcog/papers). But no one—at least I do not think so—would want to claim that C major, for example, is universally "gay and/or warlike," or that E-flat major is always perceived as "cruel and severe." This is not what my argument entails at all. It may well be that such descriptions of our responses to the keys are merely partial, occasional, meager, inadequate, or even plain wrong. They may be culture-bound; they may depend on personal circumstance (as will the strength of such responses, too). All I want to suggest by offering examples such as this one (and the one cited by Ban below) is that we attend to the principles at stake in the historical claims for the relations between particular modes, or key characteristics—call them what you will, whether in music or the visual arts—and particular responses.

16. Cf. Steblin 1983, 38, citing Rameau 1722, 157.

17. Mersenne 1967, X, 30, 33; Walker 1976, 239–40. See again D'Amasio 1999, especially 275–95, for a discussion of what he refers to as "background feelings," such as harmony, calm, etc.

18. Ban was especially interested in the "wonderful arousals of the emotions" produced by modulations to remote keys, which he alleged caused strong contrasts of emotion, thus heightening the overall emotional effect of a piece. Cf. Walker 1976, 240.

19. A topic I address in my unpublished "Giotto's Struggle," a further historical case study of a problem (the structuring and sequence of the episodes on the walls of the Arena Chapel in Padua) with considerable neuroscientific interest.

REFERENCES

Alfassa, P. 1933. L'origine de la lettre de Poussin sur les modes d'après un travail recent. *Bulletin de la Société de l'Histoire de l'Art français*, 1: 125–43.

Allard, J. 1982. Mechanism, music and painting in 17th century France. *Journal of Aesthetics and Art Criticism*, 40, no. 3: 269–78.

Atcherson, W. 1973. Music and mode in seventeenth-century music theory books. *Journal of Music Theory*, 17, no. 1: 205–33.

Bialostocki, J. 1961. Das Modusproblem in der bildenden Künsten. *Zeitschrift für Kunstgeschichte*, 24: 128–41; reprinted in *Stil und Ikonographie. Studien zur Kunstwissenschaft*, Dresden, n.p., 1966, 5–35.

Blunt, A. 1967. *Nicolas Poussin*. New York: Pantheon, Bollingen Series 25, 7.

Cropper, E., and C. Dempsey. 1996. *Nicolas Poussin: Friendship and the love of painting*. Princeton, N.J.: Princeton University Press.

Damasio, A. 1999. *The feeling of what happens: Body and emotion in the making of consciousness.* New York: Harcourt Brace.

Dempsey, C. 1989. The Greek style and the prehistory of neoclassicism. In *Pietro Testa 1612–1650* [Prints and drawings], ed. E. Cropper, lii–liv. Philadelphia: Philadelphia Museum of Art.

Félibien, A. 1725. *Entretiens sur les vies et les ouvrages des plus excellens peintres anciens e modernes.* Trevoux: de l'Imprimerie de S.A.S.

Freedberg, D. 1989. *The power of images: Studies in the history and theory of response.* Chicago: University of Chicago Press.

———. 1999. De l'effet de la musique, aux effets de l'image; ou pourquoi les *affetti* ne sont pas les modes. In *Le Tasse, Actes du Colloque . . . . au Musée du Louvre . . . . 13–14 novembre, 1996,* 311–38. Paris: La documentation Française.

Jouin, H. 1883. *Conférences de l'Académie Royale de Peinture et de Sculpture.* Paris: Quantin.

Mersenne, P. M. 1967. *Correspondance du P. Marin Mersenne,* X, ed. Cornelis de Waard. Paris: Editions du CNRS.

Montagu, J. 1994. *The expression of the passions.* New Haven and London: Yale University Press.

Poussin, N. 1911. *Correspondance de Nicolas Poussin, Archives de l'Art Francais,* ed. C. Jouanny, V. Paris: H. Champion.

Puttfarken, T. 1985. *Roger de Piles' theory of art.* New Haven and London: Yale University Press.

Ruff, L. M. 1967. M.-A. Charpentier's 'Regles de Composition.' *The Consort,* 24: 233–70.

Steblin, R. 1983. *A history of key characteristics in the eighteenth and early nineteenth centuries.* Ann Arbor: University of Michigan Research Press.

Thuillier, J. 1960. Pour un Corpus Poussinianum. In *Colloque Nicolas Poussin,* ed. A. Chastel, 49–238. Paris: Editions du CNRS, II (partly reprinted in *id., Nicolas Poussin,* Paris: Flammarion, 1994).

Walker, D. P. 1976. Johan Albert Ban and Mersenne's musical composition of 1640. *Music and Letters,* 57, no. 3: 233–55.

———. 1985. *Music, spirit and language in the Renaissance.* P. Gouk, ed. London: Variorum Reprints.

Zarlino, Gioseffo. 1589. *Le istitutioni harmoniche.* In *Opere.* Venice, 1589.

PART III

Art and the Way We Think

5

The Art of Compression

Mark Turner

*Art is universal to our species. All human cultures show impressive,
sustained, irrepressible impulses for artistic activity and understanding.
Human art is possible because human beings differ mentally from other
closely related species in having an advanced cognitive capacity for
"double-scope integration." This chapter focuses on the ways in which
double-scope integration achieves conceptual compression, a hallmark
of art.*

Cognitively modern human beings have art, language, science,
religion, refined tool use, advanced music and dance, fashions of
dress, and mathematics. Blue jays, border collies, dolphins, and bo-
nobos do not. Only human beings have what we have. This conspicuous Grand Difference constitutes a puzzling discontinuity in the
evolution of life. How could these human singularities have emerged?

In *The Way We Think* (2002), and in earlier publications beginning in 1993, Gilles Fauconnier and I put forward the hypothesis that
the Grand Difference arose in the following way. The basic mental
operation of *conceptual integration*, also known as *blending*, has been
present and evolving in various species for a long time, probably since
early mammals, and there is no reason to doubt that many mammalian species aside from human beings have the ability to execute
rudimentary forms of conceptual integration. Human beings evolved
not an entirely different kind of mind, but instead the capacity for the
strongest form of conceptual integration, known as *double-scope*

blending. Human beings are thus on a gradient with other species, but what a difference an extra step makes! Double-scope blending is the crucial incremental cognitive capacity that makes it possible for human beings to create and share art. (Technical introductions to the nature and mechanisms of blending can be found in Fauconnier and Turner 2002, 1998; Fauconnier 1997; Turner 1996, 2001, 2006.) In this chapter, I will focus on ways in which blending makes possible advanced forms of *conceptual compression* that are important for art.

As Merlin Donald observes, the brain strives "for the integration of perceptual and conceptual material over time":

> The term *large-scale neural integration* refers to the nervous system's cross-modal unification of many sources of experience into a single abstract model or percept. The canonical example of this kind of integration is event-perception, which can unify a blur of millions of individual sensations of sight, sound, touch, taste, smell, and emotions into unitary event-percepts. (Donald, this volume)

When we perceive a leaf twisting in the wind, we see it as one integrated leaf, one movement, one "wind." When we look away and back, we think we see the "same" leaf before and after. This is a miraculous compression of perceptual diversity into unity. In all such cases, whether we are at rest or in action, we face a chaos of perceptual data. Bombarded by this diversity, we perform the highly impressive mental trick of compressing great ranges of it into manageable units. We parse an ocean of diversity quickly and reliably into a few elements coherently arrayed.

Typically, we are unaware that we face this perceptual diversity. When we look at the serene marble statue, it appears to us to be a single unit, without fragmentation, instability, or diversity, despite the fact that the perceptual data we are compressing to achieve this comforting and useful recognition of an abiding, unvarying statue are themselves shifty and uncoordinated.

At moments when we actually do manage to recognize that we confront shiftiness, we nonetheless feel—provided we are not in that instant afflicted with a cerebral hemorrhage, a drug-induced breakdown, or a chronic neural pathology—that the unities of the world shine through, fundaments of perception, essentially impervious to accidents. We ascribe the tiny fraction of shiftiness that we do detect consciously to changes of viewpoint on our part or to motion or transformation on the part of the unity we perceive—events that, in our conception, leave the perceptual coherence of the world intact. The cloud moves in the wind, perhaps our view of it is blocked entirely while we walk past the tree, and probably we are looking at the road for the most part anyway, but no matter, the cloud's unity is clear to us. This neurobiological creation of stability is profound and evident in everything we human beings do, despite our obliviousness to it. It is only under sedulous discipline during an ingenious experiment, for example, that we can begin to detect hints of the literal blind spots in our vision, caused by gaps where axons dive through the retina.

The neurobiological challenge of mastering spectacular perceptual diversity to achieve regularity and constancy is faced by very many species. Human beings, as I will discuss here, compound the difficulty of this challenge in a particular way. Over the last fifty thousand years, give or take (the dating is still being worked out in the archaeological record), human beings have demonstrated a remarkable ability to create new conceptual diversity. Human neurobiology makes it possible for our species, and only our species, to create great arrays of conceptual variety and yet to compress such arrays into manageable regularities. Explaining these operations of creation and compression is a key scientific problem in the study of the mind and the study of art. I focus on it in this chapter.

I begin with misleading but memorable examples, the first a detail from Pablo Picasso's 1907 *Les Demoiselles d'Avignon* (see http://theartfulmind .stanford.edu). There are five women represented in *Les Demoiselles d'Avignon*. The one in the lower right corner has a face presented in full frontal view, with two eyes, but a nose in profile. This "wild Squatter" consists of elements that come from "alternate visibilities," as Leo Steinberg describes:

> The compression of space is greatest along the right margin,
> precisely where the rearward extension is deepest. And it is here, in
> the lower right corner, that the wild Squatter becomes the focus of
> intensified realization. In the development of this figure through its
> progressive stages, one discovers how Picasso gradually worked a
> straightforward backview, pigtail and all, towards ambiguity. While
> the end result is flat as a paper cutout, Picasso convokes alternate
> visibilities, relying in part on the punning scheme of the *Standing
> Nude*. In the final picture, an arm akimbo and one rising thigh fuse
> flat against a convenient curtain. Had these limbs been omitted, the
> rest of the figure might have been readable as a three-quarter back-
> view with head jerked over the shoulder. But with these limbs
> retained, all three-quarter logic is thwarted. The figure becomes a full-
> splayed backview, in flat contradiction to the abrupt frontality of its
> head. And the violent wrench of her simultaneities more than makes

up for abstraction and flattening. It gives her pink flesh an aggressive immediacy, brought nearer still by the shameless impudence of the pose and the proximity of an implicated observer who knows every side of her. (Steinberg 1972, 172)

This image of a woman does not point to an abstraction, if by abstraction we mean what Semir Zeki means in *Inner Vision: An Exploration of Art and the Brain* (1999) and in his article "Artistic Creativity and the Brain" (2001, 51–52). Zeki observes in those works that the brain and art obey two supreme laws: the law of constancy—"registering the constant and essential characteristics of objects"—and the law of abstraction—"the process in which the particular is subordinated to the general, so that what is represented is applicable to many particulars."

An example of abstraction is the operation of orientation tuning columns in the visual cortex. An orientation tuning column consists of neurons that respond preferentially to something linear at a specific angle. One of these orientation tuning columns, for example, prefers verticality. It will accordingly respond to anything vertical presented in the visual field—a pen, a finger, a lamppost. This is abstraction: the activation for verticality applies equally and completely to all the specific instances.

But the wild Squatter is not an abstract representation of a woman, in that sense of "abstraction." For example, even her face—a small and relatively tame detail—seems to blend multiple views. She has a nose seen in profile, which comes from one view of the woman, but two eyes, which come from quite a different view of the woman. This representation cannot apply fully and equally to every view of the woman, in the way that the activation of the orientation tuning column for verticality can apply fully and equally to the pen, the finger, and the lamppost. On the contrary, the representation of the wild Squatter cannot apply fully to *any* of those views. So it is not an abstraction in that exact sense.

To be sure, there is abstraction involved in comprehending the wild Squatter. But the "alternate visibilities" do not point to an *abstraction* in Zeki's sense. They point to a *compression*. The wild Squatter represents a compressed blend that includes elements from distinct input images—for example, from the frontal view and from the profile view in the case of the head, and from the backview as well for parts of her body, as Steinberg notes. As is typical in blending, the face of the wild Squatter leaves out many elements that could be found in the inputs to the blend. Projection from the inputs to the blend is selective. Additionally, the blend develops emergent properties that are not possessed by any of the input views. For example, in the blended face, but in none of the inputs, we have a simultaneous view of elements from the profile view, the frontal view, and the backview.

These diverse elements from different inputs are not thrown into the blend arbitrarily. Each of the inputs is organized by a shared conceptual frame. The conceptual frame in this case is the same for all the inputs: it is the anatomical form of a human body—in fact, a female human body. The face, for example, makes use of the side and front views, both organized by the anatomical form of a female human body. If we emphasize this organizing conceptual frame as something generic over inputs, we produce a scheme something like the one illustrated in figure 5.1.

Both of these inputs are organized by the frame of the anatomical form of a female human body, and this frame is in the generic space. If we were thinking in terms of brain activation, we would say that each of the inputs activates the generic space. The blend shares this same organizing frame (see figure 5.2). It compresses elements from the separate inputs into that unified anatomical outline.

All four of these spaces are organized by the same general female anatomical form. The figure in the blend has a head and torso and all the usual appendages, and their part-whole relations of adjacency are for the most part preserved in the blend: the head is above the shoulders, one leg radiates from each hip, thigh and calf are joined by a knee, and so on. Steinberg naturally is drawn to the most violent wrench: "In the final picture, an arm akimbo and one rising thigh fuse flat against a convenient curtain."

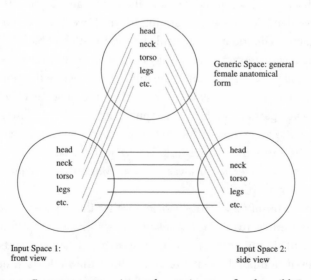

FIGURE 5.1. Cross-space mapping and generic space for the wild Squatter.

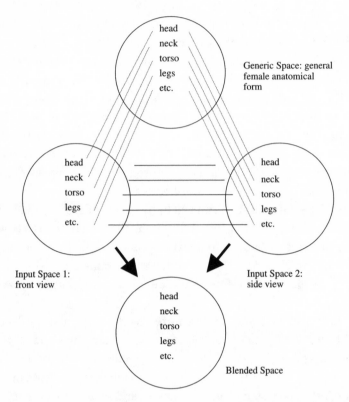

FIGURE 5.2. Part of the blending network for the wild Squatter.

The disparate views of the heads in the inputs are all projected to the one head in the blend. This is not a painting in which we have eyes on hands or a mane of hair on a doorknob. That would be quite a different blend. This painting has instead a clear morphological unity even as it compresses over diversity.

The blend is a compression of the input spaces, while the generic space is an abstraction over them. Again, if we are thinking in terms of activation, the blend activates partially both of the input spaces, and therefore activates the generic space to an exceptional degree. Indeed, the painting is remarkable for activating the entire mental network. We see just the same general method of compressing over diversity in Picasso's 1937 *Marie-Thérèse Walter* (see http:// theartfulmind.stanford.edu).

Compression of viewpoint over time rather than space is exemplified in Marcel Duchamp's 1912 *Nu descendant un escalier* (see http://theartfulmind .stanford.edu). In this case, the compressed blend has elements that come from different temporal moments of watching the nude as it descends the staircase. In the blend, but in none of the inputs, we have an extremely familiar conceptual unit, *the descent*, which remains connected to the different temporal moments. This unity-out-of-diversity can be expressed visually in Duchamp's fashion or linguistically by means of a definite noun phrase: "the descent." Duchamp's blend has emergent properties not possessed by any of the inputs. For example, in the blend, but in none of the inputs, we have a static form for the line of descent of the head.

Such compressions have occurred throughout human art since the Upper Paleolithic. A painting from the Hall of the Bulls in the Lascaux Cave (see http://theartfulmind.stanford.edu) shows the bull's head in exact profile, with one eye and one nostril, but also shows the horns from something like a three-quarters view. Similarly, we see the bull from the side but the bull's cloven hooves from nearer the front. This painting points not to an abstraction but to a compression over many quite diverse views.

In the cases of *Les Demoiselles d'Avignon*, *Marie-Thérèse Walter*, and *Nu descendant un escalier*, we recognize immediately that something is cockeyed, jumbled, or lumped. But in the case of the Lascaux bull, most people do not seem to be *consciously* aware that there is any compression at all until it is pointed out. This lack of recognition cannot be ascribed to ignorance of actual horns and hooves. I can provide evidence: although my office until recently sat at the summit of a hill in a coastal mountain range populated by wild animals, where I saw domesticated and wild hooved and horned animals in the flesh routinely, and although my children show me scores of photographic images in books and instructional films of bulls, bison, gazelles, reindeer, moose, and ibex, and although I would be quite astonished, and perhaps worried for the animal, were I to see an actual bull with horns and hooves disposed in this way, nonetheless I was not consciously aware of the oddly compressed nature of the Lascaux bull for a long time. The details of the integration network we use to understand it, with its selective projections from inputs to a compressed blend, are, as is typical, invisible to consciousness even though the product—the useful, single, human-scale, compressed bull—may be quite arresting.

Blending, even when it is remarkably creative in providing emergent structure in the blend, is always deeply conservative, anchored in what we know. The creativity is greater than we usually see, but also more profoundly anchored than we usually see. For example, although the Picasso and Duchamp and Lascaux blends are highly creative, they are rooted in what we know well—in what we, in important senses, already have. When we see a particular view of a person or an animal, we know that there are other views: we know when we see one side of the face that there is another, and that when we see the front of a person there is also a back that is not presently visible. When the person turns to face us, we are not surprised at all to see these other sides of the person. Similarly, we know when we see someone in mid-descent down a staircase that the person is at other spots at other times; indeed, if we catch only one glimpse of the person descending, we conceptually complete the action, stretching before and after. The input spaces therefore are available to us already. The creativity comes in blending them in a way that is not otherwise available to us, providing in one static view elements from distinct, but known, views.

These phenomena of compression are well known within art history. Artists also often use compression as an explicitly avowed principle of theory and practice. But compression, far from being reserved for special and remarkable effects in art, is ubiquitous and indispensable throughout human understanding. Art, in this case, exploits a basic human mental capacity.

Consider an example not from art but from everyday journalism. On July 8, 1999, the New York Times reported that Hicham el-Guerrouj had broken the world record for the mile, with a time of 3:43.13. To convey at a glance the historical significance of the performance, the New York Times provided an illustration of a one-quarter-mile racetrack with six figures running on it. The six figures represent el-Guerrouj in a race against the five other runners—namely, the fastest milers from each decade since Roger Bannister broke the 4-minute barrier in 1954. El-Guerrouj is crossing the finish line as Bannister, trailing everyone else, is still 120 yards back. This illustration prompts us to construct a conceptual packet that blends structure from six separate input mental spaces, each with a one-mile race in which the world record is broken by a runner. The blend places all six runners on a single racetrack, with a single starting time, in a kind of mythic race.

The blend is a compression, giving us an immediately intelligible human-scale unity—that is, a single footrace, with a winner. Literally, the blend is "false," obviously so in conjoining Hicham el-Guerrouj and Roger Bannister as competitors on the same track. It is also tacitly inexact in the way it locates the runners other than Hicham el-Guerrouj on the track. But it gives us a way of understanding the truth about the many different input spaces and their relationships. The integration network provides a compressed blend that lets us understand and remember at human scale a range of complicated knowledge that does not otherwise fit human-scale recognition. There is emergent dynamic structure in this compressed blend—namely, structure that cannot be found in any of the inputs: the blend is a simulation of a mythic race between legendary competitors, most of whom never in fact raced against each other. In this mythic race, Hicham el-Guerrouj "defeats" Roger Bannister by 120 yards. The compressed blend gives us the direct pleasure of immediately recognizing the competition and its conclusion.

All of the artworks and drawings I have adduced so far call up *mirror integration networks*. A mirror network is one in which all the inputs share a single organizing frame, which is projected also to the blend to organize it. The shared frame gives the inputs an analogical relation; each has the same set of roles. For example, we can frame George Washington and Abraham Lincoln using the conceptual frame *president of the United States of America*. The two resulting conceptual spaces are analogous since the frame-roles in one have identity links to the frame-roles in the other. In a mirror network, separate conceptual spaces share an organizing frame, which is also projected to organize a blended space.

It is extremely common for us to compress analogy links to identity links and identity links to unity. For example, there are striking and profound differences between me now and the male infant born to my mother many decades ago, but we construct analogy links between those two conceptual spaces. Those analogy links are almost always compressed to identity links, making not only the roles in those two spaces but also the values of the roles identical. That network with identity links is further compressed to create a blend in which there is a single unity, the person. The differences between the conceptual spaces—that is, between the baby and me now—are compressed to *change* in the blend. The result is a unified blended space in which there is a unity—the person—who undergoes change. We can thereby think of a complicated human life in the way we think of a leaf blowing in the wind: blending makes it possible in both cases for us to conceive of a single unit that undergoes change over time.

The two Picasso paintings also evoke mirror networks. Each of the input spaces is framed by the gross anatomical form of a woman, and there are identity links not only between the roles in each frame, such as *adult woman* in a *location*, but also between the values of those roles: it is the same woman, in the same place. But the details differ space to space, because each has a different view of the woman in that location. The blend keeps the organizing frame but projects conflicting details into it. The result is a mirror network. The analysis is identical for the Lascaux bull.

The painting of the nude descending the staircase evokes a mirror network in which each of the input spaces has the organizing frame of a person on a staircase, facing down, and engaged in movement. This frame is projected to the blend, but extended to incorporate several locations for the person.

The graphic illustration of the world record in the mile prompts for an integration network with six input spaces, each one framed by a mile footrace, on a standard oval racetrack, in a location and a time, and with a winner and losers. That frame is projected to the blend, giving a mirror network that, as always, compresses various disparate conceptual spaces into one unified blended space.

In any mirror network, there is always the question of which of the conflicting details from the input spaces are absorbed in the blend, and how they are incorporated there. In some cases, the conflict between alternative details is resolved by projecting only one of them. For example, in the Lascaux bull network, the input spaces have several different views of the horns, but only one of them is projected to the blend. The bull is not equipped in the blend with several different sets of horns, each from a different view. That technical possibility is not deployed in this case.

The painting of the nude descending the staircase illustrates a different technical possibility. The frame for seeing a person heading down the stairs has only one view of the person available in any instant. But the blend receives from the disparate inputs many different and conflicting views, with the result that they become simultaneously visible in the blend. We are not confused. We know that each of the input spaces has only one view of the person. But the frame is extended in the blend to include several views.

The mythic footrace deploys yet a different technical possibility. Each of the input spaces has a winner and losers. None of the specific losers is projected to the blend, although the roles for losers are projected to the blend as part of the frame of a footrace. The specific winner (Hicham el-Guerrouj) in one of the input spaces is projected to inhabit the role *winner* in the blend, but the specific winners from the other input spaces (such as Roger Bannister) are projected to inhabit slots for *losers* in the blend. In this case, the organizing frame already has slots for *losers* into which these analogous winners can be placed. Every winner in an input space is projected to the blend, but only one of them inhabits the role *winner* there.

In all of these examples, even Duchamp's painting of the nude descending a staircase, the actual visual image is static. But the principles work the same for dynamic images. The solution of the famous riddle of the Buddhist monk presents a dynamic visual blend.[1] Here is the riddle:

A Buddhist monk begins at dawn one day walking up a mountain, reaches the top at sunset, and meditates at the top for several days until one dawn when he begins to walk back to the foot of the mountain, which he reaches at sunset. Making no assumptions about his starting or stopping or about his pace during the trips, prove that there is a place on the path that he occupies at the same hour of the day on the two separate journeys.

An intuitive solution to the riddle comes from superimposing the two days—that is, imagining the Buddhist monk walking both up the path and down the path on the same day. Then there must be a place where he meets himself, and that place is clearly the one he would occupy at the same time of day on the two separate journeys. This is again a mirror network. Each of the two input spaces has the Buddhist monk walking on the mountain path from dawn to sunset. The blend has the same organization, but is now extended to have two people on the path, walking in opposite directions. The ascent from the first input and the descent from the second input are both projected to the blend, with the consequence that, in the blend, the monk is visibly in two places at the same instant, just as in Duchamp's painting of the nude descending the staircase, the body is visibly in several places at the same instant.

We are of course not confused. Just as we know that in the inputs for Duchamp's blend, the nude is in only one place at a time, so we know that in the inputs for the riddle of the Buddhist monk, the monk is in only one place at a time. But in the blend, there are two identical monks and the monk "meets" himself. The "meeting" is a compressed human-scale event inside the blend. It corresponds to an uncompressed set of links between the inputs. That is, we recognize that the "meeting" must decompress to a trio of identity links connecting the two input spaces: there is a spot on the path in the ascent that is connected by identity to a spot on the path in the descent; the time of day when the monk is located at that spot in the ascent is connected by identity to the time of day when the monk is located at that spot in the descent; and of course the monk in the first space is connected by identity to the monk in the second space. The monk's meeting himself in the blend is a human-scale compression of the input spaces and the relationships between them, and this compression allows us to have human-scale insight into something that is otherwise diverse, distributed, even impenetrable.

Now in this case, the image is not static. We run the blend as a dynamic simulation in which two people converge and then meet on a mountain path. I can only suggest this dynamic image with a static diagram (see figure 5.3). In this diagram, the generic space represents the conceptual structure that is taken as applying to both of the inputs. All four spaces have the monk traveling the mountain path. The blend has a further extension, with both monks, and the meeting.

Now consider a case where thousands of input spaces are potentially accessible by means of unpacking a blend. This blend lies in a conceptual network that provides an idea of a putative evolution from dinosaurs to birds. The artwork that prompts us to construct this conceptual integration network

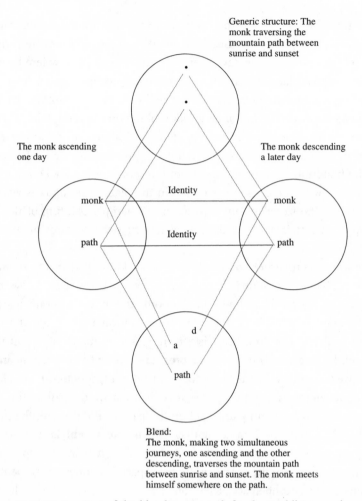

Generic structure: The
monk traversing the
mountain path between
sunrise and sunset

The monk ascending
one day

The monk descending
a later day

Identity

monk

monk

Identity

path

path

d

a

path

Blend:
The monk, making two simultaneous
journeys, one ascending and the other
descending, traverses the mountain path
between sunrise and sunset. The monk meets
himself somewhere on the path.

FIGURE 5.3. Part of the blending network for the Buddhist monk.

is taken from an issue of Zoobooks, a publication for grade-school children
(Wexo 1992).

This picture depicts a dinosaur chasing a dragonfly (see figure 5.4). We
see the dinosaur at various stages of running along a path. Note that the
dragonfly is always the same, the path is a single path, and the shadows show
that the light is always coming from the same direction. We are given a single
scene in which a single dinosaur is changing into a bird, which is at last able
to catch and eat the dragonfly. It is also easy to understand the dinosaur as
wanting to change into the bird, exactly so it can accomplish its goal.

We realize that at one level in the integration network behind this artwork, there are literally thousands of dinosaurs and birds, with no identity

FIGURE 5.4. The evolution of birds from dinosaurs. From Zoobooks' *Dinosaurs*; reprinted with the permission of Zoobooks and Wildlife Education, Ltd.

connections between them. These individual organisms are compressed into representatives of generations. There are analogy and disanalogy connections between any two generations, given that there are differences generation to generation in the dinosaur phenotype. There are also cause-and-effect connections at that level, since one generation produces the next. At this level, we have different stages of the "identical" species, somewhat different in each space.

The compression to a "species" that "changes" is already quite an arresting compression. We know that none of the actual individual dinosaurs changed genetically, although of course each of them went through ontogenetic development. On the contrary, what happened was this: the very many different individual dinosaurs had different degrees of differential reproduction, but they all died, and the dinosaurs downstream were somewhat different, because of inheritance, variation, and selection. The typical representative of the species at one time differed from the typical representative generations later, but not because there was any change in any particular organism. If dinosaurs several generations later were a little more feathery, it is certainly not because any one dinosaur changed in that direction. On the contrary, the individual dinosaurs stayed just as they were, and all died off, and their replacements looked a little different.

But compression now gives us in the final blend not a species that changes but a unique dinosaur that changes. The analogies across all the decompressed spaces become *uniqueness* in the blend, and the disanalogies across them become *change* in the blend. In the blend, we have a unique element that undergoes change. This is just the kind of compression we use to see a leaf blowing in the wind or to understand that a person changes over a lifetime, but in the case of the dinosaurs, there are no identity links across all the individual dinosaurs compressed through this cascade of integrations. Human beings are not set up to understand mechanisms of evolution operating over evolutionary time scales. In the case of the dinosaurs and birds, we use the standard compression template that has at one level analogy and disanalogy across many spaces but also has a blend in which all the analogy links are compressed to uniqueness and all the disanalogy links are compressed to change for that unique element. This template of compression allows us to understand a diffuse range of meanings that is spatially and temporally very far from the kind of thing human cognition is set up to recognize. Compression brings this diffuse, complex, and otherwise impenetrable domain of evolution into a form that fits human understanding.

Of course, we are not fooled by the blend, any more than we believe that a Buddhist monk can in fact be in two places at once or that Hicham el-Guerrouj crossed the finish line 120 yards ahead of Roger Bannister or that when we look at a woman we can see something that resembles the painting of Marie-Thérèse Walter. But the blend is extremely useful as part of an integration network. It is important to see that the kind of compression used in the integration network for the evolution of dinosaurs is not restricted to children's textbooks. The best and most careful evolutionary biologists routinely conduct serious discussions of the way in which "a species" "changes" "over time" "to become" this or that; of how a species "acquired" this or that feature or "developed" or "grew" in this or that way; of how "it" "lost" this or that capacity; of how one organ "became" something else. All of this is quite false for the most decompressed understanding of the life and death over time of individual organisms and the differences between them. But the compressions are very useful. Evolutionary biologists are usually wary of ascribing intentionality to evolutionary "development," but their caution is usually a matter of reminding the audience that the intentional language can be cashed out to a level of understanding that does not involve intentionality. That is exactly right: the blend is useful because the compression it carries can help us access, activate, remember, and use the entire network in which it resides.

Mirror networks, or near-mirror networks such as the network for the evolution of dinosaurs into birds, are impressive displays of human creativity.

Made possible by our creative capacities for integration and compression, they in turn support the further work of those capacities, and this further work increases their conceptual reach.

Even more impressive are double-scope integration networks. In a double-scope network, the two inputs have different (and often clashing) organizing frames, and the blend has an organizing frame that receives projections from each of those organizing frames. The blend also has emergent structure of its own that cannot be found in any of the inputs. Sharp differences between the organizing frames of the inputs offer the possibility of rich clashes. Far from blocking the construction of the network, such clashes offer challenges to the imagination. The resulting blends can turn out to be highly creative.

The ability for double-scope blending seems to be available to children very early. For example, in Crockett Johnson's (1983) *Harold and the Purple Crayon*, written for three-year-olds, Harold uses his purple crayon to draw, and whatever he draws is real, although it is also clearly a child's drawing.

His world is a blend, of spatial reality and its representation. In the blend, the representation is fused with what it represents. When Harold wants light to go for a walk, he draws the moon, and so he has moonlight. The moon stays with him as he moves. This blend has two inputs. One input has elements of the real spatial world as we experience it and perceive it. One of those elements is the moon. The other input to the blend has conventional knowledge about drawing. In the input with the real moon, the moon cannot be created by drawing and it does not come into existence at someone's will. In the input with drawing, a drawn moon cannot emit moonlight or float along in the sky as the artist's companion. But in the blend, there is a special blended moon with special emergent properties: you can create it by drawing, and it gives light and "moves" with you.

The mechanisms of blending that give us this special blended moon are in operation throughout *Harold and the Purple Crayon* (see figure 5.5). When he needs to walk, Harold draws a path, and then sets off on his walk, taking his big purple crayon with him. When he wants to return home, he draws a window around the moon, positioning the moon where it would appear in his window if he were in his bedroom, and so he is automatically in fact in his bedroom and can go to bed.

Child Harold's blended world has new kinds of causality and event shape that are unavailable from either the domain of drawing or the domain of spatial living. The projection to this blend, and the completion and elaboration of the blend, are not algorithmic, not predictable from the inputs, but instead have considerable room for alternatives. For example, when one draws, one

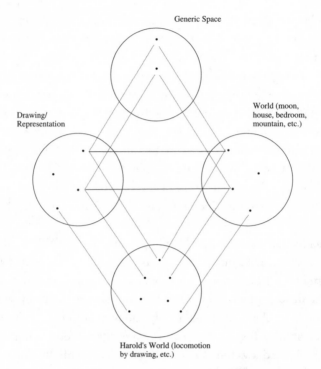

FIGURE 5.5. Blending network for *Harold and the Purple Crayon*.

often makes practice sketches, erasures, and mistakes that do not count as part of the finished drawing. Which kinds of marks made with the purple crayon shall count as reality in the blend? The answer chosen by the author of the book is "all of them." When Harold's hand, holding the purple crayon, shakes as he backs away from the terribly frightening dragon, the resulting mark is a purple line of wavy scallops: "Suddenly he realized what was happening. But by then Harold was over his head in an ocean."

The principle for connecting the purple sketches to elements of reality is, not surprisingly, image-schematic matching: if the sketch matches the iconic form of something, it is that thing. But it appears that this matching is constrained: a given purple sketch can be matched to exactly one reality. For example, once the wavy line is an ocean, Harold cannot transform the ocean into a cake by perceiving the wavy line as the icing on a cake. Yet in a differently conceived blend, in a different book, the character who does the drawing might possess the power to recast reality by perceiving the sketch first one way and then another.

In Harold's blend, all of physical space is a piece of paper on which to draw. What are the possibilities in the blend of blank paper/empty space? Can

Harold move as he wishes through it? The answer chosen by the author is that once something is drawn that gives Harold relative location, he is constrained by some of the physics of the real world. For example, once he draws the hull of a boat and part of the mast, he must climb the mast to draw the parts of the boat he could not reach from the ground. When he wants to find his house, he begins to draw a mountain so he can climb it to have a better view. He climbs the part he has drawn so he can draw more mountain to climb. But as he looks down over the other side of the mountain, he slips, and since he has been positioned with respect to the mountain, the blank space is now thin air, so he must be falling. He is obliged to draw a balloon to save himself from crashing.

Blends of the sort that we have looked at are found widely throughout art. In them, things are blended that do not in reality go together. From the point of view of evolution, to confuse things that should be kept distinct is like plucking forbidden fruit: we should not do it, on pain of death, quite literally, but also on pain of insanity. Yet, amazingly, with many mirror networks and all double-scope networks, we pluck that forbidden fruit. We put together what should be kept distinct.

Obviously, we should not confuse two different views of a woman or a bull. We should not confuse different moments in an event. We should not believe that world record holders in the mile who lived decades apart in fact all ran together on the same track at the same time. We should not believe that a Buddhist monk can in fact be in two places at once. We should not believe that a dinosaur in fact grew feathers and turned into a bird while chasing a dragonfly. We should not confuse the moon with a sketch of the moon, or paper with the world, or drawing with locomotion. But plucking this kind of forbidden conceptual fruit makes us extremely creative.

Art and literature are particularly specialized to take advantage of this kind of "forbidden fruit" blending. We recognize that the input spaces should be kept separate but nonetheless the blend is conceptually useful. It is true that sometimes this blending is aggressive and presents blends that are un-harmonious or disconcerting or in some way out of joint. A mild example, studied with great insight by Per Aage Brandt (this volume), comes from the work of René Magritte. In *La Tentative de l'Impossible* (1928), Magritte produces a blend that follows the same initial lines as the blends we saw in *Harold and the Purple Crayon*. In this painting, we see a painter who is painting a woman. I do not mean that he is applying paint to the skin of an already existing woman, nor do I mean that he is in the conventional and straightforward sense merely applying paint to a canvas to make an image. On the contrary, the body of the woman comes into existence as he paints it but there is no obvious canvas. In the blend of *La Tentative de l'Impossible*, as in the blend for Harold, reality is something one can draw on, and what one draws is real.

Forbidden-fruit integration gives us a way to keep things separate and yet to combine them. In the input spaces, they are quite separate. We understand the vital relations between them but do not compress them. Yet in the blend, we do exactly that. A forbidden-fruit integration network is a truly marvelous way to have your forbidden fruitcake and eat it, too. This is of course exactly what happens in *Harold and the Purple Crayon*. We understand very well the difference between the moon and a drawing of a moon, and in the input spaces, we understand their relationships of difference. But in the blend, they are integrated.

Every kind of art shows the power of forbidden-fruit integration. For example, if we survey high canon representations of the Annunciation, we "see" the Virgin holding, anachronistically, a lectionary, often opened to the narrative of the Annunciation. In Rogier van der Weyden's Annunciation (see http://theartfulmind.stanford.edu), the medallion on the bed represents the Resurrection. The painting in this way gives us a compression of eternity, or at least, from not yet being born to being raised from the dead, all in one momentary scene.

We have no trouble interpreting this representation as evoking a blend of a young girl and the Mother of God, which is already a blend. The Virgin's bedroom may additionally have features of a church—the lectionary stand and veil that are part of the furniture of an altar, trinitarian tracery windows in Broederlam's version, a full Gothic church interior as in one of Jan van Eyck's versions. Annunciations may have a representation of God in the upper left, although we do not interpret this to mean that God was just up and to the left of the bedroom. In the Mérode Altarpiece (see http://theartfulmind .stanford.edu), a homunculus already tolerating his own miniature cross is flying toward the womb of Mary. The representation evokes a blend of girl with Mother of God, bedroom with church, breath with life, and so on.

These Annunciations take concepts incredibly diffuse, foreign, and difficult to understand—eternity, divinity, theology, the Church, and the relationship of the immortal to the mortal—and compress them to an extremely familiar scene: a room, a woman reading in the room, and someone addressing her. What lies beyond human understanding is compressed to human scale. In this case, plucking the forbidden fruit gives us an understanding of God.

V. S. Ramachandran has encouraged us always to ask three particular questions when we discuss Art and the Mind: What? Why? and How? The What? question has by now been answered to an extent: forbidden-fruit blending happens widely throughout human art, science, religion, mathematics, culture, and indeed throughout anything done by cognitively modern human beings, and it follows a set of constitutive principles and a set of governing principles. It is what makes us cognitively modern.

The Why? question is harder to answer because we do not have a time machine to take us back fifty or one hundred thousand years or more to obtain the evidence. I am nevertheless not uncomfortable proposing that forbidden-fruit integration is an extension of integration abilities possessed prior to its evolution, and that the power of the increased creativity resulting from the ability to do forbidden-fruit blending was extraordinarily adaptive. Even small increments in that mental ability would have conferred advantage, and so the natural selection story taking us from more rudimentary forms of conceptual integration to full forbidden-fruit integration is easy to imagine, if perhaps impossible to prove.

The How? question is daunting, since our ignorance about the neuroscience of higher-order thought is profound. Yet I have more confidence in the search for an answer here than I have in the attempts to address the Why? question, exactly because we can make actual observations, however indirect, and pursue normal scientific practices in search of an explanation of how our present brains accomplish forbidden-fruit integration. (By contrast, the answers to the Why? question are entirely speculative under present methods, and nearly all the evidence related to the Why? question has vanished from the earth.) I see two, or maybe two and a half, hypothetical sources for answers to the How? question. The first, obviously enough, has to do with neural binding of the sort we do during everyday perception, location-time collocation, and other mammalian integrations. The one-half is synaesthesia, which rates only one-half since it looks as if it is probably neural binding in a different mode. The last one is special-purpose forbidden-fruit integration, tightly restricted to certain narrow domains and behaviors. Chase play, for example, is common throughout the mammalian world and evidenced even in interactions between different species, such as a human child and a dog, or a polar bear and a wolf. In this behavior, allied organisms, usually a parent and an offspring, simulate predatory behavior. During that behavior, they are simultaneously activating motor patterns, attention patterns, and motivational structures that belong to two very disparate domains. It seems not an unreasonable hypothesis that the neural circuitry subtending binding, synaesthesia, or special-purpose forbidden-fruit blending might have gotten the ball rolling in the run-up to full cognitive modernity.

I cannot supply anything more than merely suggestive evidence for the following view of the cognitively modern human brain, but I am comfortable wondering whether the human brain is not a kind of vast bubble chamber, constantly trying to blend different things. Perhaps very many of these attempts are going on in our brains all the time. Perhaps almost any two things that are activated simultaneously become candidates for an attempt at blending. I imagine that most of these attempts fail almost immediately because the constitutive principles of blending are not fulfilled or the governing principles of blending are contravened or the integration networks do not attach themselves to any purpose we have. Of the relatively very few conceptual integration networks that are successful, only fewer still ever percolate into consciousness. But this constant attempt at blending provides a robust way of introducing a strong engine of variation into our conceptual systems. Almost all of those products of variation are selected against by governing principles or by pressures and affordances of our environments or by the absence of utility of any kind. But some of them, although they begin by blending structures that one might think have no business being blended, nonetheless provide quite powerful new conceptions.

The distributed cognition question is essential here. The great virtue of any one human being's coming up with any forbidden-fruit integration is that all the other human beings stand ready to understand it, incorporate it, and propagate it. In this way, culture is an incomparably larger bubble chamber than is an individual brain. With the entire species running forbidden-fruit experiments in this vast bubble chamber, there are at last wonderful possibilities for sustained, effective, and accretive creativity.

But these hypotheses are at the outer limit of what cognitive neuroscience, evolutionary biology, and art theory can at present investigate. An aggressive and sustained program of research is needed to explain how the brain accomplishes forbidden-fruit integration in art. Inevitably—and this is the central lesson from our studies—that program of research will require intensive and sustained collaboration across researchers in many different disciplines, to design the optimum scientific system of attack and to conduct it to its goals.

NOTE

    1. A version of this riddle appears in Koestler 1964, 183–89. Koestler attributes the riddle to the psychologist Carl Dunker.

REFERENCES

Fauconnier, G. 1997. *Mappings in thought and language.* Cambridge, England: Cambridge University Press.
Fauconnier, G., and M. Turner. 1998. Conceptual integration networks. *Cognitive Science,* 22, no. 2 (April–June): 133–87.

———. 2002. *The way we think: Conceptual blending and the mind's hidden complexities.* New York: Basic Books.

Johnson, C. 1983 [1955]. *Harold and the purple crayon.* New York: Harper & Row.

Koestler, A. 1964. *The act of creation.* New York: Macmillan.

Steinberg, L. 1972. The Algerian women and Picasso at large. *Other criteria: Confrontations with twentieth-century art.* New York: Oxford University Press.

Turner, M. 1996. *The literary mind: The origins of thought and language.* New York: Oxford University Press.

———. 2001. *Cognitive dimensions of social science: The way we think about politics, economics, law, and society.* New York: Oxford University Press.

———. 2006. The Blending Web site: http://blending.stanford.edu.

Wexo, J. B. 1992. *Dinosaurs.* A volume of Zoobooks. San Diego: Wildlife Education, Ltd.

Zeki, S. 1999. *Inner vision: An exploration of art and the brain.* New York: Oxford University Press.

———. 2001. Artistic creativity and the brain. *Science*, 293, no. 5527 (July 6): 51–52.

6

The Cognitive Tango

Lawrence M. Zbikowski

This chapter explores how three basic cognitive capacities—categorization, cross-domain mapping, and the use of conceptual models—operate at the specific level of understanding music. This exploration reveals the intimate dance that takes place between music, mind, and brain.

Midway through the first act of Sigmund Romberg's 1928 operetta *The New Moon*, Philippe, a servant on the Louisiana estate of Monsieur Beaunoir, pauses to reflect on the fickleness of women. After a brief, freely sung introduction to the topic, he breaks into a tango, singing:

> Softly, as in a morning sunrise
>> The light of love comes stealing
>>> Into a new born day.
> Flaming with all the glow of sunrise
>> A burning kiss is sealing
>>> The vow that all betray.

The song, as it continues, offers a rich set of images, as much through the music as the text, and it is almost instantly memorable. Indeed, Romberg, together with his librettists Oscar Hammerstein, Frank Mandel, and Laurence Schwab, must have realized this, for they gave the song an extended reprise in the second act of the musical. Never mind the incongruity of a twentieth-century ballroom dance in the midst of an eighteenth-century southern plantation, replete with bloodthirsty pirates—there was a larger story to tell, and "Softly, as in a Morning Sunrise" was an essential part of that telling.

The effect of songs like "Softly, as in a Morning Sunrise" is immediate and profound. Which, considering the perspective developed in this collection, leads to this question: How is it that we humans can make sense of music—a complex, multidimensional sequence of patterned sound—on our first encounter with it? And, more than just make sense of such sequences, how can we have them invade our very being, leading to changes in our affective disposition and reorientations of our bodily programs (causing us to tap our toes, imagine physical gestures in response to the music, or get up and dance)?

There are a number of ways to answer this question. One approach that developed out of the pioneering work of Hermann von Helmholtz in the nineteenth century started with physiology and led ultimately to psychology (Green and Butler 2002). This has generated an impressive range of empirical research over the past hundred years, and we now know a great deal about how humans process sound. However, not all sound is music, and an account of how humans process sound is not the same thing as an account of how they understand music. Indeed, I would argue that musical understanding involves cognitive processes that occupy the *conceptual* level, which I take to be a level of cognitive activity at least potentially accessible to conscious thought. To explore this level, I want to take a slightly different approach to the question of musical understanding by showing how three general cognitive capacities crucial to our conceptual lives are specified for the understanding of music. These capacities are categorization, cross-domain mapping, and the use of conceptual models. All appear to be basic to having and, more important, using concepts. Taking "Softly, as in a Morning Sunrise" as my example, I shall describe the part each plays in our conceptualization of music. What is revealed is an intimate dance between music, mind, and brain, a cognitive tango every bit as enthralling as those that play out on the Broadway stage or the ballroom floor.

Categorization

Our ability to categorize things is a cognitive process so basic and so pervasive that it can easily escape our notice. Were you to lift your eyes from this book and survey your surroundings, you might well see chairs, lamps, tables, and other books; were you outside, you might see trees, birds, clouds, cars, and bicycles. If you considered the other things that populate your day, you might think of friends and family members, facial expressions and gestures, actions and activities. Your recognition of these things reflects the categories through which we structure our thought: to recognize a book is to identify it as a member of the category *book*; to recognize a tree is to identify it as a member of the category *tree*. Categorization occurs in all sensory modalities and throughout the range of mental activities: we categorize smells and sounds, thoughts and emotions, skin sensations and physical movement (Barsalou 1992, chap. 2).

Given that categorization is so central to our understanding of the world, what part does it play in our understanding of music? The answer to this question is a bit complicated, but we can simplify it somewhat if we restrict ourselves to two things important for musical understanding: the comprehension of a series of temporally successive events, and the ability to draw connections between such events on the basis of shared features. Let us take the second of these first, using the melody of the opening phrase of "Softly, as in a Morning Sunrise" to illustrate; the score for the entire song is given in example 6.1. (The song is cast in a highly typical 32-measure, AABA form: two nearly identical and successive phrases of eight measures each [measures 1–8 and 9–16]; a contrasting eight-measure section, known as the bridge [measures 17–24]; and a concluding reprise of the first phrase [measures 25–32].) The first phrase comprises three clearly audible falling gestures: a drop from F5 to C5 in measure 1, from F5 to A♭4 in measure 3, and from C5 to F4 in measure 5.[1] These gestures mark off measures 1–2, 3–4, and 5–7 as separate units within the larger phrase (even though none of the units seems complete unto itself). Musical analysis would characterize these units as all built from the same motive, but we don't have to rely on technical language to understand the connection between them—we can simply group them together in the category *brief musical chunks that begin with a falling gesture*. And once we do this we have an initial, if rather limited, understanding of the opening phrase of the song.

Associating the beginning of musical understanding with brief musical chunks like those evident in the opening of "Softly, as in a Morning Sunrise" has two advantages. First, such chunks have long been recognized by music theorists and composers as important for musical organization (the "motives" mentioned above; for discussion see Zbikowski 2002, chap. 1). Second, in their scope and function such chunks are remarkably similar to what researchers on categorization call basic-level categories.

The hallmark of the basic level is that it occupies a maximally useful level in the middle of a hierarchical taxonomy. The category *furniture* would occupy a rather abstract and widely inclusive level near the top of the hierarchy; the

EXAMPLE 6.1. Score for "Softly, as in a Morning Sunrise," from *The New Moon*, by Sigmund Romberg, Oscar Hammerstein, Frank Mandel, and Laurence Schwab; © 1928 Harms, Inc.

category *the Chippendale chair I inherited from my grandmother* would occupy an extremely concrete and very restricted level near the bottom. Although we could use either of these terms to categorize the thing that's in the dining room, our usual preference would be simply to call it a "chair." This description picks the object out from its surroundings (distinguishing it from the table and the sideboard, for instance) but doesn't overload us with details. *Chair* is a typical basic-level category.

There are a number of empirical operations that converge at the basic level. The basic level is the highest level whose members have similar and recognizable shapes; it is also the most abstract level for which a single mental image can be formed for the category. The basic level is also the highest level

EXAMPLE 6.2.

at which a person uses similar motor actions for interacting with category members. Finally, the basic level is *psychologically* basic: it is the level at which subjects are fastest at identifying category members, the level with the most commonly used labels for category members, the first level named and understood by children, the first level to enter the lexicon of a language, and the level with the shortest primary lexemes (Rosch et al. 1976; Rosch 1977; Tversky and Hemenway 1984).

The similarities between basic-level categories and the basic musical chunks that make up the first phrase of "Softly, as in a Morning Sunrise" are striking. Attending to these chunks, we are occupied not with individual notes or with four- or eight-measure phrases, but with a level somewhere in between. Their cognitive salience thus mirrors that of the basic level: in both cases, the focus is on a manageable whole rather than on the smallest parts. Such musical chunks have a distinctive "shape" or contour that allows us to distinguish them from other chunks; similarly, the basic level is the highest taxonomic level at which category members have similarly perceived overall shapes and the highest level at which a single mental image can reflect the entire category.

Treating the musical chunks of measures 1–2, 3–4, and 5–7 as basic-level categories offers a way to explain the salience of these chunks, as well as the basis for drawing connections between them, a capacity important for musical understanding. There remains the issue of how we relate these chunks to one another as they unfold in time—that is, how we comprehend a series of temporally successive events. To address this issue, let us take a closer look at the musical materials that make up the first phrase.

If we compare measures 1–2 with measures 3–4, and measures 5–7 with each of these, it becomes evident that the figures that make up these measures actually have little in common other than the falling gesture. Each involves different pitches and describes a different melodic interval: a descending perfect fourth in measure 1 (F5 to C5), a descending major sixth in measure 3 (F5 to Ab4), and a descending perfect fifth in measure 5 (C5 to F4). Measures 1–2 and measures 3–4 both conclude with an oscillating figure (between Bb4 and C5 in measure 2, and between G4 and Ab4 in measure 4), but measures 5–7 do not, ending instead with a highly typical cadential gesture that guides the melody to its conclusion on F4 in measure 7. Given these differences, should these various musical chunks really be in the same category? Here the answer is provided by a different line of research into processes of categorization, which has shown that, contrary to our usual impressions, membership in the categories we use in daily life is not an all-or-nothing affair (Barsalou 1987). Instead, membership is graded through a dynamic process in which the attributes of potential category members are compared with the attributes most typically found within the category.

As an example of such a graded structure, consider the category *bird*. Experimental rankings show that subjects view robins and sparrows as the best examples of birds, with owls and eagles lower down in the rankings, and ostriches, emus, and penguins among the worst examples. All are considered members of the category *bird*, but some better represent the category than others. Category structure is consequently graded according to typicality: category members range from the most typical to the least typical, with the former securely inside the bounds of the category (robins and sparrows) and the latter in danger of being excluded from the category (emus and penguins) (Rosch 1973; Rosch 1975).

Typicality effects can also be seen among our three musical chunks, which, with their repetitions across the AABA form of the song, expand to a category with nine members. Four features of the members of this category stand out:

- All members begin with a descending gesture
- For most members, the descending gesture begins on F5
- Most members conclude with an oscillating figure
- Most members are two measures long

The most typical member of this category, then, will begin with a descending gesture that starts on F5 and leads to an oscillating figure, and will be two measures long. Members that have the features first seen in measures 5–7, which begin with a descending gesture but which lack the other features, can still be included in the category but will be less typical of the category as a whole.

From this perspective, membership in the category *brief musical chunks that begin with a falling gesture*, at least to the extent that this category is manifested in the first phrase of "Softly, as in a Morning Sunrise," is something that becomes apparent only over time. The phrase begins with one chunk (mm. 1–2), the basic features of which are confirmed by the following chunk (mm. 3–4). There then follows a divergent member (mm. 5–7), which shares some but not all features with the preceding chunks. In the process of comprehending these successive musical events, two things emerge: first, certain musical features (such as gestures) will be confirmed, while others (such as the specificities of pitch) will not; second, some members better fit the category than others. The miniature drama played out in the first phrase, in which a category is first established (in the opening four measures of the phrase) and then destabilized (in the second four), is immediately reenacted in measures 9–16. Subsequent to the bridge, it unfolds once more (in mm. 25–32, with a slightly different conclusion) and brings the song to a close.

The perceptual salience of the musical chunks of measures 1–2, 3–4, and 5–7 explains why our understanding of "Softly, as in a Morning Sunrise" would start there (mirroring the salience of basic-level categories). Our capacity to organize these chunks into a category with graded membership explains why they do not need to be identical to one another and provides a basis for making sense of relationships between them as they unfold in time. The way members of this graded category are deployed in the course of the song, with the most typical members preceding the least typical, also suggests an elementary syntax for music, a topic discussed in greater detail in Zbikowski (2002, chap. 1).

What I have sketched here provides but a glimpse into how processes of categorization shape our conceptualization of music. Indeed, there is much more that could be said just about "Softly, as in a Morning Sunrise."[2] What should be apparent nonetheless is that part of the explanation for both the immediacy and the complexity of music can be found in cognitive capacities shared by all humans. Music, as an expressive medium that involves sequences of patterned sound, places some unique demands on these capacities. It also provides some unique opportunities for exploiting them, something to which extended compositions by Ludwig van Beethoven, Richard Wagner, and any number of other composers bear witness.

In my own work I have used the perspective provided by research on categorization to explain relationships among different forms of the same musical motive, to identify aspects of musical syntax and semantics, and to give an account of musical ontology (in particular, why "the same" musical work can change over time) (Zbikowski 2002). There are currently empirical studies under way to test the limits of this perspective with respect to musical themes and musical rhythm, but, given the flexibility and broad application of categorization as a cognitive process, it would seem that exploring musical categorization is an open-ended prospect. It also promises to give rise to some surprising insights into how we understand music, and how this understanding relates to other domains of knowledge.

Cross-Domain Mapping

I initially characterized the distinctive musical figures that mark the opening phrase of "Softly, as in a Morning Sunrise" as "clearly audible falling gestures." But where in fact is the trajectory through space that constitutes falling? True enough, the C5 that follows the initial F5 is placed lower on the printed page, but the actual vertical orientation of the page is of no significance: the score could be flat on the table and the C5 would still be "below" the F5. Were we to play the two notes on the piano, the C5 would be to the left of, but not really below, F5; played on the cello, the C5 would in fact be *above* F5.

These discrepancies between our characterization of musical pitch and orientations in physical space, minor though they might be, are evidence for the essentially metaphorical nature of our descriptions of musical events. Indeed, our accounts of virtually all aspects of music—from relationships between pitch and rhythmic events to characterizations of musical form to descriptions of musical structure—rely on metaphorical mappings from other domains onto the domain of music. This fact serves as further evidence that metaphor is fundamental to human thought, as George Lakoff, Mark Johnson, and others have argued for more than twenty years (Lakoff and Johnson 1980; Lakoff 1993; Lakoff and Johnson 1999; Lakoff and Núñez 2000). During the 1990s, the conception of the process of metaphorical mapping was generalized and came to be regarded as one of mapping between two different domains. The various linguistic expressions for characterizing musical pitch in terms of "high" or "low" are thus guided by the conceptual metaphor *pitch relationships are relationships in vertical space*. This conceptual metaphor correlates the domain of physical space with the domain of music, and allows us to map spatial orientations such as *up-down* onto the pitch continuum.

According to current theory, conceptual metaphors have their ultimate grounding in image schemata. In brief, an image schema is a dynamic cognitive construct that functions somewhat like the abstract structure of an image and thereby connects a vast range of different experiences that manifest this same recurring structure (Johnson 1987). The basis for the *pitch relationships are relationships in vertical space* conceptual metaphor is the verticality schema, which might be summarized by a diagram of the sort given in figure 6.1. We grasp this structure repeatedly in thousands of perceptions and activities that we experience every day. Typical of these are the experiences of perceiving a tree, our felt sense of standing upright, and the activity of climbing stairs. Our concept of verticality is based on this schema, and this concept is in turn invoked by the various conceptual metaphors that use vertical space as a source domain to structure things like relationships between musical pitches. Our characterization of musical pitch in terms of "high" and "low" is thus a manifestation of embodied knowledge—indeed, it is this knowledge that truly gives meaning to the characterization.

Mappings between music and other domains are the basis for much of the meaning construction prompted by music. And under some circumstances, the mappings can get quite a bit more complicated than the fairly simple

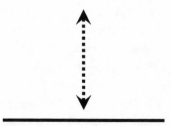

FIGURE 6.1. Diagram of verticality schema.

mapping that occurs with "high" and "low." In the bridge of "Softly, as in a Morning Sunrise," for instance, when Philippe sings, "For the passions that thrill, love, / And lift you high to heaven," the melody ascends nearly an octave, from the F4 held over from measure 15 to the Eb5 of measures 17 through 19. The compositional technique in evidence here—representing some aspect of the text through music—is conventionally called text painting: when the words of the song evoke an *ascent* to heaven, the melody *ascends* into a higher register, the music thus painting the image summoned by the text. But while this interpretation makes sense for the first line of the bridge, it doesn't make any sense for the second line. When Philippe completes his thought with "Are the passions that kill, love, / And let you fall to hell," the melody, far from portraying an infernal descent, repeats the pattern of measures 16 through 19 a whole step *higher*. Here the music argues against the text painting of the preceding measures. Even more strange, the song does not seem fragmented here: the bridge as a whole both provides an effective contrast to the first two phrases of the song and brings the story told in those phrases to culmination.

To explain how the bridge accomplishes this, we need to make recourse to work on conceptual blending.[3] Conceptual blending extends cross-domain mapping to include correlations between a number of integrated domains, and has provided a systematic way to explain how new meaning is created through interdomain and intradomain mapping. For instance, the correlation between the domain of physical space and the domain of music created by the conceptual metaphor *pitch relationships are relationships in vertical space* makes it possible to blend concepts from the two domains to create a unique imaginary domain in which pitches describe all manner of fantastic journeys through two- and three-dimensional space. A similar process is set up by Romberg's song. As shown in the conceptual integration network diagrammed in figure 6.2, one of the input spaces for the conceptual blend is set up by the text for the song. Key elements in this space are the inevitable fickleness of women (an inevitability less apparent in the lyrics for the song proper but quite evident in the conclusion of Philippe's introduction to the song: "Fickle was she, faithful never . . . So it will be forever, forever") and the tragedy of thwarted love (as one falls from heaven to hell). The other input space is set up by the music, a tango in which the bridge section (that is, measures 17–24), through two ascending passages in sequence, creates a climactic arrival on the dominant of F minor in measure 23. Elements from these spaces are then projected into the blended space, creating a true dance of seduction and summoning the intensity of a failed love affair.[4] As shown in figure 6.2, guiding the blend is a generic space structured around the paired notions of the inevitability of fate and the narrative structure of

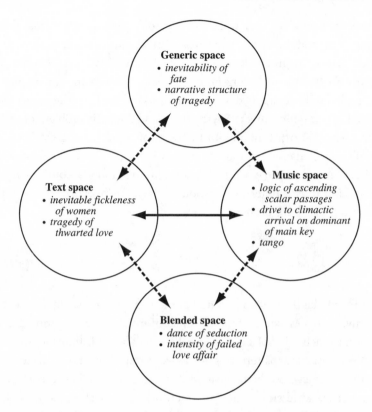

FIGURE 6.2. Conceptual integration network for the bridge of "Softly, as in a Morning Sunrise."

tragedy, both of which inform the structure of the input spaces.[5] The result is more than a somewhat simplistic representation of one or two words from the text through a stylized musical gesture—that is, having the music go "up" to depict "lift" and "heaven." By exploiting humans' capacity to blend concepts from different domains in order to create new meaning, "Softly, as in a Morning Sunrise" creates a rich domain for the imagination within which we can hear portrayed the anguish of confounded and lost love.

For at least two hundred and fifty years there has been an active discourse about whether music, as a nonlinguistic mode of expression, can mean anything. Thanks to work on cross-domain mapping, we now have a much richer and more flexible sense of how humans create meaning. Humans create meaning by using what they know about a familiar domain to structure a less familiar domain, and by blending concepts from two correlated domains together in a new domain. As I have shown, this has direct application to the process of constructing meaning in and around music.

There is now a body of work that demonstrates the part cross-domain mapping plays both in basic characterizations of musical relationships and in extended theories of music (Saslaw 1996; Zbikowski 1997; Zbikowski 1998; Cox 1999; Brower 2000). Work on conceptual blending and music proceeds apace, and has been applied to the analysis of nineteenth-century songs (Zbikowski 2002), film music (Sayrs 2003), and the basic problem of musical meaning (Cook 2001). Building on the work of cognitive linguists, an exploration of cross-domain mapping and its relationships to embodied knowledge should also make possible a much more thoroughgoing account of musical meaning, and thus a fuller explanation of the transformative effect musical compositions can have on listeners.

Conceptual Models

When I noted that the tango was a part of the mental space set up by the music for "Softly, as in a Morning Sunrise," I had in mind something more than the dry, dictionary definition of a tango: "a ballroom dance of Latin-American origin in $\frac{2}{4}$ time with a basic pattern of step-step-step-step-close and characterized by long pauses and stylized body positions." A tango is this, but it is also something more: the word summons a rich network of associations, a network that includes not only the close physical proximity of the dancers but also the aroma of sexuality and seduction, redolent of a bygone era, that swirls around the dance. This network is a manifestation of our conceptual model for the tango. Conceptual models are relatively basic cognitive structures that act as guides for reasoning and inference; each model consists of concepts in specified relationships, and pertains to a specific domain of knowledge. If, once this structure is active, we are given a bit of appropriate situational context, we have available many likely inferences concerning what might happen next in a given situation.[6] Once we know that a song is a tango and that it is sung by a solo singer, we can easily infer that it will be about seduction (if of a somewhat archaic sort), and that the lovers (like the dancers of a tango) are oblivious to all else.

In truth, the tango is even a bit more than this. Coming out of the slums and back streets of Buenos Aires in the late nineteenth century, it was only gradually absorbed by high society. During the early twentieth century it emigrated, first taking up residence in Paris and then in New York. In these metropolitan settings, it became even more of a dance of license than it was in South America, an opportunity for the spending classes to experiment with an exotic and foreign excess (Collier et al. 1995; Savigliano 1995). Romberg's use of the tango in *The New Moon*, at a time when the dance was still somewhat current, taps into this richer vein of knowledge, intending as it does to evoke a kind of dangerous sexuality equal to the subplots of insurrection and piracy that his librettists called on to energize an otherwise flaccid and predictable story line.

What is important for my argument is not whether we understand "Softly, as in a Morning Sunrise" as we might have in 1928, but that our conceptual models reflect knowledge that is basic to culture. One sort of knowledge was active in the culture of which *The New Moon* was originally a part; another sort of knowledge shapes the cultural perspective from which we view the tango (or, more to the point, *The New Moon*) some eighty years later. Put another way, culture consists of shared knowledge: as Naomi Quinn and Dorothy Holland put it, culture is "not a people's customs and artifacts and oral traditions, but what they must know in order to act as they do, make the things they make, and interpret their experience in the distinctive way they do" (Quinn and Holland 1987, 4). A tango in the early twenty-first century is not the same as it was in the early twentieth century because the conceptual models basic to culture have changed.

It is very common for conceptual models to be nested, one within another. Thus the conceptual model for the tangos that occur within *The New Moon* operates within the model of the Broadway musical. We know that such musicals often take as their premise the most unlikely of circumstances, and that their purpose is entertainment rather than edification. Thus the appearance of a resolutely twentieth-century dance within a musical play set in eighteenth-century Louisiana is not cause for alarm, but simply represents one of the licenses permitted the authors of such shows. When we hear the tango in this context we do not infer that the scene has suddenly shifted to modern times, only that the (presumably) timeless topic of sexual intrigue is now afoot.

Conceptual models, as one of the basic structures through which we organize our understanding of the world, inform most of our conscious thought processes. With respect to categorization, our conceptual models for how musical materials are most typically organized will inform what we regard as the basic musical figure of the first phrase of "Softly, as in a Morning Sunrise." Although the descending gesture of measures 1, 3, and 5 certainly has salience, our knowledge about how tunes of this sort are structured may lead us to expand the first two figures to include the oscillations of measures 2 and 4. Similarly, what counts as a typical member of a musical category is often informed by the function of category members within a broader context. For instance, while measures 1 and 3 begin with the same pitch (F5), and thus seem to set out a clear perspective for what is typical of the category of musical figures around which the first phrase is organized, measures 1 and 5 involve the same pitch classes (F and C).[7] The importance of these pitch classes to the key of F minor, along with the placement of both measure 1 and measure 5 at the head of a four-measure subphrase, might cause us to regard *them* as most typical of the category, were these factors to inform the conceptual model relative to which the categorization was made.

With respect to cross-domain mapping, the characterization of musical pitches as "high" or "low" so common among Western musicians is by no means necessary, but reflects a conceptual model that includes not only the conceptual metaphor *pitch relationships are relationships in vertical space* but also an entire network of linguistic expressions and notational conventions based on this metaphor. In contrast, musicians in Bali and Java describe pitches not as "high" and "low" but as "small" and "large."[8] Behind these descriptions is a conceptual model focused on the norms of acoustic production: small things typically vibrate more rapidly than large things. This acoustic fact is represented throughout the numerous parts of the gamelan, the collection of instruments central to the musical practice of Bali and Java.

Conceptual models, then, are not only crucial for explaining the larger context for our judgments about how musical events relate to one another; they also help to capture the uniquely cultural aspect of music. They are important to fuller accounts of the parts that categorization and cross-domain mapping play in musical understanding, and I have also used them to explain the differences and similarities between audiences' and performers' construals of works of popular music (Zbikowski 2002, 2004). Although we still have much to learn about the structure and use of such models, they will prove essential to our fuller explanation of how we understand music.

Conclusion

Discovering how humans make sense of complex and multidimensional sequences of patterned sound does not promise to be simple. This is so not only because human cognition is so staggeringly complex, but also because understanding music is not simply a matter of processing auditory signals—it involves a number of higher-order processes that humans use in a variety of ways to structure their understanding of the world. These processes include, but are not limited to, categorization, cross-domain mapping, and the use of conceptual models. It is important to emphasize that these processes are *embodied*, in two senses: first, they are part of the way the mind and brain connect to and structure interactions with the outside world; second, they arise from more basic cognitive processes that operate on a preconceptual level. The cognitive tango that mind and brain dance with music is a complicated one, and the partners intertwine—music adapted to the capacities of mind and brain, mind and brain stretched and reconfigured by music—much as dancers in Buenos Aires and elsewhere have done for over a century. Some of the steps in the dance, as well as some of the stylized gestures, are now becoming more apparent, even as many remain obscure. But the dance has much to teach us, not only about how music relates to mind and brain, but also about how mind and brain make music itself possible.

NOTES

1. The pitch designation I use is that of the American Society of Acousticians: middle C is C4; the B below middle C is B3; the octave above middle C is C5.

2. Left out of my discussion of "Softly, as in a Morning Sunrise" is consideration of the contrasting phrase that occurs in mm. 17–24, the arpeggio traced by the three descending figures of the first phrase (encompassing F5, C5, Ab4, and F4), the octave transit the melody makes from the F5 of m. 1 to the F4 of m. 7, and the harmony. One could also note the higher-order musical category formed by the A sections (a category interrupted by the B section of mm. 17–24).

3. Most of the work that has been done on conceptual blending focuses on blends set up by language. However, there is a strong argument that the process is not specific to language; see Fauconnier and Turner 2002.

4. The tango has long been associated with lovemaking in general and acts of seduction in particular. What is interesting about "Softly, as in a Morning Sunrise" is the sense of denial created when the ascending lines of the bridge are exposed as shams: these expansive gestures lead not to an escape from the jagged descents of mm. 1–15 but back to the very premise of those descents (the F5 of m. 25, equivalent to the F5s of mm. 1 and 9). This same sense of denial is lacking in the instrumental tango that introduces the song "Fair Maria" later in act 1 of *The New Moon*.

5. Note that the generic space of figure 6.2 is itself a richly blended space. Describing its structure would require a number of conceptual integration networks; for discussion, see Fauconnier and Turner 2002.

6. The conceptual model, as I construe it, is similar to knowledge structures proposed by a number of other researchers in cognitive science, such as the idealized cognitive model (Lakoff 1987), cognitive domain (Langacker 1987), frame (Minsky 1975), and mental model (Johnson-Laird 1983). From the larger perspective that I develop in recent work (Zbikowski 2002), musical concepts are a result of processes of categorization, and relationships between musical concepts are a derivative of the process of cross-domain mapping. Conceptual models are consequently the first level of organization for concepts. Although I characterize conceptual models as "relatively basic" and "fairly small," this is only within the context of higher cognitive processes

(which is where I prefer to focus). Were we to consider the whole of cognition, it would be apparent that conceptual models are hardly basic and are of a compass that is far from small. For further discussion, see Zbikowski 2002, chaps. 3 and 4.

7. Pitch class is simply a more general way to characterize pitches. Whereas F5 designates a single *pitch*, F (as a pitch class) designates a *class* of pitches that includes F5, F4, F3, and so on.

8. Benjamin Brinner, personal communication, July 8, 1997. See also Zanten 1986, 85.

REFERENCES

Barsalou, L. W. 1987. The instability of graded structure: Implications for the nature of concepts. In *Concepts and conceptual development: Ecological and intellectual factors in categorization,* ed. Ulric Neisser, 101–40. Cambridge, England: Cambridge University Press.

———. 1992. *Cognitive psychology: An overview for cognitive scientists.* Hillsdale, N.J.: Lawrence Erlbaum Associates.

Brower, C. 2000. A cognitive theory of musical meaning. *Journal of Music Theory,* 44, no. 2 (Fall): 323–79.

Collier, S., A. Cooper, M. S. Azzi, and R. Martin. 1995. *Tango!: The dance, the song, the story.* London: Thames and Hudson.

Cook, N. 2001. Theorizing musical meaning. *Music Theory Spectrum,* 23, no. 2 (Fall): 170–95.

Cox, A. W. 1999. *The metaphoric logic of musical motion and space.* Ph.D. dissertation, University of Oregon.

Fauconnier, G., and M. Turner. 2002. *The way we think: Conceptual blending and the mind's hidden complexities.* New York: Basic Books.

Green, B., and D. Butler. 2002. From acoustics to *Tonpsychologie.* In *The Cambridge history of western music theory,* ed. T. Christensen, 246–71. Cambridge, England: Cambridge University Press.

Johnson, M. 1987. *The body in the mind: The bodily basis of meaning, imagination, and reason.* Chicago: University of Chicago Press.

Johnson-Laird, P. N. 1983. *Mental models: Towards a cognitive science of language, inference, and consciousness.* Cambridge, Mass.: Harvard University Press.

Lakoff, G. 1987. *Women, fire, and dangerous things: What categories reveal about the mind.* Chicago: University of Chicago Press.

———. 1993. The contemporary theory of metaphor. In *Metaphor and thought,* ed. A. Ortony, 202–51. Cambridge, England: Cambridge University Press.

Lakoff, G., and M. Johnson. 1980. *Metaphors we live by.* Chicago: University of Chicago Press.

———. 1999. *Philosophy in the flesh: The embodied mind and its challenge to Western thought.* New York: Basic Books.

Lakoff, G., and R. E. Núñez. 2000. *Where mathematics comes from: How the embodied mind brings mathematics into being.* New York: Basic Books.

Langacker, R. W. 1987. *Foundations of cognitive grammar*. Vol. 1, *Theoretical prerequisites*. Stanford, Calif.: Stanford University Press.

Minsky, M. 1975. A framework for representing knowledge. In *The psychology of computer vision*, ed. P. H. Winston, 211–77. New York: McGraw-Hill.

Quinn, N., and D. Holland. 1987. Culture and cognition. In *Cultural models in language and thought*, ed. D. Holland and N. Quinn, 3–40. Cambridge, England: Cambridge University Press.

Rosch, E. 1973. On the internal structure of perceptual and semantic categories. In *Cognitive development and the acquisition of language*, ed. T. E. Moore, 111–44. New York: Academic Press.

———. 1975. Cognitive representations of semantic categories. *Journal of Experimental Psychology: General*, 104, no. 3: 192–233.

———. 1977. Human categorization. In *Studies in cross-cultural psychology*, ed. N. Warren, 1: 1–49. London: Academic Press.

Rosch, E., C. B. Mervis, W. D. Gray, D. M. Johnson, and P. Boyes-Braem. 1976. Basic objects in natural categories. *Cognitive Psychology*, 8, no. 3 (July): 382–439.

Saslaw, J. K. 1996. Forces, containers, and paths: The role of body-derived image schemas in the conceptualization of music. *Journal of Music Theory*, 40, no. 2 (Fall): 217–43.

Savigliano, M. E. 1995. *Tango and the political economy of passion*. Boulder, Colo.: Westview Press.

Sayrs, E. 2003. Narrative, metaphor, and conceptual blending in "The Hanging Tree." *Music Theory Online*, 9, no. 1 (March): URL: http://www.societymusictheory.org/mto/issues/mto.03.9.1/mto.03.9.1.sayrs.html.

Tversky, B., and K. Hemenway. 1984. Objects, parts, and categories. *Journal of Experimental Psychology: General*, 113, no. 2 (June): 169–93.

Zanten, W. van. 1986. The tone material of the Kacapi in Tembang Sunda in West Java. *Ethnomusicology*, 30, no. 1 (Winter): 84–112.

Zbikowski, L. M. 1997. Conceptual models and cross-domain mapping: New perspectives on theories of music and hierarchy. *Journal of Music Theory*, 41, no. 2 (Fall): 11–43.

———. 1998. Metaphor and music theory: Reflections from cognitive science. *Music Theory Online*, 4, no. 1 (January): URL: http://smt.ucsb.edu/mto/issues/mto.98.4.1/toc.4.1.html

———. 2002. *Conceptualizing music: Cognitive structure, theory, and analysis*. New York: Oxford University Press.

———. 2004. Modelling the groove: Conceptual structure and popular music. *Journal of the Royal Musical Association*, 129, no. 2 (December): 272–97.

7

Dynamics of Completion

Shirley Brice Heath

This chapter considers the mystery of how art presents gaps, disparities, and improvisations that invite—and even insist on—our participation in the act of reconciliation or completion and connection. Art seems ultimately to be about playing as if we as humans could step outside the bounds of our physical limitations by opening the imagination to take on the role of seeing and being others. Of special interest here is the power of intensive visual focus for young artists and the potential correlation of such visual attentiveness with verbal fluency.

Every piece of art not only *is* but also is *of* something. With this recognition, we have only a short distance to go before we understand that art across cultures functions to transport viewers and listeners outside themselves and beyond the immediacies of space and time. Whether dramatic play, bedtime story, Indonesian puppetry, Navajo sand painting, or portrayal of European peasant life, all art enables acting *as if*. But such acting always moves toward something perceived and conceptualized as not yet complete, whole, or fully satisfying. This human response to the mystery of what is not yet there but can be made to be there through our acting to make it so prompts us to take up the challenge of completing the tale, the scene, or the melodic line. Art always pushes toward some sense of connection and completion.

This chapter examines the developmental trajectory that enables humans to play their role as connectors when they interact with art. In the early years, play prepares children not only to interpret the immediate art before them, but also to project consequences and subsequent actions, strings of words, or extensions beyond the visual field of a picture frame, book illustration, or dramatic scene. Later learning challenges have to be met by honing the power of attentiveness, memory storage, and capacity to connect, correlate, and conceptualize. As human beings evolved, their altered social and physical environments required an increasing range of social roles and hence of language use and capacities for taking on multiple perspectives. Considered here are ways in which "tuning in" to create the hypothetical, sequential, or imaginary is catalyzed through art.

For older children, particularly those with minimal opportunity to play or engage with art, development of language fluency and empathy for the perspectives of others appears to be accelerated through immersion in collaborative creation of the arts, along with accumulation of knowledge of art and its history. This chapter closes with a summary of findings from the fields of neuroscience, visual cognition, anthropology, and linguistics that support speculation that later language development is critically supported by the enactment of role-playing and the sustained visual focus required by art. The capacity to take creative leaps and seek reconciliation among disjunctures and disparities by asking not simply "what is it?" but "what is it about?" unifies human beings and marks the course of human development.

The Disconnectedness of Art

Though cultures differ greatly in what they enable members to perceive as whole or filled in, socialization within all societies depends in large part on helping the young learn to improvise and imagine so as to fill in the gaps between what they see and what they believe to be needed for completion. Learning how to be a part of such completions comes through the hours of imitation and entertainment that play between the young and their elders provides. *Homo ludens* has to play (Huizinga 1950). It is in playing that humans assume roles—the fundamental social connectors of life. From the game of peek-a-boo and its variants across cultures, make-believe games involving role shifts, and even the manipulation of objects in games of chance, the young get the central idea that they play a part by filling in the gaps of the world around them. Art is a particular form of play that ensures ample practice for learning to manage the mental work necessary to bring what is perceived to be disconnected into some kind of whole, however temporary and shifting.

For those societies with a tradition of children's literature, the art of illustration offers extensive playful practice in handling such disconnects. Illustrators insist that children complete what is not there on the page. The running figure on page 1 (represented, perhaps, only by a disappearing foot) demands that they think ahead to possible outcomes that may not be revealed until page 10. Illustrators also expect children (generally more quickly than adults) to catch what are often tiny and subtle mismatches between text and picture on a single page. Such disparities or incongruities prod children to look ahead and anticipate completion of the story (Wolf and Heath 1992, chap. 4).

Detecting disparities or incongruities depends on carrying within the mind a host of possible congruent wholes. Sensing disparities between what we think we know and what we actually see within our visual field enables us to predict danger as well as reward. But in either case, we are always working toward some sense of completion or "what's next?"—often called *meaning*. Before children learn to transform this sense of what is to come into language, they learn both to act out and act on this meaning (Dunn 1988, chap. 1; Bruner 1990). Through mimesis, they imitate and take on the roles of others (see Donald 1991; Donald, this volume); as their sense of the pragmatic grows, they recognize that an absence of stability or the presence of disparities and incongruities offers opportunities for action. The disappearing foot in the illustration from a children's book invites rapid turning of the next few pages as well as jumping to the floor and running in mock-exaggerated form.

The making of meaning—visually and linguistically—is fundamentally, more often than not, an act of reconciliation. We work to reconcile disparities or incongruities just as we strive to fill in gaps—all in an effort to "cultivate continuity" (De Mey, this volume). Works of René Magritte come immediately to mind here, for they introduce a discrepancy between what we know through our real-world visual experience and what we are led to perceive as real within his art. Hence we juxtapose two seemingly opposed views in order to make meaning of what is before us. Artists do more, however, than call on us to fill in gaps; we must also step beyond the frame of what they portray and imagine what they may have been seeing as they painted. As Miller (1998, 75–77) has made evident, Diego Rodríguez Velázquez's *Las Meninas* portrays a monarchical pair that is present in the painting only in mirrored (or merely framed?) representation. To complete this picture requires stepping outside the stance of the viewer (and indeed all the positions in the visual field of the painting).

The making of meaning from visual art is perhaps most difficult when a work contradicts bodies of intellectual, historical, or biographical knowledge.

For example, fifteenth-century tapestries such as *Los Honores* (created for Charles V) famously illustrate a hodgepodge of characters within the same scene, in defiance of historical facts or respect for known political, literary, and biographical "truths" (Delmarcel 2000). Secular and biblical, historical and fictional exist side by side, and viewers are left to make sense of a veritable onslaught of confusion. This is a case where the more one knows of "facts," the more gaps there are to fill in between artistic rendering and completion.

Here, as elsewhere in the visual arts of all cultures, mental work must be done to bring separations together into a whole. Seemingly unrelated figures all go about their business within the same two-dimensional space. It is the task of the viewer to figure out what holds these entities together other than the physical boundaries of the artwork. Whether we are considering church art of the medieval period, Giotto's storyboarding of events leading to and through the life of Christ, Hieronymus Bosch's altarpieces, or the illustration of proverbs by artists of the Brueghel family, works of art demand that we make some kind of whole of their disparate parts. Awareness of their framing within, for example, the architecture of the church, as well as knowledge of the separate narratives captured within them, links our visual experience to a known genre, event, or tradition, creating a congruence of understanding.

Nowhere is this point more aptly illustrated than in the art of Pieter Brueghel the Elder (1525–1569). Of his *Children's Games* (1560), it has been said, "It is as if the game holds out the human bond as a synaptic gap" (Snow 1997, 3) Viewers strive for the arc that connects the range of possible completions of the many simultaneous games taking place within the painting. But what brings these separate parts together into something whole? There is no firm answer, just as there is never an absolute answer to the "what?" of art. To the extent that we can surmise across cultures any pragmatic purpose for art, it is the incentive that it provides for us to move toward filling in gaps and experiencing the mind's capacity to generate a proliferation of meanings. In our encounter with art, the immediate need to act or come to closure is momentarily suspended, yet the work inspires us to want to do both.

> Play, imaged as a pure instant, can hold the present, the almost-past, the not-yet, the about-to-be, the held-in-abeyance, the imagined-away, or the permanently translated. Things suspended run the gamut from the deferred to the undecided to the imminent to the gestating to the sublated or abolished or uplifted, become implicated in boundaries, thresholds, limits, gaps—indeed, crossings of all sorts— and enter into relation with motifs of groundedness that have their own rich problematic. (Snow 1997, 159)

This state of suspension requires us to step outside the frames of space and time into a world where the question "what is it?" carries no possibility of completion or finality.

The Need to Attend and to Learn

Instead, art forces the query "what is it about?" Within the Western canon, this aboutness most often finds its explanation within a narrative that centers on the actions of animates capable of intentionality and motivated by the agency of cause and effect. Seeing and attending to stimuli in the visual field carries a kind of "representational momentum." Once we have given our attention to an object or scene, we have the systematic tendency to remember it as extending beyond its actual endpoint—that is, we give motion to what we see as we make meaning. The ability to anticipate—to see ahead—is fundamental to perception (Meyer and Kornblum 1993; Palmer 1999; Noe 2002). But underlying this fundamental ability is our ongoing sense of our capacity to make things happen. Scenes emerge and objects move, even when they do not do so within our immediate visual field: "without a sense of self as acting in the world, sensations of external objects would be meaningless" (Newton 2000, 64).

This mental work of making fragments whole or of shaping clues and cues into a pattern is often thought of as an individual response. However, in evolutionary and developmental terms, the dynamics of thinking and being that move humans to fill in gaps, particularly in the creation and appreciation of art, depend in large part on communal membership. As science within the Western tradition has attempted to understand the human brain and mind, the primary focus, especially with respect to mental model building, has been on individuals. However, at a fundamental level, connections between perceptual and conceptual or linguistic representations have emerged and always will emerge in socially interactive situations that punctuate, underline, and enlarge individual understanding (Fauconnier and Turner 2002; see also the discussion of situational-episodic apperceptions, Brandt, this volume).

The human brain as it has evolved makes possible the pulling together of the seemingly unbounded perceptions that vision allows into conceptualizations. But individuals in every society must learn through repeated practice how to build conceptual models, whose structures depend on relationships and derive from specific domains of knowledge (see Zbikowski 2002; Zbikowski, this volume). Moreover, the sense of agency and capacity for intentionality with which humans are neurally endowed must be fostered, modeled, and instructed (Gibbs 1999). In particular, linguistic expression of the mental moves associated with making sense of a work of art depends on experience in the open-ended practice that comes through play. Verbal language has minimal units of meaning, whereas visual and (generally) gestural units do not. Hence play demonstrates the somewhat limited range of linguistic expression compared to the open, expansive possibilities of the visual and gestural. It offers the opportunity to lift actions and intentions out of the moment, into multiple versions of something else (Bateson 1973). Metacognition is, in numerous ways, play, for it is here that one sees the self as performer, supervises the current scene, and learns to improve subsequent mental acts (see especially Donald 2001, chap. 7; Donald, this volume).[1]

The importance of such play is suggested by the fact that the more extensive and inclusive art is within a society, the more that society's elites emphasize play for their own children. Play is ultimately social and is thus dependent on the presence of both artifacts and players. It therefore requires the accumulation of possessions, the establishment of places of play, and the presence of agents often engaged full time in play with the young.[2] For example, we can be certain that opportunities, agents, and resources for play characterized the early socialization of the viewers and listeners described throughout this volume as enjoying and interpreting works of art. Such play ensures that individuals "tune in" and thereby gain a sense of being able to act in the world (Gopnik and Meltzoff 1998).

Design Experiments in Learning

Much of what we have said above relates to theories of human development, cognitive science, or the mind. Some of these theories have been developed and supported through laboratory experiments, some through observations of young children, and still others through a combination of these plus an interpretive reading of human history. What if we follow young children into older childhood and adolescence and observe and record their actions, language, and socializing agents and situations? What might their learning within the arts tell us about how they come to see their capacity for filling in gaps, creating continuities from disparities, and adapting what is before them to what they know to be real or possible? Conducting such an inquiry among young people who have had, until recently, little or no access to the time, agents, or artifacts of play offers special potential for helping us learn more about the socializing power of the arts and their influence on visual perception, linguistic categorization, and a sense of the self as meaning-maker.

We know that the arts generally have little or no appeal for adults who had little play experience in their childhood or early youth. Moreover, such individuals are often described as lacking interpretive skills or talents. As students, they rarely find their way to advanced levels of academic performance, particularly in areas dependent on linguistic skills and complex kinds of conceptual integration. They are often assessed as having little capacity to make judgments based on an understanding of consequences, cause-and-effect relationships, and their own responsibility for self-monitoring. But what if extensive opportunities to participate in the arts, as creators and interpreters, were available to older children and adolescents? Is it too late to develop the range of playful imagination that children exhibit as they take on roles far beyond their "real" role as children?

Answers to these questions have come from studies of youth immersed in the arts for extended periods and followed in their conceptual and linguistic development over several years. Of particular interest here is an understanding of the dynamic processes—particularly those of the visual and verbal capacities working together—as learners complete, reconcile, and pull together what is before them in art.

I am a linguistic anthropologist whose work for the past two decades has centered on language development in environments rarely attended to by other scholars—niches beyond direct instruction by elders or experts. The population I have studied consists of young people growing up in economically impoverished communities where multiple demands on parents and teachers mean little commitment to aesthetic experiences of production or interpretation. In many situations, young people seek out the aesthetic as an environmental niche, finding their way to community arts organizations or museums, conservatories, or other settings that provide intensive experience in learning frames for viewing art. These situations therefore represent a kinship with "design experiments"—a natural way to observe and often to intervene in situations that can never be created satisfactorily within experimental and control settings.[3] Such design experiments allow us to ask what we might learn from in-depth, long-term study of the uninitiated as they come to engage intensively with the arts, especially the visual arts. Precisely because every possible feature of the learning environment and the learner is under scrutiny in these experiments, such research can tell us much about how the uninitiated, including young people who are beginning to think of themselves as artists, learn to fill in the gaps that the arts create.

Within arts organizations in the economically disadvantaged communities I have studied, young people often remain immersed for several years in high-risk learning situations through which they interpret and produce art forms as they make sense of their worlds and of the arts. They initially come to these places to be with their friends, but gradually they come because they want to enter the worlds of art and aesthetics they discover there. These young people spend much time in museums, galleries, and theaters, and in video production, sculpture, and photography studios. They engage with one another as collaborators and critics, and also with professional artists and critics. Over the past fifteen years, in more than one hundred of these arts-centered environments all over the United States and England, I have followed individuals and groups, collecting on audiotape hundreds of hours of their interactions and many hours of videotape of them at work as young artists.

Whether in the visual, dramatic, musical, or video arts, these young people spend approximately ten hours each week, for at least thirty-two weeks a year, seeing, critiquing, and creating art. They also organize human and financial resources to develop a range of contexts where others in their communities can view art and learn from and with young artists. All these features of their work are relatively visible and easily narrated. Far less visible to the casual observer, however, is the extent to which they spend time attending to and visually focusing on details of line, form, color, and movement in their own art and that of others around them. Additionally, as they spend more and more weeks engaged in art, their language use changes; lexicon, syntax, range of metaphor, register, and genre control develop according to the frequency and intensity of their occasions for acting as artists. In so doing, they transport themselves not only into the places, roles, and times of the artworks they collaboratively produce but also into the world of the viewers and listeners they anticipate for their work. They not only seek to bring about the emergent properties they have jointly envisioned in their exhibitions, performances, and productions, but they also attempt to anticipate how reactions and interpretations will emerge for viewers and audience.[4]

In short, intensive community-based work in the arts enables young people who are often mercilessly circumscribed and limited in their daily existence to act beyond themselves. Many of the young artists in this research spend their days as "at-risk" troubled or troubling students in schools and communities with few economic or social resources. When they leave their schools and go to their community-based arts organizations, they take on a range of roles, from artist to mentor to planner and organizational member.[5]

Of special interest is that these young people simultaneously show relatively rapid development of fluency in spontaneous oral text and an intensity of eye focus that is absent in their engagement at school or in their navigation of the everyday world about them. Many questions remain, of course, about this correlation between intensive and extensive practice in focusing visually on attributes of visual art (color, line, motion) and advanced language development (especially in expression of predictions, conditionals, and understanding of audience or listener response).

Seeing and Saying the Emergent

Young artists working in visual, video, or drama studios become agents of imaginative action—their own action and that of others. Together they must make properties of the final production emerge, even though neither their experiences nor their linguistic repertoires have equipped them with the knowledge and skills that professionals use in choreographing a new dance or producing a theatrical work. And indeed, these young people create—always under very tight deadlines and with minimal resources—works of art that meet the standards of local art critics as well as a range of audiences. Their general pattern of operation is to plan together, at the outset of the season, the number of shows they will create, schedule times and venues for practice and performance or exhibition, and identify and capture the human and financial resources needed to achieve their planned outcomes.

Professional artists always work with these groups, and some young members continue their participation from year to year; in addition, each community organization takes in new members each year. Therefore, within any organization, the range of expertise may be considerable at the start of the season. Studio work, whether for creating visual art (such as murals or themed exhibitions) or dramatic works (often incorporating dance, music, and other art forms), consists of warm-ups and lessons directed by professional artists. As the season moves forward and segments of the exhibition or performance begin to fall into place through joint planning, the critiques provided by other artists—both the professionals and the youth members—become more frequent and focused. The goal is a final production of the best possible work that will bring prestige, recognition, and further financial support to the group.

It is in extended sessions of creation and practice toward the final collaborative work (whether a mural, a dance number, or a dramatic scene) that the young artists focus on details, ask others to "hold it right there" or "freeze," or return to a prior step or sequence and repeat it for scrutiny. On average, after the first six to eight weeks of work in a season of thirty or so weeks, an individual young artist may spend up to thirty-five minutes each of several hours each day looking intently at a series of details. Such scrutiny often involves comparing the current portion of a piece with a portrayal in an art book or a scene from a videotape. Because the work takes place interactively and the outcome must be collaborative, verbal explanation accompanies these occasions of visual focus.

In the complex set of actions carried out by these young artists, there is no way to isolate the neural correlates of either visual or linguistic behaviors. However, the extent to which, for this population, two relatively infrequent behavioral phenomena co-occur warrants some conjectures that may stimulate the gathering of more domain-specific data. These two behavioral phenomena are the extended periods of visual focus on detail and the relatively rapid later language development.

The following dialogue, which was videotaped several weeks into the season of a youth theater and dance group, suggests the correspondences between visual and verbal behaviors. In this example, three young artists— Rodney, Andre, and Aisha—work together to develop a dream sequence that will take place stage left while the "real" events of a family argument— involving a grandfather, his daughter and grandson, and the grandson's friend—take place stage right. The purpose of the dream sequence is to suggest that the grandfather is remembering a similar scene from his own childhood, when he and a young friend did what the grandson is currently proposing to the uncooperative mother. The grandson and his friend want to spend the night camping on the street in order to get the best view for a morning parade honoring a local sports team's victory in national competition.

ANDRE   If we're in a dream, we move slow, like this [demonstrating leg and arm moves], all over and act like we can't see.

AISHA   What do you mean "can't see"? Of course you can see in a dream. Don't you know people see in dreams? Just because you got your eyes closed don't mean the folks in your dream don't see.

RODNEY   But how will they know we're in a dream, if we don't have our eyes closed? No way else they're gonna know.

ANDRE   Sure, they can see us move slow and in a trance like, and they can hear what we say and know he's just remembering or daydreaming.

AISHA   But if we talk, how will they hear what they're saying? [nodding in direction of "real" action at stage right]

The conversation continues as the three talk about how dream sequences are "shown" in cartoons, in artworks at the museum, or on television shows. Their talk includes dramatic re-enactments, drawings in the air, and, at one point, a trip to the studio library to look up the Vermeer painting *The Love*

Letter, which Aisha has interpreted as representing "a dream." She views the letter as the prompt for dreamlike reflection by the young woman to whom the maid is handing the letter. The three study the painting, conclude that no audible talk takes place there, and move back to confer with the artistic director about film sequences of dreams they can possibly view.

These young people now have, and are able to project, a conscious experience of self and other. As Andre moves in a way he considers appropriate for portraying the dream state, he stimulates a comparative framework—between here and there, the dream scene and the "real" scene, the group's collective intention and that of other artists who have created dream sequences. Here Andre is "representing" not only the world but also himself as representing the world, and both of these representations take place within the comparative context of "dream" and "real." In other words, what occurs here differs considerably from a situation in which Andre recounts his own dream. He is demonstrating his awareness of the need for mutual understanding within his group of young artists, and for understanding by the audience of the co-occurring scenes of "dream" and "real." In addition, he and the others draw on the fact that audience members will bring to their interpretation of the scene their prior experience in viewing art and "seeing" dreams. Andre is working hard both to make any gaps in understanding evident and to enable audience members to fill in the gaps and create congruity to shape their own meanings.

I can imagine two very different responses to what may seem esoteric findings about this population's viewing and production of art. Neuroscientists might wonder about the connections between the neurological organization of vision and that of meaning-making expressed in oral language. Educators and museum professionals might consider the practical implications of this research for developing audiences for the visual arts. If young people in economically stressed communities spent more time engaged with the visual and dramatic arts, would this translate into a more knowledgeable and linguistically capable population, at least somewhat habituated to seeing the world in aesthetic terms?

Either response demands caution; linkages between neural spikes and behaviors, for example, remain highly elusive. We do know, however, that learning environments—especially those offering constancy of stimuli under conditions of emotional reward—lead to adaptation in single neurons and circuits, allowing the most efficient use of those brain resources to capture and process sensory information (Clark 1997; Rieke et al. 1997, 275). With respect to both the evolution of the human organism and optimal signal processing, the full range of environmental parameters and inputs for selection by the organism warrants research attention.

Conclusions

Why is it that gaps matter so much to how we neurologically and cognitively frame the viewing of art? We have suggested an answer to this question by linking the process of interpreting the visual arts to attention, visual focus, and linguistic explanation. Vision is our most efficient way of gathering information about the world around us; hence the filling in of gaps—or the fitting together of parts to make a whole—is highly dependent on visual attention (Driver and Baylis 1998). Such visual focus, motivated by intention, enables the viewer to take on agency or to see with the anticipation that creates a narrative of dynamic events. Fluency in aspects of later language development, particularly the use of conditionals to create hypothetical scenarios, comes with increased visual focus and roles that call for an evaluative, interpretive stance. Speakers who feel a real need to communicate the emerging narrative strive for coherence, using metaphors and other verbal means to call up visual images in listeners (Gernsbacher and Givon 1995).

Through attentional selection of details and visual focus, these young viewers take on the role of the other and thereby come to have an intensified awareness of agency (Proust 2000; Gallese 2000). This point raises the challenge, for arts institutions and scholars of art and aesthetics (especially those interested in sustaining and even increasing an informed viewing audience), of generating contexts and conditions that broaden and deepen role relationships to the arts.

The research on young people working as artists reminds us that art provides content grounding and an imaginative basis for viewers and creators to practice internalizing, simulating, and verbalizing the actions and emotions of others. More practice—vital to fluency in later language development—comes with collaborative situations, whether involving interpretation or production, that require verbal explication plus simultaneous focused viewing. Such scenes enact metaphorically what may happen in the action of mirror neurons—that is, an observed action stimulates the observer to do the same. What is added, however, with joint viewing and analysis of a visual artwork, is a marked metaconsciousness of this mirroring of an agent in interaction with an object (the work of art). This metaconsciousness is driven by the participants' awareness of their role in the future replication or replaying of the current moment, and of the instructional, mentoring, or modeling function they will perform for others.

Those who work in museums, galleries, and other public arts institutions are in a position to consider the implications of the "design experiment" of youth arts organizations. Findings from the fields of neuroscience, visual cognition, and the anthropology of learning provide strong evidence that later language development is critically supported and habituated through the intense visual focus required for artistic creation and interpretation. Four related findings follow:

1. Extended time spent in visual focus contributes to an increased ability to discern details and to acquire knowledge; these two capacities enable rapid "filling in" by individuals collaborating on a work of art. The social need within groups dedicated to understanding the visual and dramatic arts and to creating joint products is met through extensive practice in seeing details and learning to categorize attributes of the visual field as these are captured and held constant. (Consider the extensive use of the "freeze" command in dramatic rehearsals.) We refer here to fractionating art and attempting to verbalize the unspeakable—its components and their effects. This activity of physical, visual focus by artists differs in degree and in attentional demand from that associated with other learning environments (such as classrooms) or with casual viewing. The extensive time spent both in rapid scanning and in holding visual focus correlates with increased capacity to store details in memory. Added to this developmental achievement is an enhanced ability to scan selectively and retrieve detailed information related to specific segments of the visual field that support preverbalized narratives or explanations (Zeki 1999).

2. Mutual "tuning in," or conjoined visual and motivational attention that frames the viewing of a piece of art, enhances and speeds up development of predictive abilities. Such development depends on perspective taking—imaginatively entering the visual artwork and talking as though its components were animates, or speaking as though one were in the role of another viewer of the work or a member of the audience (Heath and Roach 1999).

3. Coherence, to the extent that it emerges as a property of a text or visual representation in art, does so in large part for the individual and the group through a sense of "the other," or, in Virginia Woolf's terms, the "face beneath the page." Collaboration toward coherence involves negotiating verbally and gesturally in order to assemble, from things perceived as similar or different, something the viewer believes can be reconciled and perceived as a whole (see Murray, this volume, for more on this point). Initial ambiguities (as well as acknowledgment

of bodies of knowledge not well known, as in the case of the young artists struggling to learn how different art forms represent dreams) motivate the drive to some kind of resolution. The reconciliation that art requires ensures the possibility of associating components of the work with some whole and of transforming these by the assignment of one or more meanings. Talking aloud with others about what this line, this color, or that indication of motion means activates predictive abilities, not only about the perspectives likely to be taken by others, but also about the relations that may hold among components of a given piece of art or between a current work and others viewed else-where or in the past.

4. Finally, viewing a work of art involves three kinds of narration. The first of these—and the most common among the young—centers on "I." We see this simple narrative in responses such as "I don't like this or that work of art" or "I don't like art." The second kind of narrative grows more frequent as young people spend more time in the role of young artist; they speak of "I" as being *with* a generalized other. It is this capacity that enables them to see a work of art as tied to religious history or a school of art. When they talk in this type of narration, they indicate their recognition of the context out of which the artwork came. The third narrative form is that of "I" as a specific other—an artist, viewer, curator, or critic. Here the language animates not only the agent or actor (through the actions and emotions of the self) but also the specific other (through the available data about such an in-dividual). Attributions of mental states to others, as well as to the self as artist, reflect what has been called second-order representation: seeing the self as capable not only of representing the world but also of representing the self doing so. Within the frame of viewing and of thinking of the self as artist, young people appear to re-enact the mind-reading or theory-of-mind capacity so frequently studied in young children (Baron-Cohen 1995). Much of the literature that attempts to understand both when and how this endowment of humans comes into being (both in the evolutionary process and in the development of a young child) gives substantial attention to ways that we detect the intentions of others through the visual gaze and other shared attention mechanisms (Carey, Perrett, and Oram 1997; for a review, see Posner and DiGirolamo 1998).

In the end, what seems to matter most in the development of artistic perception and response is not so much the "framing" of the physical space of art as it is the individual framing of the self as an intentional, attending viewer of an artwork. This framing is reinforced in multiple ways, both neurophysiologically and socially, when the viewing takes place as individuals play roles that involve planned and projected action for the future through the interpretation of the artwork. Within the contexts studied here—young people viewing art in order to learn to function as artists within community organizations—conjoined visual focus co-occurs with increased situational (and extended) use of verbal forms that portray prediction, understanding of cause and effect, and perspective taking.

We have known for some time that responses to pictures are predicated in large part on underlying mental structures that we draw upon not only to decipher or decode visual images but also to encode these for access in short-term and working memory. What we are only now beginning to understand are the regularities of pattern, for example, in neuronal spiking for the simplest of visual feats. The limitations of PET and fMRI images, as well as EEG and MEG, are well known to us. We are very far from identifying the neural substrates necessary to build image schemas of particular sorts of connections. We understand that, given the complexities of vision and especially of language reception and production, we may never be able to say just how sustained visual focus, role-playing, and verbal explication or narration (in either inner speech or spoken language) work together in the dynamism of completion that has been at work among humans since the earliest periods of their social life.

As interdisciplinary teams increasingly work together on topics widely and variously named, but all reaching toward neural correlates of consciousness (Metzinger 2000), perhaps no other phenomenon will continue to puzzle us as much as those gaps—whether synaptic, linguistic, visual, or philosophical—over which humans can leap in their creativity. These spaces, however, speak most revealingly about what makes humans so rare among all other creatures. For in these disunities and irregularities, we begin to discern what it means to be the only animals able to ask—and to answer—the questions "what is it about?" and "what's missing here?"

NOTES

1. A critical issue in metacognition is the matter of how such mental play prepares one for risk: to what extent is metacognition actually planning of future behavior, and does such cognitive work take precedence over emotional motivations? Can the taking of risk be seen as resulting from some kind of cognitive assessment that comes from having preplayed or anticipated consequences? See Loewenstein et al. 2001. Complicating this question of internal mental states and preparation for risk is the matter of whether or not having command of a deep and varied repertoire of

linguistic access to the hypothetical makes a difference in frequency and severity of risk-taking. See Heath 1998; Heath 2000; Heath 2001, for further discussion.

2. This point has often been made of those ancient societies judged most advanced. For families in postindustrial societies, a new category of professional has emerged for the very young through commercial establishments such as Gymboree. Toy manufacturers categorize their artifacts by "play" value that will hold the attention of youngsters and thereby contribute to their learning. Video materials complement objects for manipulation and "characters" that embody certain attitudes toward learning; the world of "edutainment" intends to grab and hold onto the attention of the young and thereby to promote their learning (see Steen, this volume).

3. Design experiments are theory-driven, empirically manipulating learning environments, reflecting the belief that explanations of how learning works in complex interactive systems are essential to promoting habits of learning (Cobb et al. 2003; see *Educational Researcher*, 32, no. 1, for a review of design experiments in education and the controversies surrounding transfer learning from these settings). As postindustrial societies come to depend more and more on information and creative learning, many people working with older children and youth disenfranchised from formal schooling feel a special need to help them develop habits that will enable them to keep on learning. Though most design experiments have been carried out in schools, and the majority of these on domain-specific learning processes, some work in this direction has been done in nonschool settings.

4. For more detail on the particular syntactic forms, particularly those related to evaluation, authorial stance, and conditionals, see Heath 1999; Heath 1998; and Heath and Roach 1999.

5. Numerous reports of this research and details of the methods of data collection and analysis are available; see, for example, Heath 1998; Heath and Smyth 1999; Soep 2000.

REFERENCES

Baron-Cohen, S. 1995. *Mindblindness: An essay on autism and theory of mind.* Cambridge, Mass.: MIT Press.
Bateson, G. 1973. *Steps to an ecology of mind.* Boulder, Colo.: Paladin Press.
Bruner, J. 1990. *Acts of meaning.* Cambridge, Mass.: Harvard University Press.
Carey, A., R. Perrett, and M. Oram. 1997. Recognizing, understanding, and reproducing action. In *Handbook of neuropsychology,* ed. F. Boller and J. Grafman, 11: 111–29. Philadelphia, Penn.: Elsevier Science.
Clark, A. 1997. *Being there: Putting brain, body, and world together again.* Cambridge, Mass: MIT Press.
Cobb, P., J. Confrey, A. diSessa, R. Lehrer, and L. Schauble. 2003. Design experiments in educational research. *Educational Researcher,* 32, no. 1: 9–13.
Delmarcel, G. 2000. *Los honores: Flemish tapestries for the Emperor Charles V.* The Netherlands: Pandora.

Donald, M. 1991. *Origins of the modern mind: Three stages in the evolution of culture and cognition.* Cambridge, Mass.: Harvard University Press.

―――. 2001. *A mind so rare: The evolution of human consciousness.* New York: Norton.

Driver, J., and G. C. Baylis. 1998. Attention and visual object segmentation. In *The attentive brain,* ed. R. Parasuraman, 299–326. Cambridge, Mass.: MIT Press.

Dunn, J. 1988. *The beginnings of social understanding.* Cambridge, Mass.: Harvard University Press.

Fauconnier, G., and M. Turner. 2002. *The way we think: Conceptual blending and the mind's hidden complexities.* New York: Basic Books.

Gallese, V. 2000. The acting subject: Toward the neural basis of social cognition. In *Neural correlates of consciousness: Empirical and conceptual questions,* ed. Thomas Metzinger, 325–34. Cambridge, Mass.: MIT Press.

Gernsbacher, M. A., and T. Givon. 1995. Introduction: Coherence as a mental activity. In *Coherence in spontaneous text,* ed. M. A. Gernsbacher and T. Givon, vii–x. Amsterdam: John Benjamins Publishing.

Gibbs, R. W., Jr. 1999. *Intentions in the experience of meaning.* New York: Cambridge University Press.

Gopnik, A., and A. N. Meltzoff. 1998. *Words, thoughts, and theories.* Cambridge, Mass.: MIT Press.

Heath, S. B. 1998. Working through language. In *Kids talk: Strategic language use in later childhood,* ed. S. Hoyle and C. T. Adger, 217–40. New York: Oxford University Press.

―――. 1999. Dimensions of language development. In *Cultural processes of child development,* ed. A. S. Masten, 29: 59–75. Hillsdale, N.J.: Lawrence Erlbaum Associates.

―――. 2000. Risk, rules, and roles: Youth perspectives on the work of learning for community development. *Zeitschrift fur Erziehungswissenschaft,* 1:67–80.

―――. 2001. Three's not a crowd: Plans, roles, and focus in the arts. *Educational Researcher,* 30, no. 3: 1–7.

Heath, S. B. (with A. Roach). 1999. Imaginative actuality: Learning in the arts during the nonschool hours. In *Champions of Change,* 19–34. Washington, D.C.: The Arts Education Partnership and The President's Committee on the Arts and the Humanities.

Heath, S. B., and L. Smyth. 1999. *ArtShow: Youth and community development.* Washington, D.C.: Partners for Livable Communities.

Huizinga, J. 1950 [Originally published 1938]. *Homo Ludens: A study in the play element in culture.* Boston: Beacon Press.

Loewenstein, G. F., E. U. Weber, C. K. Hsee, and N. Welch. 2001. Risk as feelings. *Psychological Bulletin,* 127, no. 2: 267–86.

Metzinger, T., ed. 2000. *Neural correlates of consciousness: Empirical and conceptual questions.* Cambridge, Mass.: MIT Press.

Meyer, D. E., and S. Kornblum, eds. 1993. *Attention as performance XIV.* Cambridge, Mass.: MIT Press.

Miller, J. 1998. *On reflection.* London: National Gallery.

Newton, N. 2000. Humphrey's solution. *Journal of Consciousness Studies*, 7, no. 4: 62–66.

Noe, A., ed. 2002. Is the visual world a grand illusion? *Journal of Consciousness Studies*, 9, no. 4.

Palmer, S. E. 1999. *Vision Science: Photons to phenomenology*. Cambridge, Mass.: MIT Press.

Posner, R., and G. DiGirolamo. 1998. Executive attention: Conflict target detection and cognitive control. In *The Attentive Brain*, ed. R. Parasuraman, 401–23. Cambridge, Mass.: MIT Press.

Proust, J. 2000. Awareness of agency: Three levels of analysis. In *Neural correlates of consciousness: Empirical and conceptual questions*, ed. T. Metzinger, 307–24. Cambridge, Mass.: MIT Press.

Rieke, F., D. Warland, R. van Steveninck, and W. Bialek. 1997. *Spikes: Exploring the neural code*. Cambridge, Mass.: MIT Press.

Snow, E. 1997. *Inside Bruegel: The play of images in children's games*. New York: North Point Press/Farrar, Straus, and Giroux.

Soep, E. 2000. *To make things with words: Critique and the production of learning*. Ph.D. Dissertation, Stanford University.

Wolf, S. A., and S. B. Heath. 1992. *The braid of literature: Children's worlds of reading*. Cambridge, Mass.: Harvard University Press.

Zbikowski, L. M. 2002. *Conceptualizing music: Cognitive structure, theory, and analysis*. New York: Oxford University Press.

Zeki, S. 1999. *Inner vision: An exploration of art and the brain*. New York: Oxford University Press.

PART IV

Art, Meaning, and Form

8

The Neuroscience
of Form in Art

George Lakoff

*The theory of form in art presented here rests on the Cog Hypothesis:
There are neural structures in the sensory-motor system that are "secondary" in the sense that they are connected neurally to "primary" neural ensembles that are more directly involved in either perception or movement. An obvious example would be premotor cortical structures that carry out highly structured complex motor actions via connections to the primary motor cortex, which controls simple actions. When the premotor-to-motor connections are inhibited, the secondary premotor circuitry can function as a "cog"—it can still compute complex patterns that permit inferences and can evolve over time. Such patterns can structure what we see as form in art. Many kinds of cogs have been hypothesized and each type corresponds to an aspect of form.*

The idea for this chapter came from observations by Rudolf Arnheim (1969) in *Visual Thinking*. Though Arnheim could not supply the neural underpinnings for a general and explanatory theory, he nonetheless had many of the basic ideas. I first turned to *Visual Thinking* in 1975, after hearing a lecture at Berkeley by Leonard Talmy on primitives of spatial relations. In English, for example, spatial-relations terms include the prepositions (*on, in, through*, etc.). Talmy, looking at many languages, had concluded that no two languages convey exactly the same range of spatial relations in their words and morphemes. However, spatial-relations concepts can be decomposed into universal cognitive primitives that recur across languages.

For example, consider *on* in a sentence like "The glass is on the table." Here the meaning of *on* is a composite of three primitives: ABOVE, CONTACT, and SUPPORT. That is, the glass is above the table, in contact with it, and supported by it. Not every language has the complex concept that we express by *on*, but every language appears to have those three primitives. We call those primitives *image schemas*. Consider another example: "Harry walked through the kitchen into the dining room." The meaning of *into* consists of two primitives: a CONTAINER—that is, a bounded region in space—and a PATH, with a SOURCE and a GOAL. The complex image schema for *into* consists of a PATH schema and a CONTAINER schema, where the SOURCE of the path is in the EXTERIOR of the CONTAINER and the GOAL of the PATH is inside it.

The Talmy idea, shared by others such as Ronald Langacker (1990), Susan Lindner (1981), Claudia Brugman (1981), and Eugene Casad (Casad and Langacker 1985), is that these primitives are not concrete images that you can see, but "schemas"—cognitive structures that fit many scenes that you *can* see. Thus, a room fits a CONTAINER schema, and so does a cup, as does a forest. Moreover, the image schema is imposed by a viewer, as when you are thinking of bees swarming *in* a garden. There is no physical container that the bees are in, but we can impose a mental one. Image schemas, I shall argue, give form to art.

When I began to work on this chapter, I went back to the copy of Arnheim that I had read in 1975 and looked at the dog-eared pages. I was in for a surprise. I date my own understanding of the phenomenon of metaphor to 1978. Yet here, reading Arnheim in 1975, I had marked the following passage: "What makes language so valuable for thinking, then, cannot be thinking in words. It must be the help that words lend to thinking while it operates in a more appropriate medium, such as visual imagery" (pp. 231–32).

In the next section, "Words Point to Percepts," Arnheim (1969) continues:

> The histories of languages show that words which do not seem now
> to refer to direct perceptual experience did so originally. Many of
> them are still recognizably figurative. Profundity of mind, for ex-
> ample, is named in English by a word that contains the Latin *fundus*,
> i.e., bottom. The "depth" of a well and "depth" of thought are de-
> scribed by the same word even today, and S. E. Asch has shown in a
> study on the metaphor that this sort of "naïve physics" is found in
> the figurative speech of the most divergent languages. The universal
> verbal habit reflects, of course, the psychological process by which the
> concepts describing "nonperceptual" facts derive from perceptual

ones. The notion of the depth of thought is derived from physical depth; what is more, depth is not merely a convenient metaphor to describe the mental phenomenon but the only possible way of even conceiving of that notion. Mental depth is not thinkable without an awareness of physical depth. Hence the figurative quality of all theoretical speech, of which Whorf gives telling examples:

> I "grasp" the "thread" of another's arguments, but if its "level" is "over my head" my attention may "wander" and "lose touch" with the "drift" of it, so that when he "comes" to his "point" we differ "widely," our "views" being indeed so "far apart" that the "things" he says "appear" "much" too arbitrary, or even "a lot" of nonsense!

Actually, Whorf is much too economical with his quotation marks, because the rest of his words, including the prepositions and conjunctions, derive their meanings from perceptual origins also.... [H]uman thinking cannot go beyond the patterns suppliable by the human senses. (pp. 232–33)

Arnheim did not have the whole theory of conceptual metaphor by a long shot. He did not have systematic conceptual mappings that preserve inferential structure, nor did he have image schemas and the neural system that defines them. But he did have a basic understanding of metaphor as conceptual, not merely linguistic, and of the conceptual as based on the perceptual.

What is most remarkable to me in retrospect is that Arnheim did have the idea that structures like image schemas give form to art, and that metaphors apply to image schemas in paintings, to give meaning to paintings. Let's start with three examples from Arnheim. The first is his analysis of Rembrandt's *Christ at Emmaus* (1648, Musée du Louvre; see http://theartful mind.stanford.edu):

> In Rembrandt's *Christ at Emmaus*, the religious substance symbolized by the Bible story is presented through the interaction of two compositional groupings. One of them is centered in the figure of Christ, which is placed symmetrically between the two disciples. This triangular arrangement is heightened by the equally symmetrical architecture of the background and by the light radiating from the center. It shows the traditional hierarchy of religious pictures, culminating in the divine figure. However, this pattern is not allowed to

occupy the center of the canvas. The group of figures is shifted somewhat to the left, leaving room for a second apex, created by the head of the servant boy. The second triangle is steeper and more dramatic also by its lack of symmetry. The head of Christ is no longer dominant but fitted into the sloping edge. Rembrandt's thinking strikingly envisages, in the basic form of the painting, the Protestant version of the New Testament. The humility of the Son of God is expressed compositionally not only in the slight deviation of the head from the central axis of the otherwise symmetrical pyramid of the body; Christ appears also as subservient to another hierarchy, which has its high point in the humblest figure of the group, namely, the servant. (p. 269)

Let's translate Arnheim's commentary into the language of cognitive linguistics. A grouping is the imposition of a CONTAINER schema, a bounding of a region of space with figures contained within. Arnheim describes two such schemas, one without the servant boy and one with him. In the inner CONTAINER schema, Christ is in the center and highest. The metaphors interpreting this arrangement are IMPORTANT IS CENTRAL and DIVINE IS UP. Not only is Christ, the divine, the highest, but he is looking up, toward the divine God. In the upper grouping, the servant boy appears. He is painted as being in the middle of an action, serving Christ food. This puts him socially below Christ, but Christ is painted as below him, the metaphor being HU-MILITY IS DOWN. The same metaphor interprets the structure of the servant boy's body: he is bowing, tilting his body down toward Christ, showing *his* humility. The action of serving Christ food is metaphorical for serving Christ. The light emanating from Christ instantiates one of our culture's basic metaphors for God: God is the source of what is good, in this case the source of light, which is interpreted via two conventional metaphors: MORALITY IS LIGHT and KNOWLEDGE IS LIGHT. The image schemas structuring the painting are orientational: HIGH-LOW, two CONTAINER schemas, two CENTER-PERIPHERY schemas, and LIGHT-DARK. Our conventional cultural metaphors apply to these schemas structuring the painting, to give it a meaning expressing an important aspect of the Protestant religious tradition: The ordinary person serves Christ in all humility, while Christ, the most important figure as the source of goodness and knowledge, sets the example, showing his own hu-mility relative to people, and looking upward to God.

Arnheim's point is that form is not just form; metaphors apply to forms to give meaning. Form is therefore a vehicle for inference, and the content of the inference depends on the metaphor.

Let us turn now to one more of Arnheim's examples: Jean-Baptiste-Camille Corot's *Mother and Child on the Beach* (John G. Johnson Collection, Philadelphia). Arnheim compares this painting with Henry Moore's 1934 *Two Forms* (The Museum of Modern Art; see http://theartfulmind.stanford.edu for both). Arnheim includes a line drawing (his figure 73*a*, p. 273) showing the similarities in the forms of the two works. Here is Arnheim's commentary:

> The child, symmetrical and frontal, reposes like a self-contained,
> independent little monument, whereas the figure of the mother is
> fitted to a bending and reaching wave shape, expressing protection
> and concern. Moore's carving, equally complex and subtle, embodies
> a very similar theme. The smaller of the two units is compact and
> self-sufficient like Corot's infant, although it also strains noticeably
> towards its partner. The larger seems wholly engaged in its leaning
> over the smaller, dominating it, holding it down, protecting, en-
> compassing, receiving it. One can find parallels to human or other-
> wise natural situations in this work: the relation of mother and child,
> spelled out in the Corot, or that of male and female. Such associa-
> tions rely on the similarity of the inherent patterns of forces.

One of Talmy's (1988) great contributions to cognitive linguistics is his analysis of force dynamics and the way that forces enter into the meaning of language. Talmy has taught us that the image schemas that characterize meaning in language are not just about vision. They are also about action and the application of force. In short, form is embodied, and Arnheim's com-mentary shows an acute awareness of the embodiment of form. The child's symmetrical form indicates that it is grounded and sitting independently—not exerting force in any direction. The shape of the mother's body shows that she is attending to the child, bending, reaching, adjusting her balance, ad-justing her body to the position of the child. Again the mother is in the middle of an action, and the action is determined by the position, size, weight, and demeanor of the child.

We know this because we, too, have bodies—and mirror neurons, a system of neurons forming a cluster across the premotor and parietal cortices with bidirectional connections. These neurons fire when we perform a coor-dinated action or see a corresponding action performed. Our understanding of Corot's painting depends on our systems of mirror and canonical neurons; it depends on our being able to see an image of a body in mid-motion acting on something, feel what it would be to perform that motion and action, and thereby know what is involved in the motion. As Arnheim observes, our ability to do this is not dependent on the details of meaning—a mother, a child, the beach, short sleeves, a long skirt, and so on. The capacity for such understanding applies to Moore's abstract sculpture as well. How?

The Cog Hypothesis

An answer to this question requires a discussion of the Cog Hypothesis and the neural theory of metaphor. We will therefore take a bit of a detour, returning to Corot and Moore—and looking at other paintings—after a digression.

Aspect as the Exploitation of Motor Control Schemas

Any complex coordinated action must make use of at least two brain areas— the premotor cortex and the motor cortex—which are separated in the brain and linked by neural connections. The motor cortex controls individual synergies—relatively simple actions like opening and closing the fist, turning the wrist, flexing and extending the elbow, and so on. The job of the premotor cortex is motor control: structuring such simple actions into coordinated complex actions, with the simple synergies performed just at the right time, moving in the right direction, with the right force, for the right duration. That is, the premotor cortex must provide a phase structure to actions and specify just the right activations of effectors, directions, and degrees of force in just the right phases. This information must be conveyed from the premotor to the motor cortex by neural connections activating just the right regions of the motor cortex. And of course, the same premotor circuitry that governs motor control for actions must govern motor control for simulated actions in our imagination—since imagined perceptions and actions use some of the same neural substrate as actual perceptions and actions.

Narayanan (1997b) has constructed dynamic neural computational models of such circuitry, including, of course, the parameters—choice of effector, direction of motion, degree and duration of force, and so on—governing their operation. In doing so, Narayanan made an important discovery: the same relatively simple phase structures for bodily actions recur in case after case— sometimes in sequence, sometimes in parallel, sometimes embedded in one another. That is, complex motor control structures are combinations of the same simple motor-control structures. Here is such a simple structure:

- Initial State
- Starting Phase Transition
- Precentral State

- Central Phase Transition (either instantaneous, prolonged, or ongoing)
- Postcentral State*
- Ending Phase Transition
- Final State

*Postcentral Options:

- A check to see if a goal state has been achieved
- An option to stop
- An option to resume
- An option to iterate or continue the main process

To perform a motor action, you have to be in a state of readiness (e.g., your body correctly oriented, having sufficient energy, and so on). Next, you have to do whatever is involved in starting the process (e.g., to lift a cup, you first have to reach for it and grasp it). Now you are in a position to perform the main process. While the central action is still in process, you check to see if a goal state has been achieved. You may stop, and, having stopped, may resume. You can then repeat or continue the central process. Finally, you can do whatever it takes to complete the process. Then you are in the final state. Of course, some actions are even simpler, leaving out some of these phases.

These are the phases of just about any bodily movement—with more complex movements constructed by branching into parallel, sequential, or embedded structures of this form. The *grasping schema*, for example, has such a phase structure:

Initial State: Object Location: Within Peri-personal Space
Starting Phase Transition: Reaching, with Direction: Toward Object
    Location; Opening Effector
Central Phase Transition: Closing Effector, with Force: A Function of
    Fragility and Mass
Goal Condition: Effector Encloses Object, with Manner (a grip deter-
    mined by parameter values and situational conditions)
Final State: Agent In-Control-of Object

Narayanan (1997a, 1997b) called the circuitry for controlling phases of motor control the "controller executing schema," or "controller X-schema" for short. A schema using such a structure—for example, the *grasping schema*—is called an executing schema, or "X-schema" for short.

Linguists are familiar with phase structures of this kind. They occur in the conceptual structure of every language in the world, and go by the name "aspect." For example, *be + ing* marks a central phase transition: "He is drinking" indicates that he is in the central phase of the act of drinking. *About + to* marks the initial state, as in "He is about to take a drink." *Have + past participle* picks out a point in time and indicates that the final state of the action occurred prior to the given time and that the consequences of that action still hold at that time. Thus, "I have done the food shopping" indicates that, at present, the final stage of the FOOD SHOPPING schema has been reached, with the consequence that we still have food. In short, linguistic aspect markers indicate what portion of a given schema has been carried out to date. The term "state" is relative to the controller X-schema. What we experience as an ongoing state (e.g., being annoyed) would be characterized in the model as a phase transition that is ongoing for the duration of that state.

Motor control is about *actions*, which are performed. Aspect is about *concepts*, which are used in reasoning. Narayanan (1997a, 1997b) showed, in his model, that the same structures that can move a body can also be exploited for reason and language. This is not surprising for action concepts like *grasping*, given that it is a sensory-motor concept. But *all* predicational concepts have aspect. It doesn't matter what kind—actions, processes, and states, both concrete and abstract. What Narayanan showed through modeling was that the same neural circuitry that is capable of *performing motor control* in the premotor cortex is also capable of *computing the logic of aspect*. The same circuitry that can *control phases* can *compute the logic of phases* for both concrete and abstract concepts.

Here are the elements of Narayanan's theory:

- The neural system characterizing the controller X-schema structure resides in the premotor cortex, where it performs motor control. Indeed, region F5 of the premotor cortex contains neurons whose firing corresponds to phases of particular actions.
- Since the same structure is used for observing, acting, and simulating, that neural system must contain mirror neurons.
- The controller X-schema can perform its computations even when all of its connections to the motor cortex are inhibited.
- There is neural circuitry from the premotor controller X-schemas to other, nonmotor domains, allowing the premotor structure to be exploited for structuring other conceptual domains.

If there were no such exploitative circuitry, exactly the same X-schema structure would have to be duplicated in many other parts of the brain for all abstract predicational concepts, no matter what the subject matter. The reason is that there are many nonconcrete subject matters with the same aspectual structure: emotions, thinking, sensing, and so on. Narayanan's theory is plausible because we recognize, in his account of cognitive operations, the sort of things that brains do: exploit computations in one part of the brain and use them via neural connections in other parts of the brain. The theory explains why exactly the same computational structure needed to run a body will compute the logic of aspect for every kind of concept there is, no matter where in the brain it is characterized.

Narayanan's theory that motor control is exploited for aspect in this manner leads us to a new concept, what I call a *cog*.

The Nature of Cogs and the Cog Hypothesis

A cog is a neural circuit with the following properties:

- A cog provides general structuring for sensory-motor observation, action, and simulation: the specific details for this general structure are filled in via neural connections to other regions of the brain; it is in those regions that the "details" that fill in the cog structure are characterized. When functioning in this way, the cog circuit is a natural, normal, seamless part of the sensory-motor system—as when the controller X-schema is used to control the action of taking a drink.
- A cog performs its neural computations even when the connections to the specific details are inhibited.
- A cog can be exploited to characterize the structure of "abstract" concepts.
- A cog's computations, which evolved to serve sensory-motor purposes, also characterize a "logic" and can be used for reasoning. Since the cog can attach to any specific details, its computations characterize a general form of logic (e.g., the logic of aspect, which applies generally to any action, process, or state).
- A cog can function in language as the meaning (or part of the meaning) of a grammatical construction or grammatical morpheme.

Thus, if Narayanan's hypothesis is correct, the controller X-schema, which characterizes the semantics of aspect in all of the world's languages, is a cog. The Cog Hypothesis generalizes this idea further.

The Cog Hypothesis: any neural structure that characterizes the semantics of a grammatical construction is a cog.

We will give more examples of cogs shortly. But before we do, we should consider why the Cog Hypothesis is initially plausible. Grammatical constructions and morphemes have general meanings. The plural morpheme pluralizes *all relevant concepts*. The first-person morpheme indicates a speaker, no matter who the speaker is. Or consider the *Forced Motion Construction*, which consists of a Force followed by a Patient followed by a Path. It applies in general, with specific details filled in; e.g., "Harry knocked the lamp off the table," where *knock* = Force Predicate, *lamp* = Patient, and *off the table* = Path. It also applies to metaphorical forced-motion cases, where the *Event Structure Metaphor* (cf. Lakoff and Johnson 1999, chap. 11) maps forces to causes, motions to changes, and bounded regions of space to states; for example, "The home run threw the crowd into a frenzy" and "The election knocked global warming off the legislative agenda." Under the Cog Hypothesis, we would expect to find grammatical meanings to be general in this way, able to fit both concrete and nonconcrete instances.

But such generality characterizes only part of what a cog is. It should also function normally, naturally, and seamlessly as part of the sensory-motor system in which it presumably evolved. With this in mind, let us consider other potential cogs.

Other Candidates for Cogs

Image schemas and force-dynamic schemas, as discussed above, are excellent candidates for cogs. These primitives (1) all have primary sensory-motor uses; and (2) are all general, with links to specific details. Some prepositions are primarily spatial (e.g., *out, around*), while others primarily involve force (e.g., *against*). Regier (1996) has argued that the visual system of the brain provides the right kinds of structures and operations to characterize the visual components of spatial-relations concepts. He has constructed neural computational models (using structured connectionism) of such spatial primitives. The models make use of computational analogues of topographic maps of the visual field, excitatory and inhibitory connections, within-map and across-map connections, center-surround receptive fields, orientation-sensitive cells, spreading activation, gating of connections—and, in more recent work, vector-sum ensembles. Regier has tested these models on language acquisition tasks, in which a program embodying the model has to learn often complex spatial-relations words on the basis of (1) a visual input with figures in a spatial relation, and (2) a range of positive exemplars (no negative cases). The program has worked to within 99 percent accuracy on examples taken from English, Russian, Arabic, Hindi, and Mixtec. Thus far, Regier has built no models of motor- or force-dynamic primitives.

Regier's model as it stands is only two-dimensional, and is limited in other ways. It is far too simple to be ultimately correct. But Regier's insights are important. He has argued convincingly that the visual system of the brain has the right kinds of neural structures to compute the visual components of primitive image schemas and to link them to each other and to specific details, so as to handle complex cases.

The CONTAINER schema is a good case in point. The CONTAINER schema has an interior, a boundary, an exterior, and optional portals; the concepts *in* and *out* make use of it. In perception, the CONTAINER schema fits or imposes an interior-boundary-exterior schema onto entities and regions of space. For example, a cup is a container, and so is a room. The details are very different, but we perceive and conceptualize both using the same general image schema. A tube of toothpaste can be seen as a doorstop, a backscratcher, a weapon—or a container!

In Regier's model, the CONTAINER schema is computed in the visual cortex. It is general and can be fitted to objects of all sorts of shapes—shapes which are computed elsewhere in the brain (for example, the temporal and parietal cortices). There is a logic of containers: If something is in the container, it's not out; if it's out, it's not in. If container A is in container B, and object X is in A, then X is in B—and if X is outside B, then X is outside A. This is basically Boolean logic, and presumably where Boolean logic comes from. Since prepositions like *in* and *out* are among the grammatical morphemes of English, the CONTAINER schema is part of the semantics of English grammar.

Many conceptual metaphors apply to the CONTAINER schema. States, for example, are conceptualized as containers: you can be *in* or *out* of a state, on the *edge* of a state, *deeply in* a state, *far from* being *in* a state, and so on. Categories are commonly conceptualized as containers, with category members *in* the categories. Occasionally the *boundaries* of a category can be *stretched* to accommodate an *outlier*. There are many, many more cases.

As Talmy (2000) has shown, the actions using force fall into a small number of general types, what he calls force-dynamic schemas. Thus, shoving and throwing involve a propulsion force on an object away from the body, resulting in motion. Bringing and carrying involve a continuous application of force, resulting in motion. Holding force keeps an object with a tendency to move in place. Supporting force keeps an entity subject to gravity from falling. The same general force-dynamic schemas govern the occurrence of force in many different actions.

Neuroscience has studied specific systems for controlling force in the body, but it has not yet found general force-dynamic schemas. It is plausible that they, or something like them, exist in the brain. Conceptual metaphors apply to force-dynamic schemas, the most common of which is the CAUSES ARE FORCES metaphor, which maps *forces that result in motion* onto *causes that result in change*. We saw examples of this above in cases like "The home run threw the crowd into a frenzy" and "The election knocked global warming off the legislative agenda." Another force-dynamic metaphor is HELP IS SUPPORT, as in "I can count on her for support," "He is supporting five children," "I'm supporting Goldberg for Senator," where help of various kinds—emotional, financial, and political—is understood in terms of a support force-dynamic schema.

A Return to Form in Art (at Last!)

The theory of form in art we are about to present rests on the idea of a cog: there are neural structures in the sensory-motor system that are "secondary" or "general" in the sense that they are connected neurally to "primary" neural ensembles that fill in the details and are more directly involved in either perception or movement. An obvious example would be premotor cortical structures that carry out highly structured complex motor actions via connections to the primary motor cortex, which controls simple actions. When the premotor-to-motor connections are inhibited, the secondary premotor circuitry can function as a "cog"—it can still compute complex patterns that permit inferences and can evolve in time. Such secondary patterns—cogs—structure what we perceive as form in art. Many kinds of cogs have been hypothesized—for example, image schemas, force-dynamic schemas, and aspectual schemas—and each type corresponds to an aspect of form.

Let us now return to where we left off in our discussion of Corot and Henry Moore. We had just made use of the existence of mirror neurons and canonical neurons to explain how we know that the mother in Corot's painting is attending to the child—bending, reaching, adjusting her balance, adjusting her body to the position of the child. We noted, too, that we can understand the larger chunk of Moore's abstract sculpture as performing similar actions—brooding over the smaller chunk, stretching out to reach it, hovering over it, protecting it. How, we had asked, is this possible?

Cogs provide the answer. Cogs include aspectual schemas with phase structures, image schemas, and force-dynamic schemas. They inhibit connections to the primary neural structures that would fill in specific details—the beach, a long skirt, and so on—while including the secondary neural structures. These cogs are at once embodied, since they are part of the sensory-motor system, and "abstract," since they do not include details. Cogs give structure to culture, and conceptual metaphors give substantive meaning to the cogs. Cogs allow us to have an embodied understanding of the form of abstract art, and metaphors apply to cog structures to provide interpretations for abstract art.

Further Examples

After reinterpreting Arnheim in terms of cogs and conceptual metaphors, I decided to test my hypothesis on other cases. I went onto the Web and picked out a handful of paintings at random. Here they are, discussed one by one.

The first is an image, "Wounded Bison Attacking a Man," c. 15,000–10,000 B.C.E., from Lascaux, France (see http://theartfulmind.stanford.edu). What is particularly interesting in this case is the aspect cog. The various parts of the painting represent different phases of a scenario: the bison is wounded (weapon in bison at left); the bison charges the man (the bison's head is down, with horns in attack position and hackles up); the man is dead (he lies on the ground, with penis in rigor mortis). The painting is composed around the phase structure of the action, with the elements of the scenario ordered visually left to right, earliest phase to latest.

The next example is Gustave Caillebotte's *Le pont de l'Europe,* 1876 (Petit Palais, Geneva; see http://theartfulmind.stanford.edu). The first thing to notice about this painting is that although it portrays a sunny day, there is no single position that the sun can be in, given the shadows. For example, the shadows of the man and woman walking are behind them, suggesting that the sun is low and in front of them, while the shadow of the dog is to his left, suggesting that the sun is high and to the right. The shadow of the bridge is not consistent with either of those.

The organizing structure of this painting is the parallel-lines schema. There are parallels everywhere, and that explains the shadows—they are set up to form parallels. The man and the woman form parallel lines, and so do their shadows. The dog and his shadow form parallels. The support structure of the bridge is a series of parallels forming X's. The parallels are repeated in the shadow of the bridge. The top of the bridge is parallel to the top of its shadow and to the top of the railing that the man in blue is leaning against. That railing consists of ovals whose sides are parallels. The man in the cap walking in the background is parallel to the man and woman, and his shadow is parallel to the shadow of the bridge top. The line of the curb is parallel to the lines of the handrail and the bridge top. The buildings on the street going off into the distance are parallel. The buildings in the distance have parallel horizontal lines and their windows have vertical parallel lines.

Another organizing form is the aspect schema for walking: the man and the woman are in the middle phase of walking, with one foot outstretched. That is true of the dog, the man in the cap, and the man way in the distance to the left. The man leaning against the railing is not walking, but he, too, is resting his weight on one foot (his left), while the toe of his right shoe lightly touches the ground.

The next example is Wayne Thiebaud's *24th Street Intersection* (1977, private collection; see http://theartfulmind.stanford.edu). The Thiebaud painting is structured in two ways: by parallels and by a downward slope evoking the pull of gravity. Let's start by noticing the parallels. First, there are the parallel lines of the streets and the lines in the middle of the streets, then the parallel lines of the sides of the houses, then the parallel lines of the trees and the telephone poles and the shadows of the telephone poles, and finally the parallel lines of the wires. The pull of gravity is sensed in the hill streets, upper left to lower right, and the hill straight ahead. The lone bus in the distance at the top of the hill looks like it's about to roll backwards, and the car to the right looks like it's about to roll downwards. The two organizing principles—parallels and downward force—come together where the hill meets the houses. It appears as though the houses are holding up the hill.

The next example is Mark Tansey's *Derrida Queries de Man* (1990, collection of Mike and Penny Winton; see http://theartfulmind.stanford.edu). This painting is based on a Sidney Paget illustration from a Sherlock Holmes mystery (*The Final Problem*, by Arthur Conan Doyle, 1893; see http://theartful mind.stanford.edu). In the Paget illustration, Holmes and Moriarty are fighting to the death on a cliff.

Tansey has, quite consciously, created a metaphorical painting, in which Derrida (a French Jew) is the Holmes-like analytical hero and de Man (the Belgian ex-Nazi writer of anti-Semitic tracts) is the brilliantly diabolical villain. Derrida is perhaps best known for his metaphor THE WORLD IS A TEXT— something to be interpreted indefinitely, especially with respect to other texts, with no "correct" interpretations. Tansey's painting itself, by its reference back to the Holmes-Moriarty drawing, is an example of Derridean intertextuality— the dependence of one text on another for its meaning. The "query" is an intellectual battle, perhaps based on de Man's questioning of Derrida's reading of Rousseau. Tansey's painting is metaphorical in another way: If you look closely at the foreground, you can see that the cliff itself is made up of letters: in the painting, the world *is* a text. (See http://theartfulmind.stanford .edu for detail.)

The painting makes central use of force dynamics. Derrida and de Man, dressed in suits, are pushing against each other. They are high up, at the edge of a deep and rocky chasm: de Man is close to the edge, seemingly in a position where Derrida could push him off, but Derrida is in a perilous position as well. There is light peering through the chasm, but a dense fog prevents it from coming through clearly. The metaphor KNOWING IS SEEING allows us to understand the light as the light of knowledge, barely able to penetrate the fog of verbiage in the philosophers' writings. Though functioning at a metaphorically high level, de Man and Derrida are skirting the edge of sense, in danger of falling into an intellectual chasm. The "querying" is seen as Derrida exerting force intellectually on de Man, trying to push him into the chasm—a perilous place where there is no solid ground to stand on.

Here again we see how common metaphors, applying to image schemas and force-dynamic schemas, can contribute meaning to a painting.

Conclusion

Beginning with Arnheim's insights, we have arrived at a theory of form in art and its relation to substantive content. The Cog Hypothesis explains how form can be at once embodied (in the sensory-motor system), permitting inference, and subject to metaphorical interpretation, while being "abstract."

Cogs are complex neural structures that are "secondary" and provide structuring to "primary" sensory-motor content elsewhere in the brain via neural connections. When those neural connections are inhibited, cogs still function, subject to neural computation, and may have connections to other, non-sensory-motor parts of the brain. Examples of cogs are aspectual schemas, image schemas, and force-dynamic schemas. Realist art contains rich images structured by cogs. The images can be structured so that the cogs interact in interesting ways with the content of the images and with conventional metaphors applying to the cog structures.

Arnheim was right that form in art is not "mere" form. Form has inferential structure and may express content in the right context. He was also right that form is not *in* the art per se. Form has to do with us, in particular with the kinds of embodied structures we impose by virtue of our bodies and brains.

REFERENCES

Arnheim, R. 1969. *Visual thinking*. Berkeley: University of California Press.
Boroditsky, L. 1997. Evidence for metaphoric representation: Perspective in space and time. In *Proceedings of the nineteenth annual conference of the Cognitive Science Society*, ed. M. G. Shafto and P. Langley (p. 869). Mahwah, N.J.: Lawrence Erlbaum Associates.

Brugman, C. 1981. *Story of Over: Polysemy, semantics, and the structure of the lexicon*. New York and London: Garland.

Casad, E., and R. W. Langacker. 1985. "Inside" and "outside." In *International Journal of American Linguistics*, ed. C. Grammer, 51: 247–81.

Farah, M. J. 1989. The neural basis of mental imagery. *Trends in Neuroscience*, 12: 395–99.

———. 2000. The neural bases of mental imagery. In *The cognitive neurosciences*, ed. M. S. Gazzaniga (2nd. ed.), 963–75. Cambridge, Mass.: MIT Press.

Fauconnier, G., and M. Turner. 2002. *The way we think: Conceptual blending and the mind's hidden complexities*. New York: Basic Books.

Gallese, V. 2000a. The acting subject: Towards the neural basis of social cognition. In *Neural correlates of consciousness: Empirical and conceptual questions*, ed. T. Metzinger, 325–33. Cambridge, Mass.: MIT Press.

———. 2000b. The inner sense of action: Agency and motor representations. *Journal of Consciousness Studies*, 7, no. 10: 23–40.

———. 2001. The "shared manifold" hypothesis: From mirror neurons to empathy. *Journal of Consciousness Studies*, 8, nos. 5–7: 33–50.

———. 2003. A neuroscientific grasp of concepts: From control to representation. *Philosophical Transactions of the Royal Society, B*: 1231–40.

Gallese, V., and A. Goldman. 1998. Mirror neurons and the simulation theory of mind-reading. *Trends in Cognitive Science*, 12: 493–501.

Gallese, V., L. Fadiga, L. Fogassi, and G. Rizzolatti. 1996. Action recognition in the premotor cortex. *Brain*, 119: 593–609.

———. 2002. Action representation & the inferior parietal lobule. In *Attention and Performance XIX*, ed. W. Prinz and B. Hommel, 247–66. Oxford, England: Oxford University Press.

Gibbs, R. W., Jr. 1994. *The poetics of mind: Figurative thought, language, and understanding*. Cambridge, England: Cambridge University Press.

Grady, J. 1997. *Foundations of meaning: Primary metaphors and primary scenes*. Ph.D. Dissertation, University of California at Berkeley.

Johnson, M. 1987. *The body in the mind: The bodily basis of meaning, imagination and reason*. Chicago: University of Chicago Press.

Kemper, S. 1989. Priming the comprehension of metaphors. *Metaphor and Symbolic Activity*, 4: 1–18.

Lakoff, G. 1987. *Women, fire, and dangerous things: What categories reveal about the mind*. Chicago and London: University of Chicago Press.

Lakoff, G., and M. Johnson. 1980. *Metaphors we live by*. Chicago and London: University of Chicago Press.

———. 1999. *Philosophy in the flesh*. New York: Basic Books.

Lakoff, G., and M. Turner. 1989. *More than cool reason: A field guide to poetic metaphor*. Chicago and London: University of Chicago Press.

Langacker, R. W. 1986, 1991. *Foundations of cognitive grammar*. 2 vols. Stanford, Calif.: Stanford University Press.

———. 1990. *Concept, image, and symbol: The cognitive basis of grammar*. Berlin and New York: Mouton de Gruyter.

Lindner, S. 1981. *A lexico-semantic analysis of verb-particle constructions with* up *and* out. Ph.D. Dissertation, University of California at San Diego.

Narayanan, S. 1997a. *Embodiment in language understanding: Sensory-motor representations for metaphoric reasoning about event descriptions.* Ph.D. Dissertation, Department of Computer Science, University of California at Berkeley.

———. 1997b. Talking the talk *is* like walking the walk: A computational model of verbal aspect. In *Proceedings of the nineteenth annual conference of the Cognitive Science Society*, ed. M. G. Shafto and P. Langley. Mahwah, N.J.: Lawrence Erlbaum Associates.

Regier, T. 1995. A model of the human capacity for categorizing spatial relations. *Cognitive Linguistics*, 6, no. 1: 63–88.

———. 1996. *The human semantic potential: Spatial language and constrained connectionism.* Cambridge, Mass.: MIT Press.

Rizzolatti, G., R. Camarda, L. Fogassi, M. Gentilucci, G. Luppino, and M. Matelli. 1998. Functional organization of inferior area 6 in the macaque monkey: II. Area F5 and the control of distal movements. *Experimental Brain Research*, 71: 491–507.

Rizzolatti, G., L. Fadiga, L. Fogassi, and V. Gallese. 1997. The space around us. *Science*, 277: 190–91.

Rizzolatti, G., L. Fadiga, V. Gallese, and L. Fogassi. 1996. Premotor cortex and the recognition of motor actions. *Cognitive Brain Research*, 3: 131–41.

Rizzolatti, G., L. Fogassi, and V. Gallese. 2000. Cortical mechanisms subserving object grasping and action recognition: A new view on the cortical motor functions. In *The cognitive neurosciences*, ed. M. S. Gazzaniga (2nd. ed.), 539–52. Cambridge, Mass.: MIT Press.

———. 2001. Neurophysiological mechanisms underlying the understanding and imitation of action. *Nature Neuroscience Reviews*, 2: 661–70.

———. 2002. Motor and cognitive functions of the ventral premotor cortex. *Current Opinion in Neurobiology*, 12: 149–54.

Rizzolatti, G., C. Scandolara, M. Gentilucci, and R. Camarda. 1981. Response properties and behavioral modulation of "mouth" neurons of the postarcuate cortex (area 6) in macaque monkeys. *Brain Research*, 255: 421–24.

Sweetser, E. 1990. *From etymology to pragmatics: Metaphorical and cultural aspects of semantic structure.* Cambridge, England: Cambridge University Press.

Talmy, L. 1983. How language structures space. In *Spatial orientation: Theory, research, and application*, ed. H. L. Pick and L. P. Acredolo. New York: Plenum Press.

———. 1988. Force dynamics in language and cognition. *Cognitive Science*, 12: 49–100.

———. 1996. Fictive motion in language and "ception." In *Language and space*, ed. P. Bloom, M. Peterson, L. Nadel, and M. Garrett, 211–75. Cambridge, Mass.: MIT Press.

———. 2000. *Toward a cognitive linguistics.* Cambridge, Mass.: MIT Press.

9

Form and Meaning in Art

Per Aage Brandt

I distinguish two styles of perception: one is pragmatic and action-oriented, the other is aesthetic and affect-oriented. I outline a cognitive-semiotic theory of conceptual organization and semantic integration in general. Both the meaning structures found in art and the surplus meanings of things, their "connotations," are based on nonintegrated structures that tend to be integrated on higher levels of mental architecture. The emphatic splitting of experienced situational meaning into two mutually mapping mental spaces—a content space and an expression space—which is characteristic of the phenomenology of works of art and other aesthetically perceived objects, is due to this phenomenon of unintegrated surplus structures. I discuss examples from art criticism and from paintings by Monet and Magritte. I propose an epistemological view of the relationship between the cognitive approach to art and the art-historical approach and show their complementary status. In fact, autonomous art must be historical—it must elaborate ever-changing styles—because pragmatic conceptualizations would otherwise absorb the authority it necessarily generates.

Aesthetic vs. Pragmatic Perception: The Phenomenology of Form

Most people probably know the strange and involuntary shift in everyday experience of things, problems, and scenarios that can suddenly make even the most trivial and ordinary "contents of consciousness" appear to us as unique and rare phenomena, as autonomous *formal* objects. Our experiences of *form*, unfolding in abstract space and time, are distinct from our experiences of concerns and states of affairs in the ordinary world and associated with various special aspects of subjectivity: religious affect, extreme mental stress or mild depression, erotic arousal, or perceptions of art. In all of these cases, we experience a sensorily achieved presence of "beauty"—in fact, an "aesthetic" presence, although the frame is widely variable. In the specific case of perceptions of art, the experience is intentionally enhanced by the aesthetic artifact—an object elaborated under special conditions as a sign of the artist's formal attention. Artists are able to voluntarily achieve, and intentionally communicate, formal perceptions. This is what they are trying to do when they are "at work," configuring the sharply framed expressions—poems, dramas, musical performances, paintings, and so on—that we call works of art. These objects are given special treatment by our cognitive system. The mind of our species allows us both an ordinary, *pragmatic* register of extensive, unbounded (weakly framed), content-oriented perception and conceptualization, and, additionally and occasionally, this extraordinary, *aesthetic* register of intensive, bounded (strongly framed), and form-oriented hyper-perception that we experience par excellence in art.

In art, and perhaps even in some nonartistic experiences of beauty, the shift from pragmatic to formal perception has a series of immediate effects:

1. It endows the expressive source with a hyper-concrete mode of sensory presence, even as it creates a hyper-abstract mode of conceptual processing. This combination makes the expressive act an instance of *symbolization.*[1]

2. It converts the reception of the expressive source into an intensely active (or interactive) *construction* or "close reading"—a search for a "symbolic" meaning, an abstract message of some sort, supposedly built into and therefore present in the sensorily accessible source. Because this meaning is experienced as inherent in form as such, it is in principle experienced as accessible to the constructive interpreter of form.

3. It creates a transcendent, affective communal atmosphere, an intersubjective feeling of unity, intentionally oriented toward the shared unique instant in which the *epiphanic* presence of this meaning occurs. Again, this meaning (of each work of art or performance) is conveyed by the formal structure of the source, and in its presence we are touched and moved, as if by some "spirit."

4. Finally, the perceptual shift affects the "self" of performers and perceivers, momentarily creating a euphoric, even ecstatic, feeling of *disembodiment* or fading of the personal "I."

These four phenomenological aspects of formal perception—*symbolization, construction, epiphany,* and *disembodiment*—are all relevant as we seek to understand the role of art in human cognition and cultural evolution. This essay will outline some basic aspects of a theoretical and analytical approach to the issue, operating within the framework of a naturalistic project of research on meaning and human cognition.

A Neuro-Semantic "Economy" of Aesthetic Perception

When consciousness is awake and aware, our organization of what we will call *meaning* is a process that occurs on many levels simultaneously. On a scale extending from the most dense, massive, and "concrete" sensations to the most transparent and "abstract" notional conceptualizations, we may distinguish a series of strata interrelated by subprocesses of integration. There are at least five such strata that the "mind's eye" can focus on, beginning with sensory inputs and proceeding "upward" toward abstract thinking and feeling (cf. Brandt 2003, chap. 10).

Thus, we may stipulate that (1) ongoing *sensation* of *forms* in different modalities (the visual, the auditory, the tactile, the proprioceptive) feeds (2) ongoing *perception* of "gestalted" and categorized *objects,* and that these feed into (3) an ongoing *apperception* of *situations.* The latter further informs (4) our trans-situational thinking, or what we may call *evaluative reflection.* And beyond this stratum, informed by it, lies (5) a rather contemplative and always affective last level of "abstraction," which is also—paradoxically, since it re-concretizes—an embodied and *action*-oriented translation of antecedent contents that constitutes our general *feeling,* including our emotional and thymic background states ("moods"). The general dynamics of this mental architecture, or of similar architectural models that we might discuss, appear to be based on two principles:

- All strata are simultaneously active, both neurally and mentally. This is not to say that they depend on one another in a hierarchical or vertical fashion; rather, they "run in parallel," so to speak, and can be either connected or disconnected. Since our attention can focus on any level of activity, we can deliberately "pay attention to" more concrete or more abstract contents (meanings), or even to both simultaneously, as in aesthetic perception.

When we communicate, our pathways of shared focus, or styles of attention, are the central concerns of our intersubjective attunement.[2]

- In this model, there is no linear "assembly line" of integration from
  one stratum to another.[3] Instead, there is a dynamic process of sub-
  sumption which is directly related to attention.[4] "Paying attention" to
  some ongoing sensation, perception, and so on, on stratum n causes it
  to be subsumed "under" a new integrative event on stratum $n + 1$.

The nonstrict overlayering of attentional foci by which semantic integration occurs means that our minds are capable of attuning plastically to
each other, attending jointly to a single event, on some (but not necessarily all)
strata. It also means that our multi-attentional minds can hold "private" ideas
and understandings and "public" (socially shared) conceptions at the same
time, or hold multiple versions of an event, idea, situation, side by side. This is
why, on the stratum of apperceptions, our minds can even hold entire networks of *mental spaces* (Fauconnier and Turner 2002; Brandt 2004) simultaneously and can creatively achieve and share operations of mapping,
blending, and compression between these local imaginary wholes.

Even more important, the overlaying of attentional foci means that the
process of integrating input material does not entirely consume it. A basic
binding—a Gestalt process integrating sensations into a perception of "something" present—makes the input material momentarily unavailable for alternative integrations or "readings": such qualia will then "belong to" the

A MODEL OF MENTAL ARCHITECTURE

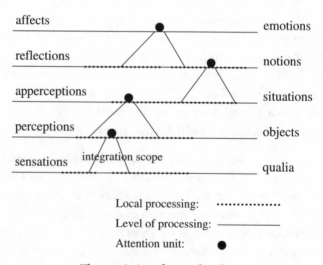

FIGURE 9.1. The semiotics of mental architecture.

things they are perceived as properties of ("orange" belongs to oranges, etc.). But even when the material is thus neutralized, it is in principle not entirely absorbed and erased by the integration. It stays "re-readable." The same principle may be at work on the next level, in the integration, or binding, of perceptions into situational-episodic apperceptions, and again at the level of evaluative reflections—for example, narrative, descriptive, and argumentative constructions. The latter are selected and reinforced as the imaginative contents of our feelings—the component that determines the *meaning* of our emotional states. All of these results of integration tend to stay flexible, "negotiable," revisable, open to change, unless the subject suffers from the *rigor mentis* characteristic of certain mental illnesses.[5]

The economy of mental construction is one of casual, short-term consumption and production, counteracted by long-term memory. It is furthermore, in this view, a "sloppy" economy, in which many early products are never used on later strata at all. Material that is processed and organized on one stratum may thus exceed or escape further integrative processing altogether. Such material may just be left here and there in the architecture, abandoned wherever it happens to be, in a state of complexity corresponding to the stratum on which it was processed. On any level, there may be a certain amount of surplus material, an *excess* of structured contents that the mental brain leaves unsubsumed, uninterpreted. This material may subsist on its own, and then either vanish or be recuperated by new integrating bindings. Or it may migrate from one construction to another, without ever "belonging to" any particular superordinate construction.[6]

My phenomenological point, then, is the following. Excess structure is experienced as

1. particularly salient and challenging, enigmatic or intriguing, calling for completion and determination: ambiguous, interrogative, even obsessive;
2. *aesthetically* relevant—that is, associated with a particular value called "beauty."

Excess structure is experienced in nature (from sunset skies and sand grooves to the ribs of leaves, the "songs" of birds, and other patterns of layered symmetries) and culturally in two predominant forms of human behavior: eroticism and expressive communication. Both of the latter can be experienced as variably "graceful"; and this aesthetic dimension is always relevant to our everyday evaluation of their manifestations.

Excess structure on level n is by definition uninterpreted on the $n+1$'th level, but may then activate recuperative integration on levels $n+2, n+3 \ldots$

In the work of art, excess structure is intentionally built into the input and is therefore likely to occur in sensory perception, from which it triggers partial sketches of higher-order integration—not on the next step, in categorial perception, but in apperception, in reflection, and most prominently in feeling. This is what we might take to be the fundamental occurrence in art and artful behavior. Art is any expressive or instrumental doing that deliberately creates excess structure. While "beauty" otherwise happens spontaneously in human life, it is intentionally *made* to happen in this genre of communication, which seems coextensive with the entire time and space of human civilization. Art is omnipresent in the human life-world, as is its contrary, the smooth functional integration of forms into useful objects, serving pragmatic purposes in our common life.

Excess structure that is stably recuperated on higher levels constitutes what we call *signs*.[7] Insofar as it stays unrecuperated, or unstably recuperated, it remains instead what we call *form*. The experience of art is therefore and by definition formal.

In the scale and scope of human cultural evolution, the semiotic recuperation of artistic form as significant may even be the main origin of *symbolization*.[8] However that may be, I would like to illustrate the neuro-phenomenological views presented here by some examples from painting and critical discourse on pictorial art.

The Cognitive Construction of Painting

On Colors, Brushstrokes, and Meaning

The American art critic Jed Perl writes the following in an article on painters Barnett Newman, Joan Mitchell, and Edwin Dickinson: "In *Vir Heroicus Sublimis*, the heat of the red is curiously counteracted or cooled by the smoothness of the paint-handling. Each quality or characteristic that Newman brings to the painting takes on an animistic power: the power of roughness or smoothness or thickness or thinness or brownness or redness or whiteness or orangeness" (Perl 2002, 28). Here, the events on the canvas are reportedly experienced as "taking on," and as either controlling or being controlled by, states or events in a noncanvas reality: "heat," "animistic power." The text continues:

> We respond to the orange and brown in *Onement I*, to the reds in
> *Vir Heroicus Sublimis*, and to the grayish-blue and off-white stripes on
> black in *The Promise* not as color orchestrations but as existential
> situations, as the inescapable nature of the painting, in much the way

that we think of a certain person as being blue-eyed or brown-eyed, a blond or a brunette. These paintings have a meaning that is encased in their most immediate and evident characteristics. (Perl 2002, 28)

Perceptions are reportedly processed in terms of "existential situations," and percepts are personalized. Likewise:

Mitchell's brushstrokes, both early and late, have a turning-back-on-themselves kind of stinging rococo power, and her finest paintings, composed of what can seem to be the infinite variety of such brushstrokes, are all elaborate flourish and steely accent. In the early work, this animated and elegant tracery sometimes has a sooty grayness that suggests a certain New York state of mind, a mentality that is at once excitable, pleasure-seeking, and world-weary. (Perl 2002, 29)

The brushstrokes, again, have "power" and can suggest a certain geographically determined "state of mind." "In Mitchell's paintings, each separate part, each stroke or group of strokes, functions with the vigor of muscle and bone and nerve, and together they give the work of art its pushing-out-from-within sense of well-being" (Perl 2002, 30). Strokes evoke concrete bodily "vigor," and they convey a "sense of well-being" that seems to proceed from within. Finally:

When Dickinson goes from working very tightly to working very loosely, I am left feeling that it is the *very*, the hyperbole itself, that really matters to him. In his drawings, which are among the high points of his art, he is carried along by the weight of the lines, whether they are the knife-edge ones or the soft, barely there ones. Dickinson is a remarkable renderer of the truths of this world, but people and places also seem to recede under the elegance of that line. (Perl 2002, 31)

There are Dickinson's lines, and there are the "people and places" that they make recede: two connected mental spaces, sometimes apparently merging phenomenologically into a strange space of strokes and ocean: "Dickinson can be at his most unruly and hyperbolic in those casual seascapes of his, in which the foaming Atlantic is reduced to a howl or growl of painterly strokes" (Perl 2002, 31). In this discourse, the strokes apparently *are* what they show, and can therefore "howl or growl."

Another critic, Peter Schjeldahl, writing on Lucian Freud, notes the following:

Hardly a painterly prodigy, as his clotted early canvases confirm, Freud taught himself to break up planes of faces and bodies into patches of color, Cézanne fashion, and to knit them together with close-toned hues and continuous textures of juicy brushwork. He achieved a distinctive, notably tactile way of modelling. It's as if his figures were brought into being by cumulative soft and rough touches—a caress here, a grab there. (Schjeldahl 2002, 72)

The Freudian brush can do amazing things to the figurative imagery involved:

No painter alive is more exciting in areas a few inches square, where Freud's brush may nuzzle into the hollow of a hip or cradle the exact weight of a sagging breast. This is more than a matter of skill, because the action symbolically unites hand, eye, mind, and sexual feeling. Too grossly frank to be conventionally erotic, the nakedness of Freud's subjects nonetheless evokes states of crude, indiscriminate arousal: mere lust. (Schjeldahl 2002, 72)

The nuzzling of the brush is an event effortlessly taking place in two realities or spaces at once—in the painting of the canvas and in a sexual situation.

In a comment on an exhibition at the National Gallery, "Fabric of Vision: Dress and Drapery in Painting," the critic Peter Campbell writes:

Drapery provides a good opportunity for a one-to-one relationship between brush strokes and the thing represented: the painter is never more free from constraint—and never more in danger of being flash—than when using a single stroke to show the crease in a sleeve or a rumpled twist of bedspread. In Fragonard's A Young Girl on Her Bed, Making Her Dog Dance it is not just the naughtiness of the subject, but the bustle of the brushwork that makes you smile. (Campbell 2002, 28)

The bustle of the brushwork—its indiscreet, daring caresses of the lovely subject—makes the critic smile: the blending of two realities, where one represents the other, triggers the humoristic affects of his mind.

We could easily go on, but these examples of the critical sensibility will suffice for our purpose. Meaning is manifestly assigned to what is happening *on* the canvas as much as it is drawn from what is being represented *by* the same canvas, and these two aspects tend to merge into a paradoxical experience of two-dimensional (2-D) expression and three-dimensional (3-D) content as aspects of one and the same event. To paint is to *touch* the things you see and show. Pictorial vision is tactile. A semantic miracle.

A Mental Space Network for Painting: Monet

In each of our examples,[9] two mental spaces blend. In one of them, the critic imagines a painter applying strokes on his canvas as intentional signs of something which is thereafter to be presented to someone. In the other space, there is a scene, a landscape, a motif or subject of some sort, and no painter.

Strictly speaking, there is, of course, a critic writing about such a "painting"; we are his readers and can go to the exhibitions he is commenting on. In terms of semiotic networks of mental spaces, this situation—where we have an exhibition, some critics, ourselves, and the physical objects called paintings—is our *base space*, from which we and the critics are now setting up the *presentation space* (painter, canvas, brushes, strokes on a two-dimensional surface) and the *reference space* (three-dimensional motif: scene, view, landscape, figure). The strokes in the presentation space are *mapped* onto the figurative events in the reference space—some strokes thereby becoming particularly fascinating. Furthermore, we have noticed the semantic existence of a *blended space* where strokes can "nuzzle" the motif, and where presentative events can thus paradoxically and humorously "be" other, referentially present events that they are not. The critic knows, of course, and knows that we know, that this blending occurs in an imaginary *as-if* mode, as a counterfactual experience. Something other than factuality must therefore make it relevant; and we know from general cultural education that the appearances of this counterfactual mode in the critic's discourse are the insignia of the work's aesthetic value. Aesthetic quality is the mode in which the viewer's attention is made to travel effortlessly between the contents of two mental spaces, the presentation space and the reference space. It is, further, the mode in which these contents are selectively brought together in a counterfactual blend and (almost) fused, in such a way that the *proximal* presence of the canvas establishes an almost bodily contact with the *distal* motif. (I am speaking here in terms of the rhetorical figure *hypotyposis*.) The vividness, the energy, and the intensity experienced through this process appear to be decisive for the subsequent aesthetic verdict. The blend must therefore additionally be somehow stabilized, independently cognized, and schematized by the relevance-making dynamics of attention. In our examples, the idea of a desiring painter whose feelings of love or something of that sort make *him* interpret a stroke as a caress, make *him* (the Model Author, as Umberto Eco would say) fuse the distal and the proximal in his erotic hallucination, transfigures the painting and produces the strong impact of an "intense thing," so to speak, a *res intensa*.[10]

Let us consider a classic instance of this universal semantic network of pictorial art: Claude Monet's early modernist paintings of reflected light—for example, his *Sunrise (Marine)*, 1873; and later his vast Giverny project, including the famous series of water lilies floating on his pond. The Orangerie set (Paris, 1916–1923) of very late works is a particularly clear case. (See http:// theartfulmind.stanford.edu for images of these works.)

The vertical (distal) figures of *Sunrise* contrast with the horizontal (proximal) reflections on the water, especially at the bottom of the picture; the strokes are much more "stroky" in the horizontal dimension than in the vertical. Strokes and reflections in the water, though they are given in separate mental spaces, locally map and match rather directly. Thus, the two surfaces, canvas and water level, are juxtaposed (or, rather, mentally superimposed), and the two dimensions meet phenomenologically in a blended representation where the surface of the water and that of the painting itself tend to fuse into an unrestful, tilting plane. The viewer is drawn toward a horizontal conceptualization both by the water motif and by the reflective strokes, but simultaneously toward a vertical conceptualization by the standard representational "window" in which the shown objects, the boats and their masts, would rise parallel to the "opening"—that is, the canvas. The phenomenological result is that the shimmering light is rendered tactile, in a sort of *photo-haptic synesthesia*.[11]

In the *Water Lilies* series, the horizontal flowers float on the invisible surface of the pond and contrast with the vertical reflections of the surrounding vegetation. This, again, creates a crossing of lines; but also, and more importantly, a conflict in the stroke qualities referring to the two properties of the smooth, transparent water, whose surface both reflects the vegetation and bears the lilies. The superposition and the crossing of vertical vegetation and horizontal water lilies are all we know (see, cognize) of this surface. The result is that the motif appears to fall forward onto the canvas and then to tilt back into its windowed space. We get once more the intensely vivid impression of standing in front of a "pond of paint" tilting between 2-D and 3-D. The physical dimensions of the *Water Lilies* canvases (cf. the reconstruction of the Orangerie walls at the Museum of Modern Art in New York) contribute to the vertiginous feeling of spatial dissolution that these paintings can produce.

A "cool" version of the same semantic mystery is given by René Magritte in his well-known *Tentative de l'impossible* (1928), showing a scene of painting: the nude stands in front of the painter, who touches her shoulder with the brush precisely where her left arm is going to be when he finishes his brushwork.[12] (See http://theartfulmind.stanford.edu for an image of this work.) The general structure of this network of mental spaces is summarized by figure 9.2.

The assumption, then, would be that all artistic painting, regardless of what else it achieves, offers this tension between its presentation and its reference, thereby creating the blend that our aesthetic sensitivity captures in its desire-based schema of attentional dynamics. Or, to put the matter differently, *we* are momentarily captured by the tilting fusion of our input spaces, and then experience an expression counterfactually coinciding with its content, a form merging with its meaning. The impact of this *res intensa* on the human mind is emotional. Art is crucial to emotional communication in the human world, and all celebrations and rituals make use of it, publicly as well as privately, from ceremonies of warfare to declarations of love. We may gain some clues to the production of this effect if we combine the outlined mental space analysis with the model of mental architecture proposed above.

Theoretically, our mental-space phenomenology unfolds on the apperceptional stratum of the architecture.[13] Consequently, the content of the input spaces is situational. One of these input spaces draws our attention to *form*, since it contains the imagined artistic activity that created the expressive events on the canvas.[14] In this input space, we focus our attention (supposedly following the artist's own intentional direction[15]) on sensory information of

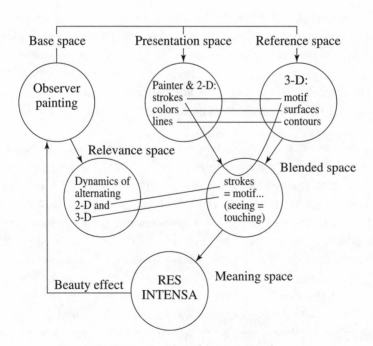

FIGURE 9.2. Mental space network.

every accessible kind. The other input space shows the scene, the landscape, the configuration of things that moved the painter's representational hand and mind. The theme of the caressing brush points to a possible determinant of this content (the "motif"). Not only is there a "mapping" going on, connecting structures in presentation space and in reference space; there is also a hyper-intentional relation of *passion* linking presentation to reference. To *paint* something is also in principle, according to human minds' cognitive schematization, to *love* it, and motifs are selected as objects of erotic passion and as the circumstances of such passion.[16] This erotic attitude toward the content of the referential input, built into the network as what foregrounds its presentation, directs our attention to the *idealization* of the content. So, while one input (presentation) orients our attention "downward," toward form, the other (reference) lets it wander "upward," toward "feeling," so that we obtain an attentional split—comparable to what happens cognitively in a real erotic experience, which is as highly "sensual" as it is highly "spiritual." The blend then overcomes or "resolves" this split by offering us a unified artful thing, the personlike, vivid, animated object, the work of art, a symbolic version of a beloved being: the opus, *res intensa*.

So What?

In this view, beauty resides in the tension between two mental spaces, a presentation and a reference, a tension maintained by the phenomenological impossibility of subordinating one of these to the other. When this conjuncture is obtained, it triggers an acute awareness both of the sensory forms of things and of their emotional meaning—a momentary polarization of attention, a split or crisis that can affect our relations to things, persons, and thoughts very deeply.

In the scope of human evolution, the early cultural presence of artistry in the visual register, and apparently also in the auditory (cf. the early appearance of musical instruments) and the motor registers (dance), may have been of great importance to the emergence of symbolization and abstraction in general. The artistic version of the iconic double-input space network leads our minds toward intentional 2-D graphics as a "scriptural" possibility—that is, the idea of intentionally and systematically producing formal events, thereby calling upon abstract forces to accomplish tasks (cf. spelling and spell-casting) in relation to the idealized referential contents.

If this hypothesis is true, then mental space semantics is an archaic semantic format which gave rise to art—and, through aesthetic semantics, perhaps to primitive mathematics (metrics, numbering, set orderings, classification, calculus) and eventually to verbal language. In the latter, pairings of form and meaning, supported only by a gestural syntax—the "shadow" image of the situational scenario, with its acts, agents, and case morphology— constitute grammars and build up wildly unrealistic, delirious, or poetic utterances as easily as they do concrete accounts of states of affairs.

But if the millennia of human cultural evolution provide the basic temporal perspective necessary to understand what art is about, what would be the role of art history, the historical development of dramatically distinct styles in painting? At a minimum, we will have to consider the dynamic historicity of manners, styles, norms, preferences, and critical discourses intimately related to art, and try to understand their "ontology": if beauty itself is trans-historical, what is it that makes artists modify their ways of pursuing it?

One factor that apparently drives artists unrelentingly is what we might call *stabilization*: any singular, beautiful, beautifully unstable work of art must inspire imitators, create epigonism, and thus give rise to a host of copies and still more predictable variations. Since forms are immaterial and can be repeated (assuming a certain level of skill), any successful formal manifestation will *spread* and create conformity, at least in the fields framed by expressive genres (stabilized as form types "for" certain meaning types). When a formal whole produces this cultural effect, it must at the end *signify* this effect. It then comes to signify and mean its own field of pragmatic influence and can no longer confine the viewer's attention to the pure, dynamic immanence of its singular aesthetic operation. Only outside of its dense history—typically centuries later, or continents away—can it again operate in this manner, and thus become "timeless" and "universal." The acclaimed and revered work and its author can never circumvent this process; they can never avoid the semiotic consumption caused by the stylistic radiation of beautiful forms and its unavoidable social effects: authority, influence, power. The only possible means of escape is *change*. Invention of new, risky concepts and forms is necessary in order to keep forms "power-free." Interestingly, this inventive necessity is extremely demanding. Invention will almost never occur unless the artist, having scrutinized his world of meaning (including his own cognitive functionings), knows the events and discourses of his time, all sorts of extreme states of mind, all available sources of sensory variations and spiritual specialties, and the sensitivities displayed in the work of his colleagues and ancestors. It takes learning, curiosity, intelligence, ambition, creative maladaptation, stubbornness, perhaps even contempt, and probably a borderline personality, to be a creative artist in this historical sense. Without such persons, we would simply not have art. We must therefore be charitable with their sometimes (in fact, mostly) discomfiting personae. Artists are cognitive researchers in the wild. It would perhaps be a scientific advantage if cognitive researchers were also artists themselves. Anyway, the study of the psychology of aesthetic sensibility, or "psycho-aesthetics," is a dimension of cognitive science that future research will need to look closely into.

A Brief Epistemology of Neuroaesthetic Research

What, Why, How?

In neuroaesthetics, as in cognitive research more generally, we have to work out and coordinate three parallel accounts[17] in order to obtain a genuine understanding. In short, we have to answer three questions: *what* are we talking about, *how* does it function, and *why* is it there? Although we seldom know enough to accomplish this triple task in a definitive way, it is a reasonable "regulatory idea," to borrow Emmanuel Kant's phrase, to consider at least these three basic dimensions of the reality we wish to explore (and, thus, three epistemological dimensions of the knowledge we hope to obtain). Indeed, we will not really have obtained any knowledge of the phenomenon at all unless we have acknowledged and at least tentatively answered the three questions. I would like, finally, to elaborate on this particular triad.

The English philosopher Barry Smith reminds us that humans live in a *mesoscopic* spatial world, the one that language is apparently made for, but above which there is a *macroscopic* world and below which we find a *microscopic* world. The two latter worlds are accessible to us only through special symbolic devices, observational prostheses, and notional hypotheses. By contrast, the mesoscopic world is our life-world, our natural one-to-one phenomenology. The other two are "constructed" worlds referred to by our abstract, mythological, and occasionally scientific knowledge, and things taking place there are understood to cause and influence—and to be caused and influenced by—most of what is going on in the mesoscopic province of reality.

We may, then, find it equally interesting to say that we live in a "mesoscopic"[18] *time*, in which narrative structures are inherently relevant and crucial to experiential reality. The "historical" time scale is mesoscopic in this sense. Art *history* is thus a huge narrative account of art, artists, institutions, conflicts, debates, markets, dramas, and intrigues running through centuries and sometimes even millennia. Historical art is our "what." But above historical time there is a macroscopic time—namely, *evolutionary* time—which we can access only indirectly by using prostheses and hypotheses. The evolution of art is a slow process running for perhaps 100,000 years; we are trying to understand its causes. This is the macroscopic "why" of the meso-scopic "what." And below it there is a microscopic time scale, corresponding to the millisecond-short neural processes of perception and mental organi-zation of cognition in art (as of everything else in human behavior). This is the microscopic "how" of the "what." The discipline of art *critique* that elaborates particular studies and analyses of single works of art—examining the micro-compositional relations of form and meaning in *singular* works of art as objects perceived and conceived (in short, experienced)—operates in this microscopic time scale, as does the neuroaesthetic analysis of, or theorizing about, the on-line processes of perceptual and mental structuring involved in art perception. But, as before, we may assume that the macro-facts of cultural evolution and the micro-facts of neural processing may explain some basic aspects, at least, of what is going on in the historical "mesoscopy" of art. Finally, the evolu-tionary causes should, of course, be related to the neuro-cognitive organiza-tions. The "why" and the "how," the macro- and the micro-scopy of the matter, should be and remain in contact.[19]

For instance, the cultural *macro*-evolution of neural *micro*-capacities for intense hyper-perception or hesitant, inconclusive[20] hypo-perception—for conceiving objects (especially artifacts) both as things and as signs—may be the over- and underlying condition that makes interpretation and social apprecia-tion of works of art, and then of other social creations, possible in general.

Transcendence

Although causal-physical stimuli and intentional information are both ap-parently processed by the same sensory neurons, the latter is precategorized as expressive. This means that it prepares the experiencer (stratum 1) for *redundant* occurrences and *elliptic* patterns that the perceiver (stratum 2) at-tempts to compensate for by re-equilibrating, through processes of reduction and completion. The cognizer (stratum 3) must then interact intentionally with the source. Aesthetic communication in a broad sense—arts and crafts, design, advertisement, humor, politeness—is based on such interaction, a collaboration in which the sender (the "maker," the "crafter") is deliberately both redundant and elliptic, and the receiver (experiencer, interpreter, user) is constantly exposed to both hyper- and hypo-perception to some extent and is supposed to respond to the sender by suggestions leading to re-equilibration. But in the genre of communication we call artistic, the exposure to redundancy and ellipsis is *maximized* and impossible to neutralize by re-equilibration. This condition creates in the perceiver the affective state from which art derives its status—namely, the impression of being momentarily in contact with things outside the triviality of spatial and temporal mesoscopy.

Accounts of the meaning of works of art universally refer to such "transcendent" perspectives. This is why we easily come to feel, and artists and even critics often claim, that art is sacred and should not be touched by profane science at all. Beauty should stay "intact," and we should not even attempt to understand it. I have two main counterarguments to this claim. First, it turns out, experimentally, that analysis does not destroy the aesthetic force of a work of art, and that, if an analysis is solid, it even enhances it; neither does weak critical work harm its object, as much as it harms the critic. Second, if one day humans abandoned all explicit attempts at understanding and evaluating art, generically and in its singularities, in order only to admire and revere its manifestations, then both the theory and history of art would soon cease to exist, and art itself would eventually disappear from the human reality. But such an eventuality is difficult to imagine.

NOTES

1. The process connects distinct levels of meaning, letting one provide mental access to the other. So, one can be said to *express* or *signify* the other. But the mental distance between signifier and signified is greater than in the case of images and indices, since the signifying item is typically a form perceived in only one sensory modality, whereas the signified item is a multimodal semantic formation of a kind which is difficult to describe: an "attitude to existence," a "metaphysical" style of thinking and feeling, etc. The resulting sign relation is of the order of symbols, and its process can be called an act of symbolization: an experiential "relation" between a hyper-concrete signifier and a hyper-abstract signified. In the aesthetic experience, this relation is still ephemeral, unstable, momentary, but when stabilization (stable coding) occurs, we get genuinely typical symbols—as in gesture, sign language, writing, numerical symbolization, etc.

2. We might say that rhetorics and the engineering of shared experience in general are essentially a matter of "grammar of attention"—I take this expression from the title of a forthcoming volume by Todd Oakley.

3. This absence of a univocal "assembly line" of informational integration is only possible because there are distinct strata and because these are relatively autonomous. Note that stratification is not modularity; it is not assumed that a stratum is a separately instantiated neuronal "plant."

4. Cf. Donald (2001, chap. 7.3), "The cultural relevance of a multifocal, multi-layered consciousness."

5. People spontaneously evaluate each other's mental health by checking the plasticity of bindings: this is probably one of the important functions of humor—the lack of which is always an alarm signal.

6. Maybe Sigmund Freud's analysis could be reassessed as such an "excess logic."

7. Again: the constitutive gap between signifiers and signifieds arises because signifiers are recuperated excess structure; gestures are thus bodily movements that exceed immediate functional acts.

8. This hypothesis opposes the view of symbolization as based mainly upon verbal language; it considers symbolic activity—such as games and all sorts of calculus—as a type of cognition *sui generis*.

9. The artist and any beholder will in principle, I claim, cognize the painting in exactly the same way as these critics.

10. In Cartesian terms, the content of the reference space could be seen as belonging to *res extensa*—namely, the physically existing or possible motif—and the content of the presentation space as belonging to *res cogitans* (the painter intending his strokes, and the strokes as intentional signs). The blended representation then activates an attentional dynamics of "figural animation," so to speak, that (in base space) lets us experience the work as matter loaded with spirit, an "inspired" thing, *res intensa*.

11. The relation between art and synesthesia is being examined by current neuroaesthetics; cf. Ramachandran and Hubbard (2001). However, the semantic phenomenon I am describing appears to me as far too abstract to be likely to directly rely on neural cross-wirings of the kind suggested by these authors.

12. Cf. Everaert-Desmedt 1999, 228, and my text in this volume, "Magritte: le théâtre robuste de la variation imaginaire."

13. Since forms and objects are not situations, they cannot constitute mental spaces on their own.

14. The formal events on the canvas must be apperceived as traces of intentional work and the display of skill. They cannot be understood as simple effects of accidental causes, because the base space determines the input spaces as built for decoding a pictorial sign. If we erased base space determinations from our theoretical horizon, the present analysis would fall apart entirely.

15. Our individual attention irresistibly follows the other's attention, as manifested by forms that express it.

16. The founder of the neuroaesthetic project, the neuroscientist Semir Zeki, insists rightly on this erotic dimension of art (Zeki 2002). But what about critical art, showing scenes of horror? The late Goya? Picasso's *Guernica?* We might need to extend the notion of "passion" to include the negative side of awe, the "awful," the terrible, and the feelings of despair and rage.

17. This is also, as I understand it, V. S. Ramachandran's "neuro-epistemological" claim (presentation and discussion, Center for Advanced Study in the Behavioral Sciences, Stanford, 2002).

19. Discourses in which the macro- and the micro-scopies do not establish any contact are typically mythological, nonscientific, arbitrary creations; here is probably a sound epistemological criterion of scientificity in discourse.

20. Cf. Semir Zeki's emphasis (this volume) on ambivalence and inconclusiveness in art.

REFERENCES

Brandt, P. A. 2004. *Spaces, domains, and meaning. Essays in cognitive semiotics.* Bern: Peter Lang Verlag, European Semiotics Series, No. 4.

Campbell, P. 2002. Fabric of vision: Dress and drapery in painting. *London Review of Books,* July, 11.

Donald, M. 2001. *A mind so rare: The evolution of human consciousness.* New York, London: W. W. Norton.

Eco, U. 1992. *Interpretation and overinterpretation.* Cambridge, England: Cambridge University Press.

Everaert–Desmedt, N., ed. 1999. *Magritte au risque de la sémiotique.* Bruxelles: Publications des Facultés universitaires Saint-Louis.

Fauconnier, G., and M. Turner. 2002. *The way we think: Conceptual blending and the mind's hidden complexities.* New York: Basic Books.

Perl, J. 2002. Circa 1950. *The New Republic.* July 8 and 15.

Ramachandran, V. S., and E. M. Hubbard. 2001. Synaesthesia—A window into perception, thought, and language. *Journal of Consciousness Studies,* 8, no. 12: 3–34.

Schjeldahl, P. 2002. Naked Punch: Tate Britain celebrates Lucian Freud. *The New Yorker,* July 8.

Zeki, S. 2002. Neural concept formation and art: Dante, Michelangelo, Wagner. *Journal of Consciousness Studies,* 9, no. 3: 53–76.

10

Slippages of Meaning and Form

Stephen Murray

*Cognitive models derive their meaningfulness from their ability to orga-
nize new experience in relation to preconceptual structures. We have
learned to recognize the importance of metaphors and figurative thinking in the formation of such mental architecture (Lakoff 1987; Lakoff,
this volume). The figurative thinking that helps organize the experience
of the thing is sometimes extended to explain the process by which the
thing came into being, producing a carry-over, or slippage of meaning.
I will explore the linkages and slippages between three types of architecture: the Gothic edifice, the forest with which it has so frequently been
compared, and the mental architecture that we create to allow us to understand the thing and the process.*

Of all the epithets invented to represent a category of artifact, *Gothic* is
at once the most powerful and the most troublesome. *Gothic*, to be
sure, continues to be applied as a conventional designation for a
particular kind of art and architecture current in the period between
the mid-twelfth and early sixteenth centuries. This uncomplicated and
unthreatening "objectivist" understanding of the phenomenon ("if
it looks like a duck, and quacks like a duck...") is based on the
recognition of a familiar and coherent combination of architectural
forms: pointed arches, flying buttresses, rib vaults, skeletal structure; and the association of these forms with a prevailing culture
(Gombrich 1985). Such an association of architectural forms, considered normative within the culture of a given time and place, has

found visual affirmation in the new European currency, where homogenized elements of Roman architecture appear on the five-euro banknote, Romanesque on the ten, Gothic on the twenty, and Renaissance on the fifty. (See http://theartfulmind.stanford.edu for images.) What clearer expression of the universal acceptance of the power of architectural form to project cultural identity could one possibly hope to find?

The academy, however, has become increasingly hostile to such taxonomic or chronological exercises, opposing all efforts to define or establish cultural "norms." Although we may continue to use the term *Gothic*, endless scholarly wrangling surrounds any attempt to assess the relative Gothicness of this or that regional or temporal variation. Why must the French always succeed in imposing their cultural norms at the expense of Italy and Germany? Why can't the English? With claims of victim status, champions of "marginalized" regional forms of Gothic have assumed their place at center stage. Surrounding such questions is the larger uncertainty as to what scholars in the field are supposed to be doing now that the old "positivism" has been declared null and void.

The forum provided by *The Artful Mind* allows us to reconsider some of the all-too-comfortable simplifications and assumptions associated with the recognition, classification, and understanding of this most important and unruly category of art, and to offer some modest suggestions as to how we can break what appears to be the current impasse. I am particularly interested in probing the tense interface that lies between what might be described as "experiential" and "objectivist" approaches (Lakoff 1987). Experientially, we may categorize a building in terms of what it *looks like* (a forest, a boat, and the like). It is well known that the founding myth for Gothic took this look-alike quality and carried it over into the explanation of the *process* of construction— asserting, for example, that the pointed look actually resulted from tying trees together. This unlikely scenario was dismissed by the "scientific" definition of the phenomenon reached in the early to mid-nineteenth century, when Gothic was defined as a category actually existing "out there" and providing an objective gauge by which the cultural value of buildings could be assessed.

Having explored the tension between experiential and objectivist models of cognition, I will proceed to the problem of finding a means of representing the phenomenon in sociological and anthropological terms—as the human responses and interactions that allowed the form of the unbuilt edifice to be fixed in the minds of the builders through the conversations that preceded and accompanied the work. This mechanism can best be represented as alternating contraction (mnemonic) and expansion (material), as existing prototypes were assessed and compressed into memories, words, and images; as modifications were identified; and as work began on a new building that might resemble those prototypes in certain respects, yet still be significantly different. That building, constructed over time, would be subject to continuing modification in the vicissitudes of local power struggles. I am also interested in the transfer of meaning that allowed levels of significance programmed into the edifice through formal similitude to be "read" by the visitor or user.

We should first consider the designation itself. The historiography of Gothic can still best be explored in Frankl (1960) and, more recently, in Rowland (1998, 226). Although we may be familiar with the process of scholarly *triage* that led to the recognition of the class of artifact so named, and the circumstances under which the epithet was first applied, the phenomenon does not lie passively still as something that we have invented. Rather, it seems to take on a disconcerting life of its own. Refusing to remain within the temporal or regional bounds assigned to it, Gothic bursts into the imagination of the nineteenth century as a vehicle for forces apparently in opposition: nostalgia for the past paradoxically coupled with the visible expression of a kind of thinking that was both modern and Modern. In the nineteenth century, Gothic (real and revival) provided, above all, an image for the expression of Northern national identity, just as Europe now seeks to reinvent itself with a reassuring procession of architectural images on its banknotes.

Gothic clearly also has its dark side: a disturbing presence in youth counterculture of our own period, synonymous with anti-rationalism or subversion, with an underlying agenda of anarchism and gratuitous violence. One hears that the young men who murdered their fellow students at Columbine High School were associated with a "Goth" counterculture. Why should the same epithet be attached to a long black trench coat and a thirteenth-century cathedral?

Students of historiography for many years took it for granted that *Gothic* was a mistaken and pejorative epithet coined by Italian *literati* of the fifteenth century who failed to understand, and had nothing but contempt for, the cultural achievements of the North. How absurd to think that barbaric Goths in their dark northern forests had anything to do with the brilliance of the architectural counterpart of the flowering of humanistic knowledge (Chenu 1968) in the twelfth century!

It seems to me, however, that we should admire the Italian humanists who first applied the term *Gothic* to architecture—they succeeded in making an astonishingly memorable connection between the "look" of the thing (like a forest), alleged cultural roots (Germans who lived and worshiped in forests), the process of construction, and the defamation necessary to assert Italian cultural supremacy in the face of threatening aliens to the north—Germans and French—all too ready to reimpose their unwanted military presence as well as their offensive cultural forms on Italian soil. Here, it is worth citing the text of Raphael's 1519 letter[1] to Pope Leo X in full (Frankl 1960, 273):

> The Germans use as ornaments for a console to carry a beam [either] a crouching, poorly executed, and even more poorly understood little figure [or] other strange animals and figures and leaves beyond natural reason (*fuori d'ogni ragione naturale*). This architecture did make some sense, however, as it was derived from trees, not yet cut down, whose branches were bent over and made to form pointed arches when tied together. And although this origin is not wholly to be despised, it is nevertheless weak: for huts made from fitted beams arranged as columns, with gables and a covering roof, as Vitruvius describes with respect to the origin of the Doric order, would be stronger than the pointed arches with two centers. For indeed, according to the law of mathematics, a semicircular arch, with each part of its line related only to one center, can carry much more. And beside this weakness, the pointed arch does not have the same grace to our eye, for the perfection of the circle is pleasing, and one sees that Nature seeks almost no other form.

Our *literati* were hard put to draw entirely negative associations from an artifact allegedly derived from a kind of forest mutation, since Vitruvius and Vasari both insisted that the basis of form in art and architecture lies in Nature.

It is clearly the experiential basis of the category that renders it so compelling. Who has not experienced that *frisson* in the Gothic space as it seems to turn into a forest and back into a cathedral before our very eyes—a sensation imaginatively explored by Baltrusaitis (1983)? Or who has walked down that wooded *allée* in the gardens at Versailles and not seen it morph into King's College Chapel Cambridge? Is the forest/cathedral a phenomenon like the man in the moon? No force has actually inscribed a human face on the cratered surface of the moon, yet our gaze may invent one there, just as we can see fantastic images in the clouds or in patterns of water. Gombrich (1960) compellingly brought our attention to the phenomenon of images that slip uncontrollably one into the other. Is this how we find the forest in the cathedral? Or did someone or some creative force put it there?

Villard de Honnecourt, the thirteenth-century graphic artist and witness of Gothic who left a little book of drawings (Bechmann 1991), set out to instruct his audience not just in the art of masonry and carpentry but also in the forms of nature. His leaf heads, in which human and foliate forms coalesce, pop out of countless Gothic edifices, which seem to put on leaf and to bloom in the most exuberant way (see http://theartfulmind.stanford.edu). Pevsner (1945), in one of his most unforgettable essays, explored the sumptuous foliage of Southwell Minster. We are here close to one of the sources of the power of our phenomenon. The natural forms of Gothic and the sense of exuberance and unruly growth induced by these buildings resonate with our own experiences of the architecture of the natural world, so that we wonder whether they are indeed the work of human hands or were rather wrought by the very Creator of that natural world.

In addition to linkages with divine creativity, the forest in the cathedral can convey ancient Northern roots. Crossley (1992) has recently suggested that such thoughts were "theorized" at the end of the Middle Ages to counter the fifteenth-century invasion of the North by the architectural forms and writings of the Italian Renaissance. It is certainly true that in fifteenth-century France, as well as in Germany, rib vaults sprouted twigs and leaves, and the double-curved forms of tracery took on an organic life. Bony (1979) explored the peculiar vegetal *fibrousness* of English Late Gothic. It was in these same years (later fifteenth century) that printed versions of Tacitus's *De Germania* began to circulate and that Germans were encouraged to think of their own cultural identity in terms of forest origins.

Is it possible that the Italian humanists who first applied the term *Gothic* to architectural forms were familiar with such Northern intentions and theorizing? The term is transformed, then, from a hostile taunt based on ignorance and prejudice to a shrewd assessment of cultural meaning projected through mimesis or formal similitude.

The idea of *Gothic* as a usefully descriptive rather than a negative epithet can be extended through a consideration of the taxonomy that, in the period following the Latin Silver Age, assigned works of rhetoric and literature to modes and periods of greater or lesser praiseworthiness. *Gothic* finds its parallel in the term applied to the rhetoric of the New Testament and the early Church: the *sermo humilis*, as explored by Auerbach (1953) and Kemp (1996). Just as the words *Gothic* or *Germanic* in the mouth of an Italian humanist might resonate with meanings of coarseness or crudity, so does *sermo humilis* designate a way of writing and talking that did not aspire to the superficial rhetorical polish of the Golden, or even of the Silver Age. In this rough mode we find stories of the life, work, and daily experience of ordinary folk. Yet the simple words characteristic of the *sermo humilis* provide a vehicle for transformative experience as well as a wealth of typological associations. A most effective illustration may be found in the Gospel story of the betrayal of Christ by Peter. Peter and his companions—far from heroes—were frightened and confused and altogether ordinary. Yet the reader of the Gospel account may anticipate in this story of humiliation and defeat nothing less than the eventual triumph of the Church.

The recognition of the rhetorical mode that we understand as the *sermo humilis* can help us understand Gothic architecture, for such architecture was not the work of architectural theoreticians but of artisans, who were not required to have an education in the liberal arts. Sauerländer (1995) has recently emphasized the historicizing language of Gothic—but that is only part of the story. Gothic was not a purely historicizing mode: the cathedrals drew upon the hereness and nowness and local flavor of the cities where they were located. Neologisms—a kind of slang—were not necessarily considered shameful. The buildings themselves achieved their affect through a set of relatively simple technical tricks. We might understand the flying buttress, for example—surely castigated by some twelfth-century critics as a crude structural fix—as a neologism of sorts. It is interesting to find that the outside supports for the flyers are designated *culée*, presumably derived from the stem *cul* (Latin *culus*), or backside (arse).

The buildings display an astonishing wealth of typological linkages through formal associations. Thus, the church looks like a forest, it looks like a human body, it looks like a boat, it looks like the cosmos, it looks like a floating canopy (*ciborium*), it looks like the tabernacle that housed the Ark of the Covenant. Existing explorations of the astonishing range of references made by the cathedral (Bandmann 1951) tend to be too restrictive. Should we also add that these edifices are capable of simultaneously pointing to the future and recalling the past? The historical epoch of principal interest to the builders and first users of Gothic was the age of the first establishment of the Church: the Christianization of the northern provinces of the Roman Empire and its subsequent invasion and transformation by the Goths. This was, after all, the founding period for Christianity in the North, the time of the martyrdom of many an evangelist who may have come from afar but who ended up on Northern soil, paradoxically expressing local identity. Gothic churches are often about the enshrinement of the relics of such a saint—a point emphasized by Grant (1998) in relation to the brilliant lantern that formed the retro-choir at Saint-Denis, intended to house the shrine of the apostles of Gaul. The very anachronism of the word *Gothic*, therefore, makes perfect sense: these are buildings synchronically layered in time. Just like the liturgical exercises with which they are intimately connected, they provide experiential mechanisms capable of carrying the user into the past—the time of the founders—even as they project him into the future with the Second Coming of Christ.

These most eloquent buildings were silent and remain silent, and during the period of their construction they provoked few direct written responses. Although inscriptions were placed, for example, at strategic points in the twelfth-century abbey church of Saint-Denis, the association between words and forms is less emphatic and direct than in Islamic or classical architecture. Part of the buildings' distinction, however, is that they make us speak for them. The abbot of Saint-Denis loved to recount to his brothers stories about the history of his monastery and the construction of the new church (Panofsky 1946; Grant 1998). Such oral storytelling doubtless lies behind the written accounts, *de Administratione* and *de Consecratione,* left by the loquacious abbot. How many other such oral accounts of Gothic remain unrecorded?

Much of the Gothic building's eloquence lies in its multiple references to entities beyond itself. And these references, in turn, compel us to become its interlocutors, explaining, interpreting, and *representing* the forms of the building to ourselves and to others, both present and absent. That person pointing here and there and talking to a group of visitors who obediently look and listen is the most common sight in the cathedral visit—one thinks of the famous Malcolm Miller at Chartres. It is worth remembering that such a person represents the building as self-appointed interlocutor rather than as attorney with powers conferred through the consent of the party represented. The building did not ask us to say a word; humility is therefore appropriate. Brilliant (1991) has demonstrated how the visual work of art can be performed, and meanings created, through narrative. However, those who attempt to represent the Gothic cathedral in words (written or spoken) may underestimate the extent to which the building is verbally impermeable. The inherent difficulty of turning buildings into words results in a limited and quite predictable range of characteristic tropes or patterns of representation.

During our brief sojourn in the building, it imposes itself as an all-encompassing present—a one-of-a-kind—inviting us to engage in an intense exploration of its forms and spaces through systematic looking. Thus, we may caress the surfaces with our gaze, moving our eyes rhythmically in vertical or horizontal patterns, and attempt to input optical data into our memories. In this exercise, the edifice quickly turns from a passive object into what feels like an active agent, impelling us to continue to move our bodies through interior space, and insidiously persuading the unself-conscious interlocutor to tell "untruths." (On the telling of lies in the Middle Ages, see Evans 1994, 73: "At the beginning of the twelfth century, writers learned to lie and reinvented the art of prose fiction. They lied about their sources, they lied about people and events, and they lied about pictures.")

I thus adopt a position diametrically opposed to that of Panofsky (1951), who represented Gothic architecture as a manifestation of visual logic or clarity. As visitors to Amiens Cathedral (figure 10.1), we might remark that the space of the interior *soars* to an incredible height; that it *expands* from the main vessel into the aisles. Or we might say that the colonnettes *ascend* to *support* the transverse arches and ribs. Or that the historicizing forms of the building *recall* prestigious prototypes of the past. Or that the forms of the choir have *changed*, no longer matching those of the nave. All these statements are, literally

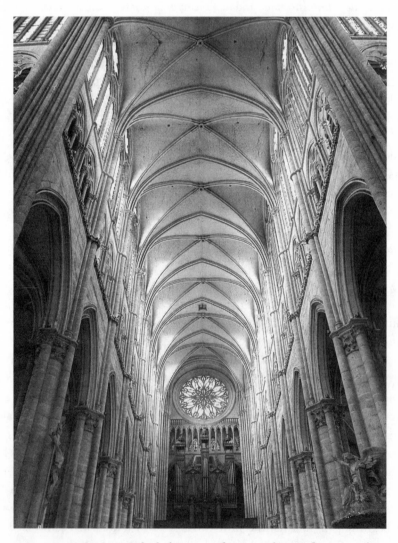

FIGURE 10.1. Amiens Cathedral, 1220–1269, general view of interior (photo by Andrew Tallon).

speaking, false, since the space of the cathedral is an inert entity, without the ability to soar or expand. The colonnettes remain where they always were—quite motionless, neither ascending nor descending. They support nothing and could be removed without threat to the arches and ribs. The building does not recall, but makes us recall—just as, still and silent though it is, it makes us move and speak. And the masonry of the edifice, except under extreme circumstances of material failure, does not change. Yet our "untruthful" rhetoric can reveal essential aspects of our experience of the building.

We become aware of the phenomenon of "change" whenever repeated experience leads to anticipation of continuity that is denied by the real object. "Change" in Gothic may be understood partly as a consequence of persistence of vision. The mechanism is similar to cinematography. More relevant for the time of the production of the cathedral, the affect is similar to that associated with a miracle, which was understood to have occurred when the expected and natural sequence of events (from summer to winter; from life to death) is disrupted.

This train of thought suggests that we are dealing with a sleight of hand, an architecture of illusionism, as was recognized by Binding (2000). The building is not what it seems, just as, in the Gospel story, Peter was not actually a defeated and insignificant fisherman; as the cornerstone of the Church, he was to become one of the most significant figures in the history of the world.

In Gothic, then, we find not one kind of architecture, but two that are in tension: one with the real capacity to bear considerable loads (buttresses and wall masses, apparent mainly on the exterior, as in figure 10.2), and one with the ability to fixate our attention and make us recount fantastic stories (the colonnettes, moldings, flora and fauna, and all the other illusionistic forms of the interior).

The efficacy of the former permits great freedom in the handling of the latter. In early Gothic we can understand the two modes as modernism and historicism. Gothic technology (modernism) performs the "magic" that allows us to see the elements of antique architecture *transformed:* columns impossibly reduced in diameter and extended like chewing gum far beyond anything possible in antiquity; slender colonnettes combined in clusters that create mind-boggling repetitions; material substance apparently denied through the powerful use of backlighting. Gombrich (1985) pointed to the parallels between this fantastic architecture and Vitruvius's disapproving account of late Roman painting that no longer depicted the "real." Vasari, echoing Vitruvius, commented: "on the façades and other decorated parts they made a malediction of little tabernacles one above another, with so many pyramids [pinnacles] and points and leaves that it seems impossible for it to

FIGURE 10.2. Amiens Cathedral, cross section (Durand, after Viollet-le-Duc).

support itself, let alone other weights. They look more as if they were made of paper than of stone or marble.... This manner was invented by the Goths" (quoted in Gombrich 1985, 84).

These are not complicated tricks, but they are astonishingly effective and affective, even to this day. What is perhaps most exciting is the builders' realization that the illusionistic structures of the interior had the power to go beyond historicism and assume a wide range of entirely new forms—from the somewhat cold and intellectual look affected by French Late Gothic, in which sharp-edged fillets catch the light and form brittle lines divided by the soft shadows of deep concavities, to the organic look achieved by the supple vegetal forms of the fifteenth-century German vault. From abstraction to mimesis.

There is a second aspect of our representation of the building where we may discern similar slippages of meaning. Frustrated by the rhetorical flatness resulting from architectural descriptive cataloguing, and urged by the need of his audience (or editor) for an animated narrative with word-images capable of conveying affect, the interlocutor will generally slip into the use of poetic and figurative language—not just in describing Gothic, but also in articulating the impact of any phenomenon that goes beyond our normal experiences and descriptive abilities: "It is as if...." Faced with describing Hagia Sophia, for example, Procopius gives us not only a laborious, factual eyewitness catalogue but also the occasional leap derived from figurative speech, saying of the great dome, for example, that "it seems not to be founded on solid masonry but to be suspended from heaven by that golden chain, and so to cover the space" (Mango 1972, 75). Or Suger in response to glistening liturgical equipment: "Thus when—out of my delight in the beauty of the house of God—the loveliness of the many colored gems has called me away from external cares... then, it seems to me that I see myself dwelling, as it were, in some strange region of the universe which neither exists entirely in the slime of the earth nor entirely in the purity of Heaven...." (Panofsky 1979, 63–65). Or Jean Bony (Congress of Medieval Studies, Kalamazoo, ca. 1973), wanting to convey the spatial expansiveness of the choir plan at Saint-Denis, suggested the metaphor of a softly inflated balloon with pressure points (corresponding to the buttresses) pushing inwards, but allowing the surface to billow outwards in a series of curves (the radiating chapels). Equally unforgettable is Bony's description of the buttresses of the transept at Laon as telescopes with sliding segments. Such figurative language mounts a kind of ambush on reality, evoking experience to convey affect: a dramatic way of forcing the receiver to envisage the as-yet-unseen thing.

Though empowering at its inception, figurative language, used to represent a single building or the complex relationship between many buildings, may eventually inhibit the originality and vigor of our perceptions. Metaphors can lose their efficacy (remember President Clinton's "bridge to the twenty-first century"?). We must learn from them, but we must also challenge them, returning to the object of study to form our own critical experience. In doing so, we will respond primarily not to the experiences and formulations of others, but to the accruing presence of our own sense-endowed body in the building.

When we expand our conceptual vision beyond the single building that we happen to occupy at the time, we face further problems of cognition. What makes Chartres Chartres is not just the peculiar architectural disposition of this particular building, but its relationship with thousands of other such buildings spread across a wide swath of geography over a considerable period of time. Our assessment of Chartres is modified in relation to whatever memory we may carry of those other buildings. The conclusion that Chartres is a dark cathedral may suggest familiarity with Amiens, which is light; the perception that Chartres is big and heavy predicates Noyon, which is small and skinny. We struggle to grasp this multitude of other buildings through systems of classification, principally by arranging them in conceptual patterns based on criteria of sameness and difference. Such is the power of an individual building like Chartres that it was, following the simple mechanism devised by Bony (1957–1958), for many years represented as the culmination of all of the trends of the earlier twelfth century and the fountainhead of all that was to follow in the thirteenth century. Edifices that did not resemble Chartres were arranged on the map as a kind of "resistance" movement: the phenomenon of "change" was thus represented as a victory ensuing from a battle between opposing forces. This kind of two-dimensional representation of a complex historical phenomenon results from the power of the individual building to persuade the visitor that its forms were the result of a "development" that had all the inevitability of the growth of a tadpole into a frog, or a caterpillar into a butterfly—that architectural forms actually possess a life of their own. Such a building also persuades us that there was, out there, a Gothic "essence" that builders in the twelfth and thirteenth centuries struggled to identify in order to achieve perfection.

To define what Gothic is, it is necessary, in this way of thinking, to lay out the characteristic elements of a "mature" or "fully developed" or paradigmatic representative. Jean Bony (1983) took Soissons Cathedral as his paradigm for Gothicness; Wilhelm Schlink (1978) took Chartres; Paul Frankl (1962) took Amiens and Cologne; Christopher Wilson (1990) took the "complete" program of the "Great Church." Having defined the various components of the "Gothic system" in the paradigmatic building(s), the interlocutor will then track the history of each element (pointed arches, rib vaults, flying buttresses, enhanced spaciousness). However, the very structure of the demonstration will obviously allow no other outcome than the paradigm itself—it is a kind of entelechy. Thus, the myth of inevitability may be understood as the result of the limits of our own conception (essentially circular) and the inadequacy of our means of representation. I should also point out that the recognition of Gothic as an "organic" combination of skeletal supports, ribs, buttresses, and tracery took place precisely as the various natural sciences coalesced to form a single living science—biology—and when notions of the evolution of the human species were being formulated (Foucault 1973). Oddly enough, our two systems of cognition, experiential and objectivist, converged in the sense that the "scientific" representation of Gothic lent to the category the aura of a natural species, just as the experiential response led back to primal forest roots.

Such patterns of representation, resulting from the need to make sense of a highly complex historical scenario, dominated the teaching of Gothic for decades. All this was swept away in the bracing atmosphere of the 1980s and 1990s; I refer the reader to two landmark pieces of revisionism in Sauerländer (1984) and Camille (1994). But very little has been done in the past twenty years to critically reassess our systems of cognition, and the "new" art history has begun to look as tired as the old. How, then, can we create a means of understanding and representing Gothic that does not slip into the same old patterns? I want to conclude with several possible avenues of approach.

First, we might note that Gothic architecture is generally defined in terms of its *difference* from the Romanesque style that preceded it. The standard narrative of Gothic suggests that the principal objective of the builders was to construct a monument that went beyond its prototypes. There is nothing wrong with this, but it is only part of the story. The powerful features that allow us to recognize Gothic obviously involve not only difference but also *sameness*—the look-alike quality that might lead the traveler to conclude that when you have seen one cathedral, you've seen them all. Look-alike buildings spread out over wide geographic expanses had, of course, been associated with the *Romanitas* upon which European cultural unity depends. Greg Woolf (1998) has explored the astonishing ability of the Romans in Gaul to project the image of a unified and widely extended empire through the multiplication of specimens of a limited number of building types: the amphitheater, the forum, the city wall, the bathhouse, and the columned portico. Later architectural waves included the white mantle of churches spread across Europe after the year 1000. The common design principles of monastic (especially Cistercian) architecture provide a precedent for Gothic not so much in architectural form (pointed arches, etc.) as in the effect achieved when considerable geographical distances are collapsed through the repetition of a unified building type.

Within the individual building, the sameness of the architectural elements (piers, capitals, window tracery, moldings, and the like) has been identified in recent scholarship (Kimpel and Suckale 1985) as a kind of natural sign—as *evidence* of a rational process of serial production. In certain ways, the building has been quite literally "stamped out"—the convex elements (supports) through the application of a template to achieve uniformity, and the concave elements (vaults and arches) through the wooden formwork used to shape the vaults. The idea that the form of the vaults has been *impressed* or printed through the temporary agency of the wooden centers interacts in the most intriguing way with medieval metaphors for memory and creativity as explored recently by Mary Carruthers (1990, 1998).

The same phenomenon (multiple stamped-out elements) can, of course, be seen as a conventional sign—a kind of language—signifying the perfect obedience of the repeated elements of the building to the dictates of its designers. Abbot Suger's allegorical thinking allowed him to see the columns of the Saint-Denis hemicycle and ambulatory as apostles and prophets (Panofsky 1979, 105). These were human beings who had formed themselves according to a human template, namely Christ (see Vicaire 1963; Schlink 1991). The sameness of the multiple elements of *ecclesia* and *Ecclesia* is therefore to be understood not just as the by-product of rational production techniques, but also as willed form. *Kunstwollen* is not a disembodied or abstract force, but the result of a shared agenda on the part of the builders.

That this agenda (driven by moral objectives as well as aesthetic) was shared by artisans and patrons over extended space and time is indicated not only by the high level of resemblance between the multiple units of an individual building, but also by the existence of "families" (not really families!) of look-alike buildings. We have not yet found the right way of representing or explaining this aspect of Gothic. Let us recognize the fact that these are inanimate objects, and that to continue to use the designation "family" is to allow ourselves to be seduced into using language appropriate only for living organisms. The term "school" is equally inappropriate, given the absence of any shred of historical evidence to suggest the existence of a formal academy established to propagate a canonical approach. Even more misleading as a means of representation are maps with arrows pointing out from the Ile-de-France purporting to show the "spread of the Gothic cathedral." Suggesting the aggressive export of the Gothic product to Spain, England, Germany, and Italy, such arrows make us think of the cultural and material imperialism of our own time.

So, if Gothic cathedrals are not literally living entities, and if they do not actually "spread" (except in cases of structural failure), what would be a more appropriate framework of cognition? We must recognize that our difficulties have resulted from an uneasy relationship between the definition of *Gothic* as a *thing* and the idea of Gothic as a *process*. Both meanings are conveyed by the Latin word *opus*. Our mistakes result from the seductive power of the thing and our lack of adequate understanding of the process. The starting point in the new understanding will be to reverse the arrows on the map. Westminster Abbey (Binski 1995) exists not because the masonry envelope of Amiens, Reims, or Saint-Denis perambulated to England, but rather because, for a complex set of reasons (spiritual as well as political and ideological), the people involved in the reconstruction of the abbey church in London agreed to turn their backs on solutions associated with recognizably English forms and to look toward France and Italy. The power of Gothic resulted very largely from its ability to project a wide range of local agendas while at the same time appearing to conform to some kind of supra-regional identity that lent the aura of legitimacy.

In this process of transmission and transformation, we have identified a sequence of alternating compression and expansion. A cathedral or abbey church is a very large entity, and its construction is a historical process involving the laborious manipulation of material—stone, iron, wood, and glass—over a period of at least a half century (and usually more). The similarity between Westminster and Reims resulted from the compression of the critical elements of the particular French cathedral (and of others, no doubt) into relatively small-scale drawings on paper or parchment that could be carried from place to place: Villard de Honnecourt's drawings of the chapels and flying buttresses of Reims provide a perfect example of the mechanism I have in mind (see http://theartfulmind.stanford.edu). The drawings might be accompanied by written observations as well as more detailed studies of pier sections, tracery patterns, and the like. The building accounts of Troyes Cathedral (Murray 1986, 172) make frequent mention of such drawings as well as of paper ("false") templates that were carried to the quarry to give the essential form to the various parts of the cathedral. An entire edifice could be compressed into a sheaf of papers that could be put in the saddlepack of a horse and taken from place to place. Construction involves a variety of participants, each bringing to the table different kinds of compressed information and different agendas. Certainly in its early days, Gothic might have brought with it the idea of a radical break with the immediate past; the desire to compete and to emulate produced the sameness that is read retroactively as reflecting a kind of *communitas*.

Change over time and place obviously results not from any kind of morphological mutation or "development" but quite simply from the *critical response* associated with the process of contraction and expansion outlined above. A building agenda will be defined first by identifying what the unbuilt edifice will look like (generally with specific references to well-known prototypes), but it will proceed—both before and after the start of construction—with the critical assessment and modification of those prototypes. Such assessment will be undertaken by multiple agents and on multiple occasions and might lead to a product significantly different from its prototypes. Critical response, moreover, will not limit itself to minor modifications: I am committed to the contention (considered quaintly romantic by some) that Gothic creativity brought the occasional spectacular leap into the unknown, as I demonstrated in relation to Notre-Dame of Paris (Murray 1999). Such a leap was made doubly challenging by the fact that the as-yet-unbuilt structure might embody great height or a spectacular new spatial configuration in the superstructure that would, in turn, demand systematic preparation in the infrastructure. How did the master mason of Notre-Dame of Paris convince the clergy, who had no prior experience of a structure of the kind that he envisaged, to invest in the enormously expensive foundations necessary to provide a secure underpinning for a vaulted superstructure rising well beyond anything that had ever been built in the North? The answer lay, of course, in that master's ability to convincingly *represent* (compressed in words and images) the unknown—that is to say, the unbuilt cathedral. It is the task of the artist to push beyond the customary limits of cognition.

It is time to try to pull together the strands of my argument. By "slippage of meaning," I intend to suggest that in our representations both of individual buildings and of the larger processes that lie behind Gothic, we have employed figurative language that has skewed our understanding of both thing and process. Should we, then, attempt to strip away such accretions of acquired meaning to allow ourselves direct access to the thing itself? Of course not. We have seen that the Gothic building resulted from a process of alternating contraction and expansion (conceptualizing and constructing), and that such a process brought exactly the kind of "slippage" that has concerned us here. We have also seen that some of the meanings that result from the similes we apply to convey the look and affect of the building ("like a forest," "like a boat") were certainly programmed in by the builders. The building "speaks" to us in this way and, astonishingly, we are sometimes still able to understand its "language."

This author owns up to two views proscribed in the restrictive atmosphere of the academy. First, the dominance of French forms in Gothic is not merely the result of skewed patterns of representation in the relatively recent past; in fact, such dominance characterized the interactions of masons in the twelfth and thirteenth centuries. Second, and more important, I believe that we must learn to rely much more heavily on our own bodily and experiential responses to Gothic.

There is, however, one area where the means of representation and analysis that we currently deploy might be profitably applied, taking us far beyond the limitations of the immediate past. When we describe Gothic in terms of a paradigmatic building (Chartres, for example), we slip into the belief that twelfth- or thirteenth-century people found Chartres just as compelling as we do, and that the buildings of the twelfth century were leading inevitably to this solution. Such a structure of interpretation results principally from the demands of the classroom or the fixed sequences of buildings that can be presented in the pages of a book. The computer, which provides a relatively untried means of holding complex data about hundreds of buildings suspended in the memory of a machine, will allow us to establish multiple patterns of linkage on multiple levels. Alison Langmead (2002), in her Ph.D. dissertation at Columbia, undertook pioneering work in the creation of a digital synthesizing framework for Romanesque churches in the southwest of France; the work continues in a series of Columbia summer field schools in the Bourbonnais, where students work digitally to gather material to facilitate the analysis of the relationships between some three hundred edifices.

Let us recognize, finally, that the great monuments—though sadly depleted in ranks and eroded by time—are still there, inviting us to return to them with new methods of investigation, understanding, and representation. Any real advance, it seems to me, demands three things: skeptical awareness of the structures imposed by existing patterns of representation and interpretation; rigorous new questions coupled with powerful new exploratory techniques; and, above all, a readiness to open our horizons—intuitive, performative, and sensory, as well as intellectual—and to return to the intense and direct study of the objects themselves. There is much to be done.

NOTES

Much of this material was worked out during the tenure of a fellowship at the Center for Advanced Study in the Behavioral Sciences, Stanford, 2000–2001. I am deeply grateful to Bob Scott and to Mark Turner for all the conversations we have shared.

1. The 1519 letter is now thought to be Raphael's. Frankl is out of date.

REFERENCES

Auerbach, E. 1953. *Mimesis: The representation of reality in Western literature*. Trans. W. R. Trask. Princeton, N.J.: Princeton University Press.
———. 1993. *Literary language and its public in late Latin antiquity and in the Middle Ages*. Trans. R. Manheim. Bollingen Series 74. Princeton, N.J.: Princeton University Press.
Baltrusaitis, J. 1983. *Aberrations. Essai sur la légende des formes*. Paris: Flamarion.
Bandmann, G. 1951. *Mittelalterliche Architektur als Bedeutungsträger*. Berlin: Gebr. Mann.
Bechmann, R. 1991. *Villard de Honnecourt. La pensée technique au XIIIe siècle et sa communication*. Paris: Picard.

Binding, G. 2000. *Was ist Gotik? Eine Analyse der gotischen Kirchen in Frankreich, England und Deutschland, 1140–1350.* Darmstadt: Primus.

Binski, P. 1995. *Westminster Abbey and the Plantagenets. Kingship and the representation of power, 1200–1400.* New Haven: Yale University Press.

Bony, J. 1957–1958. The resistance to Chartres in early thirteenth-century architecture. *Journal of the British Archaeological Association,* ser. 3, 20–21: 35–52.

———. 1979. *The English decorated style: Gothic architecture transformed, 1250–1350.* Ithaca, N.Y.: Cornell University Press.

———. 1983. *French Gothic architecture of the 12th and 13th centuries.* Berkeley: University of California Press.

Brilliant, R. 1991. The Bayeux Tapestry: A stripped narrative for their eyes and ears. *Word and Image,* 7: 98–126.

Camille, M. 1994. Art history in the past and future of medieval studies. In *The past and future of medieval studies,* ed. John Van Engen, 362–82. Notre Dame: University of Notre Dame Press.

Carruthers, M. 1990. *The book of memory: A study of memory and medieval culture.* Cambridge, England: Cambridge University Press.

———. 1998. *The craft of thought: Meditation, rhetoric and the making of images, 400–1200.* Cambridge, England: Cambridge University Press.

Chenu, M.-D. 1968. *Nature, man and society in the twelfth century: Essays on new theological perspectives in the Latin West,* ed. and trans. J. Taylor and L. Little. Chicago: University of Chicago Press.

Crossley, P. 1992. The return to the forest: Natural architecture and the German past in the age of Dürer. In *Kunstlerischer Austausch. Akten des XXVIII Internationalen Kongress für Kunstgeschichte,* 71–80. Berlin: Akademie Verlag.

Evans, M. 1994. Fictive painting in twelfth-century Paris. In *Sight and insight: Essays on art and culture in honor of E. H. Gombrich at 85,* ed. J. Onians, 73–87. London: Phaidon.

Foucault, M. 1973. *The order of things: An archaeology of the human sciences.* New York: Vintage.

Frankl, P. 1960. *The Gothic: Literary sources and interpretations through eight centuries.* Princeton, N.J.: Princeton University Press.

———. 1962. *Gothic architecture.* Harmondsworth: Pelican. (See Crossley's excellent introduction to the new edition: Crossley, P., ed. 2000. *Gothic architecture.* New Haven: Yale University Press, 7–31.)

Gombrich, E. H. 1960. *Art and illusion; A study in the psychology of pictorial representation.* A. W. Mellon Lectures in the Fine Arts. New York: Pantheon.

———. 1985. The stylistic categories of art history and their origins in Renaissance ideals. In *Norm and form: Studies in the art of the Renaissance,* 81–98. London: Phaidon.

Grant, L. 1998. *Abbot Suger and Saint-Denis: Church and state in early twelfth-century France.* London and New York: Longman.

Kemp, W. 1996. *The narratives of Gothic stained glass.* Cambridge, England: Cambridge University Press.

Kimpel, D., and R. Suckale. 1985. *Die gotische Architektur in Frankreich, 1130–1270.* Munich: Hirmer.

Lakoff, G. 1987/1990. *Women, fire and dangerous things: What categories reveal about the mind.* Chicago: University of Chicago Press.

Langmead, A. 2002. *The architectural landscape of eleventh- and twelfth-century south-central France.* Ph.D. Dissertation, Columbia University.

Mango, C. A. 1972. *The art of the Byzantine Empire. Sources and documents, 312–1453.* Englewood Cliffs, N.J.: Prentice-Hall.

Murray, S. 1986. *Building Troyes Cathedral. The late Gothic campaigns.* Bloomington: Indiana University Press.

———. 1999. Notre-Dame of Paris and the anticipation of Gothic. *Art Bulletin,* 80: 229–53.

Panofsky, E. 1946/1979. *Abbot Suger on the abbey church of Saint-Denis and its art treasures.* Princeton, N.J.: Princeton University Press.

———. 1951 and multiple reprints. *Gothic architecture and scholasticism.* Latrobe: Archabbey Press.

Pevsner, N. 1945. *The leaves of Southwell.* Harmondsworth, England: Penguin.

Rowland, I. D. 1998. *Culture of the high Renaissance. Ancients and moderns in sixteenth-century Rome.* Cambridge, England: Cambridge University Press.

Sauerländer, W. 1984. "Mod Gothic," a review of Bony's *French Gothic architecture. New York Review of Books,* November 17, 43–44.

———. 1995. Integration: A closed or open proposal? In *Artistic integration in Gothic buildings,* ed. V. C. Raquin, K. Brush, and P. Draper, 3–18. Toronto: University of Toronto Press.

Schlink, W. 1978. *Die Kathedralen Frankreichs.* Munich.

———. 1991. *Beau Dieu von Amiens. Das Christusbild der gotischen Kathedrale: Eine Kunstmonographie.* Frankfurt am Main: Insel Verlag.

Vicaire, M.-H. 1963. *L'imitation des apôtres, moines, chanoines, mendiants Ie.-XIIIe. siècles.* Paris: Editions du Cerf.

Wilson, C. 1990. *Gothic cathedral. The architecture of the great church, 1130–1530.* London: Thames and Hudson.

Woolf, G. 1998. *Becoming Roman: The origins of provincial civilization in Gaul.* Cambridge, England: Cambridge University Press.

PART V

Art and Sacred Belief

II

Making Relics Work

Robert A. Scott

The relics of medieval saints are interesting objects of art for at least two reasons. First, though mundane, often ugly, even revolting, they are nevertheless considered to be art. One purpose of this chapter is to explore how and why things such as slivers of fingernails acquire the quality of art. Second, for miracles to occur, people believed that they had to interact with saints' relics in specific ways. Understanding these ways sheds light on the power of images to affect us.

Imagine for a moment that you are an anthropologist from outer space who has landed on Earth. You find yourself in Europe during the Middle Ages. You explore the landscape and quickly discover the existence of strange edifices: buildings, often vast, always costly and ornately decorated. These buildings contain exquisitely crafted vessels watched over by members of a special class of the citizenry. They call themselves *priests* and describe their function as spiritual brokers, uniquely able to manage the relationships of ordinary people with exalted beings who dwell in heaven. The priests open the vessels they guard for your inspection and you discover that each contains one or more items that appear remarkably mundane, even ugly or downright revolting. Some hold odd bits and pieces of human remains—fragments of cartilage, bits of bone, finger and toenail clippings, strands of hair, vials of blood, teeth, skull bones. In others, you find fragments of objects that once belonged to the person in whose honor the container was built, or that were in some other way connected to that person—pieces of thorn, splinters of wood, threads from veils and blouses, fragments from sandals, purses, belts, pieces of strings and ribbon, and so on.

Lingering at these sites, you soon notice the scores of people who come to visit them. When you ask these visitors where they came from and about their journey, you learn that many have traveled great distances, over hazardous terrain, under difficult, often dangerous circumstances. Then, at the end of their arduous trek, these travelers prostrate themselves before the containers. Some camp next to them for days or weeks at a time, where they pray and then leave gifts. Talking to the visitors further, you learn another puzzling fact. What they have come to admire is not the ornately decorated container, but what it holds: the bodily and material remains of someone who has long since died.

Inside the buildings, you hear a steady din produced by people mumbling prayers in the presence of these remains. Visitors drape their bodies over the vessels or tombs that house them. If you happened to visit Salisbury Cathedral in England, you would see that the tomb of Saint Osmund (figure 11.1) has three openings on one side, matched by another three on the opposite side. Here, pilgrims may insert an injured or deformed body part that they wish healed. Some visitors insert their heads in an effort to make more direct contact with the saint.

If you happened upon the medieval city of Tours, you would learn something even more mysterious about these objects: their potential to cure even those who try to escape their miraculous powers. Here is a thirteenth-century account, by Jacques de Vitry, of an event that reportedly took place in connection with a public display of the relics of Saint Martin of Tours.

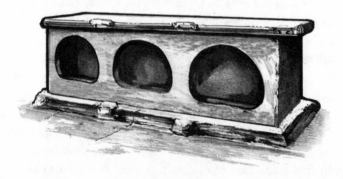

FIGURE 11.1. Drawing of Osmund's Tomb, by Cindy Davis.

[W]hen the body of St. Martin was carried in procession it healed all the sick who met it. However, near the church there were two vagabond beggars, one of whom was blind, the other crippled. They spoke together and said, "Look the body of St. Martin is now being brought in procession and if it catches up with us we shall be healed at once and from then on no one will give us alms, but we will be obliged to work and labour with our own hands." The blind one, however, said to the cripple: "Climb up on my shoulders, since I am strong and you who can see well can lead me." When they had done this they intended to take flight, but the procession overtook them and because of the crowds they could not run away and were healed against their will. (Barber 1992, 171–72)

In the building that houses these objects, the continual din of prayers is punctuated by occasional screams and hysterical shrieks. People experience seizures, or suffer fainting spells, or engage in acts of self-flagellation. Individual visitors or those accompanying them sometimes proclaim something astonishing: a blind person announces that she can now see, a deaf person proclaims that he can hear, someone with a deformed limb reports that his withered limb has been magically made whole, or a crippled person throws away her crutches and walks. With each proclamation, a great commotion ensues that includes a choir of spiritual brokers joyously singing a *Te Deum*.

Looking at all of these practices, you would be bound to ask yourself: what in the world is this about? Whatever is going on here?

You would, of course, have found yourself in the midst of what later generations of scholars would refer to as the medieval cult of saints (Abou-El-Haj 1994; Brown 1981; Finucane 1995; Geary 1978; VanDam 1993; Vauchez 1997; Ward 1982; Weinstein and Bell 1982). The cult of saints enjoyed immense popularity for a thousand years, beginning approximately in the fourth century A.D. and continuing, in fits and starts, until about the time of the Reformation. It was organized around a series of tombs, shrines, and reliquaries housed in great cathedrals, monasteries, and other grand ecclesiastical structures located throughout Europe. This chapter examines the cult of saints in an effort to understand the nature of the force that saints' relics were believed to possess; what people believed they had to do to access this force; and what they thought would happen to them (and others) if they did so. My hope is that through this analysis of beliefs people held about the powerful forces inherent in saints' relics, and the practices they spawned, I may shed additional light on the nature of the hold that objects of art generally can have on those who encounter them.

As works of art, relics of medieval saints are interesting for at least two reasons. First, whatever else one might say about them, few people would claim that saints' relics possess any great intrinsic beauty. As I have said, most relics are mundane, and many are downright revolting. And yet, because of what they signify to those who venerate them, when they are publicly displayed they are surrounded by and embedded in great art—so deeply embedded, in fact, that the quality of artfulness comes to inhabit them. As if by magic, the mundane becomes great art. How and why does this happen?

Second, when people view a painting or a piece of sculpture, or enter a grand building, it is not uncommon for them to experience powerful emotions. Beauty, it is said, stirs the soul. Yet, as David Freedberg shows in his fascinating book *The Power of Images*, how works of art come to affect us in these ways is not well understood (Freedberg 1989). It is as if profound emotional responses just happen when we encounter the art object. The impact of relics, however—with occasional exceptions, such as the remains of Saint Martin of Tours—is not, in fact, something that just happens. Relics are objects people believe will not or cannot affect them unless they, as observers, engage in specific overt actions in their company—actions that are aimed at unlocking what they believe to be the relics' inherent powers to heal or to cause other sorts of miracles. For this reason, relics provide an interesting opportunity to explore the otherwise generally opaque process by which the power attributed to images affects individuals in such profound ways. This chapter, then, will discuss the practices that were entailed in making medieval relics work.

What did medieval people have in mind when they called something "a miracle"? A miracle was interpreted as an act of God that was not subject to the laws of nature or to the usual ways in which human beings act within nature. One medieval theologian, Abbot Samson, expressed the prevailing view succinctly when he observed: "For if he [God] created the laws of matter in accordance with his will, why should he not alter them whenever he chooses to do so?" (Ward 1982, 32).[1]

What did a miracle signal? What kind of an event was it believed to be? What did it signify? According to historian Peter Brown, a miracle was viewed as an event that connected heaven and earth (Brown 1981, 1). He explains that in the medieval worldview, earth was considered the antechamber of heaven, and miracles were a way of giving the living a foretaste of the blessings that were to come. They were a way of reassuring people that they could have a friend in court, so to speak—someone who would intercede for them in times of need. In this sense, miracles associated with venerating a saint by visiting and praying before his or her relics were simply the ordinary life of heaven made manifest in earthly affairs.

In Brown's fascinating book *The Cult of the Saints*, he explains that in the medieval world there was believed to be a fault line that ran across the face of the visible universe. Heaven was imagined to be somewhere above the moon as reflected in the untarnished stability of the stars. The secular realm, at the center of which lay the earth, began somewhere vaguely beneath the moon.

This imaginary boundary line gave death its meaning. When people died, they were thought to have crossed it, going from the secular realm to the other world. The belief was that at the moment of death, the soul separated from the body and made its way to heaven (or not!). Meanwhile, the body disappeared into the earth, where it decayed into so many specks of dust.

What made saints different from ordinary people? Saints were people who had lived lives of exemplary Christian virtue. When they died, their souls went directly to heaven. However, the soul also continued to reside in the earthly remains and was therefore present at the place of burial. This belief is captured in the inscription on the tomb of Saint Martin of Tours, which reads as follows: "Here lies Martin the bishop, of holy memory, whose soul is in the hand of God; but he is fully here, present and made plain in miracles of every kind" (Brown 1981, 4).

This idea that the saint was present both in heaven and here on earth—at the site of the tomb, in bits and pieces of the saint's remains, or in fragments of clothing he or she had worn—made it possible for people to think of saints' tombs or the reliquaries housing their remains as places where, in a sense, heaven and earth joined. The saints' tombs made it possible for the faithful who worshiped at them to experience some measure of the power and mercy of heaven by experiencing or witnessing a miracle. Brown conveys the essence of the view when he writes that his book "is about the joining of Heaven and Earth, and the role, in this joining, of dead human beings" (Brown, 1981, 1).

Those considered saints were believed to be imbued with a special quality, a force termed *virtus* (Vauchez 1997, 36, 499). This quality, which God had given to them, infused their souls, their bodily remains, and objects that may have come into close physical contact with them. The force of *virtus* extended to the clothes saints wore, to their tomb, to the soil that abutted their tomb, to liquids that occasionally oozed from beneath it, and to anything else that had been in immediate or near contact with a saint.

There were some who considered *virtus* a literal force, in the sense that it could actually add mass to whatever came into contact with it. Historian Jonathan Sumption cites an account by Bishop Gregory of Tours of the procedure he recommends to a pilgrim visiting the tomb of Saint Peter: "Should he wish to bring back a relic [i.e., a contact relic] from the tomb, he carefully weighs a piece of cloth which he then hangs inside the tomb. Then he prays ardently and, if his faith is sufficient, the cloth, once removed from the tomb, will be found to be so full of divine grace that it will be much heavier than before" (Sumption 1975, 24).

Relics were treated as if surrounded by a force field of spirituality that could be transmitted to anyone who came close to it. People imagined that relics emitted a kind of "holy radioactivity" that bombarded whatever they touched. Objects placed next to them absorbed their power, and it was this that was thought to cause healings and other kinds of miraculous events. Because of this belief, people thought that the closer they could get to the relic,[2] the stronger would be the dose of the beneficial holy radioactivity they would receive. For this reason, the sine qua non of venerating saints was to go to their tomb or relics, and get as close to them as possible.

Beyond this, what did people think they had to do in order to make relics work for them? A suppliant was to visit the saint's tomb, or a reliquary containing a fragment of his or her remains, in order to venerate it, pray before it, and leave gifts. If, as a result, the suppliant successfully curried favor with the saint, the saint might then be persuaded to intercede with God on his behalf, asking God to grant a miracle to the venerate in recognition of the saint's personal merits. One authority on the subject of medieval saints, André Vauchez, explains: "it was as if the servants of God had acquired, through the sufferings they had endured during their lifetime, a means of putting pressure on God, in a sense obliging him to intervene on behalf of whoever had put themselves under their protection" (Vauchez 1997, 461).

Beliefs surrounding the force of *virtus* were elaborated in interesting ways. For example, it was believed that relics could be transported from their site at the saint's tomb to other places without in any way diminishing their potency. By the same token, disassembling a relic by breaking it into pieces and dispersing the pieces to distant locations in no way diminished its power. A single strand of hair was believed to carry the same force as the entire body; a piece of the strap from a saint's sandal, the same force as the saint's entire skeleton. Any part, no matter how minuscule, was regarded as equal in power to the body or original article of clothing from which it came.

At the same time, a relic's force and power to heal depended on enclosing it, no matter where it was. If it were left exposed, its healing powers would dissipate. For this reason, though bits and pieces of saints' relics could be found everywhere throughout the Christian world, they were always encased and displayed in tombs and boxes.

How are we to make sense of these beliefs about the forces surrounding saints' relics and the actions required to access those forces? Where did these notions come from? Out of what cultural "raw material" were they constituted? Why did (do) so many people believe in them so deeply? Why were they considered plausible? It is one thing to lay out for people how they are meant to act in the presence of a saint's remains, and to explain the kind of force the relics purportedly contain. It is quite another for people to actually believe what they have been told. Why should the preposterous notion that a sliver of toenail can possess the power to restore sight strike anyone as believable? Is it because people are gullible, or are there deeper reasons for their capacity to embrace the idea that objects contain the power to affect us in such profound ways? Any insights we may glean from the attempt to answer these questions will, I believe, help us to understand more fully what David Freedberg has aptly termed "the power of images" (Freedberg 1989).

Three lines of scholarly investigation seem especially relevant to our understanding of these issues. The first grows out of recent work by Mark Turner and Gilles Fauconnier on the phenomenon of conceptual blending (Fauconnier and Turner 2002); the second from Leonard Talmy's work on force fields (Talmy 2000) and Pascal Boyer's work on "ghost physics" (Boyer 1994, 402; Boyer 2001, 96–97); and the third from Émile Durkheim's pathbreaking work on elementary forms of religious life (Durkheim 1912).

The Turner-Fauconnier account of conceptual blending is an especially effective heuristic for elucidating the fundamental structure of ideas medieval peoples held about saints and the qualities they attributed to them. In a sense, the "job" of a saint, if one can speak this way, is to supply a mechanism by which it becomes possible for humans to connect to and gain the protection of heaven.[3] In order for this to happen, the qualities that are attributed to saints cannot be just any qualities; they must be specifically suited to the task humans have assigned them to carry out. This is an important point to emphasize, for the following reason. If saints are all-powerful and possess abilities not available to ordinary people, it should be possible for them to configure themselves however they wish. (Recall the words of Abbot Samson quoted earlier: since the Creator established the laws governing the world, he is free to break them whenever he wishes.) For this reason, one would not expect every saint to have the same set of attributes or to be like every other saint. Yet although different saints were thought to be "specialists" at healing different kinds of human ailments, the basic manner in which they performed healings did not differ. We need to understand why certain attributes and not others were given to saints, and why these attributes apply to all saints and not just to some of them. It is here that Turner and Fauconnier's work on conceptual blending is particularly useful.

To perform their mission of connecting the living with heaven, saints (all of whom were, of course, deceased) had to continue to possess attributes which are normally reserved for the living. At the same time, as intercessors between God and human beings, saints also had to possess attributes which are normally reserved for the divine. To accomplish this, elements of the concept "human" were borrowed and transported to the mental space set aside for those whom Peter Brown has termed "the holy dead" (Brown 1981, 91); and elements of the mental space termed "God" or "the divine" were borrowed and transported to this same mental space.

Turner and Fauconnier's concept of conceptual blending leads us, then, to posit the existence of four mental spaces. One contains the concept of a person who is alive and has the capacity to exert force; the second is occupied by the notion of a corpse; the third is occupied by the divine; and the fourth is the space in which elements of these three spaces are blended. From space 2, we project to space 4 the corpse or bits of the corpse; from space 1, we project personal identity and the capacity to exert force; from space 3, we project the divine power to reside in a part as well as a whole, and to penetrate barriers and other similar properties. Space 4, then, results in a blend of the deceased person (space 2) that is half-human (space 1) and half-divine (space 3). By this process of blending, the corpse inherits the identity of the living person, including, most crucially, some of its capacity to exert influence. At the same time, it also possesses certain features attributed to the divine. The ability to exert influence, part of the mental space of the living human, is extended to the corpse's body and then, borrowing powers attributed to the divine, elaborated to make possible the notion that the part acquires the power of the whole. This transference of divine powers also makes possible the potential for intercession and healing that humans consider the acid test of whether a dead human being is or is not a saint.

Though somewhat of an aside, it is interesting to speculate about what might have motivated medieval theologians to embrace the idea that the part and the whole are the same. We have said that during the medieval period, beliefs about saints' relics included the notion that a single part or piece of a saint's body, or some object or piece of an object that had touched the body, retained as much power as the whole from which it came. However, this was not always the belief. In antiquity, by which I mean the early centuries A.D., the most valued relics were of the whole skeleton and all of the remains associated with the saint, all contained within a single tomb. Only later in the history of the cult of saints did the notion begin to appear that a single tiny part had the same power as the whole.

Perhaps one reason this belief in the whole-part connection was embraced was that it provided an effective mechanism for the newly emerging religion to establish its presence in distant places. The bits and pieces of saints' relics that ended up in reliquaries throughout the Christian world helped foster a sense of unity between the most remote regions of Europe and Christianity's geographical center and source (see Brown 1981, 90).

The notion of blending provides a useful way to conceptualize the mixture of mental spaces that resulted in constructing the concept of the saint. Leonard Talmy's concept of force dynamics provides a vehicle for understanding the vocabulary with which the faithful spoke of the saints' powers. Talmy's work suggests that notions about force dynamics associated with the cult of saints, far from being idiosyncratic, are in fact an elaboration of ideas borrowed from ordinary, everyday discourse.

"Force dynamics" connotes how people conceptualize and describe the ways in which entities interact with respect to force. Examples include the impressions we have about how forces are exerted, how they are resisted, how they may be overcome, how their expression may be blocked, how we may overcome such blocking, how to tap into the forces attributed to objects and use them for the benefit of humanity, and similar ideas.

Students of the subject, of whom linguist Talmy is perhaps the foremost example, assert that notions about force dynamics figure importantly in the very structure of language and lie at the core of a speaker's basic notions of causation. Talmy writes: "Overall, force dynamics... emerges as a fundamental notional system that structures conceptual material pertaining to force interactions in a common way across a linguistic range: the physical, psychological, social, inferential, discourse, and mental-model domains of reference and conception" (Talmy 2000, 410).

Talmy shows that notions we hold about force dynamics are not an isolated domain. Rather, these notions structure the conceptual organization of other cognitive systems, such as the perceptual modalities and reason. Of special interest in the present context, Talmy notes "a striking similarity between fictive motion... and the properties ghosts or spirits exhibit in the belief systems of many traditional cultures. The anthropologist Pascal Boyer (1994) sees these properties as a culturally pervasive and coherent conceptual system he terms 'ghost physics.' Boyer holds that ghost and spirit phenomena obey all the usual causal expectations for physical or social entities, with only a few exceptions...."

Talmy offers this intriguing example of a standard conceptualization, relying on force dynamics, whose properties are also attributed to ghosts:

[I]f I, for example, am inside a windowless building and am asked to point toward the next town, I will not, through gesticulations, indicate a path that begins at my finger, leads through the open doorway and out the exit of the building, and finally turns around and moves in the direction of the town. On the contrary, I will simply extend my arm with pointed finger in the direction of the town, regardless of the structure around me. That is, the demonstrative path, effectively conceptualized as an intangible line emerging from the finger, itself has the following crucial properties: (1) It is invisible, and (2) it passes through walls. These are the very same properties that are ascribed to spirits and ghosts. (Talmy 2000, 127)

This leads Talmy to conclude, "The exceptional phenomena found to occur in ghost physics may be the same as certain cognitive phenomena that already exist in other cognitive systems and that then are tapped for service in cultural spirit ascriptions" (Talmy 2000, 126).

We have seen that the language, the metaphors, and the practices associated with relic worship are replete with ideas about force dynamics. The entire vocabulary associated with the powers that relics possess—descriptions of how to access those powers and how they act upon the suppliant, what must be done to preserve them and keep them strong, and so forth—derive from certain fundamental ideas people have about force dynamics.

I point this out for the following reason. In the modern scientific age, it is tempting to assume that belief in miracles and the role of saints' relics in facilitating them is the product of ignorance, folk myths, or both. However, once we understand that such beliefs reflect a deeper, intuitive understanding of force dynamics, we can appreciate that they are the product not of ignorance, but of notions that infuse the very structure of language itself.

If the idea of force dynamics enables us to solve one puzzle about relic worship, it immediately raises another: Why do notions about invisible forces strike people as plausible? Why is it so easy and natural for people to accept them as real? Where and how do human beings gain their impression of the existence of an external force to which they feel subject? What experiences do they have that lead them to accept this idea as intuitively and inherently plausible?

As we seek to answer these questions, the work of the great French sociologist Émile Durkheim is particularly illuminating. Durkheim was struck by a remarkable fact—namely, the parallel between the way humans think about and experience the divine and the way they think about and experience society.

Of course, the concept of the divine has its own complex conceptual history which limitations of space require us to leave aside. For present purposes we need only note Durkheim's compelling observation that many of the qualities we attribute to society are the very same ones we attribute to divine forces. The part of his argument that is most germane here relates to the ways in which society affects us as individuals and the ways in which we as members experience it.

According to Durkheim, we experience society as a force that is superior to ourselves and on which we feel we can depend. We experience it as abstract, external, powerful, and coercive. Society confronts us as an impersonal, formless, nameless, faceless, yet very real force that is simply there, a force that resists our efforts to change it or to depart from its basic ways. Ours is a world filled with preexisting rules and customs and traditions and practices, none of them of our own making; we merely incorporate, internalize, and behave in accordance with them, as a result of socialization.

Therefore, if we come to believe in the existence of invisible forces outside ourselves that act upon us and to which we are subject, there is good reason: this precisely describes our relationship to society.

Durkheim summarizes his argument in two key passages from *The Elementary Forms of Religious Life* (I quote from Fields's translation, with some corrections):

> [T]he faithful are not mistaken when they believe in the existence of a moral power to which they are subject and from which they receive what is best in themselves. That power exists, and it is society. (226–27)

> Religious force is none other than the feeling that the collectivity inspires in its members, but projected outside the minds that experience it, and objectified. (230)

Durkheim's insights also shed additional light on the equivalency in sacred objects between the part and the whole. The reason it is possible for people to accept the idea that a fragment of a relic has the same power as the whole is that the property of sacredness is not intrinsic to the object. It comes from without, and by an act of cognitive compression, we attribute it to the part no less than to the whole. Durkheim writes: "A mere scrap of the flag represents the country as much as the flag itself; moreover, it is sacred in the same way and to the same degree" (Durkheim 1912, 231).

I believe that Durkheim's insight points us toward an explanation of why people so easily accept the idea that there are invisible forces that operate on them in powerful ways. They believe this because this is precisely the way in which their relationship to the collective is experienced and understood. Relic worship is made possible because its practices are built on the very foundations of social life itself.

In sum, my aim here has been to better understand the impact art has on people by examining practices associated with the medieval worship of saints' relics. In particular, I have tried to show what people thought they had to do to activate the miraculous potential they attributed to saints' relics and to identify the origins of these beliefs and practices in basic cognitive processes, in the everyday use of language, and in certain features of communal social existence.

NOTES

1. Because miracles were considered to be inexplicable events, it became important for the Catholic Church to rule out all other causes of a natural sort. In this way, organized religion unwittingly fostered the advancement of basic knowledge in those domains of learning devoted to discovering the natural causes of things—i.e., the sciences.

2. In the beginnings of the cult of saints, the practice was to touch the relic directly. This caused damage to the artifacts and encouraged the theft of relics. As a result, later the prevailing belief was that touching a relic directly could result in burns to the skin and even death.

3. Elsewhere I explain why this was such an urgent and important matter during the medieval period. See Scott 2003.

REFERENCES

Abou-El-Haj, B. 1994. *The medieval cult of saints: Formations and transformations.* Cambridge, England: Cambridge University Press.

Barber, M. 1992. *The two cities: Medieval Europe, 1050–1320.* London and New York: Routledge.

Boyer, P. 1994. Cognitive constraints on cultural representations: Natural ontologies and religious ideas. In *Mapping the mind: Domain specificity in cognition and culture,* ed. L. Hirschfeld and S. Gelman, 211–32. New York: Cambridge University Press.

———. 2001. *Religion explained.* London: William Heinnemann.

Brown, P. 1981. *The cult of the saints: Its rise and function in Latin Christianity.* Chicago: University of Chicago Press.

Durkheim, É. 1912/1995. *The elementary forms of religious life,* trans. K. E. Fields. New York: Free Press.

Fauconnier, G., and M. Turner. 2002. *The way we think: Conceptual blending and the mind's hidden complexities.* New York: Basic Books.

Finucane, R. 1995. *Miracles and pilgrims.* New York: St. Martin's Press.

Freedberg, D. 1989. *The power of images: Studies in the history and theory of response.* Chicago: University of Chicago Press.

Geary, P. 1978. *Furta Sacra.* Princeton, N.J.: Princeton University Press.

Melczer, W. 1993. *The pilgrim's guide to Santiago de Compostela.* New York: Italica Press.

Panofsky, I. 1946. *Abbot Suger.* Princeton, N.J.: Princeton University Press.

Sargent-Baur, B., ed. 1992. *Journeys toward God.* Kalamazoo, Mich.: Medieval Institute Publications of Western Michigan University.

Scott, R. 2003. *The Gothic enterprise.* Berkeley: University of California Press.

Sumption, J. 1975. *Pilgrimage: An image of mediaeval religion.* London: Faber and Faber.

Talmy, L. 2000. *Toward a cognitive semantics. Volume 1: Concept structuring systems.* Cambridge, Mass., and London: MIT Press.

VanDam, R. 1993. *Saints and their miracles in late antique Gaul.* Princeton, N.J.: Princeton University Press.

Vauchez, A. 1997. *Sainthood in the later Middle Ages,* trans. J. Birrell. Cambridge, England: Cambridge University Press.

Ward, B. 1982. *Miracles and the medieval mind.* Philadelphia: University of Pennsylvania Press.

Weinstein, D., and R. Bell. 1982. *Saints and society.* Chicago: University of Chicago Press.

12

Architectural Space as Metaphor in the Greek Sanctuary

Gloria Ferrari

This chapter explores the power of metaphor to create images that give visual shape to cultural representations. As in Robert A. Scott's chapter in this volume, the focus is on the rise of monumental sacred architecture under particular historical and social conditions.

The topics that are central to this volume—how the mind works and what role visual images play in that process—were as crucial in ancient Greek thought as they are today. In his treatise on memory Aristotle offers the following arresting statement:

> An account has already been given of imagination in the discussion of the soul, and it is not possible to think without an image. For the same effect occurs in thinking as in drawing a diagram. For in the latter case, though we do not make any use of the fact that the size of the triangle is determinate, we none the less draw it with a determinate size. And similarly someone who is thinking, even if he is not thinking of something with a size, places something with a size before his eyes, but thinks of it not as having a size. If its nature is that of things which have a size, but not a determinate one, he places before his eyes something with a determinate size, but thinks of it simply as having size. (Aristotle *On Memory* 449B30–450A6; trans. Sorabji 1972. See also *On the Soul* 431A17)

Elsewhere in Aristotle (*Rhetoric* 1405B13, 1411B21) this capacity "to set things described before the eyes" is the special quality of the trope of metaphor. It is, then, perhaps not a coincidence that the intellectual operation described in the passage above has some significant points in common with Max Black's definition of metaphor as "interaction." This consists of the connection of two subjects in a single "frame," in such a way that one, the focal image, organizes the other, the idea in question:

> Suppose I look at the night sky through a piece of heavily smoked glass on which certain lines have been left clear. Then I shall see only the stars that can be made to lie on the lines previously prepared upon the screen, and the stars I do see will be seen as organized by the screen's structure. We can think of a metaphor as such a screen, and the system of "associated commonplaces" of the focal word as the network of lines upon the screen. We can say that the principal subject is "seen through" the metaphorical expression—or, if we prefer, that the principal subject is "projected upon" the field of the subsidiary subject. (Black 1981, 75)

Selection, implied in the figures of the screen and the network, is as critical to this process as it is to the one Aristotle envisions in the passage quoted above, where the mind is instructed to ignore the size of the diagram that makes the very thought of triangularity possible.

I reach back to Black's venerable screen metaphor for several reasons. Unlike the figure of a projection from a "source domain" onto a "target domain" that superseded it in studies of metaphor as a cognitive mechanism, the figure of the screen locates the metaphoric interaction of two terms in a frame that is distinct from the "domains" in which the terms each originate (Lakoff and Johnson 1980; Lakoff and Turner 1989, 62–64). This configuration is roughly in agreement with Turner and Fauconnier's theory of "blended space," the place where selected inputs from two other spaces combine to bring forth new understandings (Fauconnier and Turner 2002, chap. 3).[1] Black's system of "associated commonplaces" also bears comparison with that fourth "generic space" which, in Turner and Fauconnier's proposal, serves as the repository of the conceptual structure, the fund of knowledge and beliefs shared by the community of speaker and viewers. There is, however, one major difference. Whereas in the latter view the "generic space" affects equally both "input spaces," in Black's definition of metaphor the "associated commonplaces" manipulate only one, the vehicle or the focal image:

Consider the statement, "Man is a wolf." ... [It] will not convey its
intended meaning to a reader sufficiently ignorant about wolves.
What is needed is not so much that the reader shall know the standard dictionary meaning of "wolf" ... as that he shall know what I
will call the *system of associated commonplaces*. ... From the expert's
standpoint, the system of commonplaces may include half-truths or
downright mistakes (as when a whale is classified as a fish); but the
important thing for the metaphor's effectiveness is not that the
commonplaces shall be true, but that they should be readily and
freely evoked. (Black 1981, 73–74; see also Black 1962, 39)

In other words, it matters not at all that wolves are highly social and the good
parents that they are. The metaphor appeals to the folk notion that wolves are
bloodthirsty predators, and it relies on its capacity to evoke images that are as
vivid as they are familiar: the fangs, the glowering eyes, the gore.

Therein lies, to my mind, the value of the theory of metaphor as interaction
in discussing the production of what we call art. Unlike other kinds of "blends,"
metaphor typically casts thought in figurative, extralinguistic terms. It is my
thesis that images produced within the frame of metaphor indeed inform visual
representations and draw the viewer into the mental spaces that produced them
(Ferrari 2002, chap. 3). In addition, the key importance of cultural filters—
Black's "commonplaces"—in the construction of metaphors invites us to give
proper consideration to the social and historical milieu in which such representations are produced, even as we entertain globalizing explanations in
terms of the physiology of perception and evolution. My particular point of view
is that of an archaeologist charged with making sense of the material remains
of past cultures, and from that point of view I ask: if it is true that it is not
possible to think without an image, can images lead us into the conceptual
universe of a culture not our own? The emergence of the sanctuary in the
Greek Iron Age provides rich grounds on which to explore this question.

What I am concerned with is the Greek sanctuary as representation, an
artifact with formal features that map out a certain conception of the relationship of man to god, or of the citizen of the ancient Greek city-state, the
polis, to the divine. I shall argue that dominant, consistent features of the
Greek sanctuary are related to a fundamental concept in polis society, that of
"measure," or the fair apportioning of resources in both human and divine
society. Selectively recruited elements of Mycenaean palace architecture, both
real and imaginary, articulate a metaphor projecting the god as ruler of the city.

In spite of a great range of variations in the size, position, and component
elements of individual sanctuaries, certain features recur with significant

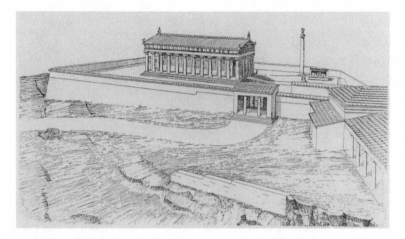

FIGURE 12.1. Aegina, Sanctuary of Aphaia. Reconstruction Drawing. After Marinatos and Hägg 1993.

consistency—namely, precinct, temple, and altar. The late sixth century B.C.E. phase of the sanctuary of Aphaia on Aegina (figure 12.1) serves as a minimal example of this model. A parcel of land that belongs to the god, the *temenos*, is marked off from the public domain by a precinct wall, and the altar stands to the east of the temple.

The Aegina sanctuary represents the point of arrival of a process whose origins we locate in the eighth and early seventh centuries B.C.E., when there become visible in the archaeological record temples on a large scale, with correspondingly large altars.[2] The sanctuary assumes canonical features in the next century, somewhere between 650 and 600 B.C.E., with further monumentalization introduced by the use of stone as building material, the canonization of the Ionic and the Doric architectural styles (which Renaissance scholars would call orders), and the development of architectural canons governing a narrow range of variations in the plan and proportions of the temple.[3]

This development marks the reintroduction of architecture on a monumental scale in Greece for the first time since the collapse of the Mycenaean kingdoms, following a series of catastrophic destructions around 1200 B.C.E. These kingdoms, centered on palaces such as the one at Mycenae, created what has been aptly named a "palace culture." Texts accidentally preserved on clay tablets attest to a highly developed bureaucracy and tell us, among other things, that the Mycenaeans spoke a form of Greek and worshiped gods that had the same names, some of them at least, as the gods worshiped by the Greeks in historical times (Burkert 1985, 43–46). But the sanctuary and its temple are unknown in the Mycenaean world, where the principal installations of cult were part of the palace itself and, we think, the

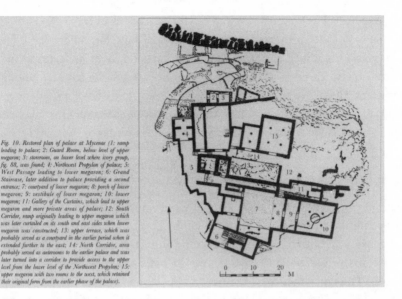

Fig. 10. Restored plan of palace at Mycenae (1: ramp leading to palace; 2: Guard Room, below level of upper megaron; 3: storeroom, on lower level where ivory group, fig. 88, was found; 4: Northwest Propylon of palace; 5: West Passage leading to lower megaron; 6: Grand Staircase, later addition to palace providing a second entrance; 7: courtyard of lower megaron; 8: porch of lower megaron; 9: vestibule of lower megaron; 10: lower megaron; 11: Gallery of the Curtains, which lead to upper megaron and more private areas of palace; 12: South Corridor, ramp originally leading to upper megaron which was later curtailed on its south and east sides when lower megaron was constructed; 13: upper terrace, which was probably served as a courtyard in the earlier period when it extended further to the east; 14: North Corridor, area probably served as anterooms to the earlier palace and was later turned into a corridor to provide access to the upper level from the lower level of the Northwest Propylon; 15: upper megaron with two rooms to the west, which retained their original form from the earlier phase of the palace).

FIGURE 12.2. Mycenae. Plan of the Citadel. Drawing by T. L. Shear, Jr. After Shear 2000.

performance of ritual was one of the prerogatives of the king.[4] Architecturally, not the temple but the palace complex is the dominant feature at Mycenaean sites, as at Mycenae itself (figure 12.2). Characteristically, access to the citadel is through a monumental gate to a ramp leading to the palace complex. In the palace, a double gate leads to the court, onto which opens the so-called *megaron,* or throne room.

The archaeological record of Greece for the three centuries or so that followed the end of the Mycenaean states gives evidence of complex trans-formations, of rupture and change, as well as a measure of permanence.[5] Fragmentation into small settlements ruled by local chiefs, depopulation, loss of literacy and other specialized technical skills, insularity—all point to for-midable disruption. If cult practices from the Bronze Age substantially sur-vived, they did so in diminished and altered form. The reformulation of sacred space in monumental terms in the eighth and seventh centuries B.C.E. is of a piece with other phenomena that signal the return of prosperity and the beginning of a new era, what has been called the Greek Renaissance in the eighth century, characterized by an increase in populations, importation of foreign goods, and the reintroduction of technical skills and literacy (Cold-stream 1977, 295–369; Hägg 1983). In the visual arts, one sees the re-appearance of figural scenes, some attesting to the circulation of myths and epic tales. We locate here an important stage of the tradition of oral poetry that we know best in Homer's *Iliad* and *Odyssey*, as well as in Hesiod's cosmogony. At the eye of the storm we locate the process of state formation that issued in the polis—the Greek city-state, defined in terms of both its territory and the citizen body. There is as well the emergence of a supra-national identity in terms of Hellas, which we translate as Greece, a Panhellenic identity that finds expression in the growth of sanctuaries such as that of Olympia, with its games, and Delphi, with its oracle situated at the center of the world (Morgan 1990).

Against this background one is justified in seeing, as most scholars do, the development of the sanctuary as an invention, one intimately connected with the emergence of the polis as a "temple culture." Our understanding of polis religion and of the role that the temple has in it, however, is riddled with paradoxes. As Sourvinou-Inwood points out, it is impossible to draw the line between the sacred and the political in polis religion (Sourvinou-Inwood 1990). The convergence of the two is apparent in the designation of a particular god as protector of the city (*polioukhos*)—Hera of Argos, Athena of Athens, Poseidon of Troizen.[6] Gods would fight for this privilege, as in the case of the contest between Athena and Poseidon over Athens (Apollodorus, *Library* 3.14.1). That is not to say that the Greek city-state was a theocracy. In fact, the reverse seems to be true, for, as is well known and often repeated, Greek religion has no priestly caste, no sacred books, no mediating body between the political and the sacred. (See Jameson 1997, 489.) It is, then, all the more remarkable that greater monumental emphasis should be given to religious structures in the city than to any others, particularly when such conspicuous display is not integral to the cult. The temple, for instance, is the most visible element of the physical plant of worship in ancient Greece, but it is not a necessary element (Burkert 1988, 36; Sourvinou-Inwood 1993, 11). As an example, scholars often point to the temple of Zeus at Olympia. The archaeological record of the sanctuary goes back to the ninth century B.C.E., and the traditional date for the foundation of the Olympic games performed there is 776 B.C.E. The earliest temple was built perhaps around that time— not to Zeus, however, but to his consort Hera. Zeus remained homeless, so to speak, over the three and a half centuries that followed. With Burkert, we may well ask: "Why did the Greeks, in the conditions of what would be third-world economy today, concentrate on elaborating the superfluous, that which at first and second glance and on their own reflection they did not really need?" (Burkert 1988, 27; see also Burkert 1996).

Although temples were accessible (but not to all and not all the time) and might house rituals, they were not congregational spaces. Cult activity principally took place outdoors, at the altar. This was the site of the central

ritual of Greek religion, the sacrifice of an animal. The beast would be dis-
membered and the parts distributed as follows: edible portions would be
roasted and distributed to the worshipers; inedible parts, including the bones,
would be burned on the altar for consumption by the gods. The foundation
legend of this ritual places its origin in a chain of fraudulent gift exchanges
that brought about the separation of men from gods and plunged mankind
into its present state (Hesiod, *Theogony* 535–89; *Works and Days* 42–89). In
the days when men and the gods lived and dined together, the story goes,
clever Prometheus slaughtered an ox and divided the carcass into two unequal
portions. He wrapped the flesh and the juiciest parts in the unappetizing ox's
paunch, and offered Zeus a bundle of shiny fat that contained only the bones
stripped of flesh. Zeus had observed how unfair the division had been, and he
saw through the deception. He took the bones wrapped in fat, nevertheless,
but in return withheld fire from mortals. When Prometheus stole the fire,
Zeus inflicted on men the worst of punishments by creating Pandora, the
creature from whom the "deadly race of women" was born. Like the bones
wrapped in fat, by which Prometheus attempted to deceive Zeus, Pandora is
made of vile matter, earth, under the appearance of a beautiful maiden tricked
out in splendid clothes and jewels.

The only necessary and sufficient installation of cult besides the altar is
the *temenos*, the site of the sanctuary itself.[7] As its etymology indicates, this
word means a portion of land "cut off," reserved for the god, and its perim-
eter may simply be marked with boundary stones or enclosed by an imposing
wall.[8] The site may contain features that bear witness to the presence of the
gods. That is the case with the olive tree and the marks of Poseidon's tri-
dent on the Athenian Acropolis, for instance, which are the visible traces of
the gods' competition over the city, or the oracular chasm at Delphi. But, as a
rule, the location chosen seems to have no inherently sacred quality. In
the foundation of colonies, it has been argued, the establishment of sanctuaries followed eminently rational criteria, which designated different areas of
the city for different functions. (See Malkin 1987, 331–44.) To cite a mythological paradigm, the *Odyssey* describes the foundation of Scheria by Nau-
sithoos in these terms: "He erected walls around the city, he built the houses,
made the temples of the gods, and he divided up the fields" (6.9–10). In the
city, the gods have their place, one that is chosen and measured by the
founder.

There are recurrent features across many sanctuaries that shape such
nonessential installations in the estate of the god as the *temenos* wall and temples. Such regularities invite an analysis of the sanctuary as representation,
a frame that organizes the city's dealings with the sacred. Most of the points

that follow are common knowledge, although they are not normally brought to bear one upon the other.

When the *temenos* is enclosed by a wall, access to the sanctuary is through an elaborate gateway, the *propylon*, that has the following consistent features: it is double, with a porch on either side of the threshold. The *Propylaea* to the Athenian Acropolis are a monumental, well-preserved example of this feature, and the restored walls and monuments of the Acropolis as a whole offer a vivid impression of the visual impact produced by a major sanctuary (figure 12.3). As a rule, the *propylon* is not aligned with the temple, nor does it feed the visitors into a processional course characterized by centrality and axiality. Instead, the faithful are confronted with a side or rear view of the buildings, and the logic of this arrangement, or lack thereof, has driven architectural historians to distraction.[9]

As Burkert playfully observed, Greek temples tend to come in groups (Burkert 1988, 34). This is a feature of Greek sanctuaries that has received less attention than it deserves. Normally sanctuaries housed several buildings, and indeed, many contain more than one temple (Burkert 1988, 34). Olympia has temples to Zeus, Hera, and the Mother of the Gods, for instance; there were two temples of Athena in her Acropolis sanctuary; on Samos, the sanctuary of

FIGURE 12.3. Overhead view of the Acropolis, Athens, Greece (c. late fifth century B.C.E.), extracted from an interactive 3-D computer model of the site created by Learning Sites, Inc.; image copyright 2003 by and used with permission of Learning Sites, Inc.

Hera presents an embarrassment of as many as eleven "temples," whose occupant is unknown (Kyrieleis 1993, 131–33); and on Delos there are three temples of Apollo, as well as one of Artemis. In view of the fact that the temple is essentially superfluous to the cult, this state of affairs raises the possibility that these monumental structures have instead the character of expensive offerings to the god (Burkert 1988, 42–44; Fehr 1996, 171–81).[10]

Votives are indeed an integral part of the cultic landscape. This is a category with which one is familiar from other places and times, encompassing a wide range of dedications.[11] Votive offerings are generally understood as "gifts" made to the gods in thanks for a favor or in hope of one. The transaction is not modeled on a commercial exchange, but is instead a matter of reciprocity; in principle, the two parties are free to give, or not, and to reciprocate, or not. That is surely the case with many dedications, and it would be a mistake to underestimate the importance of *kharis*—gratitude and the delight that the gift produces.[12]

I wish to call attention, however, to a kind of dedication that looks less like a gift than a form of taxation: the tithe, or *aparkhe*, the dedication of a percentage of a profit, or any gain. A major source of income for construction and adornment of sanctuaries was war: after a victory, a percentage (usually 10 percent) of the spoils was taken out for the god before distribution began. This was the so-called *akrothinia*, or top of the pile—the choice parts (Burkert 1985, 69). The god would also claim a share of an unexpected windfall. For instance, when the inhabitants of Siphnos became rich after discovering their gold mines, they paid a tithe to Delphi, as Apollo's oracle had advised them to do, and built a treasury-house for the god (Pausanias 10.11.2; Herodotus 3.57). A visitor at Delphi, entering the sanctuary, would find at his right a colossal statue of a bull in bronze, dedicated by the Corcyraeans, whose cost represented a percentage of a spectacular catch of tuna, to which the fishermen had been led by the bull thus immortalized (Pausanias 10.9.1).

This "accounting mentality" is nowhere more in evidence than in the monumental stone steles inscribed with detailed accounts of income flowing into the god's coffers, inventories of his property, and records of expenditures incurred in the construction of temples or the making of statues—down to the last stone and obol. A series of such inscriptions documents the construction of the Parthenon and other buildings on the Athenian Acropolis, for instance. Part of one referring to the carving of the figural frieze on the Erechtheum reads as follows:

> For placing grilles in the intercolumniations, four in number, toward the Pandroseum, to Komon, living in Melite, 40 drachmae. For

turning bosses for the coffer-lids, to Mikion, living in Kollytos,
3 drachmae, 1 obol. (Trans. Caskey 1927, 340–41)

With the erection of these steles, documents that were normally made of
perishable materials and housed in temple archives were set in stone and
publicly displayed. The inscriptions, therefore, are not only building accounts
or temple inventories, as they are called, but also monuments to the very
practice of record keeping in the management of the property of the gods.[13]

Despite a wide range of variations, the regularities I have listed in the
shape of the physical plant of worship in the polis add up to a coherent whole.
The sanctuary is a compound, encompassing both natural features and built
structures on a parcel of land. These include a circuit wall, accessible through
a double gate giving access to the altar, the temple, or temples, and other
shrines and temple-like structures. A second important formal characteristic
of the sanctuary is the appeal made by several of its features to Mycenaean
architecture.[14] We have long been aware that the plan of the temple resembles
that of the throne room, the *megaron*, of Mycenaean palaces, and that the
gateway leading into the *temenos* reproduces that of the double gate leading
into the court of the palace (Tomlinson 1976, 39–40). In addition, the model
of the Mycenaean walled citadel may explain the eccentric placement of the
gateway with respect to the temples. For obvious defensive reasons, the
monumental gate in the fortification wall was placed off-center with respect to
the palace. Finally, both capital and frieze of the Doric order have distant but
recognizable relatives in Mycenaean architecture (Jones 2002, 356–57).

For the temple builders of the archaic period, such allusions to features of
monumental Mycenaean architecture may have been a nod to the past, a
means to lay claim to the heroic age, or an advertisement of the antiquity of
cults. But their primary function, I suggest, is that of a metaphoric grid, giving
visible shape to the integration of the divinity into the polis and to its relationship to the citizenry. The quotations of particular features I have listed—
the city gate, the *megaron* plan, the *propylon*—do not add up to a reproduction,
however approximate, of either the Mycenaean palace or its citadel, as exca-
vations have revealed them to us. They do, however, find correspondences in
representations of imaginary palaces. I refer to the imagery of the residences
of gods, kings, and heroes that are contained in the epic poems, specifically in
the *Iliad* and the *Odyssey*. The correspondences are especially significant in
view of the fact that the poems surely were sung regularly at the time when
the sanctuary comes into existence, and were part of a common fund of
knowledge and ideas. In other words, the epic affords us access, albeit limited,

to the way in which palaces were imagined in archaic Greece—that is to say, entry into what Black would call the "system of commonplaces" associated with the idea of "ancient palace." In the epic we find again the image of the walled compound comprising an altar and several buildings that one enters from a double gateway.

In the *Odyssey*, gateway and court form the complex through which one reaches the palace, which consists of several buildings, as Odysseus' description to Eumaeus of his own house implies: "Building upon building, preceded by a court with wall and coping, and double doors secure the enclosure" (*Odyssey* 17.266–68). And this is what Odysseus sees as he stands on the threshold of the outer gate of the fabulous palace of Alcinous on Scheria: a court enclosed by walls with a coping of lapis lazuli, stretching from the brazen threshold to the inner part of the compound:

> And within, thrones were backed against the wall on both sides
> all the way from the inner room to the door, with fine-spun
> delicate cloths, the work of women, spread out upon them.
> There the leaders of the Phaiakians held their sessions
> and drank and ate, since they held these forever ... (*Odyssey*
> 7.95–99, trans. Lattimore 1965)

The altar, too, is a central feature of the court of epic palaces.[15] Nestor and Odysseus, standing at the gate of Peleus' palace, observe the old man performing sacrifice accompanied by a libation, and are promptly recognized by Achilles:

> Peleus the aged horseman was burning
> the fat thigh pieces of an ox to Zeus who delights in the thunder
> in the garth of the courtyard. He was holding a golden beaker
> and pouring the bright wine over the burning dedications. You two
> were over the meat of the ox attending to it, and we came
> and stood in the forecourt, and Achilleus sprang up wondering
> and took us by the hand and led us in, and told us to sit down,
> and set hospitality properly before us, as is the stranger's
> right. (*Iliad* 11.772–79, trans. Lattimore 1951)

This picture suggestively evokes the ritual of animal sacrifice at the altar in the open area, the court, as it were, of the sanctuary.

The architecture of the sanctuary lays out a metaphor that casts sacred space as the palace of the god. This is a rich and capacious screen, to return to Black's terminology, which throws into relief salient features of ancient Greek cult, recasting in metaphorical terms Victor Ehrenberg's famous statement that in archaic Greece "the god himself took the place of the king" (Ehrenberg 1960, 17). The sanctuary is the god's share of the territory of the polis, and by the grant of a parcel of land the divinity becomes, as it were, part of the polis. By these means, one might say, the sacred is configured in political terms. As the ruler, the god is assigned both rights and responsibilities. Guardianship of its domain entitles the deity to commensurate rewards—namely, shares of the city's growth and wealth, which fill the sanctuary with temples, statues, and the cash value of bullion. The relationship to the sacred thus is framed in terms of fair exchange, and its paradigm derives from the myth of Prometheus, briefly summarized above.

Besides explaining how mankind came to be separated from the gods, the myth offers a cautionary tale about right and wrong ways of dealing with the gods. The fatal error on Prometheus' part was the division of the meat into unequal portions, designed to cheat the gods out of their rightful share. What comes into play here are the notions of *moira*, allotment, and *metron*, measure. In contrast to gift exchange, a situation fraught with ambiguities, ill-defined boundaries, and potential for deceit,[16] there stands in archaic Greek thought the principle of measure, which determines one's fair share—what one is owed in return for giving something. Measure is not only the foundation of balanced exchange in human societies governed by Justice. It is as well the foundation of cosmic order, regulating even the rhythm of the seasons. One finds a brief but striking statement to this effect in a fragment of Heraclitus, a pre-Socratic philosopher: "The Sun will not transgress his measures. If he does, the Furies, ministers of Justice, will find him out."[17]

It is this notion of measure and order that I think structures the form of the Greek sanctuary as a template for dealing with the divine. The establishment of the *temenos*, the "portion" of the god of the territory of the city, in its urban space and at the margins of its territory, is the crucial step, since it assigns the god its share. In this view, the symbolic import of that accounting mentality to which I referred above becomes clearer. The kind of record keeping in stone which building accounts and inventory steles present to us attests to the scrupulous discharge of what the citizens owe. The metaphor of the sanctuary as the god's palace thus configures the sacred in political terms, according to a mentality of equity and accountability, which are the guiding principles in the polis.

NOTES

1. On the differences between "conceptual metaphor theory" and "blending theory," see Grady, Oakley, and Coulson 1999.

2. Polignac 1995 argues that the sanctuary is a new development at this time, one tied to the emergence of the polis. For the opposite view, that temples are an elaboration of the basic structure of dwellings of rulers of the Dark Age, see Sourvinou-Inwood 1993; Mazarakis-Ainian 1997, 381–92.

3. For an annotated bibliography on the Greek sanctuary, see Østby 1993.

4. On cult places in Mycenaean religion, see Wright 1994.

5. Useful reviews of this issue in Whitley 2001, 136–39; Le Roy 1984.

6. On the gods as citizens, after a fashion, see Sissa and Detienne 2000, chap. 9.

7. The point is forcefully made by Sourvinou-Inwood 1993.

8. Since at least Mycenaean times, the term *temenos* refers to the estate of a king or a hero. See Casevitz 1984, 85–87.

9. Notable attempts at an explanation are Bergquist 1967 and Doxiadis 1972.

10. In addition to temples, a variety of other structures filled the sacred space: *thesauroi* (small, temple-like buildings that housed the gods' valuable property), porticoes to shelter the faithful, dining halls, minor shrines, tombs of heroes.

11. The basic source on votives is still Rouse 1902. For an introduction to more recent literature, see Linders and Nordquist 1987; Snodgrass 1989–90; Whitley 2001, 140–46.

12. On the role of *kharis* in reciprocal exchange between men and gods, see Parker 1998.

13. Harris (1994) gives an insightful analysis of this practice "The act of setting up a costly marble stele on the Acropolis can be interpreted as a sacred act: it was within the *temenos*, and was an expensive offering to Athena and a testimony to their goddess that the treasurers had been faithful stewards of her treasures and that the Athenian citizens had performed their audit satisfactorily" (216).

14. Hanell (1932) proposed that the Mycenaean palace was the model for the Greek sanctuary.

15. For the altar of Zeus in the palace court, see *Iliad* 9.771–75; 24.306; *Odyssey* 22.333–37; 378–80. Athenaeus, *Sophists at Dinner* 5.189E.

16. On the Prometheus myth as a string of perverted gift exchanges, see Vernant 1988; Slatkin 2004.

17. Heraclitus fr. 94D-K, cited by Slatkin 2004, 25, in her seminal essay on the concept of "measure" in archaic Greek thought. Trans. Kahn 1990.

REFERENCES

Alcock, S. E., and R. Osborne, eds. 1994. *Placing the gods: Sanctuaries and sacred space in ancient Greece*. Oxford, England: Clarendon Press.

Bergquist, B. 1967. *The Archaic Greek temenos*. Skrifter Utgivna av Svenska Institutet i Athen, 40, 13.

Black, M. 1962. *Models and metaphors*. Ithaca, N.Y.: Cornell University Press.

———. 1981. Metaphor. In *Philosophical perspectives on metaphor*, ed. M. Johnson, 63–82. Minneapolis: University of Minnesota Press, 1981. Originally published in *Proceedings of the Aristotelian Society* N. S. 55 (1954–55), 273–94.

Burkert, W. 1985. *Greek religion*. Oxford, England: Blackwell.

————. 1988. The meaning and function of the temple in classical Greece. In *Temple in society*, ed. M. V. Fox, 27–47. Winona Lake, Ind.: Eisenbrauns.

————. 1996. Greek temple-builders: Who, where and why? In *The role of religion in the early Greek polis*, ed. R. Hägg, 291–99. Stockholm: P. Åströms Forlag.

Casevitz, M. 1984. Temples et sanctuaires: ce qu'apprend l'étude léxicographique. In *Temples et sanctuaries*, ed. Georges Roux, 81–95. Lyon: GIS-Maison de l'Orient.

Caskey, L. D. 1927. The inscriptions. In *The Erechtheum*, ed. J. M. Paton, 277–422. Cambridge, Mass.: Harvard University Press.

Coldstream, J. N. 1977. *Geometric Greece*. New York: St. Martin's Press.

Doxiadis, C. A. 1972. *Architectural space in ancient Greece*. Cambridge, Mass.: Harvard University Press.

Ehrenberg, V. 1960. *The Greek state*. Oxford, England: Blackwell.

Fauconnier, G., and M. Turner 2002. *The way we think: Conceptual blending and the mind's hidden complexities*. New York: Basic Books.

Fehr, B. 1996. The Greek temple in the early archaic period: Meaning, use and social context. *Hephaistos*, 14: 165–91.

Ferrari, G. 2002. *Figures of speech: Men and maidens in ancient Greece*. Chicago: University of Chicago Press.

Grady, J. E., T. Oakley, and S. Coulson 1999. Blending and metaphor. In *Metaphor in cognitive linguistics*, ed. G. J. Steen and R. W. Gibbs, Jr., 101–24. Philadelphia: J. Benjamins.

Hägg, R. 1983. *The Greek renaissance in the eighth century B.C.E.* Stockholm: P. Åströms Forlag.

Hanell, K. 1932. Zur Entwickelungsgeschichte des griechischen Tempelhofes. In *Corolla Archaeologica*, 228–37. Lund: C.W.K. Gleerup.

Harris, D. 1994. Freedom of information and accountability: The inventory lists of the Parthenon. In *Ritual, finance, politics*, ed. R. Osborne and S. Hornblower, 213–25. Oxford, England: Clarendon Press.

Jameson, M. H. 1997. Sacred space and the city: Greece and Bhaktapur. *International Journal of Hindu Studies*, 1: 485–99.

Jones, M. W. 2002. Tripods, trigliphs, and the origin of the Doric frieze. *American Journal of Archaeology*, 106: 353–90.

Kahn, C. H. 1990. *The art and thought of Heraclitus*. Cambridge, England: Cambridge University Press.

Korres, M. 1994. The history of the Acropolis monuments. In *Acropolis restoration: The CCAM interventions*, ed. R. Economakis. London: Academy Editions.

Kyrieleis, H. 1993. The Heraion at Samos. In *Greek sanctuaries: New approaches*, ed. N. Marinatos and R. Hägg, 125–53. London and New York: Routledge.

Lakoff, G., and M. Johnson. 1980. *Metaphors we live by*. Chicago: University of Chicago Press.

Lakoff, G., and M. Turner. 1989. *More than cool reason: A field guide to poetic metaphor*. Chicago: University of Chicago Press.

Lattimore, R. 1951. *The Iliad of Homer*. Chicago: University of Chicago Press.

———. 1965. *The Odyssey of Homer*. Chicago: University of Chicago Press.

Le Roy, C. 1984. Mémoire et tradition: réflexions sur la continuité. In *Aux origines de l'hellénisme. La Crète et la Grèce. Hommage à Henri Van Effenterre*, 163–72. Paris: Université de Paris I Panthéon-Sorbonne.

Linders, T. and G. Nordquist, eds. 1987. *Gifts to the gods*. Uppsala: Academia Ubsaliensis.

Malkin, I. 1987. La place des dieux dans la cité des hommes. *Revue de l'Histoire des Religions*, 204: 231–352.

Marinatos, N., and R. Hägg. 1993. *Greek sanctuaries: New approaches*. London and New York: Routledge.

Mazarakis-Ainian, A. 1997. *From ruler's dwellings to temples: Architecture, religion and society in early Iron Age Greece. Studies in Mediterranean Archaeology*, 121. Jonsered: Åström.

Morgan, C. 1990. *Athletes and oracles: The transformation of Olympia and Delphi in the eighth century BC*. Cambridge, England: Cambridge University Press.

Østby, E. 1993. Twenty-five years of research on *Greek sanctuaries: New approaches*. A bibliography. In *Greek sanctuaries*, ed. N. Marinatos and R. Hägg, eds., 192–227. London and New York: Routledge.

Parker, R. 1998. Pleasing thighs: Reciprocity in Greek religion. In *Reciprocity in ancient Greece*, ed. C. Gill, N. Postlethwaite, and R. Seaford, 105–25. Oxford, England: Oxford University Press.

Polignac, F. de 1995. *Cults, territory, and the origins of the Greek city-state*. Chicago: University of Chicago Press.

Rouse, W.H.D. 1902. *Greek votive offerings*. Cambridge, England: Cambridge University Press.

Shear, I. M. 2000. *Tales of heroes*. New York and Athens: Caratzas.

Sissa, G., and M. Detienne 2000. *The daily life of the Greek gods,* trans. J. Lloyd. Stanford, Calif.: Stanford University Press.

Slatkin, L. M. 2004. Measuring authority, authoritative measures: Hesiod's *Works and Days*. In *The moral authority of nature*, ed. L. Daston and F. Vidal, 25–49. Chicago: University of Chicago Press.

Snodgrass, A. M. 1989–90. The economics of dedication at Greek sanctuaries. *Scienze dell'Antichità*, 3–4: 287–94.

Sorabji, R. 1972. *Aristotle. On memory*. London: Duckworth.

Sourvinou-Inwood, C. 1990. What is *Polis* religion? In *The Greek city from Homer to Alexander*, ed. O. Murray and S. Price, 295–322. Oxford: Clarendon Press.

———. 1993. Early sanctuaries, the eighth century and ritual space: Fragments of a discourse. In *Greek sanctuaries: New approaches*, ed. N. Marinatos and R. Hägg, 1–17. London and New York: Routledge.

Tomlinson, R. A. 1976. *Greek sanctuaries*. London: Elek.

Vernant, J.-P. 1988. The myth of Prometheus in Hesiod. In *Myth and society in ancient Greece*, trans. Janet Lloyd, 183–201. New York: Zone Books.

Whitley, J. 2001. *The archaeology of Greece*. Cambridge, England: University of Cambridge Press.

Wright, J. C. 1994. The spatial configuration of belief: The archaeology of Mycenaean religion. In *Placing the gods: Sanctuaries and sacred space in ancient* Greece, ed. S. E. Alcock and R. Osborne, 37–78. Oxford, England: Clarendon Press.

———. 2001. *The archaeology of Greece*. Cambridge, England: Cambridge University Press.

PART VI

Art and Ambiguity

13

The Neurology of Ambiguity

Semir Zeki

The function of art is an extension of the function of the brain, namely the acquisition of knowledge about the world. The brain is often confronted with situations or views which are open to more than one interpretation. I explore the neurobiological foundations of ambiguity in art, as an aspect of a larger research program through which we seek to understand the reasons underlying the phenomena of aesthetic appreciation.

In this essay, I use the term *ambiguity* in the sense that it is understood by most people and as it is defined in the *Oxford English Dictionary*: "uncertain, open to more than one interpretation, of doubtful position." To this, I will add below a neurobiological definition. I consider ambiguity to be a characteristic of much great art, an attribute that heightens substantially the artistic and aesthetic merit of a work. In accordance with my general view that we should seek to understand the reasons underlying aesthetic appreciation and evaluation in the organization and functioning of the brain (Zeki 1999), I try to explore here some of the neurobiological foundations of ambiguity. I restrict myself to the visual brain and thus to visual art, not because I know more about the visual system but because I know less about other systems. My aim is twofold: first, to explore what ambiguity tells us about conscious processes in the visual brain. The relationship of ambiguity to consciousness is critical;

ambiguous states would indeed not be possible without consciousness. Correspondingly, a discussion of the relationship of consciousness to ambiguity may provide not only material for new experiments but also insights into how the brain is organized to acquire knowledge. My second aim is to show that the characteristic of ambiguity in art is not special to art. It is rather, a general property of the brain which is often confronted with situations or views that are open to more than one, and sometimes to several, interpretations. The artist, rather than creating ambiguity, thus uses, sometimes to exquisite effect, this potential of the brain. Equally, the viewer uses this same potential in providing different interpretations.

Of necessity, in the present highly incomplete state of our knowledge about the functions and functioning of the brain, the exploration of the relationship of ambiguity to conscious processes in the brain that I give here is nothing more than a sketch designed to stimulate further experimentation. Similarly, the neurobiologically based explanation of ambiguity in art that I give cannot be anything near complete and may even turn out to be wrong in the end. But I hope that it will nevertheless constitute the basis of further artistic explorations of how ambiguity works in neurological terms.

The Brain and the Acquisition of Knowledge

To understand the neural basis of ambiguity requires us first to understand that the brain is not a mere passive chronicler of external events and that perceiving is not therefore something that the brain does passively (Zeki 1984, 1993). Rather, the brain is an active participant in constructing what we see, through which it instills meaning into the many signals that it receives and thus gains knowledge about the world which, of course, it can only do in the conscious state. The percepts that the brain creates are the result of an interaction between the signals that it receives and what it does to them. To understand perception, and the knowledge that we acquire through it, we must therefore enquire not only into the nature of the signals that the brain receives but also into the contribution that the brain makes to, and the limitations that its characteristics impose upon, the acquisition of knowledge (Kant 1781; Schopenhauer 1859; Zeki 2001).

The primary law dictating what the brain does to the signals that it receives is the law of constancy. This law is rooted in the fact that the brain is only interested in the constant, essential and non-changing properties of objects, surfaces, situations and much else besides, when the information reaching it is never constant from moment to moment. Thus the imperative for the brain is to eliminate all that is unnecessary for it in its role of identifying objects and situations according to their essential and constant features. The search for the constant is relatively simple when the choice itself is limited, as in color vision. It becomes more complex when, in trying to instill meaning into this world and extract the essentials, the brain is confronted with several possible solutions. Here, it must first ascertain what the possible solutions are and decide which is the most likely. True ambiguity results when no single solution is more likely than other solutions, leaving the brain with the only option left, of treating them all as equally likely and giving each a place on the conscious stage, one at a time, so that we are only conscious of one of the interpretations at any given time. *Thus a neurobiologically based definition of ambiguity is the opposite of the dictionary definition; it is not uncertainty, but certainty—the certainty of many, equally plausible interpretations, each one of which is sovereign when it occupies the conscious stage* (Zeki 1999). Each interpretation therefore is as valid as the other interpretations, and there is no correct interpretation. Ambiguity therefore is the obverse of constancy. For here, the information reaching the brain is constant from moment to moment (assuming a constant viewing distance, lighting conditions and so on) while the percept shifts and is inconstant. In a sense, the brain accepts that there is no single essential and constant feature, but several instead.

In fact, whether the choice available to the brain is limited (as in color vision) or not, many have sought to account for both perceptual constancy and the ambiguity resulting from perceptual inconstancy by appealing to a "top-down" influence of higher cognitive factors and centers, and especially the frontal and prefrontal cortex. Such an influence implies a separation between processing and perception. To account for color constancy, for example, both Helmholtz (1911) and Hering (1877) invoked higher (cerebral) factors such as judgment, learning and memory. Similar higher factors have been invoked to account for ambiguous figures such as the Rubin vase. But the mandatory involvement of "higher centers" in color vision or in the perception of illusory figures is doubtful, since all imaging studies of color vision and illusory figures are united in showing that there is no involvement of frontal or prefrontal cortex (Hirsch et al. 1995; ffytche and Zeki 1996; Larsson et al. 1999; Bartels and Zeki 2000). In fact a discussion of ambiguity and its relationship to (micro)conscious processes leads us to conclude that, in some if not all instances, ambiguity may result from a fluctuation in the state of micro-consciousness within an area, without involving higher cognitive factors. This is of course not to say that higher areas are not involved in the perception of certain ambiguous figures, and as we shall see they may well play a critical role in determining which of the interpretations of an ambiguous stimulus hold the conscious stage. It is self evident that such a scenario, of many possible solutions, is closely linked to a condition in which some work or scene or narrative is left unfinished. Here again, the brain can complete the work in a variety of different ways, each one of which is as plausible as the others. But in this instance probably greater demands are made of higher cognitive factors, including memory, learning and experience. In art, the importance of this capacity to provide multiple solutions means that the importance of the work becomes more general and can cover a whole range of situations. My aim here is to show that there are different levels of ambiguity dictated by neurological necessity and built into the physiology of the brain. These different levels may involve a single cortical area or set of areas; they may involve different cortical areas, with different perceptual specializations; or they may involve, in addition, higher cognitive factors such as learning, judgment, memory and experience. Whether the result of activity in a single area or in different areas, these different levels are tied together by a metaphoric thread whose purpose is the acquisition of knowledge about the world and of making sense of the many signals that the brain receives.

Nodes and Essential Nodes in the Visual Brain

It is useful to introduce here the concept of nodes and essential nodes (Zeki 1999; Zeki and Bartels 1999a) by giving a very rough sketch of the organization of the visual brain (see figure 13.1).

In essence, a very prominent part of the input from the retina reaches the primary visual cortex, known as area V1. Signals belonging to different attributes are distributed to specialized compartments within V1. V1 is surrounded by another visual area, V2, which also has specialized compartments that receive input from their counterparts in V1. V2 itself is surrounded by further visual areas, prominent among them being V3, V3A, V4 and V5, all of them specialized visual areas that receive distinct inputs from the specialized compartments of V1 and V2. These specialized areas have diffuse return anatomical connections with areas V1 and V2 and also reciprocal connections with further visual areas, but the details do not concern us here. There are therefore many visual areas in the brain and each receives input, directly or indirectly, from area V1. By a node I mean a stage in the visual pathway, for example area V4 or area V5, or a specialized sub-compartment within the pathway, for example the compartments that feed V4 or V5 (see figure 13.1). An example of the latter would be the blobs of V1 and the thin stripes of V2, both of which contain wavelength-selective cells and project to area V4 (Livingstone and Hubel 1984; Shipp and Zeki 1985; De Yoe and Van Essen

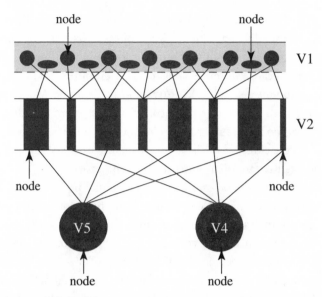

FIGURE 13.1. Diagrammatic illustration of nodes and essential nodes. Signals related to color and motion reach distinct compartments in the primary visual cortex (Vi) and the area surrounding it (V2). In the diagram, the color signals are indicated by circles in Vi and thin bars in V2, projecting to V4. The motion signals are indicated by ovals in Vi and thick bars in V3, projecting to V5. The specialized compartments of Vi and V2 constitute nodes that project to further nodes V4 (for color) and V5 (for motion). The latter are essential nodes in that the signals in them become explicit and do not necessarily need to be processed further. When V4 and V5 are destroyed the nodes in Vi and V2 become essential nodes and the subjects' perceptual capacities in color and motion now reflect the physiological capacities of cells in Vi and V2.

1985; Hubel and Livingstone 1985). An essential node is one at which activity becomes perceptually explicit without the need for further processing (Zeki 1993; Zeki and Bartels 1999A). In other words, when activity at a node has a conscious correlate, it becomes an essential node. Each node can potentially become an essential node, a supposition that receives support from the work of Logothetis and his colleagues (Logothetis 1998), who have shown that, in every visual area, including even area Vi, there are cells whose responses follow the percept rather than the visual input. I refer to the conscious correlate that is the result of activity at an essential node as a micro-consciousness (Zeki 2003), since activity at other nodes leads to a micro-conscious correlate for other attributes (Zeki 2003). Visual consciousness consists therefore of many micro-consciousnesses that are distributed in space, since they are the correlates of activity in spatially distinct locations. Moreover, different visual areas (nodes) have distinct activity time courses (Bartels and Zeki 2003), reflecting perhaps the fact that we become conscious of different attributes at different times, because different areas take different times to complete their processings (Moutoussis and Zeki 1997a and b; Zeki and Moutoussis 1997; Arnold et al. 2001). Hence, the microconsciousnesses are also distributed in time. Overall, at the level of micro-consciousnesses, there is no such thing as a unified *visual* consciousness. Visual consciousness consists of many micro-consciousnesses that are distributed in time and space.

Area V4 provides a good example of an essential node. Activity in it leads to the conscious perception of color without the need for further processing. We therefore say that a micro-consciousness for color is generated as a correlate of activity within the V4 complex. In the intact brain, the nodes that feed V4—the blobs of V1 and the thin stripes of V2—are not necessarily essential nodes as far as color vision is concerned, in that activity in them is processed further, at the level of V4. They become essential nodes in two conditions: one obtains when activity in them leads to conscious awareness of the fact that the dominant wavelength has changed, as happens when a scene is viewed under two different illuminants, with different wavelength compositions. This is a consequence of the fact that most of their chromatic cells are concerned with wavelength composition and seem to lack the machinery for long-range interactions that generate colors (Zeki 1983; Moutoussis and Zeki 2002). The other condition is when V4 is damaged, leading to a perceptual state produced by activity in the blobs of V1 and the thin stripes of V2, and characterised by an inability to construct constant colors (Zeki et al. 1999). In patients rendered achromatopsic (cortically color blind) by damage to V4, the intensity of lights of different wavebands can be detected, but no colors can be ascribed to them or, if the damage is sub-total, the attributed color is heavily dependent upon the wavelength composition of the light reflected from a surface (Kennard et al. 1995). This is in spite of recent evidence that at least some cells in monkey V1 are influenced somewhat by their immediate surrounds to suggest a perceptual color induction (Wachtler et al. 2003). Assuming a similarity between monkey and man, it is possible that, because of the limited spatial range of these interactions, such cells are not capable of effecting the long-range interactions necessary for constructing constant colors, thus leaving a patient with a damaged V4 essentially incapable of color constancy. At any rate, present clinical evidence suggests that, when V1-V2 become (in the absence of V4) the essential node for color vision, that faculty is characterized by an unstable color vision in which constancy is a primary casualty.

Processing Sites Are Perceptual Sites

Strong evidence in favour of essential nodes has recently been obtained by experiments which show directly that processing sites and perceptual sites are one and the same. There has been much evidence that favours such a view or is at least consistent with it (Zeki 1993; Zeki and Bartels 1999b; Rees et al. 2002; Dehaene et al. 2001). But perhaps the most compelling evidence comes from recent psychophysical experiments combined with imaging studies (Moutoussis and Zeki 2002).

It depends for intelligibility upon full color. In this experiment, pictures of houses, faces, and uniformly colored controls were used. (See http://theart fulmind.stanford.edu for image.) The input to the two eyes and the expected perceptual output was compared to the subjects' true psychophysical performance. Continuous fusion of the stimuli was achieved by using repetitive brief presentations. Identical stimuli of opposite color contrast were invisible when presented dichoptically to the two eyes (opposite stimulation), whereas identical stimuli of the same color contrast (same stimulation) were easily perceived. Control stimuli were never perceived either as a face or a house. In this experiment, group results of brain regions showing stimulus-specific activation under conditions of same and opposite stimulation revealed that such activation correlates with perceived and not-perceived conditions. The contrast *same houses-same faces* showed bilateral stimulus-specific activation in the parahippocampal gyrus (Talairach coordinates, 230, 244, 212 and 26, 244, 210). The contrast *opposite houses-opposite faces* showed unilateral stimulus-specific activation in the same region (238, 242, 210). The contrast *same faces-same houses* revealed stimulus-specific activation in a region of the fusiform gyrus (42, 282, 212). The contrast *opposite faces-opposite houses* revealed stimulus-specific activation in the same brain region (44, 274, 214).

The use of dichoptic visual stimulation allows us to arrange the sensory input into the visual brain in such a way that it is sometimes seen and sometimes not, even though the stimulus is identical in both situations. Thus, when an identical stimulus, such as a house or a face, is presented monocularly to each eye in turn, the presentation to one eye alternating with that to the other eye every 100 ms, the two images are fused into a single image and the subject can report consciously and correctly what the stimulus was. But if the same stimulus is presented to each eye in the same way though with opposite color contrasts, the two colors cancel each other in the fusion; the stimulus is no longer perceived and cannot be recognized by the subject, even though the visual input to the eyes is the same as in the condition when the stimulus was correctly perceived. Brain imaging experiments show that the same stimulus-specific areas are activated regardless of whether the stimulus is perceived or not. Thus when the stimulus is that of a face, the area in the brain specifically implicated in the perception of faces is specifically activated, regardless of whether the stimulus is perceived or not. A similar result obtains with stimuli depicting houses, which activate a different, specialized, part of the visual brain (Tovée 1998). This demonstration shows that the cortical perceptual sites, at least for faces and houses, are not separate from the cortical processing sites. This is not to imply that other cortical areas are never involved in the perception of houses and faces. There is little doubt that the memory system would be involved when the identification is that of a particular house or a particular face. The importance of the demonstration lies in showing that there is not a separate site specialized for perceiving, as opposed to processing, an argument that is important in what follows.

To summarize therefore the neurological context within which this article is written: There are many different visual areas in the brain, each one of which receives visual input in stages, each stage constituting a node. These nodes become essential nodes if the activity in them requires no further processing and results in a conscious correlate. An essential node is therefore a processing site as well as a perceptual site. One important conclusion that follows from this in the context of this article is that activity at a given essential node need not necessarily be dependent upon an input from a "higher" area, or what is commonly called a "top down" influence.

The Nonambiguous State

Obligate Interpretation—Color Vision

I begin by considering unambiguous conditions, when the brain has no option but to interpret signals in one way and one way alone. Color vision provides a good example. It is important to emphasize here that when I say that the brain has no option, I mean that it has no option given its genetically determined neurological apparatus and wiring (Zeki 1999). The question that we ask in color vision is: what is the formal contribution that the brain makes in acquiring knowledge about color, what is the "concept" that it applies to the incoming signals, and what are the limitations that it imposes, given its neurological apparatus.

The color of a surface remains substantially the same even in spite of wide-ranging variations in the wavelength composition of the light reflected from it, a phenomenon generally known as color constancy. The brain, in other words, is able to discard all the variations in the wavelength-energy composition of the light reflected from a surface and assign a constant color to it (Land 1974; Land and McCann 1971)[1]. To be able to do so, there must be some constant physical feature about the surface. That feature is *reflectance*. By this is meant that a surface reflects a constant percentage of light of any waveband in terms of the amount of light of that waveband that is incident on it. A green surface will reflect, let us say, 70% of middle-wave (green) light that is incident on it, no matter what the actual amount; it will reflect 20% of incident long-wave (red) light, again no matter what the amount, and so on. In normal conditions, the surrounding surfaces will have different reflectances for the same wavebands and will therefore reflect different percentages of the same intensity of these different wavebands that are incident upon them. The ratio of light of any given waveband reflected from a surface and from its surrounds will therefore always remain the same in all illumination conditions. To ascertain the reflectance of a surface, the brain simply has to take the ratio of light of a given waveband reflected from it and from its surrounds, which it must of course do for all wavebands. This provides the brain with a lightness record for the scene at each waveband. The next step consists in comparing its lightness in the three wavebands, and thus determining its color. This description is based on the Land system and the exact stages involved in the neural implementation are not known. It is possible and even likely that the brain uses a procedure different from the one envisaged in the Land algorithm but the end result of brain operations must be the same, that is the construction of a color which is independent of the precise wavelength composition of the light reflected from it, since it is significantly a matter of comparison between one surface and surrounding surfaces. By applying a brain-based, genetically inherited "concept" of ratio-taking for different wavebands, the brain can determine that a given surface (in our example the green surface) has a high reflectance for middle-wave light, and low reflectances for lights of other wavebands, *compared to surrounding surfaces and without reference to absolute values*. The knowledge that the brain thus acquires, in the strict sense, is not about color but about the constant property of a surface, namely its reflectance. Color then becomes a sort of an addition, an interpretation, *a visual language*, that the brain gives to that constant property of reflectance. What is critical to understand here is that the comparison is done by the brain and the result of that comparison, knowledge of the reflectance of a surface for lights of different wavebands, and the tagging of a visual language to that knowledge, belongs to the brain, not the world outside.

There is no ambiguity here, in that surfaces have definite reflectances for lights of different wavebands, and the brain merely has to compare the reflectances of these surfaces and their surrounds for the same wavebands and determine which has the higher reflectance for light of one waveband and of another. Given that reflectances are immutable, the brain has no option but to reach the conclusion that it does. It has developed an efficient and unfailing machinery for doing so, and a significant part of that machinery, related to long-range ratio-taking mechanisms, is vested in the color center of the brain, the V4 complex (Bartels and Zeki 2000; Wade et al. 2002). The V4 complex is thus the essential node for both the construction and the perception of colors, without any evidence that it consults other, perhaps "higher," cortical areas in this endeavor, although it of course becomes an essential node by cooperation with the nodes in V1 and V2, with which it is reciprocally connected. When the color center in the brain is damaged, or where the receptors for color vision are lacking (Zeki et al. 1991; Bartels and Zeki 2000), such long-range comparisons either become impossible or are much reduced in scope, leading to the condition of achromatopsia, or to conditions in which color vision is much impoverished (see Zeki 1990 for a review).

It is interesting to consider the apparent chaos that is caused when, through partial damage to the color center, the ratio-taking mechanism of the brain becomes imperfect though not completely non-operational. The consequence is to give the brain several options, in that the color of a surface now becomes hostage to the wavelength composition of the light reflected from it (Kennard et al. 1995; Zeki et al. 1999). But these options are not available simultaneously, in that the color of a surface will change markedly only when the wavelength composition of the illuminating light also changes markedly. These options are useless, for they cannot give a correct interpretation of the reflectance of a surface and hence of its color. The different options do not have equal validity as in truly ambiguous situations. In a healthy brain with an intact color center, there is no room for many different interpretations of what the reflectance of a surface and hence its color is, which is not to say that the color that one individual sees is the exact replica of what another sees. But for a given individual, there is no luxury of giving different interpretations to the reflectance of a surface, a luxury that in this case would only lead to confusion and false knowledge.

The Kanizsa Triangle

The same physiological straitjacket, determined strictly by the rules of the brain, is at play in interpreting other patterns of signals, which are nevertheless not as rigid as color vision in allowing no options. Orientation-selective cells are capable of responding to virtual lines. Such cells are to be found in areas V2 and V3 (von der Heydt and Peterhans 1989; Peterhans and von der Heydt 1989) but whether the orientation-selective cells of V1 respond to

FIGURE 13.2. The Kanizsa triangle.

virtual lines of their preferred orientation remains a matter of dispute (see Ramsden et al. 2001). Whichever area they are located in, these cells, by definition, respond optimally only to their preferred orientation and not at all to the orthogonal orientation. They are therefore not free to respond in other ways, thus forcing only one plausible interpretation. A more complex situation arises with the objectively "unfinished" pattern of figure 13.2.

The brain tries to make sense of this, by "finishing it off" in the most plausible way, and interprets the pattern of luminances in this Kanizsa figure as a triangle. There are of course other interpretations that the brain could give in this instance (Malach et al. 1995), but they are far less plausible. There are many variants of this Kanizsa figure and their characteristic is that they are all open to only one *plausible* interpretation. The interpretation is probably dictated by the physiology of orientation-selective cells in the cortex, and more specifically the orientation-selective cells in areas V2 and V3. But the patterns in the Kanizsa figures, though consisting of lines, nevertheless constitute objects. It is not surprising to find therefore that viewing the Kanizsa illusory figures also activates area LOC (Hirsch et al. 1995, Larsson et al. 1999; Stanley and Rubin 2003), an area that is critical for object recognition in the human brain (Malach et al. 1995). In terms of our description, LOC could be referred to as a processing-perceptual center for objects. As with color vision, LOC works in collaboration with areas V2 and V3 (Murray et al. 2002), with which it is presumably reciprocally connected.

Essential Nodes and "Top-Down" Influences in Resolving Ambiguities

To interpret the "unfinished" picture of figure 13.2 as a triangle naturally involves a semantic element, which itself is shaped through experience. This, among other reasons, is probably why many have thought that a "top-down" influence is brought to bear upon the pattern of signals, forcing their interpretation in a certain way. What is meant by "top-down" is vague in neurological terms, but what is implied is that a "higher" thought process influences the way in which we interpret things or that a "higher" area influences neural activity in a "lower" area. The meaning of "top-down" influences becomes clearer when one considers what the proponents of this view had in mind. Both Herman von Helmholtz and Ewald Hering evoked "top-down" influences (though without using the term) in trying to account for the constancy of colors. Helmholtz (1911) thought that factors such as prior knowledge and judgement were important, while Hering (1877) invoked the importance of memory. Implicit in such thinking is the supposition that processing and perception are always entirely separate, that a processing site in the brain is different from a perceptual site or, more accurately, that an interpretation has to be brought to bear upon the result of processing in an area, the interpretation emanating from a different source than the processing site. Effectively, this means that we can only become conscious of the triangle in the Kanizsa triangles, or of a color, if some "higher" area located, for example, in the frontal lobes, forces the interpretation of the ambiguous figure in a certain way. If this were invariably so, one would expect that, when the brain is constructing colors, cortical areas such as the ones in frontal lobes that have been implicated in thought processes would be engaged and that their activity could be demonstrated with imaging experiments. Yet imaging studies show that the computation of reflectances and the consequent construction of colors by the cerebral cortex is an automatic and autonomous process undertaken by a specific area in the visual brain, the V4 complex (the color center) (Bartels and Zeki 2000), without involving frontal areas or other areas implicated in memory and abstract thought. The V4 complex constructs colors in the abstract, that is to say, it is indifferent to what objects colors belong to. As much can be demonstrated by using, in these experiments, Mondrian scenes which are constituted by an arbitrary assembly of squares and rectangles of different colors, with no recognizable shapes. Additional brain areas are recruited if, in such imaging experiments, subjects are shown colors that are the properties of recognizable (semantic) objects (Zeki and Marini 1998). The V4 complex, in brief, constitutes an essential node for color, activity at which has a conscious correlate and does not need to be processed further.

In the same way, it has been supposed that the interpretation that the brain gives to the configuration shown in figure 13.2 is imposed "top-down" (Gregory 1972). If so, then "higher" areas of the brain should become engaged when subjects view such figures. But imaging experiments show that, when human subjects view and interpret such incomplete figures as triangles, activity in the brain does not involve the frontal lobes. The reason for the absence of any frontal lobe involvement, and hence the absence of "top-down" influences as traditionally understood is becoming obvious, and it entails a major shift in our thinking about perceptual and processing sites in the brain and about consciousness too. While older theories assume, either explicitly or implicitly, that a processing site is different from a perceptual site, evidence from physiological and imaging experiments, discussed above, shows that this is not necessarily so and that, in many instances relating to the perception of figures with semantic content, such as faces or houses, a processing site is also a perceptual site (Moutoussis and Zeki 2002). The consequence of this postulate, if true, is important for understanding the neurological basis of ambiguity, for it implies that some categories of ambiguity at least are generated and possibly resolved by activity in given areas, without recourse to other, or higher, areas. As we shall see below, there are other categories of ambiguity that are probably dictated (and resolved) by the intervention of "third" areas.

Simple Perceptual Ambiguity

Ambiguous Bi-Stable Images

The absence of any real ambiguity in the examples given above is occasioned by the fact that there is no more than one plausible solution to the visual problem, even if it is the brain that constructs what is perceived. The situation is rendered more complex when one considers the Kanizsa cube (see figure 13.3).

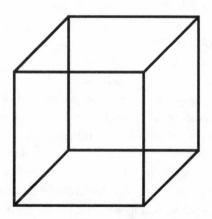

FIGURE 13.3. The Kanizsa cube.

Here there is little information in the intersecting lines. They could all be in the same plane, or some could be in a plane that is closer to the viewer than others. The brain has no means of knowing, and thus allows for all three interpretations. The important point to note is that, at any given time, only one interpretation is possible, *and this interpretation is as valid as the other interpretations.* It is a sort of interpretational flip-flop, one OR the other but not the two simultaneously. It is difficult to tell whether this interpretational flip-flop is due to any "top-down" influences or to the activity of areas beyond the ones that register and combine the oriented lines into particular groupings. Without much evidence to go by, my hunch is that it is due to activity in a single area. If true, such a supposition has important consequences, for it implies that a micro-consciousness that is due to activity at a single essential node can be in several, mutually exclusive, states. One of the reasons that leads me to this conclusion is the obligate nature of the recessional planes seen in other instances, of which a good example is provided by the work of the British artist Nathan Cohen. (See http://theartfulmind.stanford.edu for image.)

Obligate Meta-Stability

Cohen's abstract compositions make original use of a long-known perceptual effect, namely that juxtaposed rectangular forms can be interpreted by the brain as being in one of two recessional planes, either towards or away from the viewer at the point of juxtaposition, but not in both simultaneously. What Cohen's work shows compellingly is that, with the addition of further elements (rectangular shapes) of the same type, there develops an obligate perceptual relationship in the planes occupied by the contiguous rectangular forms. In the composition, when the plane at the point of convergence of the central rectangles is towards the observer, the two surrounding ones are shifted to a plane away, and vice versa.

There is no choice in this obligate relationship, which raises interesting physiological problems that are worthy of study. One would suppose, not unreasonably, that there must be some reciprocal relationship between cells that are capable of signalling recessional planes, and that that relationship depends upon the lateral connections between cells in a given area, assuming of course that there are no "top down" influences, which there may well be. Given the strong topographical relations involved, one would also suppose that the meta-stability is due to activity in an area with a good topographical map in it. Given that many cells in the third visual complex are disparity selective and capable of signaling what occurs in front of, and behind, the fixation plane (Poggio and Fischer 1977; Adams and Zeki 2001), and given the topographic representation of the visual field in the V3 complex (Zeki 1969; Cragg 1969; Lyon and Kaas 2002), it becomes reasonable to suppose that this perceptual meta-stability is due to the instability of the responses of cells in V3, in the sense that the activity of some cells dominates perceptually at one moment and that of others at another. It is important to note here that such perceptual alterations can be attenuated or even abolished if the (ambiguous) visual stimulus is periodically removed from view, suggesting that uninterrupted viewing is necessary for the physiological mechanisms that lead to multistable vision (Leopold et al. 2002). While the critical experiments have not been done, it is interesting to note what the consequence of such a demonstration is. It implies that the physiology of a single area, or a limited number of what are called "early" visual areas, allows a multiple perceptual interpretation of incoming signals. That interpretation is nevertheless strictly circumscribed by the basic physiology of the cells in the visual area, without involving factors such as memory and learning. Accepting that activity at an essential node can have a micro-conscious correlate, one is naturally led to the conclusion that the micro-consciousness can be in more than one state, though only one occupies the conscious stage at any one time. This raises the question of whether what regulates the change from one state to another of the same micro-consciousness (due to activity in the same essential node) is identical to the mechanism that regulates the change from one micro-conscious state to another when it is due to activity at two different essential nodes.

Resolution of Ambiguity by "Third" Areas

Ambiguous Interpretations of the Same Category

In the above examples, I have hypothesized that the same cortical area is engaged during the bi-stability or meta-stability where the meta-stability involves the same object or attribute. I may be wrong in this supposition and only further experiments will clarify the picture. My reason for doing so is to be found in the principle of functional specialization in the visual brain (Zeki 1978; Livingstone and Hubel 1988), which tells us that the processing of distinct visual attributes is the privilege of distinct visual areas. A cube is a cube, whether one of its planes is closer to the viewer or further away; hence one supposes that it is differences in processing *in the same area* that leads to different versions of the cube. The same reasoning holds for other and more complex bi-stable images, such as the "wife/mother-in-law" image (figure 13.4), though with a difference.

FIGURE 13.4. (left) Bi-stable figure: wife/mother-in-law. (right) An attempt to dis-ambiguate the same figure. Despite the spectacles and eyeshades to stabilize the per-ception of the "mother-in-law," the figure remains unstable.

Since each one of the two images seen in this bi-stable image is that of a face, I assume (though without much direct evidence to support my as-sumption) that the bi-stability involves activity in the same area. But here the two faces differ substantially in other attributes, principally that of age but also in viewing angle, making it plausible to suppose that other influences will be brought into play in giving one of two different interpretations. The involve-ment of other areas is even more plausible in examples such as the Rubin vase (figure 13.5), where the two images, faces and a vase, belong to different categories.

One supposes that two different areas are involved and that, as percep-tion shifts from one to the other, from the area concerned with face recog-nition to the one involved with object recognition, "third" areas may become engaged.

Imaging experiments (Lumer et al. 1997; Kleinschmidt et al. 1998) have shown that the switch from one percept to another during the presentation of bi-stable images (when the stimulus remains the same but the percept changes) is indeed accompanied by a shift in the activated areas. For example, a shift from faces to vases entails a shift in the site of activation within the fusiform gyrus, a region of the visual brain that contains areas for object recognition. However, they have also shown that the fronto-parietal cortex is engaged whenever a percept changes from one condition to another. The intervention of a higher "third area" distinguishes this kind of ambiguity from the more straightforward ambiguity that is due to activity within a single

FIGURE 13.5. Bi-stable figure: vase/faces.

area alone and renders the interpretation of these experiments awkward. One interpretation might be that the fronto-parietal cortex is the "higher" area dictating the percept and hence that we only become conscious of the interpretation through the intervention of the fronto-parietal cortex. This would be tantamount to saying that the areas in the fusiform gyrus that are activated are not sovereign in dictating what is perceived, and hence that a processing site is not really a perceptual site. But such an interpretation sits uneasily with the experiments of Moutoussis and Zeki (2002), referred to above, in which there is no demonstrable involvement of the fronto-parietal cortex. In these experiments, two conditions prevail: (a) when the stimulus remains the same but the percept changes and (b) when the percept remains the same but the stimulus changes. Collectively, they show that a processing site is a perceptual site. How is one to resolve this difficulty? Recent experiments (Sterzer et al. 2002) have shown that where the reversal is that of a single attribute—the change in the direction of motion that is perceived—the activity is restricted mainly to V5 and to V3B, the former an area that is critical for motion perception and the latter an area that is important in extracting contours (Zeki et al. 2003). But here again the fronto-parietal cortex is engaged. One conclusion that can be drawn from these studies is that the fronto-parietal cortex is involved when there is a perceptual *change* of which we become aware, without being involved in the percept that we are conscious of. The experiments of Lumer et al. (1998) and Kleinschmidt et al. (1998), referred to above, are consistent with this explanation, which leads to the following conclusion: that activity in the parieto-frontal cortex is critical for us to become aware of a change, without necessarily knowing what has changed. To become aware of what has been processed or what has changed, (heightened) activity at a specialized processing site (essential node) is critical.

The Stability of Perceptual Instability

The extent to which the machinery of the brain is programmed to allow of different interpretations, and the seeming poverty of any "top-down" influences, can be demonstrated by showing that it is not easy to dis-ambiguate these ambiguous figures. This may be readily ascertained by examining the so-called staircase illusion (see figure 13.6).

Adding features to the illusion which, one might have thought, would oblige the brain to perceive the figures in only one way does not lead to perceptual results that can only be interpreted in one way. The same is true of the "wife/mother-in-law" illusion (figure 13.4). Adding a number of features to the figure, to force the brain to interpret it in one way only, is never successful. The brain retains the options of interpreting it in two ways. This suggests that the brain does not have much choice in the multi-interpretations that its organization makes possible. *The ambiguity, in other words, is stable.* It also argues against ubiquitous "top-down" influences, even when coupled with direct visual stimulation. For the addition of further visual features that, top-down wise, would have imposed a single interpretation on the figure, fails to do so. This stability in the ambiguity, together with the fact that ambiguity may reside in a single object belonging to one category (for example, the cube) leads one to ask whether the multiple interpretations that the brain gives to a

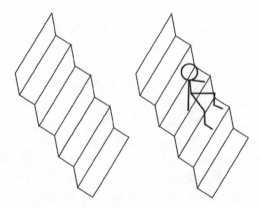

FIGURE 13.6. (left) The staircase illusion. (right) It is difficult to stabilize the staircase by placing a figure on the stairs.

figure may not, at least with some figures, be the result of reciprocal fluctu-
ations in the responses of cells in a single area.

Ambiguity and the Microconsciousnesses

We have argued elsewhere (Zeki and Bartels 1999a; Zeki 2003) that there are
many micro-consciousnesses, each the correlate of activity in a specific brain
area (a processing-perceptual site). Micro-consciousnesses are therefore distributed in space. Micro-consciousnesses are however also distributed in time,
because we become conscious of some visual attributes (e.g., color) before
others (e.g., motion) (Moutoussis and Zeki 1997a and b). In general, it would
be reasonable to suppose that attributes that are perceived at different times
are processed at different sites (or essential nodes).

The arguments I have given can be summarized by saying that activity
of different groups of cells in the same area can result in different micro-
consciousnesses for the same figure (for example of the different recessional
planes in the Kanizsa cube) or that two different micro-consciousnesses for the
same figure might be the consequence of activity in two different areas (as in the
face-vase figure). Either way, one must suppose a shift in strength of activity,
either from one group of cells to another within a single area, or from cells in one
area to those in another. This also applies in cases of binocular rivalry. Logothetis
and his colleagues have argued convincingly that binocular rivalry is the consequence of two rivalrous perceptions (Logothetis 1998). Where the rivalry is
between two gratings of different orientation or of two colors, one presented to
each eye, one can conjecture that one group of cells holds sway over the other
because of a shift in strength of activity. Where the rivalry is between two stimuli
of different category, for example a face and a house, one can conjecture that the
fluctuation in strength is between cells in different areas. This leads one to an
interesting problem: that there is a mechanism in the brain that can work on a
single area or on two (or more areas), altering the balance of the strength of
activity between cells, whether the cells themselves are located in the same or in
different areas. This mechanism allows one micro-consciousness to dominate
over the other, regardless of whether the two micro-consciousnesses are the
correlates of activity in the same area or in two different areas. In the former, it
gives activity of one set of cells conscious primacy, while in the latter it gives one
area perceptual primacy over the other. Given our conjecture and demonstration
that the shift from the unconscious to the conscious state involves an increase of
activity within an area (Zeki and ffytche 1998; Moutoussis and Zeki 2002), we
can now go further and conjecture that, where the shift in micro-consciousness

during the perception of an ambiguous figure such as the Kanizsa cube is due to activity within a single area, then the relative activity of one set of cells will be higher than that of another. It goes without saying that the demonstration that activity in a processing-perceptual site acquires a conscious correlate only when the activity at that site becomes more intense (otherwise it remains a processing site alone) does not give insights into the question whether the heightened activity is due to the recruitment of previously unresponsive cells or to the increased activity of already active cells.

Higher Levels of Ambiguity

One of the functions of the brain, as emphasized earlier, is to instill meaning into this world, into the signals that it receives. Instilling meaning amounts to finding a solution. But the brain commonly finds itself in conditions where this is not easy, because it is confronted with several meanings of equal validity. Where one solution is not obviously better than the others, the only option is to allow of several interpretations, all of equal validity. Such a higher level of ambiguity is to be found in the multiple narrative interpretations that can be given, for example, to Vermeer's painting entitled *The Pearl Earring*. (See http://theartfulmind.stanford.edu for image.)

Note that this is a single stable image, and the only variable is that the brain of the beholder can offer several equally valid interpretations of the expression on her face. She is at once inviting, yet distant, erotically charged but chaste, resentful and yet pleased. These interpretations must all involve memory and experience, of what a face that is expressing these sentiments would look like. The genius of Vermeer is that he does not provide an answer but, by a brilliant subtlety, manages to convey all the expressions, although the viewer is only conscious of one interpretation at any given moment. Because there is no correct solution, the work of art itself becomes a problem that engages the mind. "Something, and indeed the ultimate thing, must be left over for the mind to do," wrote Schopenhauer (1859). There could be no better illustration of this than the work of Vermeer, where nothing is explicit. Vermeer's *The Music Lesson* provides another interesting example. (See http://theartfulmind.stanford.edu for image.)

This revolves around the relationship between the man and the woman. Many interpretations are possible. He could be her teacher, or brother, or husband or a suitor. They could be discussing something quite banal, like the quality of her playing or something a good deal more serious, such as a separation or a reconciliation. All these interpretations have equal force and validity.

The brain must entertain them all and try to find the correct solution, except that in this instance there is no correct solution. It is this that led me to offer a neurological definition of ambiguity, namely that it is not vagueness or uncertainty, but rather certainty, the certainty of different scenarios each one of which has equal validity with the others (Zeki 1999). There is no correct answer, because all answers are correct. Schopenhauer wrote, "... through the work of art, everything must not be directly given to the senses, but rather only so much as is demanded to lead the fancy on to the right path ... for Voltaire has very rightly said, 'Le secret d'être ennuyeux, c'est de tout dire' [the secret of being boring is to tell everything]. But besides this, in art the best of all is too spiritual to be given directly to the senses; it must be born in the imagination of the beholder, although begotten by the work of art. It depends upon this that the sketches of great masters often effect more than their finished pictures."

It is obvious that there is a relation between works that display such ambiguity and unfinished works, because in both instances the brain is able to give multiple interpretations that are of equal validity to the same work. I have written elsewhere of the unfinished sculptures of Michelangelo as an example (Zeki 1999; 2002). Even in spite of their unfinished status, they have commonly led to interpretations that are so self-contained that one is left with the conclusion that they must have been "finished off" by the viewer. Charles De Tolnay's (1934) lyrical description of the Rondanini Pietà as a work which "comes to represent in the personal life of the artist that state of beatitude to which his unsatisfied soul aspired" could as well be a description of a finished work except that in this instance it refers to an unfinished work. (See http:// theartfulmind.stanford.edu for image.)

It is thus interesting to compare the unfinished triangles of Kanizsa with the unfinished sculptures of Michelangelo, although many might regard such a comparison as demeaning to the great sculptor. In trying to make sense of the Kanizsa pattern that constitutes a Kanizsa triangle, the brain "finishes it off" in the only way possible; when trying to make sense of the pattern that constitutes the Kanizsa cube, the brain can interpret the intersecting lines as being in one of three planes. In Michelangelo's Rondanini Pietà, the capacity to give multiple interpretations is taken yet a step further. Now the solutions are, by comparison, large in number. Hence the capacity to give multiple interpretations is not a separate faculty invented or used by the artist. It is instead tied to a general capacity of the brain to give several interpretations, a capacity that is important for it in its role of acquiring knowledge. It is on this physiological basis that the prized quality of ambiguity in art is built.

One can therefore conjecture that there are graded steps, not only from non-ambiguous to ambiguous stimuli, but also in the number of areas or distinct cortical sites that may be involved. At the simplest level, I am suggesting that the ambiguity may be due to activity in a single area in which the micro-conscious correlate of activity may be in more than one state. Obviously, there is no "top-down" influence here. At a higher level, the ambiguity may involve more than one area, as in the Rubin vase. This may or may not involve higher areas in the frontal lobe. At a higher level still, the ambiguous state may involve several distinct areas that are able to bring their influence. The Vermeer paintings referred to above provide a good example. Here, memory, experience, learning and much else besides can influence what is perceived at any given moment. This almost certainly involves a "top-down" influence, from diverse sources, not just the frontal lobes. Thus, opening up the capacity for a given brain area to be influenced by another areas is merely one step in opening up the capacity to be influenced by multiple other areas. Hence, the artist exploits this potential of the brain that allows multiple areas to influence what is perceived. It is not ambiguity itself, therefore, that is aesthetically pleasing, even though some artists such as Arcimboldo and Salvador Dali have deliberately made of ambiguity an artistic form. It is rather the capacity of multiple experiences, even though we are conscious of only one at any given moment, that a stimulus can provide.

Ambiguity and Contradictions

In the examples given above, of Vermeer's work, the possible interpretations are not only many but are also sometimes contradictory. Some will see the girl in Vermeer's masterpiece as being alternately chaste and erotically charged, or approachable and resentful. These of course are interpretations that my brain is giving to this composition, and it is not implausible though not certain that others will see similar contradictions or other ones. Yet we do possess a work which is in a highly incomplete state and which allowed Johann Winckelmann to perceive as embodying contradictory elements. Winckelmann, often regarded as the father of art history, had a very definite view, one might say a concept, of beauty as reflected in Greek sculpture, which he related to his view of Greek culture in general. For him, Greek art was born out of, and in, a free social and political setting, yet one that was beset by a contradiction or tension that, he thought, was reflected in its art. That tension was between "an 'active' manly freedom realized in the violent struggles of the early phases of Greek culture... and a free sensual enjoyment of things." Winckelmann, of whom Goethe interestingly wrote that "his gift was to search in the outer world what nature had laid in his inner world" chose the *Belvedere Torso* (also known as the *Belvedere Hercules*), an "unfinished" work, as representative of the highest beauty in Greek art and as one depicting most forcefully this apparent tension. (See http://theartfulmind.stanford.edu for image.)

In fact, of course, the *Torso*, which occupied a very privileged position in Winckelmann's writings on art (Potts 1994), is not unfinished but is now, and when Winckelmann saw it, badly damaged and a very incomplete fragment, so that only parts of the torso and thighs remain. It is this incomplete status that allowed Winckelmann to read so much into it and, what is more, so much that is visually compelling, at least to anyone who may not be acquainted with the history of the torso. He thought of it as "the high ideal of a body raised above nature, a nature of mature manly years, as it would appear when elevated to a state of divine contentment"(Winckelmann 1764). The *Belvedere Torso* is thus characterized as being actively heroic and passively contented. And these contradictory interpretations, united in a single figure, can compellingly become, or become acceptable, as the interpretations of the spectator as well, even though only one interpretation can occupy the conscious stage at any given moment. That Winckelmann himself attributed a primary role to the imagination (to us, the brain) in this instability becomes evident in his description of the *Belvedere Hercules*, which he asked the viewer to admire for its continuous flow of one form into another. As the viewer interprets these ever changing forms "*er wird finden, dass sich niemand im Nachzeichnen der Richtigkeit versichern kann, indem der Schwung, dessen Richtung man nachzugehen glaubt, sich unvermerkt ablenket, und durch einen andern Gang, welchen er nimmt, das Auge und die Hand irre machet* ([the artist] will then find that it is not possible to reproduce this accurately by drawing since the curve that the drawer believes himself to be following changes its direction imperceptibly and confuses both eye and hand with its new direction" (Winckelmann 1764, Volume 6: 98; quoted by Potts 1994). To him, "The apparent calm and stillness, which recall the blissful self-absorption of the ideal youth, are charged by intimations of the naked physical power of a hero laying waste all that came in his way" (Potts 1994: 179).

The important point to note here is that it is to some considerable extent, visually at least, the incomplete status of the *Belvedere Hercules* that allowed him to make, and allows us to consider, contradictory interpretations that are visually convincing. It is perhaps not entirely fortuitous, then, that Winckelmann chose an incomplete work to represent his highest ideal of Greek beauty. To generalize what Langerholc (1986) has said, these artists "relied on ancient laws of perspective and tonality *deriving from the nature of our perceptive mechanisms* [our brain] to draft their illusions. Otherwise they would not have worked" (my emphasis). This applies as much to the Kanizsa cube as to the progression of the Tristan chord in Wagner's work (Zeki 2002) and to the *Belvedere Hercules*.

Conclusion

The general point that I make in this chapter is that there is a continuum in the operations of the brain, the basis of which is to seek knowledge and to instill meaning. In this continuum, we proceed from conditions where the brain has no option in its interpretation of the signals that it receives, as in color vision, to ones in which there are two equally plausible interpretations and, finally, ones in which there are many interpretations. On the other hand, we also have a continuum in which activity in an area is almost sovereign in this context, to ones in which activity in an area is open to one or multiple influences from other areas. If, as I have written elsewhere, the function of art is an extension of the function of the brain, namely the acquisition of knowledge about the world, then it stands to reason to suppose that the mechanisms used to instill meaning into this world are the very ones used to instill meanings into works of art. It is those basic mechanisms that artists have used so successfully.

NOTE

1. In what follows, I use essentially the description given by Edwin Land (1974). I am aware that there are other algorithms besides his that have been proposed, and also that some have disputed the novelty of Land's system. These are matters that do not concern us here, for there is broad agreement that constancy is the principal characteristic of the color system and there is also broad agreement that no one really knows the precise neural mechanism by which constant colors are constructed by the brain.

REFERENCES

Adams, D. L., and S. Zeki, 2001. "Functional organization of macaque V3 for stereoscopic depth." *Journal of Neurophysiology* 86: 2195–203.

Arnold, D. H., C. W. Clifford, P. Wenderoth. 2001. "Asynchronous processing in vision: color leads motion." *Current Biology* 11: 596–600.

Bartels, A. and S. Zeki. 2000. "The architecture of the colour centre in the human visual brain: new results and a review." *European Journal of Neuroscience* 12: 172–93.

Bartels, A. and S. Zeki. 2003. "The chronoarchitecture of the human brain: functional anatomy based on natural brain dynamics and the principle of functional independence." In R. S. Frackowiak, K. Friston., C. Frith, R. Dolan, S. Zeki,

C. Price. Elsevier, eds., *Human Brain Function* (2nd ed.). San Diego (in press).

Cragg, B. G. 1969. "The topography of the afferent projections in circumstriate visual cortex studied by the Nauta method." *Vision Research* 9: 733–47.

Dehaene S., L. Naccache, L. Cohen, D. L. Bihan, J. F. Mangin, et al. 2001. "Cerebral mechanisms of word masking and unconscious repetition priming." *Nature Neuroscience* 4: 752–8.

DeYoe, E. A. and D. C. Van Essen. 1985. "Segregation of efferent connections and receptive field properties in visual area 2 of the macaque." *Nature* 317: 58–61.

ffytche, D. H., S. Zeki. 1996. "Brain Activity Related to the Perception of Illusory Contours." *Neuroimage* 3: 104–8

ffytche, D. H., C. N. Guy, and S. Zeki. 1996. "Motion specific responses from a blind hemifield." *Brain* 119: 1971–82.

Gregory, R. 1972. "Cognitive contours." *Nature* 238: 51–52.

Helmholtz, H. 1911. *Handbuch der Physiologischen Optik.* Hamburg: Leopold Voss.

Hering, E. 1877. *Outlines of a Theory of the Light Sense.* Cambridge: Harvard University Press.

Hirsch, J., R. L. Delapaz, N. R. Relkin, J. Victor, K. Kim, et al. 1995. "Illusory Contours Activate Specific Regions In Human Visual-Cortex—Evidence from Functional Magnetic-Resonance-Imaging." *Proceedings of The National Academy of Sciences of the USA* 92: 6469–73.

Hubel, D. H. and M. S. Livingstone. 1985. "Complex-unoriented Cells in a Subregion of Primate Area 18." *Nature* 315: 325–7.

Kant, I. 1781. *Kritik der reinen Vernunft,* Translated by W. S. Pluhar (1996) as *Critique of Pure Reason.* Indianapolis, IN: Hackett.

Kennard, C., M. Lawden, A. B. Morland, and K. H. Ruddock. 1995. "Colour identification and colour constancy are impaired in a patient with incomplete achromatopsia associated with prestriate cortical lesions." *Proceedings of the Royal Society (London) B—Biological Sciences* 260: 169–75.

Kleinschmidt, A., C. Büchel, S. Zeki, and R.S.J. Frackowiak. 1998. "Human brain activity during spontaneously reversing perception of ambiguous figures." *Proceedings of the Royal Society (London) B—Biological Sciences,* 265: 2427–33.

Land, E. H. 1974. "The retinex theory of colour vision." *Proceedings of the Royal Institution of Great Britain* 47: 23–58.

Land, E. H., and J. J. McCann. 1971. "Lightness and retinex theory." *Journal of the Optical Society of America* 61: 1–11.

Langerholc, J. 1986. "L'Accordo di Tristano come Immagine Ambigua: "Figure Vuote" nell'Opera di Wagner." *Rivista di Psicologia dell'Arte* VII: 55–68.

Larsson J., K. Amunts, B. Gulyas, A. Malikovic, K. Zilles, P. E. Roland. 1999. "Neuronal correlates of real and illusory contour perception: functional anatomy with PET." *European Journal Neuroscience* 11: 4024–36.

Leopold, D. A., M. Wilke, A. Maier, and N. K. Logothetis. 2002. "Stable perception of visually ambiguous figures." *Nature Neuroscience* 5: 605–609.

Livingstone, M. S., and D. H. Hubel. 1984. "Anatomy and physiology of a color system in the primate visual cortex." *Journal of Neuroscience* 4: 309–56.

———. 1988. "Segregation of Form, Color, Movement, and Depth—Anatomy, Physiology, and Perception." *Science* 240: 740–9.

Logothetis, N. K. 1998. "Single units and conscious vision." *Philosophical Transactions of the Royal Society of London B* 353: 1801–18.

Lumer E. D., Friston K. J., Rees G. (1998) Neural correlates of perceptual rivalry in the human brain. *Science*. 280:1930–4.

Lyon, D.C., and J. H. Kaas. 2002. "Evidence for a modified V3 with dorsal and ventral halves in macaque monkeys." *Neuron* 33: 453–61.

Malach, R., J. B. Reppas, R. R. Benson, K. K. Kwong, H. Jiang, W. A. Kennedy, P. J. Ledden, T. J. Brady, B. R. Rosen, R. B. Tootell. 1995. "Object-related activity revealed by functional magnetic resonance imaging in human occipital cortex." *Proceedings of the National Academy of Sciences U S A.* 92: 8135–9.

Moutoussis, K. and S. Zeki. 1997a. "A direct demonstration of perceptual asynchrony in vision." *Proceedings of the Royal Society (London) B* 264: 393–9.

———. 1997b. "Functional segregation and temporal hierarchy of the visual perceptive systems." *Proceedings of the Royal Society (London) B* 264: 1407–14.

———. 2002. "The relationship between cortical activation and perception investigated with invisible stimuli." *Proceedings of the National Academy of Sciences USA* 99: 9527–32.

Murray, M. M., G. R. Wylie, B. A. Higgins, D. C. Javitt, C. E. Schroeder, and J. J. Foxe 2002. "The spatio-temporal dynamics of illusory contour processing: combined high-density electrical mapping, source analysis, and functional magnetic resonance imaging." *Journal of Neuroscience* 22: 5055–5073

Peterhans, E., and R. von der Heydt. 1989. "Mechanisms of contour perception in monkey visual cortex. II. Contours bridging gaps." *Journal of Neuroscience* 9, 1749–63.

Poggio, G. F., and B. Fischer 1977. "Binocular interaction and depth sensitivity in striate and prestriate cortex of behaving rhesus monkey." *Journal of Neurophysiology* 40: 1392–405.

Potts, A. 1994. *Flesh and the Ideal: Winckelmann and the Origins of Art History.* Yale University Press: New Haven and London.

Ramsden, B. M., C. P. Hung, and A. W. Roe. 2001. "Real and illusory contour processing in area V1 of the primate: a cortical balancing act." *Cerebral Cortex* 11: 648–65.

Rees, G., G. Kreiman, and C. Koch. 2002. "Neural correlates of consciousness in humans." *Nature Reviews Neuroscience* 3: 261–70.

Schopenhauer A. 1859. *Die Welt als Wille und Vorstellung*, vol. 1, 3rd edn. Translated by E. F. J. Payne (1969) as *The World as Will and Representation*. New York: Dover Publications.

Shipp, S., and S. Zeki. 1985. "Segregation of pathways leading from area V2 to areas V4 and V5 of macaque monkey visual cortex." *Nature* 315: 322–5.

Stanley, D. A. and N. Rubin. 2003. "fMRI activation in response to illusory contours and salient regions in the human lateral occipital cortex." *Neuron* 37: 323–331.

Sterzer, P., M. O. Russ, C. Preibisch. et al. 2002. "Neural correlates of spontaneous direction reversals in ambiguous apparent visual motion." *NeuroImage* 15: 908–916.

Tolnay, C. 1934. "Michelangelo's Rondanini Pietà." *Burlington Magazine* 65: 145–157.

Tovée, M. J. 1998. "Is face processing special?" *Neuron* 21: 1239–42.

Von der heydt, R., and E. Peterhans. 1989. "Mechanisms of Contour Perception In Monkey Visual-Cortex. 1. Lines of Pattern Discontinuity." *Journal of Neuroscience* 9: 1731–48.

Wade, A. R., A. A. Brewer, J. W. Rieger, and B. A. Wandell. 2002. "Functional measurements of human ventral occipital cortex: retinotopy and colour." *Philosophical Transactions of The Royal Society of London B Biological Sciences* 357: 963–73.

Wachtler, T., T. J. Sejnowski and T. D. Albright. 2003. "Representation of color stimuli in awake macaque primary visual cortex." *Neuron* 37: 681–691.

Wapner, W., Judd T., and Gardner H. 1978. "Visual agnosia in an artist." *Cortex* 14: 343–64.

Winckelmann, J. 1764. *Geschichte der Kunst des Altertums.* Dresden: der Waltherischen Hof-Buchhandlung.

Zeki, S., J.D.G. Watson, C. J. Lueck, K. J. Friston, C. Kennard, and R.S.J. Frackowiak. 1991. "A direct demonstration of functional specialization in human visual cortex." *Journal of Neuroscience* 11: 641–9.

Zeki, S., J. D. Watson, and R. S. Frackowiak. 1993. "Going beyond the information given: the relation of illusory visual motion to brain activity." *Proceedings of the Royal Society (London) B* 252: 215–22.

Zeki, S., and K. Moutoussis. 1997. "Temporal hierarchy of the visual perceptive systems in the Mondrian world." *Proceedings of the Royal Society (London) B* 264: 1415–9.

Zeki, S. and L. Marini 1998. "Three Cortical Stages of Colour Processing in the Human Brain." *Brain* 121: 1669–85.

Zeki, S., S. Aglioti, D. McKeefry, and G. Berlucchi. 1999. "The neurobiological basis of conscious color perception in a blind patient." *Proceedings of the National Academy of Sciences of the USA* 96: 14124–9.

Zeki, S. and A. Bartels. 1999a. "Towards a theory of visual consciousness." *Consciousness and Cognition* 8: 225–59.

———. 1999b. "The clinical and functional measurement of cortical (in-) activity in the visual brain, with special reference to the two subdivisions (V4 and V4a) of the human colour centre." *Philosophical Transactions of the Royal Society of London B* 354: 1371–82.

Zeki, S. and D. ffytche. 1998. "The Riddoch Syndrome: Insights into the Neurobiology of Conscious Vision." *Brain* 121: 25–45.

Zeki S., Perry R. J., Bartels A. (2003). The processing of kinetic contours in the brain. *Cereb Cortex.* 13:189–202.

Zeki, S. M. 1969. "The secondary visual areas of the monkey." *Brain Research* 13: 197–226.

Zeki, S. 1978. Functional specialization in the visual cortex of the monkey. *Nature* 274: 423–8.

———. 1983. "Colour coding in the cerebral cortex: the reaction of cells in monkey visual cortex to wavelengths and colours." *Neuroscience* 9: 741–65.

———. 1984. "The Construction of Colours by the Cerebral Cortex." *Proceedings of the Royal Institution of Great Britain* 56: 231–57.

———. 1990. "A century of cerebral achromatopsia." *Brain* 113: 1721–77.

———. 1993. *A Vision of the Brain*, Blackwell, Oxford.

———. 1999. *Inner Vision: an exploration of art and the brain*, Oxford University Press, Oxford.

———. 2001. "Localization and globalization in conscious vision." *Annual Review of Neuroscience* 24: 57–86.

———. 2002. "Neural concept formation and art: Dante, Michelangelo, Wagner." *Journal of Consciousness Studies* 9: 53–76.

———. 2003. "The disunity of consciousness." *Trends in Cognitive Sciences* 7: 214–18.

14

Mastering Ambiguity

Marc De Mey

I explore the ways in which creative discovery involves mastering ambiguity. Ambiguity results when apparently incompatible data or constraints are perceived but a way is found to integrate them into a coherent whole or to toggle transparently between interpretations. Pictorial inventions exemplify the power of creative ambiguities.

The central concern of this chapter is the degree to which creative discovery in art and science involves mastering ambiguity. Ambiguity arises when one encounters apparently incompatible data or constraints but discovers a way either to integrate them into a coherent whole or to toggle transparently between interpretations.

Ambiguous figures familiar from elementary psychology textbooks provide prototypical examples of ambiguity. An example Wittgenstein seemed to like was the pelican-antelope figure (see figure 14.1). On occasion, these ambiguities are presented by philosophers of science as toylike analogs of paradigm shifts in science.[1]

An apparently simple but historically important case in the history of science can be found in the study of sunlight passing through angular apertures. When the sun shines through the rich foliage of trees during summer, the ground under the trees is covered with patches of light in a great diversity of shapes. Nevertheless, there are quite a number of patches which are perfectly circular. This puzzling observation has engrossed the minds of scholars for centuries. How

FIGURE 14.1. The pelican-antelope figure is a prototypical ambiguous picture. It indicates a pelican when seen as the head of an animal with a large bill looking upward to the left, and an antelope when seen as a horned animal looking downward to the right. Though the figure is utterly simple, people enjoy mastering the reversal forth and back between the two interpretations, thus keeping the ambiguity intact and controlling it rather than settling for either version.

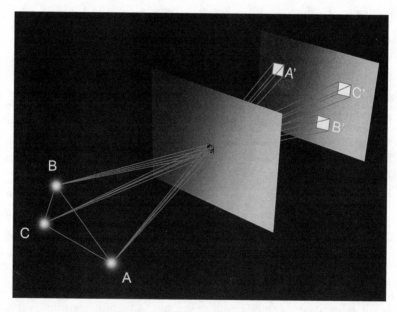

FIGURE 14.2. Kepler investigated the trajectory of the rays point by point. He realized that each point of the source of light (ABC) produces a patch of light that has the shape of the aperture (square). However, taken together, all the points of the source will produce a combination of patches that constitutes an inverted image A'B'C' of the light source (triangle).

could a circular shape be produced by rectilinear rays passing through an angular aperture? Kepler managed, in his *Paralipomena* of 1604, to overcome this ambiguity of circular shapes stemming from angular apertures (figure 14.2).[2]

The question is whether the eureka experience of triumph that accompanies a major discovery is but an amplified version of the more modest intellectual delight experienced in seeing through simple perceptual ambiguities and enjoying major works of art. Mithen (1996) claims that the most powerful feature of the modern mind is this capacity to bring together unrelated and even apparently incompatible representations. It appears to have arisen roughly 40,000 years ago as a result of a major evolutionary change in the cognitive operation of the brain, expressed in such cultural phenomena as burial rituals and art.

While art and science both appear to require this ability to bridge different kinds of representations, Mithen suggests that in the development of human beings, art was the more prototypical achievement, a kind of precursor of science. If that is so, then prior to looking into creativity in science, we should pursue and elucidate the nature of constructive ambiguity in art.

Suspense from Combinations of Composition and Perspective

A few examples will indicate how the equivocality of simple ambiguous figures is also present in well-known works of high art, even though it might not be apparent at first blush. Consider the ambiguity that can reside in a straight line, as in Giotto's representation of *The Wedding at Cana* on the north wall of the Arena chapel in Padua (for the image, see http://theartfulmind.stanford.edu).

The theme of the miraculous transformation of water into wine is anchored in the big vessels in the lower right corner of the picture. However, it is the spatial layout that is to be screened for ambiguity. Together with the organization of the tables, Giotto uses in his typical way an architectural element near the ceiling to indicate the 3-D spatial structure of the depicted room. However, the reddish curtain that provides the background for the scene and that decorates all the walls of the room is shown along a single straight line that divides the picture vertically into almost equal segments. The horizontal line by which this is accomplished approaches the status of an ambiguous figure. Though it seems to be a single homogeneous entity, only the middle segment consists of a section parallel to the picture plane, while the outer segments consist of sections orthogonal to the picture plane. While it has a major two-dimensional compositional function as a single geometrical element, in three dimensions, the curtain line arises from a more complicated composition. One could obviously conjecture that this is a coincidence resulting from the height of the viewer's vantage point. But even if the painter chose the vantage point on those grounds, there remains a mild tension evoked by this ambiguity. The disambiguation of it, without any doubt largely unconscious, is a miniature discovery, leading to unpretentious aesthetic pleasure.

The same phenomenon arises in the case of Donatello, where a similar line divides the roundel depicting the *Raising of Drusiana* in the Old Sachristi of the San Lorenzo church in Florence (for an image, see http://theartfulmind .stanford.edu).

More modern painters equally exploit ambiguity. See how, in his painting *Hospital Room*, van Gogh uses the stovepipe to amplify perspective, suggesting that it falls along a vanishing line even though it is in no way to be construed as orthogonal to the picture plane (for an image, see http://theartfulmind .stanford.edu).[3]

We can see similar and more subtle combinations of compositional principles suitable for two dimensions with depicted elements suitable for three dimensions in Masaccio's *Trinity* fresco (see figure 14.3). This fresco, which measures more than twenty-one feet high and ten feet wide, has been celebrated as the most important breakthrough in the discovery of linear perspective in art.

The ornamental capitals crowning the columns and pilasters of the depicted chapel are nicely aligned on straight lines—perspectival vanishing lines, for that matter. But while the Ionic capitals on the columns at each side are to be construed as lying in a plane orthogonal to the picture plane, the segments connecting the frontal Ionic capitals with the Corinthian capitals that crown the pilasters are to be construed as lying within the picture plane. Again, an apparently single straight line includes line segments that intersect at right angles. In this case, the tension results from the fact that what count as vanishing lines in three dimensions are simultaneously compositional lines in two dimensions.

Another more complex and extraordinary combination of two-dimensional organizational patterns and three-dimensional perspectival depth can also be found in Masaccio's *Trinity* (see figure 14.4), according to an analysis by Polzer of the method of composition (1971). Surprisingly, this milestone in the art of perspective can be constructed almost entirely along two-dimensional compositional principles. If we begin with a vertical arrangement of three squares and an inscribed circle, then a convincing three-dimensional image can result from a series of simple straightforward divisions in two dimensions, along with a single, and possibly arbitrary, three-dimensional division. The partial overlap between the lower squares can be plausibly accounted for on some

FIGURE 14.3. The pilasters in Masaccio's *Trinity* fresco have ornamental capitals in Corinthian style; the columns supporting the vault have ornamental capitals in Ionic style. All of these ornamental capitals line up along straight lines that happen to be vanishing lines. The Ionic capitals atop the front columns lie with the Corinthian capitals in a plane that is parallel to the picture plane. But those same Ionic capitals atop the front columns lie with the Ionic capitals atop the back columns in a plane that is orthogonal to the picture plane. So what look like simple straight lines in two dimensions represent segments that have very different orientations in three dimensions.

FIGURE 14.4. The reconstruction of Masaccio's *Trinity*, inspired by Polzer (1971), proceeds from a vertical organization of three squares. The circular arch that covers the front of the vault coincides with the top half of a circle inscribed in the top square. The top of the nimbus behind the head of God the Father coincides with the center of the circle. Christ's head is exactly in the middle of the lower half of the square. When a vanishing point is chosen at the location of the head of the viewer shown in the bottom square, the whole construction of this convincing perspective, including the semi-circular vault, can be done according to traditional *pre*-perspective two-dimensional rules.

Vitruvian Man model; accordingly, a construction along these lines by Masaccio himself is not to be excluded. The incision lines found in the recent restoration of this fresco might suggest a new attempt at reconstructing the genesis of this work.[4]

But whether or not the two-dimensional construction method is in any way compatible with the newly discovered incision lines, the power and fascination radiating from Masaccio's *Trinity* are undoubtedly due in large measure to this exceptional ambiguity between two and three dimensions. A perfectly balanced two-dimensional composition happens to coincide with a perfectly convincing three-dimensional perspective. We see in Masaccio's *Trinity*, then, an utterly complex and intricate version of what is after all an ambiguous straight line!

Jan van Eyck: Master of Ambiguity

The few examples indicated above refer to ambiguities that remain within the pictorial realm. Compositional geometry and perspectival space can both be characterized as sets of rules suited to encoding or decoding specific representational mechanisms or self-contained world models. They probably should be considered along the lines of perceptual modules such as virtual lines, texture, structure from movement, stereoscopy, and so on. Perspective is readily understood as a system for representing space. For David Marr (1982), it was so important that he inserted it in his model as the pivotal 2.5-D (two-and-a-half-dimensional) component. Composition might not be so easily associated with specific representational purposes, but if we want to classify it among the separate world models that Mithen distinguishes, its components should be representational in origin as well. One such important compositional device is symmetry. While one might think of symmetry as something purely ornamental, one can easily conceive of an evolutionary origin in which its detection might have had an adaptive function. After all, many living organisms tend to be symmetrical along one or more dimensions, and either for a predator seeking to locate its prey or for potential prey seeking to avoid predators, sensitivity to symmetry might be a valuable asset. In that sense, even the pure and empty perceptual categories of the brain that Zeki (1995, 1997, 1998) proposes as the objects explored in abstract art may be anchored in evolutionary psychology.

Many impressive works of art derive their perceptual ambiguity from playing off against each other the outcomes of different perceptual feature mechanisms. The more complicated versions of ambiguous figures like the devil's tuning fork or Escherian figures typically trigger simultaneously several mental computational modules whose outcomes seem incompatible. A genuine art historical example might be found in the figures of Arcimboldo— figures which derive their ambiguity from seemingly incompatible part-whole relationships but are nevertheless held together by some conceptual affinity. One of his most famous pictures is a portrait of a librarian composed entirely of books. This creates a perceptual incompatibility between the global level of the overall shape and the intermediate level of constituent parts, but the conceptual envelope is most interesting here. The perceptual incompatibility evokes surprise, just as it does in Arcimboldo's representation of the four seasons, where symbolic figures are depicted as compositions of natural products harvested in the corresponding seasons of the year (for images of the works, see http://theartfulmind.stanford.edu).[5] In the case of the seasons, however, the binding between the global shape and the components is weaker than in the case of the librarian, because the allegorical figures have anonymous faces while the librarian is an identifiable person. Higher aesthetic pleasure is evoked when the interpretation at the global level is amplified in a synergistic way by the nature of the parts—that is, when the portrait of an identifiable librarian is composed of a cunning assembly of books and library equipment. In the case of the librarian the strength of the effect depends in part on knowledge about the depicted figure; it is not exclusively the result of rivalry between perceptual modules. A major question, then, is to what degree these perceptual and symbolic ambiguities can be intertwined, as opposed to being recognized as entirely separate in nature.

A few decades ago, a notorious controversy between Svetlana Alpers and Eddy De Jongh centered on the contrast between perceptual and symbolic orientation. In her famous book *The Art of Describing*, Alpers (1983) proposed to emphasize mechanisms of perception rather than iconological interpretation. For De Jongh (1967), by contrast, following the iconological approach of Panofsky (1939), mechanisms of perception and perceptual ambiguity were beside the point. The relevant ambiguity that underlies aesthetic pleasure is the reference of the perceptually unambiguous representation to something that is conceptually hidden. Thus, for De Jongh, an important part of aesthetic pleasure is in reading the hidden meaning of the picture and knowing a private code or doctrine that furnishes the interpretation.[6]

The controversy regarding the iconological approach focused mainly on seventeenth-century Dutch painting. But Panofsky had been led in that direction through his study of earlier Flemish painting, which had improved spectacularly with the fifteenth-century work of Jan van Eyck (Panofsky 1953).

Jan van Eyck is celebrated as a preeminent example of iconological representation. Supposedly, his hyperrealistic pictorial scenes convey symbolic messages. Recently, the painter David Hockney (2001) has expressed his amazement at the realistic qualities of the chandelier in the Arnolfini double portrait in the National Gallery in London. According to him, such perspectival and optical exactness can be achieved only with the use of sophisticated technical equipment such as a concave mirror.

In figure 14.5, the chandelier of Jan van Eyck's Arnolfini double portrait is shown partly in a computer reconstruction developed at Ghent University by the author and architect Wim De Boever. It is an image from an animation that also appeared in David Hockney's *Secret Knowledge* on BBC television. The 3-D computer model was developed to check on the lighting and the perspective of the chandelier, which is very convincing. But when the vanishing lines for a few small decorative elements are checked, the perspective appears to deviate from a regular textbook case.[7]

Viewed from the perspective of the iconological school, such superb realism is part of the disguise—a trick to hide the real message. The genuine meaning of the chandelier lies in the single candle that it holds: a reference to Christ as the sole source of light and the only important witness for the marriage supposedly taking place, as depicted in the scene of a couple holding hands.[8]

FIGURE 14.5. The chandelier of Jan van Eyck's Arnolfini double portrait.

The bifurcation between two kinds of ambiguity, one perceptual and one symbolic, seems unfortunate. It introduces divergence and antagonism between two kinds of mechanisms that might have a strong affinity with each other. Furthermore, while van Eyck is certainly intelligent and playful enough to confront the viewer of his panels with puzzles, the idea that he would bedevil the viewer with extreme realism as a superb camouflage for an entirely different meaning seems unfair. Van Eyck is playful and witty, yes, but treacherous or misleading, no.

A careful examination of van Eyck's largest work, the Ghent Altarpiece (see figures 14.6 and 14.7), reveals a great variety of intended ambiguities, and this suggests a continuity between the perceptual and the symbolic references. Here, I will explore these ambiguities to investigate the possibility of a continuous transition from perceptual to symbolic blending.[9]

If the Ghent Altarpiece were located now where it once was, within the Vijd chapel of the choir of St. Baafs Cathedral, and one were standing in front of it, and one could think away the baroque fence that isolates the chapel from the interior of the church, one might be reminded of a passage from Ingmar Bergman's introduction to the script of his film *The Seventh Seal*:

> Regardless of my own belief and my own doubts, which are unimportant in this connection, it is my opinion that art lost its basic creative drive the moment it was separated from worship. It severed the umbilical cord and now lives its own sterile life, generating and degenerating itself. In former days the artist remained unknown and his work was to the glory of God. He lived and died without being more or less important than other artisans; "eternal value," "immortality," and "masterpiece" were terms not applicable in his case. The ability to create was a gift. In such a world flourished invulnerable assurance and natural humility. (quoted in Bragg 1993, 9)

Not all of this characterization of the artist could be applied to van Eyck. He was already well known in his time, highly reputed and highly paid. Natural humility? He had this somewhat mysterious motto that combines modesty and ambition: *Als ik kan* (freely translated as "If I manage"). Plenty of ambiguity already! But the global impression that Bergman alludes to—the sense of being confronted with a complexity to which we must relate—seems to emanate from those twenty panels of the Ghent polyptych.

There has been much debate about the heterogeneity of the Altarpiece. Some figures, including the Holy Virgin and Saint John the Baptist, appear twice, the latter depicted once as a statue in grisaille and once as a living being in color. Although these double appearances resemble many others, such as

FIGURE 14.6. The closed panels of the Ghent Altarpiece, with the Annunciation scene deployed over four panels.

the double appearance in van der Weyden's *Altarpiece of the Seven Sacraments*, discussed by Turner (2001, 48), van Eyck's figures evoke more puzzled reactions. Contemporaneous with the introduction of linear perspective in art—the Ghent Altarpiece was created in the same decade in which Masaccio executed the *Trinity* fresco—it apparently shows poor organizational coherence

FIGURE 14.7. The open panels of the Ghent Altarpiece, with the Adoration of the Lamb as the central panel of the lower tiers.

and a lack of spatial coherence. The depicted figures vary greatly in size. But the harmony and vividness of the colors, together with perceptual features such as a continuity of background, unite the panels and prompt the viewer to wonder what holds the representation together.

What Is the Thread That Connects All Those Panels?

At the University of Ghent, we have compared van Eyck's Altarpiece and Masaccio's *Trinity*, with an emphasis on the early fifteenth-century scientific scholarly background in which they arose. The two artists share themes but have different scientific sensibilities. In the fifteenth century, optics was a popular scientific discipline. From antiquity to Kepler and Newton, the science of optics was preoccupied with the question of "how we see." Based on a breakthrough achieved by the Arab astronomer Al-Haytham (Alhazen) circa A.D. 1000, thirteenth-century European scholars developed a theory of light and vision closely associated with theology (Sabra 1989). This theory, called *perspectiva*, held that light is a phenomenon that heaven and earth have in common. The crisp and clear geometric principles that govern the behavior of light are analogous to the distribution of grace that radiates from God as a point source of illumination. The scientific component of this doctrine is relatively solid. According to a scheme developed by Ptolemy, standard treatments of optics offered analyses of the visual cone, of reflection in plane, convex, and concave mirrors, and of refraction. These subjects are now considered basic fields of physics, but at the time, they belonged to the psychology of visual perception. While the visual cone explained authentic perception, reflection and refraction were associated with "errors" of perception. As devices for seeing, mirrors show you something standing in a location where, in fact, it is not present. Similar apparent displacements are caused by refraction. Thus, reflection and refraction were invoked to explain *false* perceptions.

The geometric notions involved in the development of linear perspective in the early fifteenth century may have come directly, as applications, from thirteenth-century optical knowledge about the visual cone. The visual cone is the pyramid of lines connecting the surface of a visual object to the center of the eye. Al-Haytham's theory explains vision as a section through the visual cone by the lens of the eye. Functioning as a screen, the lens captures a reduced but upright image of the object. Linear perspective as conceived by Brunelleschi and Alberti involves a similar slice of the visual cone, cut out slightly in front of the eye, exactly at the distance from the eye to the picture plane.

The development of linear perspective in art is a technical elaboration and expansion of these concepts. But these were simple concepts in standard optics. A typical textbook at the time would have presented them in the first chapter, to be followed by a second chapter on plane mirrors, a third chapter on convex mirrors, and a fourth chapter on concave mirrors. Van Eyck was probably as fascinated by optics as Alberti,[10] but instead of adopting the geometry of the visual cone, he embraced the geometry of reflection. It offered him intriguing possibilities as a painter and provided him with a vehicle for expressing the theological concepts that his patrons wanted to see expressed in his religious paintings. Let us explore the logic of van Eyck as he blends perception with optics and religion.

The doctrine that van Eyck illustrates and explores in pictures comes down to the assertion that ultimately God is the sole source of light. He is *the* Light. Applying the rules of optics to this belief yields a perfect guide for understanding and tracing light on earth. After all, every effect of light noticed on earth should, when followed completely, lead to God, its ultimate source. On earth, the painter observes how effects of light manifest themselves on earthly objects and in earthly settings. These earthly entities are accidental, perishable things, compared to the light that makes them visible and shines on them.[11] That light is essential and eternal. Tracing the effects of light on objects back to their origin is a matter of establishing the various anamorphic shapes that connect reflections and shadows in a lighted scene. Instead of seeing light as a device that helps to reveal the structure of objects, we should see the structure of objects and the various ways light is reflected by their surfaces as a means of tracing light closer to its origin. This conception of light is linked to an extended interpretation of Saint Paul's letter to the Corinthians: "For now we see through a glass darkly" (1 Cor. 13, 12). Our earthly vision presents us with a deformed and anamorphic view of reality. In heaven, having arrived at the source and facing the light directly, instead of inferring it via reflection, we will achieve full vision and full knowledge. Indeed, in heaven, seeing and knowing will become identical. The ultimate goal and final successful outcome of life is the *seeing of God*. This is the key to the riddle of the Ghent Altarpiece. Van Eyck provides it in readable text on the closed polyptych, as if to tell the viewer from the very first glance what to look for and what to expect. The Latin phrase *de visione Dei* is to be found in the book next to the Virgin Mary in the Annunciation scene of the four upper panels, which have been integrated into a single space. Van Eyck's depiction of an open book (see figure 14.8) looks at first like a representation of authentic text, but closer inspection reveals that most of his lines consist of undecipherable pseudo text. However, on occasion, such an imitation of the texture of a text will be interspersed with fragments that are in

FIGURE 14.8. The page of the book next to the Holy Virgin in the Annunciation scene on which one can detect the legible phrase *de visione dei* (highlighted), *the seeing of God*, as the final destination of man according to Christian doctrine, the key phrase for understanding the polyptych.

fact readable. The phrase *de visione dei* is such a readable fragment on the lower half of the page, prominently written in red ink.

Once we have grasped the meaning of this Platonic approach whereby the earthly entities are but the anamorphic reflections or shadows of genuine realities to which we have, for the time being, only indirect access, we can understand light as the connecting link throughout. Indeed, every patch of light must be welcomed as a reference to the ultimate Source, regardless of the amount of backtracking it might involve along a great variety of fascinating chains of reflections. This celebration of Light is, in the Ghent Altarpiece, the all-embracing presence that pervades all panels.

With the *de visione dei* key, we should be able to disclose the whole series. The panels should not be read serially, like Giotto's Arena chapel frescoes, each depicting a selected scene within the sequence of a biblical story. If the book of the Holy Virgin on the closed polyptych indicates the goal, its fulfillment is in the middle of the upper panel, where a divine figure—crowned and in red clothing, accompanied by the Holy Virgin and Saint John the Baptist—looks directly at the viewer.[12] At each side, angels provide either song or instrumental music. At the periphery we find Adam and Eve, the parents of mankind who, through original sin, spoiled the relationship with God. Their presence here demonstrates that the relationship has been restored and that they are again on good terms with their Creator. This restoration has been brought about by Christ's offering, an achievement that is commemorated in the celebration of the Mass, depicted here in the shape of the bleeding Lamb on the altar depicted in the lower central panel. On earth, the celebration of the Mass reminds believers of this instrumental act of Christ, which makes the God of the upper panels again accessible to them.

To summarize, the central theme on the closed polyptych is the Annunciation, promising the restoration of access to God, the single source of light. The lower central panel of the open polyptych indicates how that restoration is effectuated through Christ's sacrifice, an event to be recapitulated with gratitude in the Mass by all peoples, joining in along the side panels, from everywhere. The upper panels of the open polyptych show the result: God is again accessible, to be contemplated by every true observer.

On Pursuing the Light

With the key notions in mind that to see God is the final goal and that God is the ultimate Light, let us trace the light from within the Vijd chapel for which the Ghent Altarpiece was designed.

The natural light enters the pentagonal Vijd chapel through two windows, one oriented to the south and one to the southwest. For the spectator looking at the polyptych, this means that the light is coming from the right at an angle of about 45 degrees, both horizontally and vertically. By having shadows and reflections of the depicted figures and scenes lighted accordingly, van Eyck has this light penetrate his painting. The shadows projected by the figures of God, the Holy Virgin, and the Baptist on the upper panels of the open po-lyptych are to be found left of them (see figure 14.9). On the red cloak of the divine figure, the short segments of shadow of the slender strings of rope dangling in front are used to reveal the complicated folds and bends of the cloth (see figure 14.10).

The highlights indicating reflection on various objects also point to the two windows of the Vijd chapel as the light sources. Reflections of these windows are everywhere in the Ghent Altarpiece. One sees them in the eyes of the depicted figures looking in the direction of the windows; the spherical surface of their globular eyeballs functions as a convex mirror. Figures depicted as looking in the other direction—that is, away from the windows— do not display these reflections (see figure 14.11).

FIGURE 14.9. The shadows of the heads of the three main figures of the upper panels in the open polyptych indicate the orientation of the incoming light.

FIGURE 14.10. The shadows of the strings of rope on the cloak of God the Father illustrate subtle optics: as the light source is not a point but the plane of the window, shadows are not sharp and are identifiable only very close to the surface on which they project (in late medieval optical treatises, a large light source combined with a small lighted object implies a very short shadow cone). The painter uses this effect to detail the sculptural qualities of the cloak.

FIGURE 14.11. The eyes of the depicted figures function as reflecting spheres which produce a reduced image of the light source. The highlights seen in the eyes of figures looking in the direction of the windows show this effect, here demonstrated with the eyes of Adam. Those that look in the other direction do not show this effect.

The depicted jewels exhibit these highlights in the same consistent fashion. The globular pearls and the multifaceted precious stones all have highlights on the right side, indicating that the light is coming from that direction. This effect is most prominently displayed in the brooch of the singing angel of the upper panels in the open polyptych. The cylindrical stone clearly bears a mirror image of one of the Vijd chapel windows (see figure 14.12).

Van Eyck's sensitivity to subtle applications of optical principles is evident in the different representations he provides of reflection on the kettle as a convex mirror and the basin as a concave mirror (see figure 14.13). Refraction, too, is represented, in addition to shadow and reflection. Small clear crystal spheres, mixed among the pearls and the transparent scepter held by God (shown in figure 14.14), produce secondary reflections and focal points, just like burning glasses.

All of these effects are meticulously traced and depicted according to the local situation of the Vijd chapel. It is the natural light of this space that is represented as penetrating the painted scenes. However, inside the depicted scenes, reflections do not stop. The red spear of the knight is reflected on the metallic plates of his armor. A similar optical effect on the metallic pipes of

FIGURE 14.12. Cylindrical surfaces provide an image of the light source, elongated along the axis of the cylinder. On the cylindrical brooch worn by the singing angel, the light source can clearly be identified as a window of the Vijd chapel.

FIGURE 14.13. Reflection is different on convex and concave surfaces. The kettle in the Annunciation scene reflects light like a sphere, with a single small highlight disclosing the light source. In the interior of the basin, which qualifies as a concave surface, repeated highlights reflect the light source accordingly.

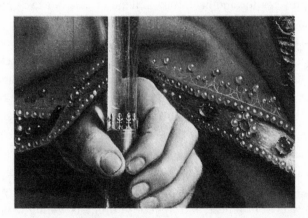

FIGURE 14.14. The scepter of God the Father is a transparent cylindrical object. The fine whitish vertical line on the right side shows the light that is reflected at the first optical barrier it encounters: the outside of the cylinder. Light penetrating the cylinder hits a second optical barrier at the concave outer boundary of the left side and is more diffusely scattered, as optics predicts. The light that overcomes these two barriers and that traverses the crystal staff undergoes refraction and results in focal spots on the hand of God the Father and on the pearls and folds of his cloak along the line of the incoming light.

289

FIGURE 14.15. In principle, the metallic organ pipes should have been made by folding a flat metallic plate into a cylinder, leaving a visible seam where the two edges form a joint. By showing two seams, van Eyck requires the viewer to sort out for himself what is meant to represent a genuine seam and what is only presented as a mirror image of a seam in his painting.

the organ provides for another subtle ambiguity that van Eyck presents as a mild challenge to his viewers. It is difficult to distinguish between the genuine seam of each cylinder and the seam it reflects from the adjacent tube. The viewer is forced to do some further inspection to distinguish between what represents the real thing (the seam) and its mirror image (see figure 14.15).

Another indication of internal mirroring is the reflection of the red cloth that covers the altar in the top of the wing of the metallic angel decorating the fountain on the central panel. These effects demonstrate the continuity of optical principles within the depicted scenes. The same rules according to which the light of the Vijd chapel could enter the painting keep operating within the painting and continue to govern the further trajectory of light. It can be followed from reflection to reflection if one is willing to decipher the various anamorphic forms that reflection produces on various surfaces and textures.

The Hierarchy of Lights and Reflection Devices

The natural light of the Vijd chapel enters the painting and penetrates the interiors and landscapes of every panel. A single light source—the light

FIGURE 14.16. While, in the Annunciation scene, the room with the Holy Virgin is still lighted from the windows of the viewer's space (the Vijd chapel), the light entering the oriel behind her comes from another direction.

source of the viewer's space—is consistently applied and persistently followed through a series of steps that illustrate various principles of the advanced optics which already existed in van Eyck's time.[13] In one scene, however, a second light source appears. Surprisingly, the street that can be observed from the small window in the Annunciation room depicted on the closed polyptych is clearly receiving light from another direction. Also, the patches of light produced on the wall of the oriel behind the Holy Virgin clearly indicate the alternative light source (see figure 14.16).

As a matter of fact, the clash of lights occurs right at that location! The room occupied by the Holy Virgin is still lighted according to the conditions applying to the Vijd chapel. The body of the Holy Virgin projects a shadow on the floor and the wall segment behind her. The shadow of the frame for this panel projects into the depicted room. The oriel, on the contrary, has the light enter through the window from the other direction. The way this light affects the carafe with water on the window ledge clearly indicates that it is coming from the left, diametrically opposed to the light of the Vijd chapel (see figure 14.17).

The way optics affected theology can be seen in the popularity of the carafe metaphor. The fascinating phenomenon of light passing through a liquid, leaving it unchanged and yet producing intriguing optical effects, was seen as the physical counterpart of the Incarnation. Gottlieb (1981, 135–36) assumes that the Dominican Vincent Contenson paraphrases Bernard of Clervaux when he compares the Incarnation of Christ with the union of God's light and the color of the earth contributed by the Holy Virgin: the color of

FIGURE 14.17. The optics of the carafe on the window ledge indicate that the light entering from the back comes from the opposite direction of the light entering at the front.

flesh. "As a pure ray enters through glass and emerges incorrupted, but has acquired the color of the glass which it irradiates, likewise the Son of God, who entered the most pure womb of the Virgin, emerged pure but took on the Virgin's color, that is, human nature and a comeliness of human form, and He garbed Himself in it" (Gottlieb 1981, 136). The carafe paradigm, together with the two-dimensional arrangement with which van Eyck makes the light patch of the oriel appear just next to the womb of the Holy Virgin, makes it clear that the light coming from the left is a superior light interfering with the natural light. It is God's light entering the scene directly.

Having emphatically demonstrated how a single light pervades both the picture and the room in which it is exposed, van Eyck is all the more capable of dramatizing the event of the Incarnation by having this ubiquitous light overruled by another one. This affirms both God's power and the exceptional character of the event. The regular light source on earth is the sun, which God has created, in a sense, as his deputy. Normal practice takes this dominant single light source into account when extending the experienced world into a pictorial world. However, when God finally decides to intervene in the world in order to reestablish a broken relationship, He has to interfere directly with the devices that He himself has created for the benefit of mankind. From this derives the exceptional clash of two lights and the overruling of the sun by the divine light of the Incarnation (see figure 14.18).

FIGURE 14.18. The Annunciation scene on the Ghent Altarpiece, with arrows added to indicate the two lights: the natural light from the sun, entering from the viewer's space, and the divine light, entering from the opposite direction in the back, affecting the Holy Virgin.

To enter the world and to take part in mankind, God acts through an instrument superior to the sun: the Virgin Mary. That this intervention introduces permanent changes in the hierarchy of divine creations is manifest from the text on the aureole behind the Virgin's head in the open polyptych:

> She is more beautiful than the sun and all stars, she is purer than
>   the light;
> She is the reflection of eternal light, a spotless mirror of God.

That van Eyck has quoted these lines in several other works as well confirms the importance he assigns to them. The text is a conflation of two verses from the Book of Wisdom:

> For she is a reflection of eternal light,
> a spotless mirror of the working of God,
> and an image of his goodness. (7:26)

> She is more beautiful than the sun,
> and excels every constellation of the stars,
> Compared to the light she is found to be superior. (7:29)
> (*The New Oxford Annotated Bible with the Apocrypha* 1989)

Although these biblical exclamations refer to Wisdom, van Eyck reverses their order and makes them apply to the Holy Virgin. In doing this, he accentuates the *optical scope* of the verses. God, ultimately remaining the unique source of light, inserts the Holy Virgin into the hierarchy of the vicarious lighting devices in his service, all of them being *mirrors of His light*. The Holy Virgin becomes second only to Him, and as a "light," she is *superior to the sun and the stars*. This superiority led to an image of the Holy Virgin popular for many centuries, in which she stands with her feet on the moon while the sun radiates behind her and an aureole of stars shines around her head (for an image, see http://theartfulmind.stanford.edu). Many times, a mirror is added as an attribute to indicate her status as a "reflector" of God's light.

The clash of lights can be seen only on the closed polyptych, in the dramatic Incarnation scene that coincides with the Annunciation. The other panels receive their light from the windows of the Vijd chapel. But through the circle of stars and the statement on the aureole of the Virgin, the hierarchy of lights and mirrors is also securely established on the open polyptych![14]

Performative Painting?

With the natural light of the spectator's space seeping into the painting and passing through it to meet the direct light of God that comes from the other direction, the light is breaking through the barrier between the spectator and God, the separation between the viewer and the depicted scene. The cultivation of continuity in van Eyck develops in contrast with the cultivation of the window that his contemporary Alberti cherishes. The Albertian notion of a window, coinciding with the section through the visual cone, upholds a clear-cut distinction between the depicted world and the world of the viewer. Even when the painted view should fit seamlessly into reality, as in Brunelleschi's lost panel of the Florence baptistery, the picture plane remains a glass barrier, like the glass barrier in one of Dürer's instruments for drawing perspectives. But van Eyck clearly wants the picture plane to be an open passage through which the spectator can reach the more solid world of revelation. He wants that picture plane to be permeable so that the viewer can step in, like Alice in Wonderland, to explore the perplexingly promising realm beyond that familiar but less pretentious viewing space. In the Annunciation panels of the closed polyptych, the frames of the panels throw a shadow into the depicted space to indicate the merging of these two spaces: the room of the Holy Virgin and the viewer's space. Thus, *following the lead of the light*, the spectator can step into the picture and follow it through all the way to an encounter with

God, who, descending in the Annunciation along his own light, directly provides part of the way himself.

Philippot (1966) interpreted the bringing together of donors and saints (the Vijds and the two saints John) in a single picture as another means of dissolving the boundary between the viewer's reality and the depicted reality. Compared to its Italian pendant, Masaccio's *Trinity*, where portraits of the donors situate them outside the depicted chapel with its divine persons and saints, the donors of van Eyck's polyptych have indeed entered the picture. Could this also imply the expression of a more active involvement expected from the viewers?

Recently, Yvonne Yiu (2001) has demonstrated that within several of van Eyck's religious paintings, a definite place has been assigned to the viewer. She focuses in particular on the Arnolfini double portrait, in which the purported self-portrait of van Eyck accompanied by a friend is supposedly present as an image reflected in the depicted convex mirror right in the center. But the figures in the mirror are indeed so unspecified that they could count for any two spectators standing in front of the couple. A similarly reflected image, this time of the viewer, may be hidden in a more subtle way on the shield of Saint George in the panel of *The Virgin with Canon Van der Paele* in the Groeninge Museum in Bruges.

In the van Eyck panel preserved in the Louvre, *The Virgin with Chancellor Rolin*, two spectators are integrated within the picture, again quite in the center. However, concealed in the arrangement of tiles is also the suggestion of a path onto which the viewer of the panel might step in order to join the depicted spectators. Apparently, the painter not only wants to dissolve the boundary between the viewer's space and the depicted space, thereby making the latter as real as the former. He also expects the viewers to enter the depicted space, and even offers them a path. Do these pictures exemplify a sort of performative painting, going beyond the purposes of depiction or description? Are they meant to make the viewer do something, mentally? Could van Eyck compel the viewers of the Ghent Altarpiece to move mentally toward the painting and to penetrate those inviting worlds underlying transient earthly reality?

The viewer is given easy access into the painting in the Annunciation scene, but there the light of God has to come half of the way. The Altarpiece's capacity to make the viewer enter the painting and embark upon a visual path that finally traverses the entire collection of panels might have been better expressed in the central panel of the open polyptych. Technical analysis has revealed that van Eyck may have intended this central panel to be less crowded and less busy than it is. Reflectography by Van Asperen de Boer (1979) has disclosed that the regular underdrawing, present for most of the objects and

FIGURE 14.19. Central panel of the Ghent Altarpiece.

FIGURE 14.20. The original plan of the central panel of the Ghent Altarpiece might not have contained the fountain. There is no underdrawing for it, as there is for most of the other components. Without the fountain, the Ghent Altarpiece provides ample room for the viewer to step into the picture to join the assembled believers who witness Christ's offering, which reopens the way to (seeing) God.

figures, is not present for the fountain, which is right in the middle under the altar. Furthermore, beneath the layers of paint that depict that fountain, one detects grass and foliage similar to that surrounding the fountain and the altar. These findings strongly suggest that the fountain was probably a late addition that did not belong to the original design. Once that possibility is accepted, it makes sense to entertain the hypothesis that the space in the middle, between the two large frontal groups, was initially conceived as empty. Would this signify some Eyckian pragmatics, equivalent to a Gricean maxim, where a statement is meant to evoke some action? Had van Eyck already provided a space for the viewer in the Ghent Altarpiece? Was the inviting area in the middle of the open polyptych meant to allow the viewer to step in? In her paper "Blended spaces and performativity," Eve Sweetser (2000) has explored the power of the word to affect the world: linguistic expressions can bring about effective changes. To the degree that he makes the viewer mentally active, van Eyck genuinely transcends his reputation as a meticulously descriptive realist painter (see figures 14.19 and 14.20).

Did we realize that his apparently contemplative art could so decisively have been meant to evoke action?

Concluding Remarks

In the complexity of its twenty panels, the Ghent Altarpiece contains a wide range of pictorial inventions that exemplify the power of blended lights to put creative ambiguities on a single continuum. Natural light entering through the windows of the Vijd chapel combines with divine light coming from the center of the church building to constitute an optical ladder along which the distinction between perceptual and conceptual ambiguity dissolves. Van Eyck is involved with "seeing" broadly considered: from perception of sensory details far more subtle than the common observer would ever notice, to conceptual interpretation far beyond what that same observer is mostly aware of. Over this range, light is preeminent, and its physical presence coincides with its theological meaning.

The controversy between Alpers and De Jongh concerning the Golden Age of Dutch painting found its origin in the distinction between observation and interpretation. For Alpers, seventeenth-century Dutch painters were most of all fascinated by *the art of describing*, the careful rendering of light and detail that is based on careful examination of objects and scenes and that we would associate with van Eyck's apparent hyperrealism. For De Jongh, the painters of the Golden Age are, in the first place, concerned with moral meaning, messages that we would associate with van Eyck's capacity to express spiritual concepts and religious values. Overcoming the controversy, Mieke Bal (1994) has comfortingly reconfirmed that Dutch seventeenth-century painters can expand meaning beyond the confines of their realist pictures and combine both attitudes. But perceptual attributes and spiritual meaning have never been welded together so strongly as they are in van Eyck's work. It is as if, after the unique conjunction attained by van Eyck, the two components—perceptual veridicality and spiritual meaning—begin to drift apart and, after centuries of increasingly loose connections, finally go their separate ways.

For their analysis of the *Proverbs* by Pieter Breughel the Elder, Dundes and Stibbe (1981) chose the title *The Art of Mixing Metaphors*.[15] This is undoubtedly a most appropriate designation for successful art in general: to combine the alternatives of an ambiguity into a new unit. Perhaps the loss of unity in art that filmmaker Bergman deplores is the loss of a unity of the scope and power present in the Ghent Altarpiece. The fragmentation that he bemoans may be due to the lack of a single unifying feature that, in van Eyck's picture, permeates everything and keeps it all together. Breughel's *Proverbs* contains a treasury of apt visualizations of single maxims, but the collection is not held together by the sustained use of one single feature that unites it all, such as the light in the Ghent Altarpiece. That the dynamic handling of light could be superior to static perspective in unifying an entire picture is Jan van Eyck's greatest discovery.

NOTES

Figures 14.6 to 14.19 from the Ghent Altarpiece are based on photographic negatives from the late Alfons Dierick, currently in the Fonds Alfons Dierick at Ghent University, reproduced here with permission from the copyright owner of the polyptych (Kerkfabriek Sint-Baafskathedraal, Bisdomplein 1, 9000 Gent, Belgium) and the Reproductiefonds (Bijlokekaai 1, 9000 Gent, Belgium), owner of the copyright for photographs.

1. The pelican-antelope figure is mentioned in Hanson's *Patterns of Discovery* (1958). Simple ambiguous figures of this kind began to symbolize so-called paradigm shifts after Kuhn introduced that notion in his quite influential *The Structure of Scientific Revolutions* (1962). More on their scope and role in philosophy and history of science can be found in my book *The Cognitive Paradigm* (De Mey 1992, chaps. 6 and 10).

2. Kepler's historical solution in his *Paralipomena* (1604/2000) recognizes the *camera obscura* nature of circular shapes on the ground when the sun shines at noon through the angular apertures of the summer foliage of trees. To arrive at the solution, he systematically explored to what degree the shape of bright spots depended on the shape of the light source and on the shape of the aperture. In Chapter Two of the

Paralipomena, Kepler uses the geometric example of a triangle for a convincing demonstration. With the sun being circular, it is less obvious that the circular patch is an inverted image (though for astronomers, such as Kepler, it becomes very obvious on the occasion of a lunar eclipse). In describing the process of his discovery, Kepler tells us that he actually explored the case by taking a book as representing the light source. He held the book above a hole in a table, and attaching sequentially a piece of string to each corner of the book, he traced on the floor the shape of the figure formed by following with the string the contour of the hole in the table. He saw that for each point, his drawing represented the shape of the hole, but all together these shapes constituted an image of the book. Various authors have suggested that this particular exploration by Kepler might have been inspired by Dürer's 1525 illustration, in *Unterweysung der messung mit dem zirckel und richtscheyt Linien ebnen und gantzen corporen . . .*, of the use of strings in an instrument designed for perspective drawing (see Durand 2003 for an introduction to this topic). A Ghent University Web site provides relevant illustrations and animations developed by the author in collaboration with W. De Boever and Gitte Callaert. A link to this site is available at http://theartfulmind.stanford.edu.

3. The stovepipe at the ceiling in van Gogh's *Hospital Room* appears to lie on a vanishing line, suggesting a simple symmetrical perspective. In fact, it falls at an angle with respect to the back wall. Thus, the perspective is complicated even though the slanted pipe segment, which could even be parallel to the picture plane, misleadingly makes it look simple. Van Gogh was actually quite intrigued by perspective and used a device to trace out his preferred views. A dynamic illustration of how such a device might apply to van Gogh's *Bedroom at Arles* is available at http://theartfulmind.stanford.edu.

4. In 2001, on the occasion of the six-hundredth anniversary of Masaccio's birth, the *Trinity* was restored and celebrated with an exhibition in the Galleria degli Uffizi organized by the Instituto e Museo di Storia della Scienza. Some technical aspects of the restoration are reported in the exhibition catalog, edited by Filippo Camerota (2001). More elaborate reconstructions and animations illustrating our own points made in this chapter can be found at http://theartfulmind.stanford.edu.

5. *The Librarian* and the allegorical representations of the seasons are Arcimboldo's most famous paintings. For Arcimboldo's works, see http://theartfulmind.stanford.edu.

6. De Jongh (1999) provides some larger background information on the iconological approach and the controversy with Svetlana Alpers, while still stressing the scope and importance of the symbolic orientation.

7. A similar reconstruction has recently been developed by Stork (2004). Although we sent him our chandelier material at his request, he preferred to have it redone in order to be able to draw the vanishing lines for the small decorative hanging quatrefoils of the chandelier, carefully checking the preciseness of the linear perspective. Apparently Stork does not consider our reconstruction and animated representation of it in any way convincing or relevant, as he leaves out in his article any reference to the materials we sent him. We agree, however, that his test confirms the

exultant but hackneyed claim that van Eyck did not use linear perspective in the strict sense of that specific criterion. Once again, vanishing lines are used as deadly arrows to hit what some prefer to consider van Eyck's Achilles' heel! So what? Apparently, Stork's major concern is to falsify Hockney's claim for the use of the concave mirror. Does he?

8. The Arnolfini double portrait in the National Gallery in London has been thoroughly studied by Lorne Campbell, whose results reported in the 1998 catalogue *The Fifteenth Century Netherlandish Schools* provide the most current information on that painting. The interpretation of the scene as representing a marriage is rather doubtful. See Lorne Campbell's analysis, "NG 186. *Portrait of Giovanni [?] Arnolfini and his Wife*," in Campbell (1998, 174–211). See also Yiu (2001).

9. The Ghent Altarpiece has been the subject of numerous studies. Elisabeth Dhanens's *Hubert and Jan van Eyck* (1980) remains a standard reference. In it, expanding on her earlier work *Van Eyck: The Ghent Altarpiece* (1973), she situates the polyptych in the oeuvre of the van Eyck brothers. Although there is scant evidence concerning Jan van Eyck's older brother Hubert, Dhanens has no doubt about his existence and his participation in the Ghent Altarpiece. On the other hand, Volker Herzner's *Jan van Eyck und der Genter Altar* (1995) argues that the polyptych is the work of a single painter, Jan van Eyck. Despite some indications in archival sources, many uncertainties and ambiguities remain. Based on a reinterpretation of known materials and additional archival research, Hugo van der Velden argues in his forthcoming book that 1435 rather than 1432 should be taken as the year in which the Ghent Altarpiece was finished.

10. The influence of late medieval optics on Alberti is manifest in his monograph *De Pictura* (Alberti 1435). This small book is considered a turning point in the history of art, codifying a method for constructing linear perspective as a section through the visual cone. Earlier on, this geometric notion was developed around the year 1000 by the Arab astronomer Ibn Al-Haytham (Alhazen) as the core concept in his theory for the optical workings of the eye and visual perception (for a translation of Al-Haytham's book on vision, see Sabra 1989). Concluded in 1435, Alberti's book came only after some of the major perspective innovations had already been achieved, by Brunelleschi and Donatello and, most importantly, by Masaccio. His *Trinity* fresco in the Santa Maria Novella in Florence probably dates from around 1425 and could not be later than 1428, the year in which he died. An edition of the Grayson translation of Alberti's book, with introduction and notes by Martin Kemp, is published as a Penguin Classic. Its role and position in the history of linear perspective in art is to be found in Martin Kemp's *The Science of Art* (1991).

11. That the familiar everyday world of sensory experience is but a transient, anamorphous image of a not yet directly accessible spiritual reality is obviously a version of Plato's parable of the cave in the *Republic*. A progress to various levels of vision opens up when the prisoner, previously fixed in a position from which he could see only shadows, is freed and can gradually turn directly toward the light:

> When he approaches the light his eyes will be dazzled, and he will not be able to see anything at all of what are now called realities.... He will require to

grow accustomed to the sight of the upper world. And first he will see the shadows best, next the reflections of men and other objects in the water, and then the objects themselves; then he will gaze upon the light of the moon and the stars and the spangled heaven; and he will see the sky and the stars by night better than the sun or the light of the sun by day.... Last of all, he will be able to see the sun, and not mere reflections of him in the water, but he will see him in his own proper place, and not in another; and he will contemplate him as he is.

Then, explaining the allegory, Plato continues: "The prison-house is the world of sight, the light of fire is the sun, and you will not misapprehend me if you interpret the journey upwards to be the ascent of the soul into the intellectual world...." (Plato, *Republic*, Book VII, paragraphs 35–40). This notion of a stepwise upgrading of vision was expanded by Plotinus, the leading neoplatonist philosopher (third century). Through his influence on the church fathers, it also became ingrained in Christian doctrine. According to Plotinus, "the ascent from the cave and the gradual advance of the souls to truer and truer vision" (Plotinus, *Six Enneads*, second Ennead, ninth tractate, paragraph 50) will ultimately lead to seeing the light itself: "the vision floods the eyes with light, but it is not a light showing some other object, the light itself is the vision" (sixth Ennead, tracts 6–7, paragraph 225). Notice that this kind of progress in vision, whereby the light becomes gradually more important than the lighted object itself, establishes a hierarchy of light-revealing objects. Van Eyck's undeniable fascination for jewels and gems is probably akin to Abbot Suger's enthusiasm for them: such objects allow the light to reveal its power and beauty.

> Thus, when—out of my delight in the beauty of the house of God—the loveliness of the many-colored gems has called me away from external cares, and worthy meditation has induced me to reflect, transferring that which is material to that which is immaterial, on the diversity of the sacred virtues: then it seems to me that I see myself dwelling, as it were, in some strange region of the universe which neither exists entirely in the slime of the earth nor entirely in the purity of Heaven; and that, by the grace of God, I can be transported from this inferior to that higher world in an anagogical manner. (Suger, quoted in Panofsky 1979, 63–65)

Thus, there is an optical reason for seeing gems and jewels as instruments for religious meditation.

   12. One of the many controversies that remain unsettled is the identity of the divine figure on the upper central panel of the Ghent Altarpiece. The attributes are certainly ambivalent: some are clearly associated with Christ, others refer to God the Father. That the identity of this figure could have been changed during the execution of the work should not be excluded. While at the outset the Deësis group might have been theologically most indicated, pressures from patrons or religious or political advisors might have induced a change into God the Father. Coremans (1953) considers the dove on the top of the lower central panel as a later addition. It might well have

been an element added at the time the Trinity option was chosen to replace a previous Deësis option.

13. As argued above, the optics of reflection and refraction were well developed in van Eyck's time. In antiquity, Euclid and Ptolemy had developed optics into a solid discipline. It was significantly improved by Arab refinements, advances, and corrections around the turn of the first millennium. It remained popular as *perspectiva* after it was reconsolidated as an important and fascinating field in the thirteenth century by Grosseteste, Bacon, Pecham, and Witelo, who were motivated by theological considerations. It should be emphasized that the discipline of *perspectiva* included much more than "perspective in art" as that subject was developed in the fifteenth century. *Perspectiva* dealt with seeing in a wider sense, including errors of perception supposedly induced by mirrors and lenses. The *perspectiva artificialis* of the painters (codified by Alberti) dealt with more than the small subclass of the theorems (the visual cone) that *perspectiva naturalis* addressed (i.e., the treatments of reflection and refraction that aroused the interest of Jan van Eyck).

14. Although not particularly focused on the light hierarchy, Carol Purtle's *The Marian Paintings of Jan van Eyck* (1982, 168) provides a thorough and balanced analysis of the figure of the Holy Virgin in van Eyck's works. With a powerful grip on the unifying force of the religious theme, she finds "a consistent Eyckian interest in dealing with the mystery of the Incarnation, *the entrance of God into human history*, and with the impact the Incarnation exercises on his own life and on the lives of people around him" [emphasis added]. In the Ghent Altarpiece, the two lights twined together, along with their optical paraphernalia, constitute the path along which God enters human history.

15. The title of Dundes and Stibbe's (1981) *The Art of Mixing Metaphors* was taken over in a German version by Frank Detje as the title for a collection of Internet materials in which he assembled a nearly complete compilation of studies on the various versions of the Brueghels' *Proverbs*. His collection of materials is entitled *Über die Kunst, Metaphern zu mischen. Einladung zu einer Diskussion über Pieter Bruegels Bild "Die holländischen Sprichwörter"* 1559. It can be consulted at http://www.deproverbio .com/DPjournal/DP,5,1,99/DETJE/Bruegel.html.

REFERENCES

Alberti, L. B. 1435/1991. *On painting*, trans. C. Grayson, intro. and notes M. Kemp. London: Penguin Books.

Alpers, S. 1983. *The art of describing*. Chicago: University of Chicago Press.

Bal, M. 1994. *Reading Rembrandt: Beyond the word-image opposition*. Cambridge, England: Cambridge University Press.

Bragg, M. 1993. *The seventh seal*. London: British Film Institute.

Camerota, F. 2001. *Nel Segno di Masaccio. L'Invenzione della Prospettiva*. Florence: Giunti.

Campbell, L. 1998. *The fifteenth century Netherlandish schools*. London, England: National Gallery Publications.

Coremans, P. 1953. *L'Agneau mystique au laboratoire*. Antwerp: De Sikkel.

De Jongh, E. 1967. *Zinne- en minnebeelden in de schilderkunst van de zeventiende eeuw.* Den Haag, Netherlands: Openbaar Kunstbezit.

———. 1999. The iconological approach to seventeenth-century Dutch painting. In *The golden age of Dutch painting in historical perspective,* ed. F. Gijzenhout and H. van Veen, 200–223. Cambridge, England: Cambridge University Press.

De Mey, M. 1992. *The cognitive paradigm: An integrated understanding of scientific development.* Chicago: University of Chicago Press.

Dhanens, E. 1973. *Van Eyck: The Ghent Altarpiece.* London: Allen Lane.

———. 1980. *Hubert and Jan van Eyck.* Antwerp: Mercatorfonds.

Dundes, A., and C. Stibbe. 1981. *The art of mixing metaphors.* Helsinki: FF Communications nr 230.

Durand, F. 2003. The art and science of depiction: Linear perspective. MIT Lab for Computer Science. Web presentation. See http://theartfulmind.stanford.edu.

Dürer, A. 1525 and 1538/1995. Instruction sur la manière de mesurer, trans. J. Bardy and M. van Peene. Paris: Flammarion.

Gottlieb, C. 1981. *The window in art: From the window of God to the vanity of man.* New York: Abaris Books.

Hanson, N. 1958. *Patterns of discovery.* Cambridge, England: Cambridge University Press.

Herzner, V. 1995. *Jan van Eyck und der Genter Altar.* Worms: Wernersche Verlaggesellschaft.

Hockney, D. 2001. *Secret knowledge. Rediscovering the lost techniques of old masters.* London: Thames and Hudson.

Kemp, M. 1991. *The science of art.* New Haven: Yale University Press.

Kepler, J. 1604/2000. *Optics: Paralipomena to Witelo and the optical part of astronomy,* trans. W. H. Donahue. Santa Fe, N.M.: Green Press.

Kuhn, T. 1962. *The structure of scientific revolutions.* Chicago: University of Chicago Press.

Marr, D. 1982. *Vision: A computational investigation into the human representation and processing of visual information.* San Francisco: W. H. Freeman.

Mithen, S. 1996. *The prehistory of the mind.* London: Thames and Hudson.

New Oxford Annotated Bible with the Apocryphal/Deuterocanonical Books 1989. New York: Oxford University Press.

Panofsky, E. 1939. *Studies in iconology.* New York: Oxford University Press.

———. 1953. *Early Netherlandish painting: Its origin and character.* Cambridge, Mass.: Harvard University Press.

———. 1979. *Abbot Suger on the abbey church of St.-Denis and its art treasures.* Princeton, N.J.: Princeton University Press.

Philippot, P. 1966. Les grisailles et les "degrees de réalité" de l'image dans la peinture flamande des XVe et XVIe siècles. *Bulletin des Musées Royeaux des Beaux-Arts de Belgique,* 15: 225–42.

Plato. *The Republic.* 1991, trans. B. Jowett. World Library: Electronically Enhanced Text.

Plotinus. 1991. *The Six Enneads,* trans. S. Mackenna and B. S. Page. World Library: Electronically Enhanced Text.

Polzer, J. 1971. The anatomy of Masaccio's Holy Trinity. *Jahrbuch der Berliner Museen,* 13: 18–59.

Purtle, C. 1982. *The Marian paintings of Jan van Eyck.* Princeton, N.J.: Princeton University Press.

Sabra, A. I. 1989. *The optics of Ibn Al-Haytham.* London: Warburg Institute.

Stork, D. G. 2004. Optics and realism in Renaissance art. *Scientific American,* 291: 76–83.

Sweetser, E. 2000. Blended spaces and performativity. *Cognitive Linguistics,* 11: 3/4 (special issue on mental spaces and blending).

Turner, M. 2001. *Cognitive dimensions of social science: The way we think about politics, economics, law, and society.* New York: Oxford University Press.

Van Asperen De Boer, J.R.J. 1979. A scientific re-examination of the Ghent Altarpiece. *Oud Holland,* 93: 141–214.

Van der Velden, H. forthcoming.

Yiu, Y. 2001. *Jan van Eyck Das Arnolfini-Doppelbildnis. Reflexionen über die Malerei.* Frankfurt am Main und Basel: Stroemfeld.

Zeki, S. 1997. The Woodhull lecture: Visual art and the visual brain. *Proceedings of the Royal Institute of Great Britain,* 68: 29–63.

———. 1998. Art and brain. *Daedalus, Journal of the American Academy of Arts and Sciences,* 127: 71–103.

Zeki, S., and Balthus. 1995. *Balthus ou la quête de l'essentiel.* Paris: Les Belles Lettres.

Epilogue

It was in 1902 that Emile Cartailhac, an influential French archae-
ologist who had vehemently contested the authenticity of the finds that had
been made in the French and Spanish caves, recanted and published his
now-famous article Mea culpa d'un sceptique. *The widespread, though*
not complete, skepticism that had denied the prehistoric people of the
Upper Palaeolithic period the ability to produce art at once fell away. At a
stroke, the study of Upper Palaeolithic art became respectable, and a new
academic industry was born.

Now, just over a century later, we ask how much we have learned
since Cartailhac changed his mind.... [T]he greatest riddle of
archaeology—how we became human and in the process began to
make art—continues to tantalize.

—David Lewis-Williams, The Mind in the Cave:
Consciousness and the Origins of Art (*London:*
Thames and Hudson, 2002)

What are the operations of the human mind that make it artful?
Why did the human mind evolve so as to be artful? How do neurobiological operations of the brain subtend the operations of the artful
mind?

The what, why, and how of the artful mind remain tantalizing
mysteries, but the contributors to this volume have shown that we are
now far beyond the stage of Emile Cartailhac a century ago. The pace
of research has increased dramatically over the last decade.

There are overarching settled conclusions: that the artful mind has been with us on the order of at least fifty thousand years; that all human cultures show comprehensive impulses toward artfulness; that the artful mind is subject to scientific investigation through a variety of methodologies.

But settled conclusions within the questions of what, why, and how are harder to find. Although the available answers do not yet constitute a body of established knowledge, the culture of scientific investigation into the artful mind *is* established and by now indomitable. We look forward to its increase and diffusion.

Index

24th Street Intersection (Thiebaud),
 166

abstraction, 96–9, 173, 182, 198; law
 of, 96
Acropolis (Athens), 232
acting, 23, 63, 133, 137, 140, 157,
 160
adaptation, 26
aesthetic faculty, 21, 25, 64
aesthetics, 28–31, 43, 57, 61, 186;
 and appreciation, 38; and
 cognition, 26–31, 37–8, 41, 44,
 57, 184; and evolution, 57, 60;
 neuroaesthetics, 184; and
 perception, 173
agape, 38
Alberti, Leon Battista, 283, 294,
 300, 302
Al-Haytham (Alhazen), 282, 300
Alpers, Svetlana, 278, 299
Altarpiece, Ghent, The (*Adoration of
 the Mystical Lamb, The*) (van
 Eyck) 280–302
ambiguity, 95, 243–5, 251, 255, 258,
 260–4, 271–80, 290, 297–8; of

figures like the devil's tuning
 fork or Escherian figures, 278;
 and microconsciousness, 261;
 of pelican-antelope figure,
 271, 298
ambiguous bi-stable images, 255
Amiens, Cathedral church of
 (Cathedral of Notre-Dame,
 Amiens), 196
animal communication, 34
Annunciation, high canon
 representations of, 110
Annunciation scene of the Ghent
 Altarpiece (van Eyck), 284–5,
 291–5
Aphaia on Aegina, sanctuary of,
 227
appreciation, aesthetic, 38
Arcimboldo, Giuseppe, 264, 278,
 299
Arena Chapel, 88; frescoes (Giotto),
 285
Aristotle, 77, 225–6
Arnheim, Rudolf, 153–7, 165–7
Arnolfini double portrait (van Eyck),
 279, 295, 300

art; and emotion, 40, 57; and excess structure, 176; function of, 3, 243, 266; Islamic, Jewish, Buddhist, and Hindu, 8; and language faculties, 27; and pleasure, 57; representational, 67–9

Art of Describing, The (Alpers), 278, 297

Art of Mixing Metaphors, The (Dundes and Stibbe), 298, 302

aspect, 159; aspectual schemas, 164

Asperen de Boer, J. R. J. van, 295

Auerbach, Erich, 19

awe, 38

Bal, Mieke, 298

Ban, Johan Albert, 86

Bannister, Roger, 100, 102, 106

basic-level categories, 117–9, 120–1

Bateson, Gregory, 30

beauty, 3, 39, 57–64, 69–70, 172, 175–6, 182–3, 199, 214, 264–5, 301; in the tension between mental spaces, 182

Bedroom at Arles (van Gogh), 299

Beethoven, Ludwig van, 84, 122

Belvedere Hercules (or *Torso*) (Greek sculpture), 264–5

Bergman, Ingmar, 280

Bernard of Clervaux, Saint, 291

Bernini, Gian Lorenzo, 81

binding, neural, 111, 174–5, 278

bisociation, 21, 42–4

bi-stable images, 255

Black, Max, 226

blended space, 43, 48, 101–4, 129, 179, 226

blends and blending (conceptual integration), 4, 5, 13, 21, 40–51, 93–112, 124–9, 139, 171–9, 186, 217–9, 227, 234–6, 280, 283; compressed, 96–100; double-scope, 40, 41, 43, 93, 94, 107, 109; of self and other, 52

Blunt, Anthony, 78, 81, 87

Bosch, Hieronymus, 136

Boyer, Pascal, 217–9

Brandt, Per Aage, 109, 171

Breughel, Pieter, the Elder, 298

Bronze Age, 229

Brown, Peter, 214, 218

Brunelleschi, Filippo, 6, 283, 294, 300

Buddhist monk blend, 102–3, 106, 109

Caillebotte, Gustave, 165

Carruthers, Mary, 202

Cartailhac, Emile, 305

categories, basic-level, 117–9, 120–1

categorization, 116–7

Cathedral church, at Amiens, 196; at Chartres, 195, 199, 200, 204; at Salisbury, 212; at Troyes, 203

Cézanne, Paul, 178

Chambray (Fréart de Chambray, Roland), 76

Chantelou (Fréart de Chantelou, Paul), 75–9, 85

Charpentier, Marc-Antoine, 84

Chartres, Cathedral church of (Cathedral of Notre-Dame, Chartres), 195, 199, 200, 204

chase play, 111

Christ at Emmaus (Rembrandt), 155

Christian civilization, art and ritual, 8

cognition *passim*; distributed, 4, 12, 19, 112; models of, 189; principles of, 3, 20

cogs, hypothesis of, 153, 158, 161–2, 167

Cohen, Nathan, 256

Colbert, Jean Baptiste, 76

color vision, 245, 248, 250, 252–3, 266

communication, 4, 22, 24, 31, 33–4, 49, 66–7, 129, 175–6, 181, 185; animal, 34

compression, conceptual, 93–110, 174, 203, 221

conceptual blending. *See* blending

Condillac sequences, 11–2

consciousness, 11, 17, 51, 59, 62, 67, 99, 112, 147, 173, 186, 243, 247, 248, 255, 256, 257, 261; contents of, 172; and processing, 5

constancy, law of, 96, 244
Corinthians, First Letter to the (Saint Paul), 284
Corot, Jean-Baptiste-Camille, 157
cortex, 258; premotor, 15, 153, 158, 160
counterfactual, 67, 179
cross-modal unification, in nervous system, 4, 94
Cult of the Saints, The (Brown), 215

Dali, Salvador, 264
Damasio, Antonio, 75, 87–8
dance, xv, 3, 8, 22, 23, 48, 93, 115, 116, 124, 126–7, 129, 141–2, 182
De Germania (Tacitus), 193
De la propriété des modes & des Tons (Rameau), 85
Demoiselles d'Avignon, Les (Picasso), 95, 99
Dennett, Daniel, 30
De Pictura (Alberti), 300
Derrida Queries de Man (Tansey), 166
"de visione Dei" (key phrase in van Eyck's Ghent Altarpiece), 284
dialogue, 142
disembodiment, 173
distributed cognition. *See* cognition
Donald, Merlin, 3–7, 11, 14, 94, 135, 138, 186
Donatello, 274, 300
Dorian mode, 77–8
double-scope blend. *See* blends and blending
Doyle, Arthur Conan, 166
drawing, 23
Duchamp, Marcel, 98, 99, 102, 103
Dürer, Albrecht, 299
Durkheim, Émile, 217, 220–2

Eco, Umberto, 179
Elementary Forms of Religious Life, The (Durkheim), 221
el-Guerrouj, Hicham, 100
emotion, 37, 73

engineering, cognitive, 4, 19
Enneads (Plotinus), 50, 301
epiphany, 173
ethics, 52
Euclid, 302
eureka experience, 38
euro, 190
event-perception, 4, 94
evolution, cognitive and cultural, 14; Eyck, Jan van, 110, 277–302; hominid, 19; human cognitive and neural, 26; and origins of art, 14; theory of, 7, 57

face, recognition of, 258
face-vase figure, 261
Fauconnier, Gilles, 40–2, 52, 93–4, 129, 137, 174, 217–8, 226
figure-background shift, 34
Final Problem, The (Doyle), 166
Finding of Moses (Poussin), 75, 76
Fodor, Jerrold, 17
force dynamics, 219
Fragonard, Jean-Honoré, 178
frame, conceptual, 47, 97, 101
Fréart de Chambray, Roland, 76
Fréart de Chantelou, Paul, 75–9, 85
Freedberg, David, 73, 214, 217
French Academy of Painting, 79
frescoes of the Arena Chapel, 285
Freud, Lucian, 177
Freud, Sigmund, 30
fronto-parietal cortex, 258
fusiform gyrus, 249, 258

games, imaginary, 16
gaps, disparities, and improvisations, 133–5
George, Saint, 295
gestalt, perceptual-emotional, 34
Gestalt psychology, 42
Ghent Altarpiece, The, 280–302
Giotto, 88, 136, 273, 285
Girard, René, 19
Giverny project (Monet), 180

Goethe, Johannes Wolfgang von, 42, 264
Gombrich, E. H., 189, 192, 197
Gothic, 110, 189–204
Gregory, bishop of Tours, 215

habitat, choice of, 58
Hagia Sophia, 199
Hall of the Bulls, 99
Hammerstein, Oscar, 115
Harmonic Institutions (Istitutioni
    harmoniche) (Zarlino), 79
Harold and the Purple Crayon (Johnson),
    107–10
Hegel, Georg Wilhelm Friedrich, 42
Helmholtz, Hermann von, 116, 245, 254
Heraclitus, 236–7
Hering, Ewald, 245, 254
Herzner, Volker, 300
Hesiod, 230–1
Hockney, David, 279
Holland, Dorothy, 127
Holmes, Sherlock, 166
Homer, 230, 234
Homo ludens (Huizinga), 134
Honnecourt, Villard de, 192, 203
Hospital Room (van Gogh), 274, 299
human scale, 99–100, 103
humor, 38, 43, 47–8, 185–6
Hypolydian mode, 78

iconic, 18, 30, 34, 40–1, 58, 66, 108,
    182
Iliad (Homer), 230, 234
illustrators, 135
image schemas, 155–6, 164, 167
imitation, 135
indexical, 31, 34, 41
indignation, 38
integration, conceptual. See blends and
    blending
integration, semantic, 174
irony, 38
Israelites Gathering the Manna, The
    (Poussin), 79–80

Johnson, Crockett, 107
Johnson, Mark, 123
joke, 43, 47
Jongh, Eddy De, 278, 297, 299
juxtaposition, 21, 36, 39–52, 256

Kanizsa cube, 255, 261, 263, 265
Kanizsa triangle, 252
Kant, Immanuel, 42
Keats, John, 58
Kepler, Johannes, 273, 282, 298
Koestler, Arthur, 42–4, 49, 112
Koko, 65–6
Kuhn, Thomas, 298

Lakoff, George, 123, 153
Land, Edwin, 266
landscape preferences, 58
language, xv, 8, 14–36, 52, 93, 106, 117,
    119, 129, 134–47, 154–62, 183–7, 194,
    199, 202, 204, 219, 220, 222, 251
language adaptations, 29
language faculty, 29
Lascaux, 99, 101–2, 165
Las Meninas (Velásquez), 135
laughter, 47
Le Doux, Joseph, 75
Leo X, Pope, 192
Le pont de l'Europe (Caillebotte), 165
Lewis-Williams, David, 305
Los Honores (fifteenth-century tapestry
    created for Charles V), 136
Love Letter, The (Vermeer), 142–3

Magritte, René, 109, 135, 171, 180, 187
mammals, 4, 15
Mandel, Frank, 115
mapping, cross-domain, 122
Marian Paintings of Jan van Eyck, The
    (Purtle), 302
Marie-Thérèse Walter (Picasso), 98,
    99, 106
Marr, David, 277
Martin of Tours, Saint, 214–5

Masaccio, 274, 277, 281–2, 295, 299, 300
Mazarin, Jules, Cardinal, 76
Mea culpa d'un sceptique (Cartailhac), 305
memory, long-term, 175
mental space, 67, 100, 171, 174, 177, 179, 180–2, 187, 218–9, 227; beauty in the tension between, 182; Mersenne, Marin, 86; network, 179–81; semantics of, 182
metacognition, 5, 138
metaphor, 8, 42, 123–8, 140, 154–8, 163–7, 199, 225–7, 235–6, 291
meta-stability, obligate, 256
Michelangelo Buonarroti, 263
mimesis, 7–9, 14–20, 86, 135, 193, 198
mind-reading, 146
mirror networks, 106
Mithen, Steven, 273, 277
mode, modes, 75–84
model author, 179
model, conceptual, 126
Mondrian scenes, 254
Monet, Claude, 171, 179, 180
Morris, Desmond, 66
Mother and Child on the Beach (Corot), 157
mother-in-law/wife image, 257
motor actions, 119, 153, 164
motor control, 15, 158–61
motor cortex, 47, 153, 158, 160, 164
music, xv, 3, 17, 22–3, 48, 51, 73–88, 93, 115–7, 121–8, 141, 285
Music Lesson, The (Vermeer), 262
Mycenae, 228
Mycenaean palace, 227, 234, 237
mythic culture, 7–8; forms of thought, 9

Narayanan, Srini, 158–61
natural aesthetics, 60, 63, 64, 65, 69
natural selection, 18, 60–9, 111
network of mental spaces, 179–81
neural binding, 111, 174–5, 278

neural evolution, 26
neural integration, 4, 13, 20, 94; large-scale, 13
neural structures in the sensory-motor system, 153, 164
neuroaesthetics, 184
New Moon, The (Romberg), 115, 126–9
New Testament, 156, 193
Newton, Isaac, 137, 282
nostalgia, 38
Notre-Dame, Cathedral church of, Amiens, 196; Paris, 204
Nu descendant un escalier (Duchamp), 98–9

object recognition, 253, 258
"Ode on a Grecian Urn" (Keats), 58
Odyssey (Homer), 230, 234
Olympia, 230–2
On Memory (Aristotle), 225–6
Orangerie set (Monet), 180
Ordination (Poussin), 75, 76
orientation-selective cells, 252
orientation tuning column, 96
Orléans, Philippe I, duc d', 84

Paget, Sidney, 166
Panofsky, Erwin, 195–202, 278, 301
pantomime, 8, 16
Paralipomena (Kepler), 273, 298
Paul, Saint, 284
Pearl Earring, The (also known as *Girl with a Pearl Earring, The*) (Vermeer), 262
peek-a-boo, 31, 134
pelican-antelope figure, 271, 298
perception, 6, 10–5, 26, 37, 39, 47, 59, 73, 94, 111, 137–8, 153, 163–4, 171–6, 185, 200, 227, 244–62, 278, 283, 297, 300–2
perceptual ambiguity, 255
perceptual-emotional gestalt, 34
performative painting, 294
Perl, Jed, 176–7

Perona, Pietro, 73
perspective in art, 274, 281–3, 300–2
photo-haptic synesthesia, 180
Phrygian mode, 77–8
Piaget, Jean, 31
Picasso, Pablo, 95–9, 101, 187
Piles, Roger de, 87
pitch relationships are relationships in
    vertical space (metaphor), 123–8
Plato, parable of the cave in the *Republic*,
    300
play, 29, 30, 136, 138; chase play,
    111; cross-species, 30; and
    representational stance, 29; simple,
    48; skill-related, 16
Plotinus, 50, 301
Pointel, Jean, 75
Poussin, Nicolas, 73–87; proposal of, 73
Power of Images, The (Freedberg), 73, 81,
    214
Pozzo, Cassiano dal, 76
predators, 33, 227, 277
premotor cortex, 15, 153, 158, 160
pretense, 66–8
primary adaptation, 26
Procopius, 199
Propylaea to the Athenian Acropolis, 232
psychoaesthetics, 184
Ptolemy, 283, 302
Purtle, Carol, 302
Puttfarken, Thomas, 87

Quinn, Naomi, 127

Raising of Drusiana (depiction in the Old
    Sachristi of the San Lorenzo church
    in Florence) (Donatello), 274
Ramachandran, V. S., 110, 187
Rameau, Jean-Philippe, 85
Raphael Santi, 192, 205
reference, symbolic, 32–7, 42, 49
reflectance, 251, 252
Reflectography (Asperen de Boer), 295
Regier, Terrence, 162, 163

relics of medieval saints, 211, 214; of
    Saint Martin of Tours, 212
religion, xv, 8, 93, 110, 219, 222, 230–1,
    237, 283
Rembrandt van Rijn, 155–6
representation, symbolic, 30, 33, 37,
    39–40
representational art, 67–9
representational momentum, 137
representational stance, 26, 30–1
res cogitans, 187
res intensa, 179–82, 187
Richelieu, Armand Jean du Plessis, duc
    de, cardinal, 76
Rodin, Auguste, 7
role-playing, 16, 17, 18, 134, 147
Romberg, Sigmund, 115
Rondanini *Pietà*, 263
Rules of Composition (Charpentier), 84

Saint-Denis, Abbey church of (now
    Cathedral church of), 194–5, 199, 202
Salisbury, Cathedral church of, 212
sanctuary of Aphaia on Aegina, 227
scale, human, 99–100, 103
schemas, 41–50, 147, 154–7, 160–7;
    motor control, 158
Schjeldahl, Peter, 177
Schopenhauer, Arthur, 244, 262, 263
Schwab, Laurence, 115
scientific discovery, 43, 47
self-construction, 57, 62–3, 67–8
self-other blend, 52
semantic integration, 174
semiotics, 39, 47
sensation of forms in different
    modalities, 173
sensory-motor system, 153, 164
Seven Sacraments, Altarpiece of the (Rogier
    van der Weyden), 281
Seventh Seal, The (Ingmar Bergman), 280
singing, 23, 49, 115, 213, 288
skill-related play, 16
Smith, Barry, 184

social mammals, 4, 15
spatial-relations concepts, 154, 162
stabilization, 183
Steblin, Rita, 84
Steinberg, Leo, 95
storytelling, 8, 22, 195
Structure of Scientific Revolutions, The (Kuhn), 298
Suger of Saint-Denis, Abbot, 301
Sunrise (Marine) (Monet), 180
Sweetser, Eve, 297
symbol, 32
symbolic communication, 33
symbolic juxtapositions, 21
symbolic reference, 32–7, 42, 49
symbolic representation, 30, 33, 37–40, 50
symbolic technologies, 6
symbolization, 38, 172–6, 182, 186–7
symbols, 36, 40
synaesthesia, 111; photo-haptic, 180

Tacitus, 193
Talmy, Leonard, 153–7, 163, 217–9, 220
Tansey, Mark, 166
temenos, 227, 231–7
Temple of Zeus at Olympia, 230
Tentative de l'Impossible (Magritte), 109–10, 180
Theogony (Hesiod), 231
theoretic modes of thought, 7–9
theory of mind, 146
Thiebaud, Wayne, 166
"Tintern Abbey, Lines Written a Few Miles above" (Wordsworth), 63
tokens, 34, 36, 41
Tolnay, Charles de, 263
tomb of Saint Osmund, 212
tomb of Saint Peter, 215
Traité de l'harmonie (Rameau), 85
Trinity fresco (Masaccio), 274, 277, 281–2, 295, 300
Tristan chord, 266

Troyes, Cathedral church of (Cathedral of Saint-Pierre, Troyes), 203
Turner, Mark, 40, 52, 60, 93–4, 205, 217–8, 226, 281; and Gilles Fauconnier, 217–8, 226
Two Forms (Moore), 157

uniqueness, human, 14, 24, 32, 52
universal cognitive primitives, 154
Upper Palaeolithic, 99, 305

van Gogh, Vincent, 274, 299
van Schuurman, Anna Maria, 86
Vasari, Giorgio, 192, 197
Velázquez, Diego, 135
Velden, Hugo van der, 300
Vermeer, Joannes, 142, 262, 264
verticality schema, 123
Vijd chapel (Cathedral church of Saint Bavo, Ghent), 280–94
Virgil, 78
Virgin with Canon Van der Paele, The (van Eyck), 295
Virgin with Chancellor Rolin, The (van Eyck), 295
Vir Heroicus Sublimis (Newman), 176
visual and gestural units, 138
visual brain, 243, 246, 249, 254, 257–8
visual consciousness, 247
visual thinking, 153
Vitruvian Man (da Vinci), 277
Vitruvius, 192, 197
Vitry, Jacques de, 212
Voltaire (François-Marie Arouet), 263

Wagner, Richard, 122, 266
Walker Art Gallery (Liverpool), 87
Water Lilies (Monet), 180
Way We Think, The (Fauconnier and Turner), 93
Wedding at Cana, The (Giotto), 273
Westminster Abbey, 202
Weyden, Rogier van der, 110, 281

Why Cats Paint: A Theory of Feline Aesthetics (Busch and Silver), 24–5
wife/mother-in-law image, 257
wild Squatter (from *Les Demoiselles d'Avignon*, Picasso), 95–6
Winckelmann, Johann, 264, 265
window, Albertian notion of, 294
Wittgenstein, Ludwig, 271
Wordsworth, William, 63
worldviews, Stoic, scientific, Puritan, and Romantic, 5

Works and Days (Hesiod), 231
Wounded Bison Attacking a Man (Lascaux cave painting), 165
writing systems, 6

Young Girl on Her Bed, Making Her Dog Dance, A (Fragonard), 178

Zarlino, Gioseffe, 79, 81, 82, 83, 87
Zeki, Semir, 11, 96, 145, 187, 243–66, 277
Zoobooks, 104